Global Elites

Global Elites

The Opaque Nature of Transnational Policy Determination

Edited by

Andrew Kakabadse

and

Nada Kakabadse

First published 2012 by
PALGRAVE MACMILLAN

Palgrave Macmillan in the UK is an imprint of Macmillan Publishers Limited,
registered in England, company number 785998, of Houndmills, Basingstoke,
Hampshire RG21 6XS.

Palgrave Macmillan in the US is a division of St Martin's Press LLC,
175 Fifth Avenue, New York, NY 10010.

Palgrave Macmillan is the global academic imprint of the above companies
and has companies and representatives throughout the world.

Palgrave® and Macmillan® are registered trademarks in the United States,
the United Kingdom, Europe and other countries.

ISBN 978–0–230–27873–8

This book is printed on paper suitable for recycling and made from fully
managed and sustained forest sources. Logging, pulping and manufacturing
processes are expected to conform to the environmental regulations of the
country of origin.

A catalogue record for this book is available from the British Library.

A catalog record for this book is available from the Library of Congress.

10 9 8 7 6 5 4 3 2 1
21 20 19 18 17 16 15 14 13 12

Printed and bound in Great Britain by
CPI Antony Rowe, Chippenham and Eastbourne

In Memory

Professor Alex Kouzmin

Our dear friend and esteemed colleague Professor Alex Kouzmin regrettably died during the later stages of the preparation of this book. Alex was a highly talented, globally renowned intellectual in the fields of social, business and political science. His discourse ranged far and wide and his arguments were deeply penetrating. We shall all surely miss his sharp mind, his infectious wit and his warmth of heart.

Alex, your presence and extensive contribution have benefited us all.

Contents

List of Figures, Tables and Boxes

Figures

Tables

Boxes

Notes on Contributors

Andrew Kakabadse is Professor of International Management Development, Doughty Centre, Cranfield University's School of Management in the UK. Andrew has held and also holds visiting appointments at the Centre for Creative Leadership and Thunderbird, the Garvin School of International Management, USA; at the University of Ulster, UK; and at Macquarie Graduate School of Management, Australia. He has consulted and lectured in every region of the world. His bestselling books include *Leading the Board* and *Rice-Wine with the Minister*.

Nada Kakabadse is Professor in Management and Business Research at the University of Northampton, Business School and Visiting Professor at US, Australian, French, Kazakhstani and Chinese universities. She has co-authored seventeen books (with Andrew Kakabadse) and has published over 140 scholarly articles. Her current areas of interest focus on leadership, strategy, boardroom effectiveness, governance, CSR and ethics, and ICT impact on individual and society. Nada is co-editor of the *Journal of Management Development* and the *Corporate Governance* journal. For further information see http://www.kakabadse.com.

Akram Al Ariss, Champagne School of Management, France

Elif Ünal Çoker, Department of Statistics, Mimar Sinan Fine Arts University, Turkey

Ali Ergur, Department of Sociology, Galatasaray University, Turkey

Robert Galavan, Chair in Strategic Management, Head of the School of Business and Law, National University of Ireland, Maynooth, Ireland

Dimitria Groutsis, University of Sydney, Australia

Shaowei He, Lecturer in Economics/Contemporary Chinese Studies, Northampton Business School, UK

Kalu N. Kalu, Professor of Political Science, Auburn University Montgomery, USA

Alexander Kouzmin, formerly Professor in Management, School of Commerce and Management, Southern Cross University, Australia

Peter Lawrence, Emeritus Professor, University of Northampton, UK

Eddy Louchart, Postgraduate Researcher, University of Northampton, Business School, UK

Mustafa F. Özbilgin, Professor, Brunel Business School, Brunel University, UK

Jelena Petrovic, Principal Lecturer and Course Director, Leadership, HRM and Organisation, Kingston Business School, UK

Ian N. Richardson, Researcher, Stockholm University Business School, Sweden

William I. Robinson, University of California-Santa Barbara, USA

Barbara Russell, Postgraduate Researcher, University of Northampton, UK

Richard Sanders, Professor of Contemporary Chinese Studies, Northampton Business School, UK

Arthur Sementelli, Florida Atlantic University, School of Public Administration, USA

A. G. Sheard, Vice-President, Fan Technology, Fläkt Woods, UK

Thomas Sigel, T Sigel Consulting, USA & UK

Jon Stobart, Professor of History, School of Social Sciences, University of Northampton, UK

Philip Sugarman, CEO, St Andrew's Healthcare, Northampton, UK

Kym Thorne, Senior Lecturer, School of Commerce, University of South Australia, Australia

Artun Ünsal, Department of Political Science, Galatasaray University, Turkey

Joana Vassilopoulou, Norwich Business School, University of East Anglia, UK

Sibel Yamak, Department of Management, Galatasaray University, Turkey

Preface

For many years little was written about the particular but contentious topic of this book; then out of the blue a special *Economist* issue on 'The Few' (2011). In effect, this was an in-depth analysis of elites.

The *Economist* special issue is impressive. It shies away from the conspiracy theory perspective and attempts to diagnose and dissect the nature of that exclusive group, the world's leaders. The special issue discusses the nature and positive contribution of elites. Equally, it analyses the antics of the spoilt rich. Further, elitism is not just viewed from the perspective of wealth and status. An additional group of outstandingly clever people, termed 'cognitive elites', are also given serious attention.

Great stuff, except for the fact that the *Economist* special issue stretches the imagination just a bit too far by arguing that elites serve the people and not the other way around. Perhaps a bit more in-depth analysis could have explored whether elites primarily serve themselves first, and only then others.

And that is the question, do elites master and amass resources to enrich themselves, or do they offer economic and socially beneficial value? In fact, who are these elites and just what is the reach of their influence? And if they are so important, why has this subject been neglected for so long?

It is evident that the world's leaders (one element of elites) do frequently meet and interact with each other, such as at Davos. More commonly, however, what they do is meet behind closed doors. Yet, politicians on the world stage are not the only elites for there are also other elites from business, medicine, education, sports, the arts and so the list continues, that one rarely hears about except in specialist forums.

The question is do elites really shape society? Well, the purpose of this book is to explore this question. Getting straight to the punch line, the conclusion from this collection of original essays is that elite networks are healthy, are operating at full steam ahead, with the Bilderbergs and the Trilateral Commission being two prominent examples, and they do shape local and global society.

Perhaps because of Washington Consensus politics where all is negotiated to reach a common shared and often lowest common denominator viewpoint (resulting in little diversity of opinion), elites have managed to keep out of the limelight due to the absence of sharp discourse. Also perhaps because of the increasing concentration of news and media ownership in fewer hands, attention has been diverted from the conversations of the great, to the daily distractions (better known as tittle-tattle) of everyday life better known as TV soaps and fascination with celebrities and the like.

So, on the basis that we see some of them just sometimes, but more often than not do not know who they are, are elites simply a rich fodder feeding conspiracy theorists?

In one sense, the opaque nature of the global movers and shakers feeds the conspiracy arguments. One prominent view is that anything can be arranged once into these exclusive elite network(s), or at least that is how it feels from the outside. This point was particularly well captured in 'The Week' (2011) outlining the antics of Colonel Gaddafi of Libya. The story goes that Gaddafi, peeved with being asked for a head and shoulders photo for a visa to enter the USA, supposedly refused to hand over a supply of enriched uranium (as part of a weapons decommissioning programme) to which he had agreed. Under high temperatures, this toxic load sat on a local airport tarmac for over a month. It was reported that only a personal call from Hillary Clinton, reassuring the Libyan leader of America's support and friendship, had the consignment released and shipped off to a safer destination. So amongst elites, government contradicts its own government. The pull of elite connections does seem to be all powerful.

Elite connections are powerful and the Gaddafi story reinforces the strongly held view that the elite serve each other's self-determined needs simply because they are 'members' of a self-serving club. One school of thought, however, counters this view and argues that elites are a vital link to the effective economic and political functioning of democratic regimes. The argument is taken further by highlighting that elites form a constructive bridge between democratic and non-democratic regimes and this link minimises the incidence of wars. In this sense, corrupt and untrustworthy elites are eventually removed. The current conflict in Libya and the attempts to remove Gaddafi add weight to this argument.

Raymond Duch (1995) epitomises such thinking by highlighting that regime change, particularly of non-democratic regimes, leads to economic crisis which in turn leads to an unwelcome sequence of events. The two most predominant reasons for crises are:

- Weak internal cohesion amongst the ruling elites, prior to the crisis.
- Weak civilian control over the military, emphasising the divided nature of elites in that regime.

So one strongly held view is that well-integrated elites promote stability. Along the line of realising long-term sustainable peace, Brownlee (2007) identified elite trust of each other as a primary requirement for post-conflict stability. Further, in order to maintain social cohesion, Brownlee (2007) also considered that the benefits of in-group attachment outweigh the gains from pursuing out-group linkages.

And here lie the two sides to elitism: the self-seeking, conspiratorially inclined rich and powerful whose sole aim is to promote their own ends, versus the socially minded leaders whose contribution to this world is to nurture and protect the one requirement that we all crave for, the stability for enduring peace. Whichever interpretation is made, the one undisputable fact is that elites exist, there are few of them and their influence has a huge reach.

Overview

Both the extent of their influence and the neglect of this subject catalysed us, the editors, to invite contributions to examine the nature of elites. The range of submissions has been broad but intellectually, powerfully penetrating. This original collection of essays spans from, at one end, a theoretical discourse on the nature of elites to, on the other, the provision of practical study on the composition of elites in different contexts across the world. In fact, even a treatise on how to conduct elite interviews in order to extract meaningful insight from these encounters is included in this collection of original works.

The book is composed of eighteen chapters. The first eight chapters examine the nature of elites from a broader, theoretical perspective. Outlined are the demographic nature of elites, the penetrating spread of elite ownership of resources, the capacity of elites to influence the direction of market forces, and the impact of elites on democracy and the ruling of the nation state. The following eight chapters take a more practical view of how elites function. The shape, values and contribution of elites in newly emergent economies are given attention. Case studies of China and Turkey are presented with discussion focusing on how these emergent elites are attempting to position themselves to realise global reach. In fact, these later chapters explore the skills and abilities of elites and their likely influence over the global scene in the future. The debate on how the very successful can penetrate exclusive networks is contrasted by a contribution examining how the underprivileged can reposition themselves and also adopt elite status. Attention is also given to how to go about researching elites, bearing in mind that insufficient scrutiny has been given to this exclusive population.

Specifically, Chapter 1 provides a historical analysis of elite formation and the influence of elites in shaping national and global policy. A critical dilemma is highlighted: while society needs elites to provide stability, elites need to be removed when their self-seeking nature accumulates resources exclusively for their benefit. The chapter also points out that the new elite can come from both the top and bottom of society, either as a result of progressive or because of revolutionary change. Despite the source of elite formation, the same concern is faced, and that is unchallenged elite control of resources leads to institutionalised corruption, which, in turn, requires a change, often a violent removal of the elite strata.

The theme of power and influence is captured in Chapter 2. Who are these elites and why their invisibility? The chapter discusses how the economic and political elites have gained from the information and communication technology revolution. Ironically it is argued that technology innovation provides the cloak by which elites remain invisible and continue to promote their agendas and, in particular, their self-supporting values.

Despite their opaque nature, Chapter 3 highlights a particular tension prominent in elite circles, namely that between the older, nationally orientated elites and the ever more prominent transnational elites. The chapter emphasises the inevitability of global market integration thus challenging national loyalties, national values and national wealth-creation mechanisms. The message is that the whole nature and shape of elites is changing.

Yet whether national or transnational in inclination, Chapter 4 draws attention to a particular concern of elites and that is how elites protect themselves and their properties from capture or loss. Drawing on Bentham's Panopticon, the development of a fortress mentally amongst elites is posited as a real prospect for the future. The current phenomenon of gated communities is considered as only the beginning of a society dominated by surveillance and covert investigation, fundamentally to protect the very rich. The case put forward is that by being cut off from the life of the 'ordinary' majority, elites become insensitive to the effect of inequitable wealth distribution. Rather than elites providing stability, the contention is that elites will contribute to ever greater societal disaggregation.

Along the same lines, Chapter 5 captures the enormous impact the economic and political elites have in determining the nature and the shape of the current and future global markets. In so doing, the question is raised of whether the invisible hand of the market is still a force in its own right, or whether the invisible hand is deliberately kept so in order that markets are pushed in the direction desired by the Anglo-American neo-liberal elites. The inaccessibility of elites to investigation leaves this question open.

In response to the debate about who and what are the elites, Chapter 6 is emphatic that elite analysis is a critical issue, but is under-researched in contemporary social science. In this chapter the term 'elite theory' is introduced into the discussion. Through a better understanding of elites, the case presented is that society at large will be enabled to decide whether they wish to buy into 'the brand' of the current elites, and if not, then a change of taste amongst the population will stimulate a change of elites. The message from Chapter 6 is that understanding elites is important because when you do so and you wish to change them, the change steps to take become that much easier.

Implicit in the discussion of who and what are the elites is the question of what value elites really offer. In addressing this question, Chapter 7 offers a supportive viewpoint, highlighting the diverse background of elites and how through transparent discourse elites can provide substantial value to the functioning of an open society.

In contrast, Chapter 8 comes to a different conclusion. Using the American republic as a case study, the point is made that historically, representative democracy was preferred over direct democracy. It was considered that the latter fell too much into the camp of 'rule by the rabble'. Thus who controls the American state is posited as a key question. Whoever 'they' may be, Chapter 8 identifies that throughout American history, the top 1% of the population of the USA had, and continues to have, 40–50% of the wealth of the nation. So yes, who does control the American state?

The next cluster of chapters concentrates less on the bigger question of who and what are elites, but examines elitism in particular contexts. Chapter 9 discusses how the newly emergent Turkish corporate elite have attempted to penetrate and integrate with international elite networks. The push for acceptance in global networks is extensive and has been realised through substantially drawing on the nation's economic, social and cultural resources. A refreshing point is made that the new elite, i.e. the first generation of the upper echelons of Turkey, have more 'common' tastes than the 'refined' tastes of the global elites. At least in this way the current generation of Turkish elites are more grounded and in touch with developments in their society.

Away from national context to that of the boardroom, Chapter 10 examines the nature of elite interactions amongst board directors in international joint venture structures. It is concluded that elite status distinctly influences director role, contribution and effectiveness as opposed to director skill and experience. The call for further research to examine the status versus functionality divide is emphasised.

The challenges facing elites in different circumstances are the theme of the next five chapters. Chapter 11 explores the particular circumstances of Chinese elites and the particulars of their transitional journey to international prominence over the last three decades. Their higher living standards, their more open society and the focus on science and innovation to promote China's growth, have had a powerful impact on the upper strata of Chinese society. The point made is that political controls will become reduced and the requirements for greater transparency and autonomy will increase. How the Chinese will embrace such social change is the question. What is clear is that unless the Chinese elites continue to adapt their behaviour, then their acceptance by the global, political, economic and scientific elites will wane as will the country's transition onto the global stage.

The previous chapter's discussion on how to politically master change in China highlights a particular skill required by elites and that is to strategise. Chapter 12 examines the nature of how strategy is made to work. Enacting strategy requires the elite leader to transverse a number of contrasts, ranging from being broad and outward-facing to being detailed and inward-looking. Based on a qualitative study of elites in strategic roles, the chapter emphasises what it takes to realise meaningful engagement, for without that elites will not continue to remain in their present leadership roles. Accomplishing the skill of being creative and yet having one's feet firmly on the ground, sets global elites apart from others.

The functionality required to survive and continue as an elite member is also examined in Chapter 13, namely a case study of political elites in the state of Ohio, USA. The study focuses on the leadership requirements for reversing the economic and political decline of Ohio. Despite all the positive comments made by the political leaders of the state, the reality is a lack of leadership and the continued decline of Ohio. Not listening and not critically examining current circumstances emerge as two reasons why the political leadership of that state does not rise to the challenge of driving through change for the better. To not adapt either means a change of elite or the persistent deterioration of the state. Sadly, the latter seems to be the more likely.

On a more upbeat note Chapter 14 reports a study of the mind-set, skills and drive of high-performing entrepreneurs. In fact, nine performance considerations are identified. The proposition made is that if elites are going to continually provide value, then meeting performance challenges has to become a daily discipline.

The theme of the determination, drive and willingness to succeed whatever the odds continues in Chapter 15. The experiences of minority ethnic groups in their host countries are examined. Comparative studies of France and Germany are reported. The social and employment challenges facing migrants in these two countries are discussed. Despite having acquired the relevant skills and qualifications in both countries and for different reasons, migrants are denied access to positions of responsibility commensurate with their intellectual and performance accomplishments. Therefore finding alternative pathways to expressing each individual's ability has become a necessity. The personal qualities to overcome inbuilt social prejudice and to then become successful in such a context is the basis for the migrants to form their own newly emergent elite.

So far all chapters have provided analysis of elites today or ventured into a historical policy design overview of elite development. Chapter 16 is different in that it provides an insightful and practical historical, socio-graphic analysis of the social capital of elites in eighteenth-century Northamptonshire, a county of England. Drawing on archival material, the chapter captures a study of elite networks in formation and in operation in the 1770s. The same critical message emerges and that is that the guardians of that local community 240 years ago were a combination of business and political elites intermingled with people from inherited family networks and positions of privilege. New elites rubbed shoulders with old elites. What kept them together was the trust engendered through their continuous membership of exclusive networks. Then, as today, it is social capital that binds elites together.

The final two chapters again take a different slant. Chapter 17 captures the experience of having conducted studies of elites and highlights the lessons learned from pursuing research of elites. Gaining understanding of the context within which elite groupings operate is considered fundamental.

Furthermore, adopting qualitative methodologies for the study of elites is strongly recommended as insightful penetration of elite contexts supersedes the knowledge gained from broad-brush surveys. How then to conduct elite interviews becomes the focus of the chapter. The reader is taken through four stages of interviewing with practical tips on how the interviewer should conduct themselves. One point is emphasised and that is, make the encounter (i.e. the interview) a learning experience for the elite study participant, otherwise the interview may be prematurely terminated.

The final chapter, Chapter 18, offers a study of the dark side of elites. Leadership hubris is presented as an underexamined aspect of leadership but one that is necessary to explore in order to appreciate the damaging nature of elites. The conclusion reached is that governance safeguards against elite excess are only partly useful. Self-determined and self-reasoned control are the only real safeguards and these have to primarily come from the leader. To mediate against leadership abuse, shared leadership is proposed as the infrastructure for a more sustainable distribution of accountabilities. Only when responsibilities and accountabilities are equitably shared amongst the leadership cadre, can the negative outcomes of investing power in one person or a small group be minimised.

So from what elites are, to how to interact with elites, to how to control their darker nature, this book provides a comprehensive overview of those who shape our lives. The publishing of this book acts as call for more work to be undertaken in this area. This topic is too important to be left neglected, not because elites, as a form of celebrity, have the right to continuous attention, but because we should all have greater control of our lives and not allow elites to determine our future.

At the time of 'putting the final touches' to this book, the covert and exceptionally well-directed 'jasmine' revolutions of the Middle East (Egypt, Tunisia, Bahrain, Libya – who are not playing ball – and Yemen) were underway without even a murmur from Europe. What was witnessed was soft power at its best, and all to promote the Anglo-American neo-liberal resource capture agenda. Most believed what was said on television and in the newspapers of spontaneous, grassroots uprisings against tyrannical directors. Most, however, did not know of the hundreds of millions of dollars that had been spent over the last five or six years on social groups to ferment regime change favourable to neo-liberal interests. Once regime change is accomplished, the very same who demonstrated in the streets will be hounded or shot by their new, even more Western-friendly rulers. And all for what? – Continued supplies of cheaper oil and regimes supportive of the expected bombing and consequent dissection of Iran. If only all this disruption could bring about an improvement to people's lives.

As this book repeats, one all-too-common experience is that one tyrannical group of dictatorial elites substitutes another but with the winners better organised and likely more repressive than their predecessors. However, should reading be too arduous but your curiosity about elites drives you to learn more, then pick up a newspaper, switch on the television or read a more serious professional journal, and you will find out about today's elites at their most proficient, namely amassing resources while the other side are labelled the bad guys.

References

Brownlee, J. (2007) *Authoritarianism in the Age of Democratization* (New York: Cambridge University Press).

Duch, R. M. (1995) 'Economic Chaos and the Fragility of Democratic Transition in Former Communist Regimes', *Journal of Politics*, 57(1): 121–58.

The Economist (2011) 'The Few: A Special Report on Global Leaders', 22 January.

The Week (2011) 'What a Touchy Despot Gaddafi is', Issue 797, 18 December.

1
From Local Elites to a Globally Convergent Class: A Historical Analytical Perspective

Nada K. Kakabadse, Andrew Kakabadse and Alexander Kouzmin

Introduction

Since the Roman Republic, members of groups at the top of the social stratum have interacted and continue to interact with each other socially and business wise, deeply conscious of and responsive to each other's interest (Mills, 1956). These intricately connected networks, the so-called elite connections, come about through the influential roles individuals hold in the political, commercial and/or military structures of the day. Yet, despite their intimate knowledge of each other and the closed-shop nature of their exalted position, elite groupings are not necessarily a cohesive whole. Considerable tensions exist between those who shape whole societies. Even Athenian democracy was twice interrupted by oligarchic coups organised by elites against elites during the turbulent period of the Peloponnesian Wars. And why? Because one cluster of elites viewed democracy as inherently arbitrary government by the masses (Morrow, 1962). The Athenian coup of 411 BC, led by a number of prominent and wealthy Athenians holding positions of power over the Athenian army, overthrew the democratic government and replaced it with a short-lived oligarchy. Within several days, that was thwarted by Samian democrats and pro-democratic leaders controlling the Athenian fleet (Kagan, 2003). Previously in 404 BC, a small group of thirty pro-Spartan oligarchs, installed in Athens after its defeat in the Peloponnesian War, organised a coup which was overcome within the year and democracy restored (Rhodes, 2006). Plato watched with horror as constitutional justice degenerated into a reign of terror (Morrow, 1962).

From this brief glimpse into history, what lessons can be drawn? Elites interact and support elites. Elites overthrow elites. But the overwhelming lesson from history is that elites are ever-present and are one, if not *the*, predominant force shaping societies throughout time.

From previously local elites and in an increasingly interconnected world, elite influence has stretched considerably. The previous local elite of the USA – as first illustrated by McAllister's list of 'Metropolitan 400' (containing about 300 names) and being a simple roll-call for the Patriarch Ball of 1892 – became superseded by the first *Social Register* of New York (comprising some 881 families). In a relatively short period of time, the old European moneyed class of America blossomed into an international elite, interacting today with the global rich through a number of interconnected networks such as the Trilateral Commission; the Bilderberg group; the World Economic Forum; the Council on Foreign Relations; the Paris Club; the G7/8; and the British–American Project, amongst others. Seemingly, a small elite group of about 6,000 people (Rothkopf, 2008) has vastly more power than any other group on the planet, of which the richest 1,000 have more than twice the wealth of the poorest 2.5 billion. Such gross and blatant disparity is considered to create a damaging imbalance within any individual state that aspires to have an effective democracy. So what is the impact of elites? Does their intimacy of interaction circumvent war, substituting destruction with a series of tradeoffs? Alternatively does elite control of resources foster deep societal tensions that ultimately lead to state-wide and ultimately global-level disturbance?

This chapter addresses these questions by examining the power base of elites and the consequences of elite interaction and their control of resources. The scope of the chapter stretches from a historical perspective to the present day.

Who are the elite?

Elite (Latin, *eligere*, 'to elect') refers to a relatively small, dominant group within society who enjoy a privileged status envied by others (Parenti, 2007). Depending on the theoretical perspective and political persuasion adopted, elites have been variously categorised (see Table 1.1). For example, Aron's (1985) inquiry into what constitutes an elite concluded that elites are the minority that fulfil the functions of leadership within society. According to Aron, an elite strata encompasses five groups: political leaders; administrators of the state; those in charge of the economy; leaders of the people; and military chiefs. Aron holds that in a democracy the elite must be composed of a number of contrasting groupings in order to ensure a balance of power. Scott (1995), on the other hand, on the basis of critical theory, compared sixty important studies carried out in the English-speaking world dealing with political and economic elites and concluded that elite influence is in decline.

However, the predominant view is that elites are 'omnipotent, in their powers', harbouring a 'great hidden design' (Mills, 1956: 16). Perhaps it is an elite's 'amorphous power situation' (Mills, 1956: 17) that makes their examination difficult. Or perhaps it is the manner of industrialisation and private enterprise that 'has made it possible for men to occupy such strategic positions that they can dominate the fabulous means of man's production; link the owners of science and labour; control man's relations to nature and

Table 1.1 Elite theoretical perspectives

	Classical theory	Critical theory	Democratic theory	Network theory
Structure	Hierarchical	Structural-functional	Democratic	Polymathic and polymorphic cluster of individuals (network webs) bound by strong social, political or professional ties
Composition	A class of people who have the highest indices in their branch of activity ('the strongest, the most energetic and the most capable') within society (social, political and economic arenas), hence, a governing elite (directly or indirectly) plays a part in government and a non-governing elite (the rest) leads in other social and business arenas.	Those who rule through the greatest access to wealth and power and are able to utilise that power to establish and amass greater power over others – constitute and control the means of power. In the USA, military and large business corporations constitute critical elements of power.	Elites have accrued skills that can be utilised in specific tasks for the good of the whole community. Pressure from other interest groups places responsibility on the elites to produce an adequate outcome, which benefits both community and business interests.	Network interaction – those who have access to resources (rather than just those who control resources) – the network webs which an individual or group has access to, and is able to mobilise – both the recognised elite and the non-elite from a community: 'those actors who are in some way perceived to be more influential or more privileged than some undefined group'.
Stability	Groups and individuals are transitory, destined to be usurped by a new elite as economic and social conditions change.	Power elite cannot be easily removed from their positions in society.	Democratic process of selection and removal of elites from positions of power.	Fluid – evolving, dynamic process, but relatively stable.
Influential authors	Pareto (1968: 36); Mosca (1884/1925)	Scott (1995)	Lasswell (1966: v); Aron (1985)	Woods (1998: 2101, 2105); Windolf (1998); Grewal (2008)

make millions out of it' (Mills, 1956: 98). In contrast to the total domination perspective, Petit and Scholz (2002) conceptualise elites as resulting from a dichotomy that appears in social groups, namely those that are the 'best' and the 'less good'. Yet whether elites are the great and the good or the wealthy and villainous, the notion of elites raises two considerations, the legitimacy of any elite grouping and the pathways to membership of an elite cluster.

Arguing from the nineteenth-century classical perspective, Pareto (1935) and Mosca (1884/1925) noted that an entire elite can be replaced by a new one and that any single individual can drop from elite to non-elite status. Although elites are not hereditary by nature (though hereditary elites exist) and people from all classes of society can, at least theoretically, become a member of an 'elite', the replacing of one elite group by another is either slow or distinctly rapid through coups and bloody revolutionary action. The exceptions are the bloodless coups of the 'velvet and colour revolutions' of the twenty-first century (Kakabadse et al., 2006; Sussman and Krader, 2008), with Egypt, Bahrain and Tunisia being the latest targets. The colour revolutions of Ukraine, Serbia, etc. have been superseded by the scented revolutions of North Africa.

UK and European elite formation and restructure has been both slow and bloody. The transition process from a hegemonic, aristocratic society (landed or old money) to a more pluralist society began during the Middle Ages but gained momentum from the sixteenth century onwards, as new groups of individuals, such as merchants and bankers, sought to gain social status and power (Cannadine, 1999). That is not to say that the aristocracy was and is no longer an influential elite, but rather that the hegemony of power is now more inclusive of other elite groups such as wealthy, non-landed individuals, corporate leaders, political leaders and others who control, or who have access to, critical resources.

Examining the structure of elite networks in Germany and Britain, Windolf (1998) concluded that the resources on which the dominance of the economic elite depends are bureaucratic power, ownership of physical capital and influence over social capital. Woods (1998: 2106) suggested that elites may be better defined to include 'those who have access to resources rather than simply those who control resources, where individuals and interest groups can be networked and directed towards a specific action, for an intended outcome'. Iglic and Rus (2004) found that although elite networks have high reproduction rates, in time there exist fluctuations within the old elite networks. Drawing from various strands of political and social thought, Grewal (2008), using a network perspective, explained how globalisation is best understood in terms of a power inherent in current and emergent social networks.

For example, a UK inquiry led by the then Secretary of State, Alan Milburn, examining the barriers and pathways to employment in the professions regardless of background, found that professionals tend to come from wealthier than average backgrounds (UK Cabinet Office, 2009). The inquiry found that although only 7% of the population attended 'independent' schools (UK private schools), well over half the members of the professions have done so. For example, 75% of judges, 70% of finance directors, 45% of top civil servants and 32% of MPs have been privately educated (UK Cabinet Office, 2009). In France, since the nineteenth century, many top executives share a common education, namely attendance at the elite schools of higher education, the *Polytechniques* and, consequently, share common career paths (Bourdieu, 1986). Elite engineering schools (*Écoles Polytechniques*) have trained elite managers for French firms for approximately 150 years. Further former and retired high-ranking civil servants join the business elite as a common practice. Since the Second World War, French public servants have attended training at the *École Nationale d'Administration* (ENA) which has been recognised as having a profound influence on civil servant thinking and sense of cohesion. Overall, these institutions have traditionally produced a significant percentage of France's high-ranking civil servants, politicians and executives, as well as many scientists and philosophers.

In France, being a member of an elite means access to privileged social relations. An exclusive and privileged education and a career in the civil service nurture shared values and strong social bonds (Suleiman, 1974). Similarity of educational experience leads to privileged friendships which in turn become shared political affiliations (Kadushin, 2006). Such commonality of privileged and shared experience leads to invitations and also to boardroom cross-directorships (Bauer and Bertin-Mourot, 1999). Chief Executive Officers (CEOs) from *Grandes Écoles* and from the civil service run 20% of French firms, but a huge fraction of French assets (80%). Over 20,000 senior executives of the industrial and business community of France hold degrees from *Grandes Écoles*. Over 60% of the managing directors and CEOs of France's 100 largest firms are graduates of the *Grandes Écoles* (Smith, 2005). Exposure to privileged courses of study enables these individuals to assume top positions as well as offering them different career possibilities. In France, for example, the graduate engineer enjoys a prestigious social status and is destined for senior level decision-making.

Furthermore, most of France's political leaders, on both the right and the left, have come from the *Grandes Écoles*. For example, President Jacques Chirac and his prime minister, Dominique de Villepin, studied at the National School of Administration, which has produced most of the political technocrats who have run France for the last thirty years (Smith, 2005). Two opposition leaders, François Hollande and Laurent Fabius, also graduated from the same institution (Smith, 2005).

With such a wealth of evidence emphasising their all-powerful influence, what is surprising is the lack of extensive debate on the impact of elites on society. Few commentators have examined elite interaction and impact (Table 1.2).

Table 1.2 Elite debate

Author	Focus on	Key argument
Pareto (1935)	Psychological and intellectual superiority of elites	Elites are the highest accomplished in any field. Two types: • governing elites; • non-governing elites.
Mosca (1884/1925)	Sociological and personal characteristics of elites	Elites are an organised minority with superior organisational skills, whilst masses are the unorganised majority.
Michels (1911/1915)	Social and political organisations	Social organisation and division of labour allows elites to rule through three basic principles: • need for leaders, specialised staff and facilities; • utilisation of facilities by leaders within their organisation; • the importance of the psychological attributes of the leaders.
Mills (1956)	Macro-scale	Power elite groups are a triumvirate – political, economic and military – forming a distinguishable body wielding power in the American state.
Hunter (1953)	A structural-functional approach on micro-scale in community power (city)	Hierarchies and webs of interconnection operating within the city reveal relationships of power between businessmen, politicians and clergy amongst others.
Burnham (1941)	Managerialism	Power elite is in the hands of modern managers rather than politicians or businessmen due to separating ownership and control.
Putnam (1976)	Competencies	New elite of scientists, mathematicians, economists and engineers harnessing new intellectual technology.
Bourdieu (1986)	*Noblesse de robe* ('state nobility')	Elite as a dominant class maintains and justifies its supremacy through a formal elite education system of schools and universities – in France the *Grandes Écoles*, in the United States the Ivy League schools, and in England Oxford and Cambridge universities.

What is clear is that elite rule is not exercised in a consistent manner across a whole privileged class. Rather, it is manifest through the activities of a wide variety of organisations and, as such, is less visible and certainly more difficult to discern as a singular influence (Domhoff, 1997: 2). However, organisations and institutions are directed by the members of the power elite and in so doing:

> have the interest and ability to involve themselves in protecting and enhancing the privileged social position of their class. Leaders within the upper class join with high-level employees in the organizations they control to make up what will be called the power elite. This power elite is the leadership group of the upper class as a whole, but it is not the same thing as the upper class, for not all members of the upper class are members of the power elite and not all members of the power elite are part of the upper class. It is members of the power elite who take part in the processes that maintain the class structure. (Domhoff, 1997: 2)

Mills (1956: 147), on the other hand, sees 'the managerial reorganization of the propertied classes into the more or less unified stratum of the corporate rich'. And therein lie the range of perspectives on the composition of elites; the dynamic/ever-changing as opposed to the established/self-protective.

Yet, irrespective of the perspective adopted, and as already stated, there still exists a general paucity of empirical data on the nature of elite groupings and how they operate across their networks. This is, perhaps, unsurprising given the obvious political sensitivities and the almost uniform veil of 'invisibility'/privacy that surrounds these privileged groups (Thorne and Kouzmin, 2010).

Many scholars have tried to define the mechanisms by which the elite is constituted, reproduced and dissolved. Bourdieu (1979), who holds that individual chance of success depends above all on the way the social system works, found that the mechanisms for elite reproduction is through networks and the privilege of sharing distinct social roots which shape future success. Studying the ruling class in the north of France under the Second Empire (1849–71), Barbier (1989) found that the mechanism by which the elite absorbs new members and develops them is through inbreeding. By such unity and belief in the elite's own common values, both simultaneously representing strengths and weaknesses, Barbier (1989) also illustrated how sons lacking their fathers' qualities and preferring the charms of social life, inhibit innovation. Unable to progress in the old elite, the 'new man' in frustration turns to innovation and becomes armed with technological ingenuity. Despite those new skills, the new man, however, is kept well outside elite groupings. Through lack of innovation, existing social network ties are preserved, at least for a while. Thus, elite membership and continuity is through prestige, achieved by 'getting in with and imitating those who posses power as well as prestige' (Mills, 1956: 43). In a way, elites become a caste within the upper classes, assuming the responsibility for making major decisions and determining the parameters within which any debate takes place.

Focusing on the Americans, Parenti (2007) argued that there is no one grand secret power elite governing the USA. In fact there are numerous coteries of corporate and governmental elites which communicate and coordinate across various policy realms. He suggested that behind their special interests are the common overall interests of the moneyed class, which is not to say that differences never arise among these elites. Parenti (2007: 181) argued that:

> like technology, money has a feedback effect of its own, advantaging the already advantaged, liquefying wealth and making it easier to mobilize and accumulate. With the growth of moneyed wealth comes a greater concentration and command over technology by the moneyed class. To understand the elite, one needs to understand the economic and political structure of the nation in which the elite resides as, 'the very rich circumvent or violate existing laws and also have laws created and enforced for their direct benefits' (Mills, 1956: 99).

The only exception in history to the hierarchical and controlling nature of elites is the horizontal organisation of the Jewish people, facilitated by two fundamental principles. The first principle, stated in the Hebrew Scriptures, refers to every human being as created in the image of God, guaranteeing equality for all and thus placing human rights as inherently given (Faur, 2008). The second principle is the Sinai Covenant which establishes the Law (constitution) as the supreme authority. The implication is that the ruling authorities are not hierarchically superior to anyone, as they too are equally bound by the same Law (Faur, 2008). By these principles, the individual does not depend on the state as it is the individual who creates the household which will then create the state, i.e. the evolution is from individual to household to law and then to state and citizenship (Faur, 2008). Biblically, these two principles were captured by Samuel who was reluctant to introduce the institution of *melukha* (monarch) despite the fact that the people desired the institution of kingship. Samuel gave warning of too readily accepting the institution of government through monarchical rule (1 Samuel, 11:14–12:22):

> This is what the king who will reign over you will do: He will draft your sons to make an army, and force others to farm to feed it, and still others to make weapons for it [...] He will take your daughters to be perfumers and cooks and bakers. He will take the best of your fields and vineyards and olive groves and give them to his attendants. [...] He will tax your grain

and give it to his officials. Your servants will be conscripted to be his servants, and take the best of your labour for his own use. He will take a tenth of your means of production, and you will become his slaves. When that day comes, you will cry out for relief from the king you have chosen.

What Samuel described was the relationship (social contract) between the ruler (government) and the people. In order to maintain social order the people need to give up certain rights to government in order to preserve social stability (Kakabadse et al., 2009). Samuel implies that the people need to recognise that they cannot function solely as individuals for in order to ensure the defence of the nation, the will of government and the rule of law must predominate (Kakabadse et al., 2009). What Samuel also highlights is that the social contract between ruler (government) and ruled is likely not to be equitable or just, but shielded from criticism by the need for collective sacrifice in order to preserve the state and provide security for its people. Samuel strongly emphasises power and might as the source of authority despite the fact that in Judaism authority is technically limited by the Law (Faur, 2008).

As already indicated, with such a wealth of historical precedence, it is interesting to note that scholars have tended to shy away from the subject of elites. This is noted by Sklair (2001: ix–x):

> It is somewhat surprising to discover that of all the social classes, however defined and categorized, the group that has attracted the least serious research is the class at the very top of the pile. Terms like elite, ruling class, and capitalist class have been out of favour in the social sciences for some time and the idea of a 'global ruling class' appears, frankly, ridiculous to many capable scholars.

This may be due to the difficulties faced by researchers in gaining access to often high-profile, busy individuals. In the words of Kahl (1957: 10), 'those who sit amongst the mighty do not invite sociologists to watch them make the decisions about how to control the behaviour of others'. Hence, there exists little public documentation regarding elite contribution to, or overall control of, corporate strategy or their influence on corporate behaviour, political processes or the overall policy design of the nation state.

However, some literature does exist. According to Rothkopf (2008), the transnational elite comprises mostly top businessmen, mainly from the USA and the EU. The elite is attributed with engendering a concentration of capital, leading to giant firms, banks and private equity organisations. This super-class advances its interests through self-regulation, liberalised markets, privatisation and the free movement of capital and control over labour and privatised services (Rothkopf, 2008). Increasingly, private firms now decide what public elected bodies used to determine, thus spawning an imbalance of power which undermines democracy. Through the globalising agenda, the super-class has created this hugely unjust system of accumulation of wealth at one pole of society and of poverty at the other.

The historical interpretation of the phrase 'balance of power' implies seeking to ensure an equality of power amongst interested parties. This has been equated with Greek democracy and the doctrine of the harmony of interests, rather than positional power and status as exercised in the Roman Republic, and in the modern era by the USA. This is a critical point to raise as the philosophy that underpins Congress is that of elite theory. It is strongly argued that members of Congress were and continue to be elected from the local upper classes and are not representative of the interests of the varying income groups of society (Mills, 1956). Within Congress, power comes through seniority and the prestige of sitting on particular congressional committees, thus mitigating dissent (Mills, 1956). Mills (1956: 277) uses the term 'power elite' rather than 'ruling class', as 'class' is an economic term; 'rule' is a political one. The phrase 'ruling class' purports that the economic class rules 'politically'. Influential corporate interests, through concentrations of political and economic power, are in the control of small, interlocking elites, which operate according to informal, personal ties which defend this unequal distribution of wealth. These networks also act as a proxy for a foreign policy elite, where informal networking and coordination of policy is accomplished through the tools of formal organisation and institutions whose members are *ex officio* representatives of the major institutions regulating national life.

Elites: self-fulfilling and self-regulating

Collective ownership has existed in various forms throughout history. Ancient Eastern despotism was based on the pre-eminence of the state's or the king's property. In ancient Egypt after the 15 BCE, arable land passed to private ownership. Before then only homes and their surrounding buildings were privately owned. State land was handed over for cultivation while state officials administered the land and collected rent. Canals and installations were also state-owned. The Roman state treated newly conquered land as state land and as a result also owned a considerable number of slaves. The medieval churches also had collective property. 'Capitalism by its very nature was an enemy of collective ownership until the settlement of shareholder organizations' (Djilas, 1957: 55).

The English Civil Wars (1641–51) were one of the first organised attempts to challenge elite control of land. They were a conflict between the 'middle class' and the landowning Parliamentarians and Royalists with the purpose of making better use of land, enhancing trade and redistributing resources from the hands of the monarch and aristocracy to other landowners. The Parliamentarians challenged the 'Divine Right of Kings' and monarchical rule. Charles I resisted for he hoped to unite England, Scotland and Ireland into one kingdom with the wealth of the realm remaining in royal and aristocratic hands. The Parliamentarians, operating almost as a temporary advisory committee, challenged the Crown's prerogative to use Parliament as a tax collection vehicle (Johnston, 1901). Three civil wars ensued followed by Cromwellian rule which unknowingly laid the basis for a constitutional monarchy to this date (McClelland, 1996).

The French Revolution was also initiated by a small elite consisting of the 'Committee of Thirty', a body of largely wealthy, liberal Parisians, who agitated against voting by estate. The argument was that ancient precedent was not sufficient cause for political control, because 'the people were sovereign' (Neely, 2008). In the 1789 election, suffrage requirements were that of being 25 years of age and over and having paid six *livres* in taxes. The election produced 1,201 delegates, including 291 nobles, 300 clergy and 610 members of the Third Estate, namely those who represented the rest of France (Hibbert, 1980).

The National Guard (representing the centre or centre-left of the Assembly) under La Fayette also emerged as a power in its own right. Other self-generated assemblies, Jacobins and *sans-culottes*, were all led by an elite. Similarly, the Roman Catholic Church, the largest landowner in the country, instead of championing the cause of the poor, levied high taxes (known as the *dîme* or tithe) on crops. While the *dîme* lessened the severity of the monarchy's tax increases, it worsened the plight of the poorest who faced a daily struggle with malnutrition (Chisholm, 1911). In effect, the French Revolution politicised the *sans-culottes*, whilst 'the Industrial Revolution industrialized them and despite all this, the under privileged remained and the elites continued as before' (Furet, 1996). Supporting the notion that elites do not easily let go of resources despite conflicts with each other, certain writers have argued that the French Revolution was planned by Adam Weishaupt, a German philosopher and founder of the Illuminati movement (1776). The movement was based on Jesuit thought and consisted of freethinkers (an offshoot of the Enlightenment) and financed by the money changers of Europe (Barruel, 1797/1799; Scott, 1827/1843).[1]

The American Civil war was also a war between elites. Abraham Lincoln used private money residing in bonds to finance the war.[2] He had to deal with treason, insurrection and national bankruptcy during his first days in office. Despite this he managed to build the world's largest army, take the first steps to abolish slavery and create the greatest industrial giant in the world – the steel industry. In addition, a continental railroad system was created, the Department of Agriculture was established and a new era of farm machinery and cheap tools was promoted. However, in a letter to

Colonel William F. Elkins, Lincoln (1864/1950: 40) expressed his fear concerning what he had unleashed:

> I see in the near future a crisis approaching that unnerves me and causes me to tremble for the safety of my country. [...] corporations have been enthroned and an era of corruption in high places will follow, and the money power of the country will endeavour to prolong its reign by working upon the prejudices of the people until all wealth is aggregated in a few hands and the Republic is destroyed.

In many ways, Lincoln's fears have been realised. The US Founding Fathers' idea of checks-and-balances was grounded in the belief that the American middle class would act as the stabiliser and the pivotal point of the class balance in society. In contemporary US economy, the political and economic influence of small entrepreneurs has been replaced by a handful of large corporations, creating an imbalance of power (Mills, 1956). The 'checks-and-balances' system assumes that the contrasting purposes of the Executive, Judiciary and Congress keep society in a dynamic equilibrium. That assumption does not seem to hold as today major interests not only compete with each other, but also extensively cooperate to promote shared interests, for example through the lobbies that are supposed to be part of the checks-and-balances compact but are now part of the system promoting the agendas of elite interests (Mills, 1956; Dalton, 2004).

In terms of their role and impact, the middle classes have come to be dependent on the state. Their jobs cannot provide them with the tools for political freedom, economic security and independence (Mills, 1956). Labour unions themselves have become weak. The inability of government to discharge its duties due to its being controlled by corporate and military interests is visible through the rise of federal public debt (Table 1.3). In his final analysis, Mills (1956) concluded that from the American War of Independence onwards and through the administration of John Adams, the military, the state and the corporate entities have became more or less united, allowing the American power elite to move from one identity and agenda to another. American democracy is now only a formality as the state and corporate entities have became largely indistinguishable. In effect, democracy is dominated by corporate chiefs (Mills, 1956).

What of other countries? Before the 1917 Russian Revolution, three-quarters of the capital of the large banks in Russia was in the hands of foreign capitalists (Lenin, 1902/1970, 1916/1948, 1970; Brovkin, 1994). Foreigners controlled 40% of the shares of the industrial capital of Russia (Trotsky, 1932). Paradoxically, it was elite foreign funding that promoted the Russian Revolution by sponsoring an intellectual and revolutionary elite. Lev Davidovich Bronstein, later known as Leo Trotsky, was one of the first group of Russians living abroad to be sent to Russia to incite riot and rebellion

Table 1.3 US Expenditure and public debt

Year	Expenditure of the federal government (in dollars)	Federal public debt (in dollars)
1870	309.6 million	2.4 billion
1940	8,998.1 million	43.0 billion
1950	40,155.8 million	257.4 billion
1978	478.1 billion	771.5 billion
1988	1,118.5 billion	2,602.6 billion
1998	1,771.4 billion	5,614.2 billion
2008	2,537.9 billion	10,699.8 trillion

Source: Compiled from Clough (1953); Bureau of Labour Statistics (2009); Department of the Treasury (2009).

(Wilson, 1940). On 29 March 1919, *The Times* of London reported on 'one of the curious features of the Bolshevik movement [being] the high percentage of non-Russian elements among its leaders', since some twenty or thirty commissars who provided the central machinery and leadership to the Bolshevik movement were not less than 75% non-ethnic Russians. Moreover, it was German, German-American and British interests that sponsored and sent Vladimir Ilyich Ulyanov Lenin, and his 224 associates into Russia in 1917, to induce defection from the Russian armies. The editor of *The Times*, Steed (1924, 11: 301) noted this in his writings:

> potent international financial interests were at work [at the Peace Conference] in favour of the immediate recognition of the Bolshevists. Those influences had been largely responsible for the Anglo-American proposal in January (1919) to call Bolshevist representatives to Paris at the beginning of the Peace Conference ... and Tehitcherin, the Bolshevist Commissary for Foreign Affairs, had revealed the meaning of the January proposal by offering extensive commercial and economic concessions in return for recognition.

In particular, the top man at the US Federal Reserve, Max Warburg, was behind the financing of Trotsky, whilst Olof Aschberg of the Nya Banken, Stockholm, played a major role in the funding of the revolution (Allen and Abraham, 1976).

Overall, Marxism was promoted by Western monopolistic capitalism for the economies of the industrially underdeveloped East, such as Russia, China and Yugoslavia, and for Cuba and Latin America. Although the revolutionary movements existed in semi-feudal Russia some fifty years earlier, it was elite promotion of agents provocateurs that made the difference (Carr, 1950). Of course, elite influence on its own could not have created revolution. These economies desperately needed industrial change, and because their capitalism was not fully developed, peasant-based revolutionary change could be induced (Meisner, 1967). However, what was underestimated by the West was that the socialist movement also created a new class – the party elite (Djilas, 1957).

Like the socialist revolutions, the post-socialist revolutions have been sponsored by foreign interests (see Table 1.4). For example, between 2000 and 2005, the Russian-allied governments of Serbia, Georgia, Ukraine and Kyrgyzstan were overthrown through bloodless upheavals which the Western media portrayed as spontaneous, indigenous and popular ('people power') uprisings, termed 'velvet' or 'coloured' revolutions. In fact they were outcomes of extensive planning and considerable financial investment much of which originated in the West (Sussman and Krader, 2008). Among the key foreign agents involved in the process of nurturing 'transitional democracies' are the United States Agency for International Development (USAID), the National Endowment for Democracy and its funded institutes, the Open Society Institute, Freedom House, and the International Center on Nonviolent Conflict (Sassman and Krader, 2008). These agencies offered four types of foreign assistance: political, financial, technical training and marketing propaganda (Sussman and Krader, 2008). For example, in the Ukraine in 2004, the USA spent about $US34 million on regime change initiatives (US Department of State, 2004), whilst George Soros is purported to have invested about $US1.6 million in support of a local 'Freedom of Choice' NGO coalition and Ukraine's 'New Choice 2004' (Wilson, 2006: 184).

As anthropologist Margaret Mead (quoted in Szakos and Szakos, 2007: xiii) poignantly observed, 'never doubt that a small group of thoughtful, committed citizens can change the world; indeed, it's the only thing that ever has'. She voiced a historical truism that major social changes have been led by an elite. Mills (1956) too concluded that from Caesar onwards each subsequent elite has more power and, with advanced technology, a greater capacity for destruction. Moreover, with each new generation, 'the facility of power is enormously enlarged and decisively centralized, meaning that the decision of small groups is now more consequential' (Mills, 1956: 23).

Whether conflict is initiated from above (elites on elites) or from below (the new elite), history emphasises that a new power elite takes control through centralising the levers of power. Despite the source of the revolution, the emergent (new or old) power elite is more unified and resourceful than the previous fragmented 'mass society' (Mills, 1956). The new society is controlled through organs of government, particularly that of social services, such as health and education, which possess the administrative and human means to exercise close supervision of the so-called 'problem populations', those usually at the bottom of the social scale. These services are encouraged to collaborate with the police and judicial system which turns them 'into extensions of the penal apparatus, instituting a *social panopticism* which, under cover of promoting the well being of deprived populations, submits them to an ever-more precise and penetrating form of punitive surveillance'

Table 1.4 Elites and social change

Country and event	Power base of old elite	Drivers for change	Power base of new elite	Outcomes
Religious revolutions Kingdom of Judea (167 BCE) – uprising led by a *kohen* of the Hashmonaim, Mattityahu[3]	Jerusalem (priests of the second Temple) and the cities of Judah (i.e. upwardly mobile Jews); Syrian–Greek military administration	Helenisation of Jews under the Syrian–Greek leadership, Antiochus IV[4]	Judea's countryside	• Daring military victories of the Hasmoneans • Re-established Jewish sovereignty in the Land of Israel • The Hasmonean leadership that lasted for some 200 years – temporary custodians of Jewish leadership, high priests, and priest-kings • Celebration of *Chanukah*
Bourgeois revolutions England – English Civil War (1641–51), achieved from above	Royalists (i.e. absolute monarchy with feudal privileges for the aristocracy)	• Charles I's 'Eleven Years' Tyranny' (i.e. 'Charles's Personal Rule) • Tax illegality • Political system out of keeping with wealth creation sector • Penalties on Puritans for not attending Anglican church services	• Parliamentarians (i.e. gentry, religious Puritans) • Puritans led by Cromwell (religious sects – dispersed dialogical views)	• Parliamentary victory[5] • Short period of dictatorship • Constitutional monarchy[6] • New Model Army[7] • Ending the monopoly of the Church of England on Christian worship • Elite kept power

(continued)

Table 1.4 Continued

Country and event	Power base of old elite	Drivers for change	Power base of new elite	Outcomes
France – French Revolution (1789–99) achieved by the proletariat below	• Absolute monarchy • Feudal privileges for the aristocracy and Catholic clergy • Supported by the 'right wing' in Assembly	• Economic factors included widespread famine, national debt,[8] conspicuous consumption of the noble class, high crop tax levied by the Roman Catholic Church and an undeveloped internal trade with too many customs barriers • Protests (i.e. riots, chaos) and widespread looting	• Third estate (i.e. people representatives, middle-class and the Royalist democrats) • Jacobeans (a federation of clubs – of dispersed dialogical view) • Napoleon and his elite	• Violence and terror • Resources placed in the hands of the revolutionary authorities • Structural change: Enlightenment, citizenship and inalienable rights[9] • French Republic
American Civil War (1861–5) achieved from above	The Confederacy (agrarian South)	• Slavery • Sectionalism • Economic differences between North and South	The Union (i.e. industrialised/ corporate North)	• Ending slavery[10] • Restoring the Union (i.e. Reconstruction) • Strengthening the role of the federal government • High casualty rate[11] • Rise of corporate power[12]

Irish Civil War (1922–3) achieved from below	Anti-Treaty (i.e. *Fianna Fáil* party)[13] – Republican opposition, for whom the Treaty represented a betrayal of the Irish Republic	• Independence from British rule • Conflict between two opposing groups of Irish nationalists prompted by the Anglo-Irish Treaty[14]	• Pro-Treaty factions – Irish nationalists (i.e. *Fine Gael* party with stronghold in the cities – the forces of the new Free State, who supported the Anglo-Irish Treaty under which the state was established) • Strong social capital • Religious bonding	• Victory won by the Free State forces • Establishment of the Irish Free State, independent from the UK but within the British Empire • The Anglo-Irish Treaty • Two main parties in the *Fianna Fáil* and *Fine Gael*[15]
Socialist revolutions Russian Revolution (1917) – through foreign financial support achieved from above and below.[16]	Constitutional monarchy 1906 – supported by the landed class, aristocracy and the White (all non-Bolshevik) factions[17]	• Economic factors; • High foreign control of resources • Peasant hardship • Foreign financial support of revolution[18]	The Reds (i.e. national network of Soviets, led by socialists, the allegiance of the lower-class citizens and the political left which controlled the levers of government)[19]	• New monolithic party – the Communist Party • New class – new inequalities[20] • New social and political order
China – Chinese Civil War (1927–36 and also 1946–50), achieved from below and above	Control of land by several major and lesser warlords	• Economic factors • Foreign support for revolution through training and know how	Both city and countryside through rebalancing of wealth distribution	• The Communist army confiscated property and weapons from local warlords and landlords, while recruiting peasants and the poor, solidifying its appeal to the masses • Creation of People's Republic of China

(continued)

Table 1.4 Continued

Country and event	Power base of old elite	Drivers for change	Power base of new elite	Outcomes
Post-socialist revolutions (i.e. coloured revolutions)[21]				
Ukraine – Orange Revolution (2004–5)	*Siloviks* ('strongmen' – politicians from the old security or military services, often linked to the KGB)	• Western finance and expertise • *Pora* ('It's Time') a civic youth organisation and political party • Extensive grassroots campaigning and coalition-building among the opposition	• Western alliances • Advocacy of increased national democracy	• Amended constitutional law • New round of elections • Ongoing pandemic corruption[22]
Capitalist revolutions of the Middle East (i.e. scented or jasmine revolutions)[23]				
Tunisian Jasmine Revolution (2010–11)	Autocratic regime led by Ben Ali's, Constitutional Democratic Rally (RCD) party originally supported by the United States and France	• Western finance and expertise • Intensive campaign including youth and labour unions • Protest with relatively little violence between security services and protesters	• Western alliances • Advocacy of increased national democracy	• Interim government supported by USA • Continued discontent • Promised election in mid-2011

Source: Compiled by authors.

(Wacquant, 2008: 22). This is best captured by Orwell's (1946: 1) summary of political theory put forward by James Burnham (1941):

All historical change finally boils down to the replacement of one ruling class by another. All talk about democracy, liberty, equality, fraternity, all revolutionary movements, all visions of Utopia, or 'the classless society', or 'the Kingdom of Heaven on earth', are humbug (not necessarily conscious humbug) covering the ambitions of some new class which is elbowing its way into power. The English Puritans, the Jacobins, the Bolsheviks, were in each case simply power seekers using the hopes of the masses in order to win a privileged position for themselves. Power can sometimes be won or maintained without violence, but never without fraud, because it is necessary to make use of the masses, and the masses would not co-operate if they knew that they were simply serving the purposes of a minority. In each great revolutionary struggle the masses are led on by vague dreams of human brotherhood, and then, when the new ruling class is well established in power, they are thrust back into servitude.

Thus, from whatever perspectives they are analysed and whatever the reasons for their existence, the emergent view is that elites are, historically were, and will continue to be, self-serving. Such seems to be the case today with the expansion of the means of mass persuasion of public opinion through the emergence of new information and communication technology (ICT). ICT has been used to promote a deceptive picture of choice. In reality, choice has been considerably limited to just a few options concerning political, social and economic concerns all of which favour the current elites. The remote possibility of debate and discussion, let alone action, is disappearing as the experience of the public turns into a narrowing of routines and structural environments. The mass has no escape from institutions tightly owned by the few. It is the agents of authorised institutions that penetrate this mass, reducing free thought through minimal discussion and replacing it with mindless information such as 'big brother' television programmes and chat shows, where the realisation of opinion in action is 'guided' by the authorities who organise and control the channels of such action. As Gioia (2003: 278) notes, 'the reality people confront is the reality they construe'.

The uncomfortable truth of today is that the social construction of organised life is determined by increasing privately owned communication channels. These influence not only how citizens think and feel, but also how each relates to the other. More often than not fear, uncertainty and doubt are spread through dramatic accounts of military and economic crisis. The net result is that individuals in society are defenceless whilst, as groups, they have been minded to be politically indifferent (Mills, 1956). As David Rockefeller observed in 1993 (*Telegraph*, 2008), 'we are on the verge of a global transformation – all we need is the right major crisis and nations will accept the New World Order'. This message was later reinforced by Mikhail Gorbachev arguing that 'the threat of environmental crisis will be the "international disaster key" that will unlock the New World Order' (*Telegraph*, 2008). However, this new world order will seemingly be controlled by the not so new global elite.

Global elites

Although for centuries elites were confined to local contexts, they nevertheless exercised colonial/imperial aspirations. Now with globalisation and the tight control of information and capital, these elites operate within a created context of the global milieu. In the past, one could talk of the French social system characterised by the importance it attached to its elite and the importance of belonging to the 'state' (D'Iribarne, 1989). Now the same elite belongs to the world. French society, which traditionally functioned according to an 'honour system' rather than a 'contract system' typical of the USA, and the 'consensus system' typical of the Netherlands (D'Iribarne, 1989), is increasingly integrating a 'contract system' with its established status and honour preoccupation. Thus, global elites today can be viewed as the locally rich but with extensive global reach.

In the present, three trends amongst the newly emergent global elites differentiate them from traditional elites. First, the locally rich elites are buying land in foreign economies on a massive scale, the consequences of which have not yet been understood. The World Conservation Bank owns many titles to lands across the globe through the World Wilderness Land Inventory Trust (Sweatman, 1987). Moreover, World Bank loans that are not collateralised may undergo loan-swaps where, for example, the bank may own sections of the Amazon by default.

Secondly, the ruling elite of one country is using the ruling elite of another country to initiate proxy wars. Once an invaluable Anglo-American policy tool, proxy wars are increasingly becoming a well-utilised policy lever. For example, in the past the UK used proxy wars/conflicts to divide many Arab states. Similarly the USA has used proxy wars in South America and South Korea, as well as in Poland, Hungary and other states. Now China has adopted this strategy through North Korea and Iran. It will be interesting to observe whether, through the invasion of Iraq and the future possible bombings of Iran, the USA will shape the new state of Kurdistan in order to provide a home base for Anglo-American operations.

Thirdly, the phenomenon of multi-polarity is gaining ground. In the past, the globally rich elites were more bipolar (Britain vs. Spain, Britain vs. France, Britain vs. the Netherlands), all competing for global resources. There were exceptions where multi-polar blocs emerged at times of conflict, such as the Thirty Years War and the Seven Years War. Now multi-polar interrelationships and networks (USA and its allies vs. Russia–China) are constantly competing in the same space. All have global reach and, as a result, these elites via their networks are coming together to negotiate and progress their individual agendas but also to avoid direct confrontation with each other at all costs.

These multi-polar relationships can be witnessed through the phenomenon of outsourcing. By the 1980s there was a strong drive by the West for transferring technology to developing countries, utilising cheap labour and 'outsourcing' the dirty industries. This was followed in the 1990s by the outsourcing of routine information technology. In the twenty-first century, outsourcing is more focused on leveraging cost efficiencies particularly for staple diets (or bio-fuels) such as wheat, maize, rice and jatropha. For example, Egyptian and South Korean projects in the Sudan are as much for resource exploitation as for food production. Libya has leased 100,000 hectares from Mali for rice cultivation (*The Economist*, 2009a). Previous farming ventures involved private investors purchasing land for the growth of cash crops (coffee, tea, sugar, bananas). The trend has continued, for example in Russia, where privatised land is being bought by foreign investors for similar agrarian purposes (*The Economist*, 2009a).

Private investors are no longer single rich individuals. Now, corporations and governments act in a similar manner to the state-sponsored monopolistic companies of the past such as the East India Company, the Dutch COC, etc. In 2008, a Swedish company, Alpcot Agro, bought 128,000 hectares of Russian land; South Korea's Hyundai Heavy Industry paid US$6.5 million for a major stake in Khoral Zerno, a company that owns 10,000 hectares of eastern Siberia (known for its richness in natural resources), and the US-based bank Morgan Stanley bought 40,000 hectares of the Ukraine in March 2009 (*The Economist*, 2009a). Piva, the first Russian grain processor to be floated, plans to sell 40% of its landowning division to investors from the Gulf, giving them access to 500,000 hectares of land (*The Economist*, 2009a). Cambodia leased land to Kuwaiti investors in August 2008 after mutual prime ministerial visits. In 2008, the Sudanese and Qatari governments set up a joint venture to invest in Sudan. Saudi officials have visited Australia, Brazil, Egypt, Ethiopia, Kazakhstan, the Philippines, South Africa, Sudan, Turkey, Ukraine and Vietnam to talk about land acquisitions. The majority of the new deals have been government-to-government either directly or indirectly through corporations. The acquirers are foreign regimes or companies closely tied to sources of wealth such as sovereign wealth funds. The sellers are host governments dispensing land they have owned.

In terms of elite influence, particularly over land acquisition, the balance between the state and private sectors is heavily skewed in favour of the state. When private investors invested in cash crops, they tended to boost world trade and international economic activity – at least in theory. Now, governments are investing in staple crops but from a protectionist impulse to circumvent world markets. These land deals are in response to food-market turmoil. For example, *The Economist* index for food prices highlights rises of 78% from 2007 to 2008, with soybean and rice both increasing by more than 130%. Even more important is the drive for land acquisition due to water shortages (*The Economist*, 2009a). Control over resources as well as control over the means of production gives elites the power base needed to reshape the geo-politics of the globe. Electrical based transport using lithium-ion batteries will be promoted according to who controls big lithium deposits in Chile, Australia, Russia and Bolivia. Underneath its salt flats, Bolivia holds between one-eighth and one-half of the global total of lithium deposits (*The Week*, 2009). Mitsubishi and French interests have already approached the Bolivian government regarding the construction of lithium plants. Publicising environmental concerns over lithium mining, particularly the poisoning of the water supply in parts of Chile and the environmentally protectionist nature of South American socialist government policies, are considered unfriendly to the West, by the West (*The Week*, 2009).

Nature of social capital

One powerful exposition on the nature of elites is that drawn from social capital theory. As we have seen, the social capital perspective of elites is that they are individuals with similar interests who give support to one another. For example, Dewey (1899/1956) drawing on the work of Madison (1788/1961) and de Tocqueville (1840/2000) to integrate the concepts of social cohesion and connectedness into the pluralist tradition of American politics, adopted the terms 'social capital' and 'social spirit' in his exposition of democracy and education. Dewey (1899/1956: 30) recognised that all children have 'natural resources, namely un-invested capital, which when effectively exercised enhances the active growth of the child'. The 'impulse to communicate, to construct, to inquire, and to express in a finer form' is a central aspect of social capital and social spirit. Yet, when social spirit is replaced with 'positively individualistic motives and standards' such as fear, emulation, rivalry and judgements of superiority and inferiority, then 'the weaker gradually lose their capacity to exercise such strengths and accept continuous and persistent inferiority', whilst 'the stronger grow to glory, not in their strength, but in the fact that they are stronger' (Dewey, 1899/1956: 64–5). Dewey's line of argument can be extended to the rest of society on the basis that 'education is the fundamental method of social progress and reform' (Dewey, 1899/1956: 93). Later Hanifan (1916: 130), in referring to social cohesion and personal investment in the community, and in differentiating social capital from material goods, argued that this

> tends to make these tangible substances count for most in the daily lives of people: namely good will, fellowship, sympathy, and social intercourse

among the individuals and families who make up a social unit ... The individual is helpless socially, if left to himself ... If he comes into contact with his neighbour, and they with other neighbours, there will be an accumulation of social capital, which may immediately satisfy his social needs and which may bear a social potentiality sufficient to the substantial improvement of living conditions in the whole community. The community as a whole will benefit by the cooperation of all its parts, while the individual will find in his associations the advantages of the help, the sympathy, and the fellowship of his neighbours.

The political scientist Salisbury (1969) further advanced the concept of social capital as a critical component of interest group formation. Along the same lines, Bourdieu (1972) differentiated social capital from cultural, economic and symbolic capital. He later acknowledged that social capital, and similarly cultural capital, is the possession of the individual first and the group second (Bourdieu, 1986). However, the role that groups, associations and, in particular, entrenched institutions play in the accessibility and distribution of assets, produced for Bourdieu (1986) a negative opinion of social capital. For example, the great US Civil War Commander Andrew Jackson noted that, 'the rich and the powerful too often bend the acts of government to their selfish purposes', whilst Franklin Roosevelt noted that 'private enterprise is ceasing to be free enterprise. Private enterprise indeed became too private. It became privileged enterprise, not free enterprise.'

As can be seen, social capital lends itself to multiple definitions and interpretations through its duality in accommodating understanding of both economic and social interactions. In so doing, the concept has both structural and individual aspects. Whilst social capital facilitates collective action, generated by networks of relationships, reciprocity, trust and social norms, it can operate within the existing social structures and yet mould new social structures. Communication is the primary tool for building, activating and leveraging social capital. Communication is needed to access and use social capital through exchanging information, identifying problems and solutions to these problems, and also through finding pathways through conflict (Hazleton and Kennan, 2000). Equally, social capital in the institutional sense can also lead to undesired outcomes if the political institutions and nature of democracy in a particular country are not sufficiently robust and, as a result, are overpowered by particularly driven social capital groups (Putnam, 2000). This fear was particularly visible in Lincoln's (1864/1950) regrets and, later on, echoed by Woodrow Wilson (1913/2006: 185):

I am a most unhappy man. I have unwittingly ruined my country. A great industrial nation is controlled by its system of credit. Our system of credit is concentrated. The growth of the nation, therefore, and all our activities are in the hands of a few men. We have come to be one of the worst ruled, one of the most completely controlled and dominated Governments in the civilized world, no longer a Government by free opinion, no longer a Government by conviction and the vote of the majority, but a Government by the opinion and duress of a small group of dominant men.

Putnam (2000) noted that social capital is not always invested towards positive ends, as cartels as well as violent or criminal groups' activities are encouraged through the strengthening of intra-group relationships or the 'bonding of social capital' to pursue their singular ends. The bonding of social capital perpetuates sentiments which can lead to a variety of consequences, such as ethnic marginalisation, social isolation (Putnam, 2000), social deprivation and war.

The notion of social capital has permeated through to a multitude of academic disciplines, and has been segmented into three different forms: cognitive, relational and structural. There are no hard lines of delineation between these categories, which often overlap thus ensuring further confusion of empirical research results (Fine, 2008). Nevertheless, there appears to be an agreement that networks and trust have a major role in the construction and use of social capital regardless of the variety of definitions.

However, as noted by Fine (2008), current social capital literature barely addresses the issues of class and the state. This is particularly evident in post-Second World War deliberations, where in the Anglo-American system of oligarchic and financial hegemony, elites have used elaborate networks of financing and impersonal forms of control through a constellation of interests (i.e. internal investors) to build up a shareholding that has given them influence and/or control over various firms (Scott, 1987). Control through a collection of interests is characteristic of Anglo-American economies where financial leverage particularly through the use of credit has encouraged the building of large financial intermediaries. For example, the UK economy is represented by an inter-corporate network in which 'City' enterprises (financial services) are closely aligned with 'non-financial enterprises' (Scott, 1987).

Examination of FTSE 100 and 250 companies by Froud et al. (2008) revealed that, in 2005, 60% of FTSE 100 companies had at least one executive from another FTSE 100 company sitting on their board as a non-executive director (NED). Similar spheres of influence were found within FTSE 250 companies (Froud et al., 2008).

Thus social capital thinking has a cohesive and dynamic nature, both of which provide explanation of the nature of elites. Certainly, there has been a preoccupation with the cohesive effect of social capital. However, the dynamic perspective to social capital indicates that, at the time of revolution, the elites rotate. As already stated, the elite that takes over is often more oppressive than the previous elite. Yet, there are exceptions when change of the old regime is replaced by a new, more progressive one, as in Ireland and Australia. The Irish Civil War of the 1920s was fought by essentially two divisions of the working classes and although one side won, no particular elite took over, thus providing an example of the few more egalitarian societies that exist today. The Irish took exceptional dislike to the intervention of the British in the Irish Civil War and since then have vowed to maintain their political neutrality. This is seen today with Ireland demanding special status in the Treaty of Lisbon concerning political neutrality and also its refusal to be a member of NATO. In Australia, the very first federal Prime Minister, Sir Edmond Barton, brought the six British colonies into a federated Australia without violent conflict.

Conclusion

What seems clear is that a new and increasingly globally oriented, technically sophisticated elite uses its mass-organisational skills to promote its interests and power. This new global elite sees any vestige of traditional society as an obstacle and uses all means at its disposal, including political influence, financial clout, technology, propaganda as well as military and religious manipulation to undermine the previous order(s) and recreate a political order in its favour.

The danger, as captured by Mills (1956: 310) is that, with the

> broadening of the base of politics within the context of a folk-lore of demo-
> cratic decision-making, and with the increased means of mass persuasion
> that are available, public opinion has become the object of intensive efforts
> to control, manage, manipulate and increasingly intimidate.

This can be seen through governments' efforts across the globe that use fear under the pretext of terrorism, whether that narrative is imaginary or real, to increase control over people (Wacquant, 2007; Thorne and Kouzmin, 2010).

In reaction to elite supremacy, *vertical* society (Friedman, 1999) is supposedly being reformed by ICT, particularly through the spread of a global mass culture, into a purportedly more *horizontal* society. ICT and cyberspace offer utopian myths about the end of dysfunctional politics (Thorne and Kouzmin, 2008). However, although ICT has the potential to liberate communication, this potential is not fully utilised as IT mediated communication follows existing patterns of norms and regulations and, as such, more invisibly centralises control (Kakabadse et al., 2008; Kouzmin and Thorne, 2010). Moreover, as Nathanson (1969: 230) notes, the military R&D complex and 'experimentation with new processes of production and new products' has been fundamental to this development. What has emerged is a centralised and complex network of laws which allow particular institutions such as trade associations to forge a privileged relationship with government, thus minimising the influence of the individual entrepreneur (Sweezy, 1983).

The technologically savvy elites see new ICT as a means for the fulfilment of some of the nineteenth-century 'bourgeois public sphere' (club and coffee-house) functions, where individuals were able to exchange their views through 'reasoned argument' and, in so doing, develop opinions on the basis that everyone had an equal right to speak (Habermas, 1979). In one sense, that is the case; an interactive debate facilitated by ICT between citizens and their representatives offers the representatives a likely realistic view of citizen opinion on practical issues. In this way, links are provided for the politician to access groups with whom there was no previous contact. Thus the opportunity for increasing citizen participation is available (Klein, 1995).

The counter to such a reality is that electronically mediated interactions are embedded in broader social processes, wherein the Internet itself is only one element of the ecology of the media. From space satellites such as the Global Positioning System (GPS) to the Internet, from mobile telephones and public CCTV to office and home electronic gadgetry, every minutia of human activity is monitored. Moreover, the under-the-skin radio-frequency identifier (RFID), VeriChip, has been implanted in many high security employees, destitute people and those in elderly care homes for the purpose of control (Kakabadse et al., 2010). These newly emergent structures, variously named as 'Virtual Feudalism', 'Post-national State', 'New Serfdoms', 'IT-Harems' and 'Electronic Shoguns', depict increasingly invisible, all-seeing, all-powerful control mechanisms over citizens first envisaged by the British philosopher, Jeremy Bentham (1787) in his essay on the need for social control in prisons, asylums, nursing homes, work places and schools – the 'Panopticon' (Kakabadse et al., 2007). It should be remembered that the Internet is both an instrument for, and result of, the institutionalised practices of those that use it (Mosco and Foster, 2001). The original Internet community custom of sharing information freely is slowly diminishing as the Internet is becoming an increasingly controlled commodity by both big business and governments.

The debate between ICT determined freedom and control is captured in the dual theories of technology amplification and technology reinforcement. 'Technology amplification theory' (Agre, 2002) holds that ICT has the ability to amplify citizen's democratic participation by providing electronic public forums and electronic voting. 'Technology reinforcement theory', sometimes termed technology enactment theory (Fountain, 2004), holds that ICT provides new mechanisms to further reinforce existing power structures and social controls and identifies problematic structural aspects to the polity through ever-increasing surveillance systems. Both theories provide different analytical frameworks but come to the same conclusion – that ICT does not create a new political order, it reinforces the existing one.

The rhetoric of the 'communication revolution' is, in reality, a 'functional amplification' (Morrison et al., 1999). As such, ICT is a tool for 'reinforcement politics' and is less applicable to the 'creation of new forms of democratic public spheres than to the support of already existing ones' (Buchstein, 1997: 260). The public sphere is and always was a much larger phenomenon than any ICT-mediated forum. New 'political forms will emerge only by counter-balancing or transcending a regime of political integration and category of the political subject that ICT is rapidly amplifying' (Agre, 2002: 331). The propagation of cyberspace as a mythical space rests on three powerful beliefs about radical and transcendent disjunction celebrating the end of history, the end of geography and the end of politics. Yet, deeper analysis shows that the marriage between ICT and capital, which seeks to dispel old means of doing politics, is in fact distinctly skilled at practising old politics (Mosco and Foster, 2001). In this sense, capital as we know it today, wins.

The concepts of 'self-service democracy' and 'new public management' (NPM) are borrowed from the private sector primarily for the purposes of reinforcing cost discipline practices. Firms that employ 'service' use the mythical language of customer empowerment but are in fact driven by cost savings. It costs $7.00 to answer a query through a call centre, but only 10 cents to deal with the issue online. Each self-service checkout at a grocery store replaces around 2.5 employees (*The Economist*, 2009b). In a similar vein, e-government is going the same route. Political governance, by virtue of controlling societal behaviour through consumerism and personal choice packaged in electronic format, is powerful (Passavant, 2005). The promoters of e-democracy, such as the Progressive Freedom Foundation (PFF), backed by large electronic technology enterprises, are advocating a regulatory regime where the focus that will shape behaviour and mould opinion in cyberspace will be technological code rather than traditional legal regulation (Mosco and Foster, 2001).

In societies such as the USA and the UK which operate mission-oriented public policies based on 'big science deployed to meet big problems' (Weinberg, 1967: 24), technology is used strategically and is 'intimately linked to the objectives of national sovereignty', including that of national defence and national pride such as atomic energy, weapons and aeronautics. However, the technology application debate is removed from the public sphere (Ergas, 1987: 193). For example, the Strategic Defence Initiative (SDI) promotes the pretext of security, but also increasingly impinges on individual freedom, by deploying intrusive technology (Mosco and Foster, 2001). In societies with diffusion-oriented public policies, such as in Sweden and Switzerland, deci-sion-making is decentralised and citizens are involved in public debate over the introduction of new technology (Ergas, 1987).

As emphasised and regardless of the theoretical perspective adopted, namely ICT amplification or ICT reinforcement, ICT does not provide a solution to the shortcomings of current democratic processes. Analysis of the impact of ICT on democracy concludes that unequal power relations emerge whereby the corporation's influence on public policy development far supersedes that of the citizen (Kakabadse et al., 2007).

There is a need to change political processes from the principle set by the Roman Republic (citizen rights) but distorted by the elites for their own ends, to that based on the principle of Athenian democracy. Ireland and Australia have minimised elite control through their political governance design (proportional representation, elected upper houses). Sweden, Denmark and Finland have also minimised elite influence through the mechanism of wealth redistribution (high taxation rates, tax simplification and stability, minimisation of tax avoidance/evasion, tax efficiency) and an all-embracing social welfare system. Hence, these economies have achieved a higher degree of egalitarian culture where there is minimal elite control of the various strata of society. The UK, the USA, Russia and France, in contrast, have adopted minimal mechanisms for effective wealth redistribution to keep at bay self-seeking elites. Moreover, the UK, the USA and Russia have competitive tax systems to attract corporations and wealthy individuals to relocate to their countries, thus encouraging the cult of elitism. Ironically, Ireland has also adopted a similar practice, which goes against the culture of a down-to-earth society, but that practice has not spawned an over-dominant elite that drives public policy towards satisfying particular agendas.

There is a need to invoke a debate about how far, and in what areas of the socio-economic sphere, organs of government need to be involved (Kakabadse et al., 2007). The inherent paradox of representative democracy is expressed as the dilemma between government control versus citizen freedom. Thus the question that is raised is whether the power conferred on institutions to engender a balanced society is at the point of destroying the very freedom it sought to protect (Amato, 1997: 3). In order to debate meaningfully the state of the realm (Post, 1964: 322), there is a need for an effective and free communicative infrastructure. There is a need for a 'new birth of freedom; [so] that government of the people, by the people, for the people, shall not perish from the earth' (Lincoln, 1864/1950: 1). In order to uphold democratic values, it is the duty of government organs to maintain and enhance honourable and prosperous conditions on behalf of the state (Viterbo, 1901: 232). Unfortunately, the emergent patterns of elite behaviour that are being reported are those of evident 'oligarchic convergence and isomorphism' (Kouzmin and Thorne, 2010). The need for further, informed debate and in-depth research on the impact of elites is imperative.

Notes

1. The Illuminati (Latin *illuminatus*, 'enlightened') were the group's given name, although they called themselves 'Perfectibilists'. The group has also been called the Illuminati Order and the Bavarian Illuminati Group was founded on 1 May 1776, in Ingolstadt, Upper Bavaria.

2. Prior to the Federal Reserve Bank's creation, the House of Morgan was dominant in contrast to the early colonists' model. Operating out of Philadelphia, the nation's first capital, it favoured state-issued and loaned-out money, collecting the interest and 'return(ing) it to the provincial government' in lieu of taxes (Lendman, 2009).

3. Mattityahu, a *kohen* (high priest) of the Hashmonaim family who lived in Modi'in west of Jerusalem and his sons including Judah Maccabee (the 'Hammer') gave vent to 'righteous anger', a revolt against Antiochus IV, which won independence for Jerusalem and allowed Mattathias to rule until 166 BCE (Josephus, *Antiquities of the Jews*, XII, vi, 2). The revolt was not only against Greek rule, but also against fellow Jews and other priests who became Hellenists (Josephus, *Antiquities of the Jews*, XII, vi, 2). Many *kohanim* (priests) were among the first to assimilate, probably because their high socio-economic status brought them into close contact with the Greeks. This revolt was later called the Zealot movement, an anti-Hellenistic, Hassidic movement, which advocated the strict enforcement of Jewish Law.

4. Loss of traditions of *Shabbat, kashrut* and circumcision, and sacrificing to God in the Temple.

5. Trial and execution of Charles I, the exile of his son, Charles II, and replacement of English monarchy with first, the Commonwealth of England (1649–53) and later with a Protectorate (1653–9), under Oliver Cromwell's personal rule.

6. Constitutionally, this established the precedent that an English monarch cannot govern without Parliament's consent, although this concept was established only later in the century.

7. In 1645, Parliament reaffirmed its determination to fight the war to the finish. It passed the Self-denying Ordinance by which all members of either House of Parliament laid down their commands, and reorganized its main forces into the New Model Army, led by Sir Thomas Fairfax, with Cromwell as his second-in-command.

8. Louis XV fought many wars, bringing France to the verge of bankruptcy. Furthermore, Louis XVI supported the colonists during the American Revolution, exacerbating the precarious financial condition of the government. The national debt amounted to almost two billion *livres*.

9. The Revolution managed to give practical application to the ideas of the *philosophes* of equality before the law, trial by jury, and the freedom of religion, speech and the press. Furet (1996: 215) notes that, 'On both sides there was the implicit demand for a king, but one who was radically different from other kings, since he would be born of the sovereignty of the people and of reason. This was where Napoleon Bonaparte, King of the French Revolution, was born. In 1789, the French had created a Republic, under the name of a monarchy. Ten years later, they created a monarchy, under the name of a Republic.'

10. Slavery effectively ended in the USA in the spring of 1865 when the Confederate armies surrendered. All slaves in the Confederacy were freed by the Emancipation Proclamation. Slaves in the border states and Union-controlled parts of the South were freed by state action or (on 6 December 1865) by the Thirteenth Amendment.

11. Three per cent of the population (i.e. the war produced about 1,030,000 casualties, including about 620,000 deaths of soldiers—two-thirds through disease) (Nofi, 2001).

12. Discussing a particular case, Lincoln speaking to the Illinois legislature, argued that 'These capitalists generally act harmoniously and in concert to fleece the people, and now that they have got into a quarrel with themselves, we are called upon to appropriate the people's money to settle the quarrel' (Nicolay and Hay, 1897/1905: 1: 24).

13. Civil war broke out when Michael Collins was sent by de Valera to negotiate and agree with the British to keep Ireland (south) independent but not the north. Many did not accept this, arguing that the war with the British did not go far enough to realise a united independent Ireland. There were two main parties: *Fine Gael* (city – traders) and *Fianna Fáil* (country) who continued the war. The Irish emerged with a democracy but without an elite stronghold. *Fianna Fáil* ('Soldiers of Destiny' or 'Warriors of Fál' – 'Fál' is the legendary name for Ireland) was founded by Éamon de Valera who led it from 1926–59. The war of independence against the British which sparked the Irish Civil War was a political and social movement. The underlying sentiment inspired the need to preserve Irish culture, language, history and religion. Historically the desire for political independence from Great Britain has been associated with the Irish Catholic community, but in reality it was also supported by many Irish Protestant nationalists.

14. The Second Dáil (16 August 1921–8 June 1922) (i.e. Dáil Éireann) was the revolutionary parliament of the self-proclaimed Irish Republic. One of its most important acts was to bring an end to the War of Independence by ratifying the controversial Anglo-Irish Treaty. Officially called the 'Articles of Agreement for a Treaty between Great Britain and Ireland', the treaty between the government of the United Kingdom of Great Britain and Ireland (David Lloyd George) and representatives of the de facto Irish Republic (Michael Collins, Arthur Griffith) was signed on 6 December 1921 and concluded the Irish War of Independence. It established an autonomous dominion, known as the Irish Free State, within the British Empire, and provided Northern Ireland, which had been created by the 1920 Government of Ireland Act, with the option to opt out of the Irish Free State, which it exercised.

15. *Fine Gael* ('United Ireland Party' meaning 'Family of the Irish or Tribe of the Irish') was formed in 1933 following a merger of its parent party, the *Cumann na nGaedhael* with the Army Comrades Association (ACA or 'Blueshirts') and the Centre Party. Its origins lie in the struggle for Irish independence and the pro-Treaty side in the Irish Civil War, identifying, in particular, Michael Collins as the founder of the movement.

16. In 1905 there was a wave of mass political unrest through vast areas of the Russian Empire which led to the establishment of a limited constitutional monarchy, the establishment of the State Duma of the Russian Empire, a multi-party system and the Russian Constitution of 1906. The Russian Revolution was the result of a series of revolutions in Russia in 1917, which destroyed the tsarist autocracy and led to the creation of the Soviet Union. The first revolution took place in February 1917, in the context of the First World War, with much of the army in a state of mutiny. The tsar was deposed and replaced with a provisional government. The second revolution was in October 1917, when the provisional government was removed and replaced with the Bolshevik (communist) government. Numerous socialist revolutionaries participated in the October Revolution. After the revolution, these collaborating parties were dispersed, or dissolved of their own accord and merged with the Communist Party.

17. After 1906, landlords of large properties, terrorised by the revolutionary farmers, sold their possessions, either directly to their tenants or through the agency of the so-called 'farmers' banks' (Krestjansky Bank), a government institution that previously functioned as the business agency of the nobility. In this way a small part of the possessions of the great landed nobility passed into the hands of even wealthier farmers. By this so-called agrarian reform programme, Stolypin, the

tsarist minister, dissolved the old 'mir' (peasant communities), and divided the community lands in such a way that the best portions everywhere fell into the hands of a thin layer of agricultural bourgeoisie. The result was a visible strengthening of this new class, whose members organised everywhere on a cooperative basis.

18. The return to Russia of Lenin and his party of exiled Bolsheviks, followed a few weeks later by a party of Mensheviks, was financed and organised by the German government (Katkov, 1956; Futrell, 1963; Possony, 1966). The necessary funds were transferred in part through Nya Banken in Stockholm, owned by Olof Aschberg. The dual German objectives were: removal of Russia from the war and control of the post-war Russian market.

19. The Bolsheviks, led by Lenin, took workers' militias and formed them into the Red Guards (later the Red Army) over whom they exerted substantial control.

20. The average pay of a worker in the USSR in 1935 was 1,800 roubles annually, while the pay and allowance of the secretary of a rayon committee amounted to 45,000 roubles annually (Orlov, 1951/1953). Discrepancies between the pay of workers and of party functionaries were extreme in Russia as well as in other communist societies.

21. Between 2000 and 2005, the governments of Serbia, Georgia, Ukraine and Kyrgyzstan were overthrown through bloodless revolutions. Each of these social movements included extensive effort by student activists. In Serbia, the most famous of these was 'Otpor' ('Resistance'), a youth movement formed in 1998 as a symbol of anti-Milošević that helped bring in Vojislav Koštunica. In Georgia there was a movement called 'Kmara' – trained by the Belgrade-based Centre for Nonviolent Resistance and several other Western organisations, and founded by Freedom House, the National Democratic Institute, the European Union, the National Endowment for Democracy, the International Republican Institute, the Organisation for Security and Co-operation in Europe, USAID and the Council of Europe (Sussman and Krader, 2008). In the Ukraine there was 'Pora' ('It's Time'). Each of these revolutions included election victories followed up by public demonstrations. Although Western media generally portrayed these coups as spontaneous, indigenous and popular ('people power') uprisings, these 'coloured revolutions' were in fact outcomes of extensive planning. Currently similar supported movements operate in Belarus under the name 'Zubr', in Albania under the name MJAFT ('enough') and in Russia under the name of 'Oborona' ('Defense'). For example, in Serbia (with a population of 10 million), with a commitment of $23 million in USAID spending towards the strategic objective of 'democratic transition', the opposition was empowered and emboldened to contest the election and force Milošević from power (Bacher, 2002). In particular, 'Otpor', the Democratic Opposition of Serbia received $10 million in 1999 and $31 million in 2000 (Bacher, 2002). The first application of a Western template for regime change was in Bulgaria in 1996, where the US National Endowment for Democracy and the International Republican Institute (IRI) 'discovered' that 'NGOs could tilt an election in favour of America's preferred candidate' (MacKinnon, 2007: 30) by unifying the opposition and then creating and funding citizen-based polls. As further example, the Chair of the Georgian Parliamentary Committee on Defence and Security, Givi Targamadze, a former member of the Georgian Liberty Institute, as well as some members of 'Kmara', acted as consultants to Ukrainian opposition leaders drawing on the techniques of non-violent struggle (Mielnikiewicz, 2004). Georgian rock bands, Zumba, Sof Eject and Green Room, which earlier had

supported the Rose Revolution, organised a solidarity concert in central Kiev to support Yushchenko's cause in November 2004 (Mielnikiewicz, 2004).

22. As an example, Yushchenko failed to constrain pandemic corruption. In Georgia, Saakashvili 'replaced "super presidential" institutions with even more highly concentrated "hyper presidential" ones', even attempting to ban all parties opposed to his pro-Western policy agenda (Hale, 2006: 312).

23. Scented or fragrant revolutions originally referred to the Portuguese revolution of 1974 named the 'carnation revolution'. The term 'jasmine revolution' is used to describe nostalgia for purity, a return to creating political desires that link purity to exclusiveness and self-determination. However, 'nostalgia is never neat, and its meanings are both polyvalent and contested' as evident in the 'Turkish-Cypriot nostalgia with a seeming cosmopolitanism, or longing for a multi-cultural past' (Hatay and Bryant, 2008: 424). The sense of smell (or olfaction) is our most primitive sense and is located in the same part of our brain that affects emotions, memory and creativity. Pungent scents, like smelling salts, can jolt the mind. The scent of flowers is fourth on the list of the top twenty smells which make people happy (Hatay and Bryant, 2008).

References

Agre, P. E. (2002) 'Real-Politics: The Internet and the Political Process', *The Information Society*, 18(5): 311–31.

Allen, G. and Abraham, L. (1976) *None Dare Call it Conspiracy* (New York: Buccaneer Books).

Amato, G. (1997) *Antitrust and the Bounds of Power* (Oxford: Hart Publishing).

Aron, R. (1985) *Études sociologiques* (Paris: Presses Universitaires de France).

Bacher, J. (2002) 'Review: Bringing Down a Dictator', *Peace Magazine*, July–September, http://archive.peacemagazine.org/v18n3p28.htm (accessed 5 June 2009).

Barbier, F. (1989) *Le Patronat du nord sous le second empire* (Paris: Eyrolles).

Barruel, Abbé Augustin (1797/1799) *Mémoires pour servir à l'Histoire du Jacobinisme* [*Memoirs Illustrating the History of Jacobinism*] (Hartford: Hudson & Goodwin).

Bauer, M. and Bertin-Mourot, B. (1999) 'National Models for Making and Legitimating Elites: A Comparative Analysis of the 200 Top Executives in France, Germany and Great Britain', *European Societies*, 1(1): 9–31.

Bourdieu, P. (1972) *Outline of a Theory of Practice*, trans. R. Nice (Cambridge: Cambridge University Press).

Bourdieu, P. (1979) *La Distinction, Critique Soicale du Jugement* (Paris: Les Éditions de Minuit).

Bourdieu, P. (1986) 'The Forms of Capital'. In J. Richardson (ed.), *Handbook of Theory and Research for the Sociology of Education* (New York: Greenwood Press), 241–58.

Bourdieu, P. (1996) *The State Nobility: Elite Schools in the Field of Power*, trans. L. C. Clough, Foreword by S. L. J. D. Wacquant (Stanford: Stanford University Press).

Brovkin, V. N. (1994) *Behind the Front Lines of the Civil War: Political Parties and Social Movements in Russia, 1918–1922* (Princeton: Princeton University Press).

Buchstein, H. (1997) 'Bytes that Bite: The Internet and Deliberative Democracy', *Constellations*, 4(2): 248–63.

Bureau of Labour Statistics (2009) *Federal Government Receipts and Expenditures, 1978–2008*, http://www.infoplease.com/ipa/A0104655.html (accessed 16 June 2009).

Burnham, J. (1941) *The Managerial Revolution: What is Happening in the World* (New York: John Day Company).

Cannadine, D. (1999) *Decline and Fall of the Aristocracy* (London: Vintage).

Carr, E. H. (1950) *A History of Soviet Russia: The Bolshevik Revolution, 1917–1923*. 3 vols. (London: Macmillan).

Chisholm, H. (ed.) (1911) 'Second French Empire'. In *Encyclopaedia Britannica* (11th edn.) (Cambridge: Cambridge University Press).

Clough, S. B. (1953) *The American Way: The Economic Basis of Our Civilization* (New York: Crowell).

Dáil, É. (1921) *Ratification of Plenipotentiaries*, Volume 4 (14 September), http://historical-debates.oireachtas.ie/D/DT/D.P.192109140003.html (accessed 8 June 2009).

Dalton, R. J. (2004) *Democratic Challenges, Democratic Choices: The Erosion of Political Support in Advanced Industrial Democracies* (New York: Oxford University Press).

Dewey, J. (1899/1956) *The School and Society* (Chicago: University of Chicago Press).

D'Iribarne, P. (1989) *Le Logique de l'honneur: Guestion des Entreprises et Traditions Nationals* (Paris: Seuil).

Djilas, M. (1957) *The New Class: An Analysis of the Communist System* (London: Thames & Hudson).

Domhoff, W. G. (1997) *Who Rules America Now?* (New York: Waveland Press).

Ergas, H. (1987) 'Does Technology Policy Matter?' In B. R. Guile and H. Brooks (eds.), *Technology and Global Industry: Companies and Nations in the Worked Economy* (Washington, DC: National Academy Press), 191–245.

Faur, J. (2008) *The Horizontal Society* (Brighton: Academic Study Press).

Fine, B. (2008) 'Social Capital verses Social History', *Social History*, 33(4): 442–67.

Fountain, J. (2004) 'Enacting Technology in Cross-Agency Initiatives: Structure, Transformation or Consolidation?' Paper presented at the Fourth Social Study of IT workshop at the LSE, London, 22–23 March.

Friedman, L. M. (1999) *The Horizontal Society* (New Haven: Yale University Press).

Froud, J., Leaver, A., Tampubolon, G. and Williams, K. (2008) 'Everything for Sale: How Non-Executive Directors Make a Difference'. In M. Savage and K. Williams (eds.), *Remembering Elites* (London: Blackwell), 162–86.

Furet, F. (1996) *The French Revolution, 1770–1814* (London: Blackwell).

Futrell, M. (1963) *Northern Underground* (London: Faber and Faber).

Gioia, D. (2003) '"Give it up!" Reflections on the Interpreted World', *Journal of Management Inquiry*, 13: 285–92.

Grewal, D. G. (2008) *Network Power: The Social Dynamics of Globalization* (New Haven: Yale University Press).

Habermas, J. (1979) *Communication and the Evolution of Society* (Cambridge: Polity Press).

Hale, H. E. (2006) *Why Not Parties in Russia? Democracy, Federalism, and the State* (Cambridge: Cambridge University Press).

Hanifan, L. J. (1916) 'The Rural School Community Center', *Annals of the American Academy of Political and Social Science*, 67: 130–8.

Hatay, M. and Bryant, R. (2008) 'The Jasmine Scent of Nicosia: Of Returns, Revolutions, and the Longing for Forbidden Pasts', *Journal of Modern Greek Studies*, 26(4): 423–49.

Hazleton, V. and Kennan, W. (2000) 'Social Capital: Re-conceptualizing the Bottom Line', *Corporate Communications: An International Journal*, 5(2): 81–6.

Hibbert, C. (1980) *The Days of the French Revolution* (New York: Quill, William Morrow).

Hunter, F. (1953) *Community Power Structure: A Study of Decision Makers* (Chapel Hill: University of North Carolina Press).

Iglic, H. and Rus, A. (2004) 'Elites, Social Capital, and Regime Change: Network-based Theory of Elite Adaptation'. Paper presented at the Annual Meeting of the American Sociological Association, San Francisco, 14 August.

Johnston, W. D. (1901) *The History of England from the Accession of James the Second*, vol. 1 (Boston and New York: Houghton Mifflin).

Kadushin, C. (2006) *The American Intellectual Elite* (New York: Transaction Publishers).

Kagan, D. (2003) *The Peloponnesian War* (London: Penguin Books).

Kahl, J. (ed.) (1957) *The American Class Structure* (New York: Rinehart).

Kakabadse, A., Kakabadse, N., Kouzmin, A. and Afanasyev, D. (2006) 'Pathway to Dictatorship: Parallel Democratic Convergence to Oligarchy'. In N. Kakabadse and A. Kakabadse (eds.), *Governance, Strategy and Policy: Seven Critical Essays* (Basingstoke: Palgrave Macmillan), 166–212.

Kakabadse, N., Kakabadse, A. and Kouzmin, A. (2007) 'Designing Balance into the Democratic Project: Contrasting Jeffersonian Democracy against Bentham's Panopticon Centralisation in Determining ICT Adoption', *Problems and Perspectives in Management*, 5(1): 2–28.

Kakabadse, N., Kakabadse, A. and Lee-Davis, L. (2008) 'Smart Technology: The Leadership Challenge', *Strategic Changes*, 17(7–8): 235–49.

Kakabadse, A., Kakabadse, N. and Kalu, K. N. (eds.) (2009) *Citizenship: A Reality Far From Ideal* (Basingstoke: Palgrave Macmillan).

Kakabadse, N., Kouzmin, A. and Kakabadse, A. (2010) 'Radio-Frequency Identification and Human Tagging: Newer Coercions', *International Journal of E-Politics (IJEP)*, 1(2): 29–45.

Katkov, G. (1956) 'German Foreign Office Documents on Financial Support to the Bolsheviks in 1917', *International Affairs*, 32(2): 181–9.

Klein, H. K. (1995) 'Grassroots Democracy and the Internet: The Telecommunications Policy Roundtable'. Paper presented at the Internet Society's International Networking Conference, Honolulu, Hawaii, 28–30 June, http:///ralph.bmu.edu/ ~pbaker/klein.txt (accessed 20 October 2001).

Kouzmin, A. and Thorne, K. (2010) 'Refocusing the Problematics of "Invisibility", Oligarchy, Values and Cyberspace in Neo-liberalism'. Paper presented at the University of Tasmania/ANZSOG 4th Annual Public Leadership Workshop on 'Public Leadership in Australia: Global, State and Local', Hobart, 25–26 November.

Lasswell, H. D. (1966) 'The Unnamed Revolution: The Permanent Revolution of Modernizing Intellectuals'. In H. D. Lasswell and D. Lerner (eds.), *World Revolutionary Elite: Studies in Coercive Ideological Movements* (Cambridge, MA: MIT Press), 80–93.

Lendman, S. (2009) '"Web of Debt": The Inner Workings of the Monetary System', http://www.sott.net/articles/show/183986-Web-of-Debt-The-Inner-Workings-of-the-Monetary-System (accessed 20 June 2009).

Lenin, V. I. (1902/1970). *What is to be Done?* (London: Panther).

Lenin, V. I. (1916/1948) *Imperialism, the Highest Stage of Capitalism* (London: Lawrence & Wishart).

Lenin, V. I. (1970) *The State and Revolution* (Beijing: Foreign Language Press).

Lincoln, A. US President (1864/1950) 'Letter to Col. William F. Elkins, Nov. 21, 1864'. In Archer H. Shaw (ed.), *The Lincoln Encyclopaedia* (London: Macmillan), 40.

MacKinnon, M. (2007) *The New Cold War: Revolutions, Rigged Elections, and Pipeline Politics in the Former Soviet Union* (New York: Carroll & Graf).

Madison, J. (1788/1961) '29 articles: nos. 10, 14, 18–20, 37–58, and 62–63'. In A. Hamilton, J. Madison and J. Jay, *The Federalist Papers*, ed. Charles S. Rossiter (New York: New American Library).

McClelland, J. S. (1996) *A History of Western Political Thought* (London: Routledge).

Meisner, M. (1967) *Li Ta-Chao and the Origins of Chinese Marxism* (Cambridge, MA: Harvard University Press).

Michels, R. (1911/1915) *Political Parties: A Sociological Study of the Oligarchical Tendencies of Modern Democracy*, trans. E. Paul and C. Paul (New York: Free Press).

Mielnikiewicz, J. (2004) 'States in Caucasus – Central Asia Closely Monitor Developments in Ukraine', *Eurasia Insight*, 30 November, http://www.eurasianet.org/departments/ insight/articles/eav113004.shtml (accessed 5 June 2009).

Mills, C. W. (1956) *The Power Elite* (Oxford: Oxford University Press).

Morrison, G. R., Lowther, D. L. and DeMeulle, L. (1999) *Integrating Computer Technology into the Classroom* (Upper Saddle River, NJ: Prentice Hall).

Morrow, G. (1962) *Plato's Epistles* (Indianapolis: Bobbs-Merrill).

Mosca, G. (1884/1925) *Sulla Teorica dei Governi e sul Governo Parlamentare* [*Theory of Governments and Parliamentary Government*], 2nd edn. (Rome: Loescher).

Mosco, V. and Foster, D. (2001) 'Cyberspace and the End of Politics', *Journal of Communication Inquiry*, 25(3): 218–36.

Nathanson, C. E. (1969) 'The Militarization of the American Economy'. In D. Horowitz (ed.), *Corporations and the Cold War* (London: Monthly Review Press), 205–35.

Neely, S. (2008) *A Concise History of the French Revolution* (Lanham, MD: Rowman & Littlefield).

Nicolay, J. G. and Hay, J. M (eds.) (1897/1905) *Abraham Lincoln Complete Works, Vol. 1* (New York: Francis Tandy).

Nofi, A. (2001) 'Statistical Summary of America's Major Wars: Statistics on the War's Costs', Louisiana State University, http://web.archive.org/web/20070711050249/ http://www.cwc.lsu.edu/other/stats/warcost.htm (accessed 20 May 2009).

Orlov, A. (1951/1953) *Stalin au Pouvoir* [*The Secret History of Stalin's Crimes*] (New York: Random House).

Orwell, G. (1946) 'James Burnham and the Managerial Revolution'. In *Collected Essays*, Project Gutenberg Consortia Centre, http://worldebookfair.com/eBooks/ Adelaide/o/o79e/part40.html (accessed 18 June 2009).

Parenti, M. (2007) 'Technology and Money: The Myth of Neutrality'. In *Contrary Notions: The Michael Parenti Reader* (San Francisco: City Lights Books), 179–83.

Pareto, V. F. D. (1935) *The Mind and Society* (Trattato di Sociologia Generale) (New York: Harcourt Brace).

Pareto, V. F. D. (1968) *The Rise and Fall of Elites: An Application of Sociology* (Totowa: Bedminster Press).

Passavant, A. (2005) 'The Strong Neo-liberal State: Crime, Consumption, Governance', *Theory and Event*, 8(3): 1–48.

Petit, M. and Scholz, C. (2002) 'Highfliers in Germany'. In C. B. Derrr, S. Roussillon and F Bournois (eds.), *Cross-Cultural Approaches to Leadership Development* (London: Quorum Books), 86–108.

Possony, S. (1966) *Lenin: The Compulsive Revolutionary* (London: George Allen & Unwin).

Post, G. (1964) *Studies in Medieval Legal Thought* (Princeton: Princeton University Press).

Putnam, R. D. (1976) *The Comparative Study of Political Elites* (New Jersey: Prentice Hall).

Putnam, R. D. (2000) *Bowling Alone: The Collapse and Revival of American Community* (London: Simon & Schuster).

Rhodes, P. (2006) *A History of the Classical Greek World, 478–323 BC* (London: Blackwell).

Rothkopf, D. (2008) *Superclass: The Global Power Elite and the World They are Making* (Boston: Little, Brown).

Salisbury, R. H. (1969) 'An Exchange Theory of Interest Groups', *Midwest Journal of Political Science*, 13(1): 1–32.

Scott, J. (1987) 'Inter-Corporate Structures in Western Europe: A Comparative Historical Analysis'. In M. S. Mizruchi and M. Schwartz (eds.), *Inter-Corporate Relations* (Cambridge: Cambridge University Press), 208–32.

Scott, J. (1995) 'Les élites dans la sociologie Anglo-Saxonne'. In E. Suleiman and H. Mendras (eds.), *Le recrutement des élites en Europe* (Paris: La Découverte), 9–17.

Scott, W. Sir (1827/1843) *The Life of Napoleon Bonaparte*, 2 vols. (Edinburgh: Robert Cadel).

Sklair, L. (2001) *The Transnational Capitalist Class* (Oxford: Blackwell).

Smith, C. S. (2005) 'If French Education is Democratic, Marianne is a Bedouin: Elite French Schools Block the Poor's Path to Power', 18 December, http://adamash.blogspot.com/2005/12/if-french-education-is-democratic.html (accessed 14 September 2009).

Steed, H. W. (1924) *Through Thirty Years, 1892–1922: A Personal Narrative*. The Peace Conference, The Bullitt Mission, vol. 2 (New York: Doubleday).

Suleiman, E. N. (1974) *Politics, Power, and Bureaucracy in France: The Administrative Elite* (Princeton: Princeton University Press).

Sussman, G. and Krader, S. (2008) 'Template Revolutions: Marketing U.S. Regime Change in Eastern Europe', *Westminster Papers in Communication and Culture*, 5(3): 91–112.

Sweatman, I. M. (1987) *World Conservation Bank: A Project of the International Wilderness Leadership Foundation* (New York: International Wilderness Leadership Foundation).

Sweezy, P. M. (1983) 'Competition and Monopoly', *Monthly Review*, May: 1–16.

Szakos, L. and Szakos, J. (2007) *We Make Change: Community Organizers Talk About What They Do and Why* (Norman, OK: Vanderbilt University Press).

Telegraph (2008) 'Quotes and the New World Order', http://my.telegraph.co.uk/antireptilian/blog/2008/02/20/quotes_and_the_new_world_order (accessed 17 June 2009).

The Economist (2009a) 'Outsourcing's Third Wave', 391(8632) (23 May): 65–6.

The Economist (2009b) 'The Recession Spurs Self-Service: Help Yourself', 392(8638) (4 June): 65–6.

The Week (2009) 'Lithium and the Bolivian question', 716 (23 May): 13.

Thorne, K. and Kouzmin, A. (2008) 'Cyberpunk – Web 1.0 "Egoism" Greets Group – Web 2.0 "Narcissism": Convergence, Consumption, and Surveillance, in the Digital Divide' (Symposium on 'The Internet and Public Affairs'), *Administrative Theory & Praxis*, 30(3) (September): 299–323.

Thorne, K. and Kouzmin, A. (2010) 'The USA PATRIOT Acts (et al.): Convergent Legislation and Oligarchic Isomorphism in the "Politics of Fear" and State Crime(s) against Democracy (SCADs)', *American Behavioural Scientist*, 53(6) (February): 885–920.

Tocqueville, A. de (1840/2000) *Democracy in America*, trans. and ed. Harvey C. Mansfield and Delba Winthrop (Chicago: University of Chicago Press).

Treasury Direct (2009) *Government – Historical Debt Outstanding – Annual*, United States Department of the Treasury, http://www.treasurydirect.gov/govt/reports/pd/histdebt/histdebt.htm (accessed 16 June 2009).

Trotsky, L. (1932) *The History of the Russian Revolution, Vols. I–II*, trans. Max Eastman (London: Victor Gollancz).

UK Cabinet Office (2009) 'Unleashing Aspiration: The Final Report of the Panel on Fair Access to the Professions', 11 August, http://www.cabinetoffice.gov.uk/accessprofessions (accessed 14 September 2009).

US Department of State (2004) 'US Assistance to Ukraine – Fiscal Year 2004', http://www.state.gov/p/eur/rls/fs/36503.htm (accessed 20 October 2007).

Viterbo, Giovani da (1901) 'Liber de Regimine Civitatum' ['Liberty of a Civilised Regime']. In C. Salvemini (ed.), *Bibliotheca Iuridica Medii Aevi* (vol. 3, ed. A. Gaudenzi) (Bologna: Società Azzoguidaina), 215–18.

Vovelle, M. (1974) *L'Élite ou le mensonge des mots* (Paris: Messidot).

Wacquant, L. (2007) *Punishing the Poor: The Neoliberal Government of Social Insecurity* (Durham, NC: Duke University Press).

Wacquant, L. (2008) 'Ordering Insecurity: Social Polarization and the Punitive Upsurge', *Radical Philosophy Review*, 11(1): 9–27.

Ward, C. (1973) *Anarchy in Action* (London: Allen & Unwin).

Weinberg, A. M. (1967) *Reflections on Big Science* (Oxford: Pergamon Press).

Wilson, A. (2006) 'Ukraine's Orange Revolution, NGOs and the Role of the West', *Cambridge Review of International Affairs*, 19(1): 21–32.

Wilson, E. (1940) *To the Finland Station: A Study in the Writing and Acting of History* (London: Collins).

Wilson, W. (1913/2006) *The New Freedom: A Call for the Emancipation of the Generous Energies of a People* (Lenox, MA: Hard Press).

Windolf, P. (1998) 'Elite Networks in Germany and Britain', *Sociology*, 32(2): 321–51.

Woods, M. (1998) 'Rethinking Elites: Networks, Space, and Local Politics', *Environment and Planning A*, 30(12): 2101–19.

2
On Values, Invisibility(ies) and Elites

Kym Thorne and Alexander Kouzmin

Introduction

Issues of 'visibility' and 'invisibility' are not new. Constructing 'realities' has always involved a manipulation of what is seen and not seen. One must be aware of the invisible behind what is permitted to be visible and how one must deal with the invisible before efficaciously reacting to the visible. The visible and the invisible and the graduations/shadows between them are interrelated realities of the political condition. The most important power struggles and gambits are over the ability to control or flux '(in)visibility'.

Yet, the importance of fluxing visibility and invisibility continues relatively unrecognised. Neo-liberalism continues to benefit from fluxing (in)visible manifestations of visible management/sovereign individual triumph and 'invisible' ministrations of 'free markets' (Chandler, 1977; Thorne and Kouzmin, 2006; Thorne, 2010a, 2010b). At the same time the post-modern narrative underwrites a fragmented, multiple, socially and linguistically, de-centred subject, favouring relativism, indeterminacy and de-totalisation over coherence, linearity and causality. Post-modernism prefers political strategies that involve identity, culture and the realm of everyday life over political strategies that involve agency, the state and the political economy. This evidences a fundamental mutuality of interest between the neo-liberal and the post-modern approaches to economic globalisation – the 'Imperial Project' (Klein, 2007: 343; Thorne, 2009, 2010b), virtuality (Thorne, 2005) and an unrestrained individualism (Thorne, 2010a). Such mutuality distrusts communal activities and political action, luxuriates in the liberating possibilities of technology and celebrates hybridity, self-absorption and transparency (Kouzmin et al., 2009).

This chapter draws on Weberian (Freund, 1972) ideal type formulations and Selznick (1952, 1957, 1965, 2000, 2002) to position the hegemony conjured by elites in the cyberspace epoch. This chapter suggests that the hegemonic use of visible and invisible power in cyberspace locates the missing Weberian (Satow, 1975) 'ideal type' of authority – (in)visible hegemonic values. This chapter also considers that there is a need for a Dahrendorf-like (1968) 'sociology of values' to be extended into public affairs in order to provide an ongoing understanding of elite manipulations of visibility and invisibility.

A missing ideal type

Satow (1975) identifies within Weber's related general categories of social action a value-rational action associated with legitimacy but one that has no clearly identified form of authority. According to Satow (1975), both purposive-rational and value-rational social action and their associated forms of legitimacy and authority were subsumed under Weber's (1947) concept of rational organisation. Weber (1947) did not seem to associate value-rational social action and/or legitimacy with any form of authority. Satow (1975) did not find any discussion of the organisational structure of any organisations based on value-rational authority and considered that this omission was the result of Weber's (1925) view that all authority must be legitimate and all legitimate authority involves very specific forms of economic and political domination.

Furthermore, relying on Bendix (1962), Satow (1975) considered that everything not directly connected to the economic and political realm, including religion, was focused on the connection between 'material interests and ideas, rather than questions of domination and administration' (Bendix, 1962: 286, cited in Satow, 1975: 527). So, it is not surprising to Satow (1975) that 'while [Weber] accepted the value-rational orientation to social action and legitimacy based on rational belief in an absolute value in religion, he never considered the possibility of an administration based on value-rational authority' (Satow, 1975: 527). However, even allowing for these sharp distinctions between the economic and political realm and all other possible realms including religion, Satow (1975: 527) thought that it is possible to 'construct a fourth type of authority'. This missing form of authority could be based on a 'faith in the absolute value of a rationalized set of norms' (Willer, 1967, cited in Satow, 1975: 527). What was required is to extend Weber's emphasis on obedience to formal laws and rules into obedience to *ideological norms*.

Willer (1967: 237) also believes that ideological authority is possible and 'like legal-rational authority, implies a bureaucratic administrative structure'. Satow (1975) found this approach simplistic and restrictive. Value-rational organisations were not deviant forms of bureaucracies. Instead, value-rational organisations were inherently complex requiring the simultaneous balancing of requirements to rationally ensure survival and to ensure commitment to an absolute goal. The requisite balancing could be achieved in two possible ways – the church response and the sect response. The church response 'is to adapt at the expense of the goals' and the sect response 'is to maximize goal commitment at the expense of adaption' (Satow, 1975: 528).

In Satow's (1975) estimation, both the church and the sect were cut from the same cloth. Additionally, both represented Nahirny's (1962) division of ideological organisations into formal ideological groups (churches) and informal ideological groups (sects). Formal ideological groups are not bureaucracies; participation is not based on functionally specific official roles and total commitment is still required to 'authoritatively defined and institutionalized' causes (Satow, 1975: 528). In contrast, informal ideological groups most commonly composed of zealots are essentially unstable, even ephemeral, and their survival involves some eventual accommodations with the church.

Adapting Hammond and Mitchell (1970), Satow locates examples of this relationship within the Protestant church which found 'room for radicals rather than expelling them' and, thereby, 'minimizing disruption without sacrificing the potential contribution of the radicals' (Satow, 1975: 528). Satow also located other examples of the segmentation of radicals in the approach to research and development groups within corporations and to research institutes within universities. This

[s]egmentation allows the organization to maximize maintenance of its goals while adapting to changes in the environment. The segmented groups can retain a rather sect-like, collegial character within the parent organization which is basically bureaucratic. (Satow, 1975: 528)

Satow (1975) draws particular attention to autonomous, professional organisations whose members exist within and outside of other organisations and juggle 'self-government for their professions and autonomy for each member' (Satow, 1975: 529). Professional status is conferred by 'the degree to which practitioners conform to a set of moral norms' (Wilensky, 1964: 140). These groupings of professionals are essentially secular 'moral communities' (Satow, 1975: 529) notable for the primacy of professional ethics, 'a horizontal pattern of authority, a decentralised distribution of power and an emphasis on colleague control' (Hall, 1968, cited in Satow, 1975: 530). These characteristics are also evident in virtual organisations (Thorne, 2005).

This restrictive segmentation was not the most appropriate depiction of authority within value-rational organisations. Satow (1975) had overemphasised Weber's purported emphasis on technocratic or even socio-technic 'technique' as being fundamental to the 'rationalization' of societies of the future. As Freund (1972: 282) demonstrates, Weber located technique and techniques everywhere and did not reduce 'all human values, including intellectual and ideal values, to pure technique and the laws of energy' (Freund, 1972: 282). Satow (1975) should have consistently positioned the missing ideal type within Weber's far more distinctive emphasis on values and agency as 'technique is no more able to escape the tensions and antagonisms of values peculiar to every civilization than is any other human activity' (Freund, 1972: 282). For Weber, meaningful action was 'reserved for activities whose intent is related by the individuals involved to the conduct of others' and this behaviour was 'the primary form of more complex types of behaviour, such as those of [elite] groups, institutions, and associations' (Freund, 1972: 103).

Few of the technocratic sects responsible for the information and communications technology (ICT) 'revolution', for example, have stayed within the 'skunk works' of their original corporate employers. Similarly, monetarist economists did not stay within academe but colonised the economic levers of the global economy (Thorne, 2010b). More generally, cyberspace is dominated by the hegemonic ambitions of those elites/sects that stand to gain the most from projections of globalisation, virtuality and individual sovereignty. Sects may be extensive and diverse, may require little or no physical presence and may adapt to external events such as the 'war on terror' (Thorne and Kouzmin, 2010) and the global financial crisis (GFC) (Thorne, 2010b).

According to Freund (1972: 155), Weber considered a sect-like 'monopoly or the closed system as the defender or initiator of privilege'. The trend towards monopoly may of course take different forms according to the social structure involved:

> depending on whether it promotes the privileges of an order, corporation, social class, category, officials/employees social stratum (peasant, notables, traders, liberal professions), or of a religious fraternity of an ascetical or other nature. [...] The typical form of the closed relationship of earlier times was the [closed] guild. (Freund, 1972: 156)

Even where the 'capitalist enterprise' was most visible for being more 'open':

> offering free scope to both internal and external competition, it has also come to create other monopolies (licenses, patents, manufacturing secrets), and, in certain cases, has led to industrial concentration and has even revived protectionism, no longer at the level of a particular branch of business but at that of the wider [elite] groupings of the state. (Freund, 1972: 156)

Economic/social groupings become fundamentally about 'depending on the circumstances, whether to form a closed or an open relationship' (Freund, 1972: 157). The use of closed/open, visible/invisible means by groups/elites after economic/political advantage may be counterpoised by Weber's approach to 'supernational forces' outside of 'normal observation': 'for if one believes that behind the things of everyday are hidden forces which do not reveal themselves directly, means must be found to give them significance' (Freund, 1972: 187). These 'symbols' become 'the instrument of a wordless language which enables men to understand the will of beings who do not speak' (Freund, 1972: 187).

In Freund's (1972) analysis of Weber's work, the hidden and non-hidden, the rational and the irrational, the religious and the non-religious could all be involved in the formation of formal and informal ideological, elite groupings distinctive for visible and invisible values. 'The man motivated by political conviction must know that no one active in public affairs can avoid either violence or compromise with the powers of darkness' (Freund, 1972: 30). What is decisive is the advantage and utility to any individual person's value orientation of the evident open/closed, visible/invisible play of other value orientations (especially hegemonic value orientations) emanating from other individuals and elite groups.

Satow's (1975) highly circumscribed approach to value rationality is not surprising. Weber's life work is most often reduced to being about technocratic, instrumental rationality. This predominately Western form of rationality 'is not confined to a particular or privileged sector of human activity, but permeates the whole of life' (Freund, 1972: 143) and 'the world becomes increasingly the artificial product of man, who governs it much as one controls a machine' (Freund, 1972: 143–4). Not only does this hubris indicate the continuing relevance of the irrational within the rational and the spiritual within the practical, but suggests a 'rational civilization' that still focuses 'on appearances' and relies on 'artificial things controlled by specialists' (Freund, 1972: 146).

This rampant rationalisation just brings the sense that individuals are master of their own destiny. 'Rationalised' persons populate cyberspace. Many are evident in post-human cyborgs (Haraway, 1985); the info-persons (Zuboff, 1988); symbolic analysts (Reich, 1992); creatives (Florida, 2003); sovereign individuals (Davidson and Rees-Mogg, 1997); the multitude (Hardt and Negri, 2004; Thorne and Kouzmin, 2004; Thorne 2005, 2010a) and monetarist economics (Klein, 2007) and their free market adherents (Thorne, 2010b) that seek salvation via the manipulation of digital, monetary and other information flows in cyberspace. Pervasive is the promise of a new, electronically enabled, non-physical life, infinitely flexible, free of frictions and involving the postponement of death. This promise is essentially empty and the cyberspace epoch is another flux in hegemonic visible and invisible power.

Values permeate Weber's notion of social action, legitimacy, authority and the nature of organisations. These adjustments reveal that the missing ideal type of value-rational authority is not just restricted to a partial existence within segmented organisations but may have many forms, may be able to act visibly and invisibly within and outside of organisations and may engage fully in economic/political/religious/social processes, including elite hegemonic actions. Given these adjustments, Satow's (1975) missing Weberian ideal type is better expressed as value authority in the epochal context of (in)visible hegemonic values.

Dahrendorf and (in)visible values

Dahrendorf (1968) also notes ambiguities in Weber's conception of the 'increasing rationality of the modern world' (Dahrendorf, 1968: 218) – distinguishing tension between the rationality of economic scarcity and the rationality of the 'just society' leading to conflicting forms of social organisation – the market and the plan. Dahrendorf (1968) places norms and values (visible and invisible) as fundamental to social compacts and to all forms of social action, legitimacy and authority. Dahrendorf accepts Parsons' (1954) proposition that society is made possible 'by virtue of some assumed general agreement on a set of values that define the boundaries and coordinates of the social order and of individual identity in social groups' (Dahrendorf, 1968: 139). However, he explicitly rejects Parsons' (1954) emphasis on equilibrium and the marginalisation of power. For Dahrendorf (1968: 140), the extent of continuity within social life is often puzzling but this is more to do with constraint and force than equilibrium. Societies are 'moral entities [...] definable by normative structures [...] [and] norms are established and maintained [sanctioned] only by power, and their substance may well be explained in terms of the interests of the powerful'.

> Norms are values associated with the 'binding force' of sanctions and the translation of values into norms, the application of sanctions and the maintenance of stability all refer back to power as a constraining force rather than a currency of exchange or an expression of social integration. (Dahrendorf, 1968: 140)

In this 'trinity of norms, sanction and power' (Dahrendorf, 1968: 174), conflict is not to be unexpected. Rather than being a *'diabolus ex machine'*, conflict is the result 'of necessity from the resistance provoked by the exercise of power' (Dahrendorf, 1968: 140). Conflict is a 'great creative force' and '[n]ot the presence but the absence of conflict is surprising and abnormal'. Dahrendorf (1968: 127) presents a Machiavellian (the deft, purposeful manipulation of visible and invisible power) approach to (in)visible values as 'ruling rather than common [stabilising], enforced rather than accepted at any given point of time'. Since 'conflict generates change' then 'constraint may be thought of as generating conflict' and 'it is always the basis of constraint that is at issue in social conflict' (Dahrendorf, 1968: 127).

Dahrendorf (1968) advances an anti-utopian, conflict model of society that is the basis of an 'open' society. Epochal change occurs when the powerful become weak and opponents act 'to take over and translate their interests into norms' (Dahrendorf, 1968: 145). The most successful individuals and groups in any society will be those best able to 'adapt [...] to the ruling norms' (Dahrendorf, 1968: 174). Dahrendorf (1968: 168) assumes that 'the number of values capable of regulating human behaviour is unlimited'. Gossip, secrets, scandals and transparency may become norms and those who do not engage in these norms will be discriminated against. Norms could be false or accurate, further reinforcing the need to obtain approval tokens or safety warrants from rulers/elites. During wartime, and even economic competition, 'spreading plausible but false information is a legitimate strategy' (Dahrendorf 1968: 235). In every society – even cyber-society – some groups are more advantageously placed than others. Dahrendorf (1968: 201) thought that this advantage could be countervailed by a rational legitimisation of power that gave everyone a chance to access power via equality of citizenship rights and responsibilities. However, Dahrendorf (1968: 214) 'resolutely oppose[d] all social levelling and uniformity, and as resolutely advocate[d] institutional pluralism, social differentiation and diversity'. When stripped of the (visible) veneer of constant change, innovation and flexibility, supposedly amorphous, non-territorial and non-political cyberspace exhibits many of the negative aspects Dahrendorf (1968: 110) associates with utopias – 'utopias [being] monolithic [globally connected cyberspace?], homogeneous communities, suspended not only in time but also in space, shut off from the outside world, which might, after all, present a threat to the cherished immobility of [existing] social structure'.

Despite the professed intention to supplant Weber's 'iron cage' of industrial capitalism, cyberspace (as with other utopias) emerges from nowhere and not from any 'familiar reality or realistic patterns of development' (Dahrendorf, 1968: 108). Liberty and fulfilment are only available to those adopting these utopian prescriptions. There is no conflict (apart from the constant, yet enriching competition in cyberspace) and no need for any resistance. There is no 'depersonalization, the yielding up of man's absolute individuality and liberty to the constraint and generality of social roles' (Dahrendorf, 1968: 57). These utopias are most distinctive for the 'universal consensus on prevailing values and institutional arrangements' (Dahrendorf, 1968: 108). Cyberspace and other utopias are equilibrated systems where 'every disturber of the equilibrium, every deviant is a "spy" or "imperialist agent"' (Dahrendorf, 1968: 117). The only things required are those things that keep the system functioning. Human physical mortality is served by a minimum of institutions and other arrangements (Dahrendorf, 1968: 110) as utopian cyberspace promises an escape from all possible constraints, especially one's 'bodily nature and its consequences' (Dahrendorf, 1968: 183).

A society with universal consensus? A society without conflict? One knows that 'without the cooperation of secret police it has never been possible to produce such a state, that even the threat of police prosecution can, at best, stifle dissent and conflict for limited periods of time' (Dahrendorf, 1968: 111). What is most unusual, most utopian and most 'unreal' about cyberspace is that it contravenes Dahrendorf's (1968) expectation that 'every society also produces within itself the resistance that brings it down' (Dahrendorf, 1968: 174). In cyberspace, for example, even the opposition aims for the assimilation of the technocratic multitude into the cyberspace elite. This is most concerning when, as Dahrendorf (1968: 117) observes, utopian formulations have an 'un-explained gap' which must be interpreted in the light of 'arbitrary and permanently adapted documents prepared by the Ministry [church/sect] of Truth'.

It is also possible that cyberspace is a form of extreme market rationality – another one of the various Marxian 'character masks' (Dahrendorf 1968: 31) worn by capital and capitalists. This extreme market rationality ignores the central social and political conflict of our time 'between market-rational and plan-rational methods' (Dahrendorf, 1968: 219). There is no place in the real world for markets without periodic adjustment or supplement by plans (see Dahrendorf, 1968: 221–31). This extreme market rationality escaped into constantly changing, innovative, flexible, frictionless cyberspace promising a market-clearing equilibrium based on the certainly of perfect informa-tion and the instantaneous conversion of ideas into productive enterprises. However, frictionless markets do not lead to frictionless societies. This extreme market rationality is flawed by the existence of (in)visible power.

If the central substantive norm of human society is the 'creation of agencies of power' then there can be no such thing as equal chance of participation in the political process (Dahrendorf, 1968: 226). Under all conceivable social conditions, 'the market is a fiction; the game always takes place in front of city hall' (Dahrendorf, 1968: 226). This cyberspace-extreme-market rational-ity is just another, more dynamic, version 'of the many versions of the utopia of the powerlessness' (Dahrendorf, 1968: 226). Cyberspace serves technocrats and their theorists and is just another 'conservative ideology of a stagnant society' (Dahrendorf, 1968: 226n). Cyberspace is a 'scientific civilization [...] the image of a world steering itself decisionally by the rules of a technical rationality – the technological utopia' (Dahrendorf, 1968: 267). A 'chimera' of a computer-directed [cyberspace] world is in fact nothing but the wishful or fearful dream of the unpolitical.

Selznick, invisible elites and isomorphism

It is important to comprehend how prevailing hidden, and autonomous, elites (Selznick, 1957) operate to render self-interest as a fundamental organis-ing principle of not just economic activity but of all contemporary social and political compacts. There is convergence in the development of political oligarchies, together with their economic counterparts, within the global/ cyberspace epoch (Kakabadse et al., 2006; Klein 2007). There are now more 'democratic' governments than ever before and there is more political disil-lusionment with democracy than ever before. There is also a 'dramatic lack of trust in democratic institutions, global and large, national companies as well as NGOs, trade unions and media organizations around the world' (Kakabadse et al., 2006: 191). Oligarchic convergence (Kakabadse et al., 2006: 192) is not new. 'Who says Organization, says Oligarchy' must be one of the twentieth century's best repressed, empirical and 'inconvenient', truths (Michels, 1962).

Institutional leadership, as outlined by Selznick (1957), refers to 'critical' decision-making rather than routine, administrative, policy, even, strategic decision-making (Simon, 1957; Barnard, 1968). Institutional leadership explicitly involves invisible, political intangibles – a 'proper' ordering of human affairs; the establishment of a 'social order'; a determination of 'public interest'; and a defence of 'critical' values are agenda issues usually beyond the expectations, even mechanisms, of transparency and democratic accountability (Thorne and Kouzmin, 2010). These invisible agenda issues typically involve dominant organisational values and ideologies designed to effect hegemony; the creation and protection of value-defining elites and the resolution of any conflict between these political/organisational processes.

Institutional leadership is a 'special kind of work done' (Selznick, 1957) to design and protect institutional values and polities – it is not associated with holding office, high prestige or even policy-making. Instead it is connected to comprehending the flux in the visible and invisible 'ways and means' by which oligarchic elites and interest groups protect their values and identity and attempt to manipulate the conditions of existence (Thorne and Kouzmin, 2010). Selznick (1957) suggested that if leadership is determinate, one should be able to distinguish its presence from its absence. Intriguingly, this meant that Selznick (1957) thought that 'failure' in institutional leadership was by default – that leadership is visibly lacking when it is most needed. Successful institutional affairs are driven by an invisible efficacy and failure is rendered part of the very visible, political and accountability realm. Such purposeful fluxing renders a clear indication of the interplay between transparency and hegemonic values and authority.

Selznick's (1957) intriguing insights and observations about invisible and strategic oligarchic/elite behaviour provide an important 'communitarian' antidote to the increasingly ideologised convergence between the public and the private within neo-liberal-driven discourses – blatantly ignorant of, or indifferent to, the institutional imperatives of many public organisations/institutions. 'A market mentality invades much of social life, undercutting *values* that need *special protecti*on. It is hard to sustain the difference between liberty and license' (Selznick, 2002: 3) (emphasis added). Selznick's ontological and epistemological positions partly flow from earlier research work on the Tennessee Valley Authority (TVA) (Selznick, 1965) and, quite remarkably, even earlier research work on Lenin's Bolshevik Party (Selznick, 1952) (see Thorne and Kouzmin, 2010 for a fuller account of these linkages).

Most presciently, Selznick (1957) pointed to the critical role of 'invisible' and autonomous elites in the design and maintenance of precarious social values and elite, political ergonomics. His 'theory of elite autonomy' goes remarkably undiscussed in managerial and political discourses. Especially in the convergent context of elite manipulations, knowing one's 'counterpart' has always been a source of considerable strength – of political advantage. Selznick's (1957) generic investigations into leadership and administration are directly connected to his work on combating Leninist/Bolshevist agitation in the USA (Selznick, 1952) which also points to the isomorphic, organisational and political underpinnings of the prescriptions of institutional leadership under conditions of paranoia, Soviet, McCarthyist or 'war on terror' style.

Selznick's (1957) work appears as an 'executive summary', or an oligarch's 'training manual', for countering institutional vulnerability to radical agitation. Transposed into democratic discourse and context, such training raises some concern about invisible elites within democratic institutions bred 'tactically' on Leninism (Lenin, 1970a, 1970b). For example:

> We are necessarily interested in social pathology, in appraising the capacity of institutions to meet, within their own terms, the requirements of self maintenance. [...] the central preservation of *central values and purposes* as well as to the bare continuity of organizational existence. We shall deal with this problem by considering: the role of *creative and culture sustaining elites*. (Selznick, 1952: 276, emphasis added)

> The 'Theory of Elite Autonomy' permits us to deal with [the differential capacity of subordinate units to defend the integrity of their functions] systematically and openly. [...] Many decisions that do in fact face up to this issue must now be *justified obliquely, and be half hidden* since there is no *accepted administrative principle allowing organizations to be different according to the strength of their values*. (Selznick, 1957: 128, emphasis added)

As 'elites find it difficult to sustain their own standards and, hence, ultimately their special identity and function' (Selznick, 1952: 279), 'institutional vulnerability should focus attention upon the conditions that affect the ability of elites to maintain those standards and self images which invest the institution as a whole with its cultural meaning' (Selznick, 1952: 281). In combination, Selznick (1957) and Selznick (1952) leave one with powerful isomorphic suggestions for the current role of invisible elites within the cyberspace epoch, the mutating 'new world order' and related work on legal frameworks prosecuting terrorism (Thorne and Kouzmin, 2010).

Contemporary (in)visibility

One might look to a critical awareness able, and willing, to calibrate whether the enveloping flux of visibility/invisibility is destructive to social capital, public domains and the public interest. It is to be expected that Selznick's (1957) hidden and autonomous elites would flux both visibility and invisibility to serve oligarchic interests. Corporate capitalism, especially in its current technocratic, neo-liberal form, revolves around such fluxes. Western, liberal governance regimes invoke a heavy cloak of anonymity and secrecy provisions on the oligarchic activities of 'men of reason' (McSwite, 1997). Within and outside contemporary cyberspace, the increasing reliance on intelligence and covert operations, extraordinary rendition, outsourcing, 'black budgets', 'black sites', torture and gulags suggests that the Cold War has not ended and there is an ongoing state of permanent war thriving on the purposive fluxing of private/public realms by elites (Bacevich, 2005; Bargeant, 2007).

Apart from the ever-widening contemporary provision of surveillance in the name of national security requirements for elites and functionaries of the state (Bogard, 1996), there has emerged a newer, more insidious, form of the fluxing of (in)visibility – a massive scale of outsourcing, offshoring, partnering and privatisation operating under hidden, 'commercial-in-confidence' coercions within the privatised state (Klein, 2007; Kouzmin, 2007, 2009; Scahill, 2007; Shane and Nixon, 2007). Visibility/transparency in elite contestation is increasingly problematic and promotes the need for a high degree of scepticism, a 'hermeneutic of suspicion' (Ricoeur, 1970: 32–5), in attempts at neutralising propaganda and the 'big lie' (Kellner, 2007: 639) of official, elite voices.

The systemic collapse of the financial and banking system, for example, should be considered as a consequence of the deliberate destruction of government and regulatory oversight by the invisible and interlocked economic/ideological/political components of neo-liberalism and free market economics. The view that 'economic-financial securitization, or global financialization of the economy, could be the strategy to overcome the structural crisis of the 1970s, was an enchanted belief that the expansion of finance alone – money in its purest form, free from both production and consumption – could continue and save capitalism and U.S. dominance of the world economy' (Royrvik, 2009). Newer criminogenic (deHaven-Smith et al., 2010) and racketeering (Royrvik, 2009) elites have emerged and have largely gone unchallenged by the 'too big to fail' bailouts of major banks/financiers and other corporations by public funds (Johnston et al., 2010). The new 'Keynesian moment' (Thorne 2010b) may be over quickly. Neo-liberalism and monetarism have not been eliminated and many adherents and 'fellow travellers' are entrenched in corporations, academia and government. The post-GFC reform of the economic, and especially the financial, system remains notable for insufficient monetary or other penalties imposed on criminogenic organisations and individuals. Curtailing the ability of the finance industry to use derivatives, 'shadow' banking, 'dark pools' and other means to act visibly and invisibly in relation to financial transactions further obscures the fluxing of power by financial and political elites (Johnston et al., 2010).

Conclusion

Post-9/11 public affairs now requires a Selznick-like (1957) 'definition of mission' which promotes and protects values which inform on how the actions of fundamentalists, visibly creating and confronting terror and dissent, not only harbour their own theocratic ambitions but, also, invisibly support economic and political elites capable of profiting from global disintegration, just as much as from any global integration and continuance of the cyberspace epoch. However, it is questionable whether Selznick's (1952, 1957) hidden, oligarchic imperatives for institutional leaders – 'class warriors' – effectively translate into a resistance to the economic and cybernetic 'babble' of the neo-liberal project. Does an oligarchic defender against alienated 'Stalinoids' of the Cold War such as Selznick (1952, 1957), successfully reinvent himself as an oligarchic protector against the exploitation of a growing mass of equally alienated 'netizens' of the cyberspace epoch and/or its 'new world order' mutations?

Selznick's (1957, 2002) contributions to the study of leadership as a vehicle for articulating elite and institutional vulnerability suggest that he may be the leading theorist of invisible elites tackling the institutional dimensions of an undisciplined, feckless, libertarian, consumer-sovereign, cybernetic-anarchic, liberal democracy. Everything in Selznick's work, however, is permeated with an invisible and strategic import. Selznick (1952, 1957) resonates with Lenin's *What is to be Done?* (Lenin 1970a) in a pre-cybernetic age of corporate capitalism – a pantheon to invisible, oligarchic imperatives.

Selznick (1952, 1957) certainly does not resonate with democratic norms. Even later, Selznick (2000, 2002) does not fully resonate with democratic norms. Democratic responsiveness may have become 'communitarian', but it remains nonetheless elitist and manifestly antagonistic to change and surprisingly silent on the plight of 'netizens'. Selznick (1952, 1957, 2000, 2002), like other elites (Thorne and Kouzmin, 2010), distrusts the 'masses' and does not consider that there is any link between democracy and collective intelligence. He also distrusts the imperative link between democracy and bureaucracy. In a Weberian (1947) sense, both are doomed to the 'Iron Law of Oligarchy' (Michels, 1962). Unfortunately, it is not sufficient to identify visible elites/ oligarchs whilst disparaging participative democracy. Society – even within cyberspace – 'requires institutions set up in such a way as to accommodate change, conflict and the interplay of power and resistance' (Dahrendorf, 1968: 149). These institutions should allow for conflict; they should be designed to control power rather than to camouflage it behind an ideology of consensus.

This chapter suggests that what is required is a public affairs alert to the purposive misuse of governments, markets and social/intellectual commons by hegemonic interests fluxing visible and invisible power whilst, at the same time, demanding transparency. This will require the type of 'moral reflection' and 'authentic hesitation' (Farmer, 2005) which conjoins a materialist political economy with a post-structuralist (even post-modernist) linguistic/symbolic analysis in order to recover the arena of norms/values from the deadening embrace of technocratic neo-liberals, free-market fellow travellers, technological pundits and the conservative dogma of religious and other fundamentalists resistant to conflict and democratic participation.

This is the type of imaginative, critical public affairs representative of what Dahrendorf (1968: vii) refers to as 'a social science of values'. This involves 'big range', 'morally committed' theorising that 'weave[s] historical awareness into sociological generalizations' (Dahrendorf 1968: vii) in order to enhance 'institutional pluralism, social differentiation and diversity' (Dahrendorf, 1968: 214) – akin to Habermas' (1963) expansive 'critical sociology' which 'keep[s] us aware of what we are doing, irrespective of whether we are doing it consciously or blindly and without reflection'. A critical sociology 'in this sense should view its subject precisely from an imagined *a priori* perspective, as a generalized subject of social action' (Habermas, 1963: 228, cited in Dahrendorf, 1968: vii).

However, there is minimal room in global cyberspace for democratic involvement in society. The Internet/cyberspace 'provides an ideal (or rather model) world for economic, political and cultural control – one which is already conquered and colonized' (Nunes, 1997: 165). For those who understand the imperative of hidden values and autonomous elites, cyberspace is a dream come true. It is a highly fluxable, control space – invisible, elitist and highly value driven. To put this in direct terms, seeing through the 'emperor's new clothes', escaping from the conjuring of the (in)visible, requires a renewed vigilance that prevents religious/ideological formulations of economic/technocratic utopias ever becoming 'a welcome ideology for ruling elites which like to remain invisible' (Dahrendorf, 1968: 267).

For many positivists and empiricists, invisibility in public affairs is an anathema – ontologically and epistemologically. For what cannot be measured, or directly observed, is unknowable and irrelevant to 'scientific' wisdom or professional/academic legitimacy. However, the contours of visible and invisible power in hegemonic cyberspace and the diachronic and synchronic historical examples of this fluxing of (in)visible power by elites suggest that visibility and invisibility must be grounded in the critical realism of political contestation (Bhasker, 1986).

According to Freund (1972), research involves the difficult feat of perceiving beyond what is apparent (visible) and recovering what is missed (invisible) by others and he suggests there should be a related, interpretive modesty amongst researchers. Freund (1972) considers that Weber's ideal type methodology resolves much of the problematic nature of research, especially in relation to human subjects and social existence, but even this exceptionally valuable research requires modesty. In the study of elites:

> the complexity of human relationships and modes of behaviour forbids any one-sided interpretation, save on ideal-typical lines [...] designed to facilitate an understanding of the human reality as far as it is possible to do so. Knowledge is never commensurate with reality, whose variations are both extensively and intensively infinite; it can only offer guidelines to facilitate understanding. (Freund, 1972: 250)

Like Weber, this chapter considers history without conviction about inevitable destinations – history is a genuine random walk, full of 'surprises, disguises and reversals' (Freund, 1972: 13). This chapter abhors prophecy and is a critique of one looking for a more general meaning, in line with what they take to be the direction of world evolution on the basis of a defined system of hegemonic values. However, it is no accident that 'cybernetic eternity is one of the recurrent themes in a discourse in which the physical world dissolves and the cosmos finds itself planted squarely in the *computer*' (Virilio, 2005: 40).

References

Bacevich, A. (2005) *The New American Militarism: How Americans are Seduced by War* (Oxford: Oxford University Press).

Bageant, J. (2007) *Deer Hunting with Jesus: Dispatches from America's Class War* (New York: Crown).

Barnard, C. (1968) *The Functions of the Executive* (Cambridge, MA: Harvard University Press).

Bendix, R. (1962) *Max Weber: An Intellectual Portrait* (Garden City, NY: Doubleday).

Bhasker, R. (1986) *Scientific Realism and Human Emancipation* (London: Verso).

Bogard, W. (1996) *The Simulation of Surveillance: Hyper-Control in Telematic Societies* (Cambridge: Cambridge University Press).

Chandler, A. D. (1977) *The Visible Hand: The Managerial Revolution in American Business* (Cambridge, MA: Belknap Press).

Dahrendorf, R. (1968) *Essays in the Theory of Society* (London: Routledge & Kegan Paul).

Davidson, J. D. and Rees-Mogg, W. (1997) *The Sovereign Individual: The Coming Economic Revolution and How to Survive and Prosper in it* (London: Pan Books/Macmillan).

deHaven-Smith, L., Kouzmin, A., Thorne, K. and Witt, M. (2010) 'The Limits of Permissible Change in US Politics and Policy: Learning from the Obama Presidency', *Administration Theory & Praxis*, 32(1): 134–40.

Farmer, D. J. (2005) *To Kill the King: Post-traditional Governance and Bureaucracy* (Armonk, NY: M. E. Sharpe).

Florida, R. (2003) *The Rise of the Creative Class: And How It's Transforming Work, Leisure, Community and Everyday Life* (New York: Basic Books).

Freund, J. (1972) *The Sociology of Max Weber* (London: Penguin).

Habermas, J. (1963) *Theorie und Praxis: sozialphilosophische studien* (Berlin: Luchterhand).

Hall, R. (1968) 'Professionalization and Bureaucratization', *American Sociological Review*, 33(1): 72–104.

Hammond, P. and Mitchell, R. (1970) 'Segmentation of Radicalism: The Case of the Protestant Campus Minister'. In P. Hammond and B. Johnson (eds.), *American Mosaic: Social Patterns of Religion in the United States* (New York: Random House), 162–76.

Haraway, D. (1985) 'A Manifesto for Cyborgs: Science, Technology and Socialist Feminism in the 1980s', *Socialist Review*, 80: 65–107; republished in D. Haraway, *Simians, Cyborgs and Women: The Re-invention of Nature* (New York: Routledge, 1991), 149–81.

Hardt, M. and Negri, A. (2004) *Multitude: War and Democracy in the Age of Empire* (New York: Penguin).

Johnston, J., Kouzmin, A., Thorne, K. and Kelly, S. (2010) 'Crisis Opportunism: Bail Outs and E-SCADs in the GFC', *Risk Management: An International Journal*, 12(3): 208–34.

Kakabadse, A., Kakabadse, N., Kouzmin, A. and Afanasyev, D. (2006) 'Pathways to Dictatorship: Parallel Democratic Convergence to Oligarchy'. In N. Kakabadse and A. Kakabadse (eds.), *Governance, Strategy and Policy: Seven Critical Essays* (Basingstoke: Palgrave Macmillan), 166–212.

Kellner, D. (2007) 'Bush Speak and the Politics of Lying: Presidential Rhetoric in the War on Terror', *Presidential Studies Quarterly*, 37(4): 622–45.

Klein, N. (2007) *The Shock Doctrine: The Rise of Disaster Capitalism* (New York: Allen Lane/Penguin).

Kouzmin, A. (2007) 'Ideology, Vulnerability and Regulation in the Privatized State'. In United Nations Department of Economic and Social Affairs (ed.), *Managing Knowledge to Build Trust in Government* (New York: United Nations), 28–46. See also http://unpan.un.org/intradoc/groups/public/documents/unpan/usnpan025949.pdf.

Kouzmin, A. (2009) 'Market Fundamentalism, Delusions and Epistemic Failure in Policy and Administration', *Asia-Pacific Journal of Business Administration*, 1(1): 23–39.

Kouzmin, A., Witt, M. and Thorne, K. (2009) '"Killing the King" in Public Administration: From Critical Epistemology to Fractured Ontology and Limited Agency – A Review Essay', *Public Administration Quarterly*, 32(3): 341–72.

Lenin, V. I. (1970a [1902]) *What is to be Done?* (London: Panther).

Lenin, V. I. (1970b) *The State and Revolution* (Beijing: Foreign Language Press).

McSwite, O. C. (1997) *Legitimacy in Public Administration: A Discourse Analysis* (Thousand Oaks, CA: Sage).

Michels, R. (1962) *Political Parties: A Sociological Study of the Oligarchical Tendencies of Modern Democracy* (New York: Collier Books).

Nahirny, V. (1962) 'Some Observations on Ideological Groups', *American Journal of Sociology*, 67: 397–405.

Nunes, M. (1997) 'What Space is Cyberspace? The Internet and Virtuality'. In D. Holmes (ed.), *Virtual Politics: Identity and Community in Cyberspace* (Thousand Oaks, CA: Sage), 163–78.

Parsons, T. (1954) *Essays in Sociological Theory* (Glencoe, IL: Free Press).

Reich, R. (1992) *The Work of Nations: Preparing Ourselves for Twenty-first Century Capitalism* (New York: Random House, Vintage Books).

Ricoeur, P. (1970) *Freud and Philosophy: An Essay on Interpretation*, trans. D. Savage (New Haven, CT: Yale University Press).

Royrvik, E. (2009) 'The Sociability of Securitization: Symbolic Weapons of Mass Deception', *iNtergraph: The Journal of Dialogic Anthropology*, 2(2), http://www.intergraph-journal.com/enhanced/vol2issue2/8.html (accessed 5 March 2010).

Satow, R. L. (1975) 'Value Rational Authority and Professional Organizations: Weber's Missing Type', *Administrative Science Quarterly*, 20(4): 526–31.

Scahill, J. (2007) *Blackwater: The Rise of the World's Most Powerful Mercenary Army* (London: Serpent's Tail).

Selznick, P. (1952) *The Organizational Weapon: A Study of Bolshevik Strategy and Tactics* (Glencoe, IL: Free Press).

Selznick, P. (1957) *Leadership in Administration: A Sociological Interpretation* (New York: Harper & Row).

Selznick, P. (1965) *TVA and the Grass Roots: A Study in the Sociology of Formal Organization* (Berkeley: University of California Press).

Selznick, P. (2000) 'On Sustaining Research Agendas – Their Moral and Scientific Basis: An Address to the Western Academy of Management', *Journal of Management Inquiry*, 9(3): 277–82.

Selznick, P. (2002) *The communitarian persuasion* (Washington, DC: Woodrow Wilson Center Press).

Shane, S. and Nixon, R. (2007) 'In Washington, Contractors Take On Biggest Role Ever', *New York Times*, 4 February, http://www.nytimes.com/2007/02/04/Washington/04contract.html (accessed 25 May 2010).

Simon, H. (1957) *Administrative Behaviour* (2nd edn.) (New York: Free Press).

Thorne, K. (2005) 'Designing Virtual Organizations? Themes and Trends in Political and Organizational Discourses', *Journal of Management Development*, 24(7): 580–607.

Thorne, K. (2009) 'Will the People in Cyberspace Never be Defeated? Reflections on the Global Multitude in the Epoch of American Empire', *Critical Perspectives on Accounting*, 20(2): 255–66.

Thorne, K. (2010a) 'Narcissistic and Dangerous "Alphas": "Sovereign Individuals" and the Problem of Cultivating the "Civic" in Cyberspace', *International Journal of Critical Accounting*, 2(1): 96–109.

Thorne, K. (2010b) 'Does History Repeat? The Multiple Faces of Keynesianism, Monetarism and the Global Financial Crisis', *Administrative Theory & Praxis*, 32(3): 304–26.

Thorne, K. and Kouzmin, A. (2004) 'Borders in an (In)Visible World? Revisiting Communities, Recognizing Gulags', *Administrative Theory & Praxis*, 26(3): 408–29.

Thorne, K. and Kouzmin, A. (2006) 'Learning to Play the "Pea and Thimble" Charade – The Invisible and Very Visible Hands in the Neo-Liberal Project: Towards a Manifesto for Reflexive Consciousness in Public Administration', *Administrative Theory & Praxis*, 28(2): 262–74.

Thorne, K. and Kouzmin, A. (2010) 'The USA PATRIOT Acts (et al.): Convergent Legislation and Oligarchic Isomorphism in the "Politics of Fear" and State Crime(s) against Democracy (SCADs)', *American Behavioural Scientist*, 53(6) (February): 885–920.

Virilio, P. (2005) *The Information Bomb*, trans. P. Turner (New York: Verso).

Weber, M. (1925) *Law, Economy and Society* (New York: Clanon).

Weber, M. (1947) *The Theory of Social and Economic Organization*, trans. A. M. Henderson and T. Parsons (New York: Free Press).

Wilensky, H. (1964) 'The Professionalization of Everyone?', *American Journal of Sociology*, 70(2): 137–58.

Willer, D. (1967) 'Max Weber's Missing Authority Type', *Sociological Inquiry*, 37(2): 231–9.

Zuboff, S. (1988) *In the Age of the Smart Machine: The Future of Work and Power* (New York: Basic Books).

3

Global Capitalism Theory and the Emergence of Transnational Elites

William I. Robinson

Introduction

My objective here is to offer as theoretical reflection a 'big picture', that is, a macrostructural perspective through which to approach the theme of elites and development. A genealogy of inquiry into global inequalities and development in the modern era is a study in the original and evolution of the critique of capitalism and the distinct social forces and class agents that this system generates. Hence, how we conceptualise the role of elites in development will be tied to how we analyse capitalism as a world system and more specifically how we analyse its distinct social forces and class agents. In a nutshell, I suggest that globalisation represents a new epoch in the ongoing evolution of world capitalism distinguished by the rise of a globally integrated production and financial system, an emergent transnational capitalist class and incipient transnational state apparatuses. Structural changes in the world economy associated with globalisation have contributed to a new fractionation among elites in the former Third World between nationally oriented and transnationally oriented groups. These two overlapping yet often competing sets of elites pursued distinct development strategies in the late twentieth and the early twenty-first centuries. The former sought to build up national circuits of accumulation while the latter sought to integrate local circuits into new transnational circuits of accumulation. These contrasting strategies for development involved distinct sets of policies: the one, policies that would protect local agents from global competition; the other, policies that integrate local agents into emergent transnational circuits.

My propositions on globalisation and in particular on national and transnational fractions of the elite grounded in distinct strategies of accumulation depart from conventional wisdom yet grow out of a rich history of intellectual and political debate. The theme of the role elites play in development is as old, or older, than the concept of development itself. Early Enlightenment and bourgeois thinkers saw rising middle and commercial classes from whence many of them came as the agents of progress and modernisation. Sociologists in the nineteenth and early twentieth centuries such as Compte, Spencer and Weber, would develop these views into theoretical constructs. But as the middle classes of the early capitalist era achieved political power and became the new ruling groups Marx and other nineteenth-century radical thinkers critiqued the new order as generating the social conditions associated with underdevelopment. As Europe unleashed a new round of imperialist expansion in the late nineteenth and early twentieth centuries a new generation of Marxist thinkers, from Hilferding to Lenin, Bukharin and Luxemburg identified the leading capitalist states as the agents behind the colonisation and plunder of what would later be called the Third World. Among this generation, Leon Trotsky developed perhaps the most coherent theoretical explanation for inequalities between rich and poor countries in his theory of combined and uneven development.

In the wake of the Second World War and decolonisation newly independent countries from Africa and Asia joined with their Latin American counterparts in shifting international political attention to global inequalities (see, inter alia, Prashad, 2007). How to account for this inequality and what to do about it became the focus of heated intellectual and ideological battles and formed the backdrop to the rise of development studies. US president Harry Truman famously launched the 'era of development' in a 1949 speech, declaring that 'we must embark on a bold new program for making the benefits of our scientific advances and industrial progress available for the improvement and growth of underdeveloped areas' (Esteva, 1991: 7). Behind the Truman declaration was the effort to open up the former colonial world to an expanding international capitalism. The story of the rise of modernisation theory in the wake of the Truman declaration, largely in the US academy with ample support from the policy-making establishment, is now well known. The theme of enlightened elites leading societies into development and progress became a fundamental tenet of modernisation and concomitant political development theories that dominated the social sciences from the 1950s into the 1970s. But alternative explanations for development and underdevelopment challenged the hegemony of modernisation theory in the 1960s and on to the drumbeat of anti-colonial and revolutionary struggles across the Third World that challenged the very structures of the world capitalist system. From the perspective of new dependency, world-systems and radical international political economy theories elites in the Third World were largely seen as agents of a world capitalist system whose very constitution and reconstitution was founded on the unity and antagonism of core and peripheral or developed and underdeveloped regions of the world.

My own theory of global capitalism shares much with this radical intellectual tradition in development studies but also diverges on several key counts. I see globalisation as a qualitatively new epoch in the ongoing evolution of world capitalism, characterised above all by the rise of truly transnational capital and the integration (or rearticulation) of most countries in the world into a new global production and financial system. The leading strata among national capitalist classes, both North and South, have experienced ongoing integration across borders into an emergent transnational capitalist class, or TCC, and at whose apex is a transnational managerial elite. The nation state, while it does not disappear or even become 'less important', is undergoing transformation. The institutional apparatus of national states has become increasingly entangled in transnational institutional webs that bring them together with inter- and transnational institutions into what can be conceived as incipient transnational state apparatuses. During the 1980s and 1990s capitalists and elites around the world became fractionated along new lines: nationally oriented and transnationally oriented. Transnational fractions of local elites in competition with nationally oriented fractions vied for and in many countries around the world won state power. They utilised that power to push capitalist globalisation, to restructure national productive apparatuses and integrate them into the new global production and financial system.

These are complex propositions that I have written about extensively elsewhere (see, in particular, Robinson 2003, 2004, 2008). Here I want to focus on the implications of this theory of global capitalism for elites and development. I want to suggest, in particular, that nationally oriented elites who promoted developmentalist projects in the twentieth century often depended on the social reproduction of at least a portion of the popular and working classes for the reproduction of their own power and status, and therefore on local development processes however so defined and however deficient. In distinction, transnationally oriented elites who pushed restructuring and integration into global capitalism were less dependent on such local social reproduction. With the shift in elites came a shift in discourse from national industrialisation and expanding internal markets to global market integration and macroeconomic, principally neo-liberal, policies that facilitated such integration.

There is little consensus on the appropriate terminology for inter-state and global inequalities. Here I will use interchangeably First and Third World, developed and developing/underdeveloped, core and periphery, and North and South, although I find *all* these terms problematic. Also, how to conceive of elites is a contentious matter in political sociology that I cannot take up here. Suffice it to observe that much debate has centred on the relationship between classes and elites and whether or not these are commensurate analytical categories. By elites I refer to dominant political, socio-economic and cultural strata, and in particular, to capitalists and landlords, along with top level managers and administrators of the state and other major social institutions and leadership positions in the political system. Capitalists are elites who own or manage means of production as capital. Elites who are not necessarily capitalists occupy key decision-making positions in institutions, whether in private corporations, the state, political parties or cultural industries. However, in my view the status of elites that are not capitalists proper is dependent on the reproduction of capital.

Nation state capitalism and the turn to globalisation

Diverse Fordist–Keynesian models of national corporate capitalism spread throughout the twentieth century from the cores of the world capitalist system to the former colonial domains in Latin America, Africa and Asia. These countries tended to pursue a multi-class development model along radical Keynesian lines, often referred to as developmentalist, populist or corporatist. Developmentalist capitalism took on a form distinct from its First World New Deal and social democratic variants, often involving a much greater role for the state and the public sector, mass social mobilisations growing out of anti-colonial, anti-dictatorial and national-liberation movements, and populist or corporatist political projects. Both First and Third World models were predicated on a redistributive logic and on incorporation of labour and other popular classes into national historical blocs. The legitimacy of elites in the Third World may have been even more closely tied to the logic of this redistribution and the social reproduction of popular classes than their counterparts in the First World.

World capitalism developed in this period within the nation state and through the inter-state system. Nation states were linked to each other through the international division of labour and through commercial and financial exchanges in an integrated international market regulated, at least in theory, by the Bretton Woods institutions. In this way the system provided for more insulated forms of national control over economic and social policy and greater autonomy in internal capitalist development, even as the international market disciplined countries into supporting the international rules of exchange rates and exchange and reproduced the world capitalist power structure. The world economy experienced a sustained period of growth in the quarter century after the Second World War – the so-called 'golden age' of capitalism. But the illusion of prosperity burst with the world economic downturn that began in the 1970s and which threw national corporate capitalism into crisis.

The social origins of this crisis were to be found in the relative strength that working and popular classes won worldwide in relation to capital after many decades of class and social struggles in both the First and the Third Worlds. Organised labour, increased taxes on profits and income, state regulation, revolutions in the Third World and the explosion of social movements and counter-hegemonic cultural practices everywhere constricted private capital's real or perceived capacity for accumulation. The expansion of collective rights, the institutionalisation of Keynesian–Fordist class compromise, and the prevailing norms of a 'moral economy' that assumed capital and state reciprocities with labour and citizens and an ethnical obligation to minimal social reproduction – all this burdened capital with social rigidities that had to be reversed for a new phase of capitalist growth. Capital and its political representatives and organic intellectuals in the core countries organised a broad offensive – economic, political, ideological and military – that was symbolically spearheaded by the Reagan–Thatcher alliance. Emerging transnational elites from the centres of power in the world system launched a global counter-revolution that would be as much political and economic as social, cultural and ideological, and that was still being fought out in manifold arenas in the twenty-first century.

In structural terms, this crisis was not merely cyclical. Cyclical crises eventually accumulate into more generalised crises involving social and political upheavals and ushering in periods of restructuring. *Restructuring crises* result in novel forms that replace historical patterns of capital accumulation and the institutional arrangements that facilitated them (see, inter alia, Aglietta, 1979; Kotz et al., 1994). The world capitalist crisis that began in the 1970s is generally identified as the turning point for globalisation and in my view signalled the transition to a new transnational stage in the system. For much of the twentieth century First World Keynesian capitalism and Third World developmentalist capitalism shared two common features: state intervention in the economy and a redistributive logic. The crisis that began in the 1970s could not be resolved within the framework of these post-Second World War social structures of accumulation. In the First World there was a progressive breakdown of the Keynesian–Fordist welfare states and in the Third World developmentalist projects became exhausted as manifest above all in economic contraction and the debt crisis of the 1980s.

Globalisation became a viable strategy as capitalists and state managers searched for new modes of accumulation. 'Going global' allowed capital to shake off the constraints that nation state capitalism had placed on accumulation; to break free of the class compromises and concessions that had been imposed by working and popular classes and by national governments in the preceding epoch. The decision by the US government to abandon the fixed exchange rate system in 1973 effectively did away with the Bretton Woods system and, together with deregulation, opened the floodgate to transnational capital movement and the meteoric spread of transnational corporations (TNCs). Capital achieved a new-found global mobility, or ability to operate across borders in new ways, which ushered in the era of global capitalism. The renewed power to discipline labour that this afforded transnational capital altered the worldwide correlation of class and social forces in its favour. What was international capital in the preceding epoch metamorphosed into transnational capital.

Emerging global elites and transnational capitalists set about dismantling the distinct models associated with national corporate capitalism to construct a new global 'flexible' regime of accumulation. In broad strokes, Keynesianism was replaced by monetarist policies, deregulation and a 'supply side' approach that included regressive taxation and new incentives for capital. The Fordist class compromise was replaced by a new capital–labour relation based on deunionisation, flexible workers and deregulated work conditions and the welfarist social contract was replaced by social austerity and the law of the market in social reproduction. More specifically, the prospects for capital to accumulate and make profits were restored during the 1980s and on and on by four key developments associated with capitalist globalisation.

First was a new capital–labour relation based on the deregulation, informalisation and 'flexibilisation' of labour. Second was a new round of *extensive* and *intensive* expansion. Extensively, the system expanded through the reincorporation of major areas of the former Third and Second worlds into the world capitalist economy, so that by the 1990s no region remained outside the system. Intensively, public and community spheres that formerly lay outside (or buffered from) the logic of market relations (profit-making) were commodified and opened up to accumulation through privatisation, state deregulation and reregulation, including the extension of intellectual property rights, and so on. Third was the creation of a global legal and regulatory structure to facilitate what were emerging globalised circuits of accumulation, including the creation of the World Trade Organization. And fourth was the imposition of the neo-liberal model on countries throughout the Third and the former Second worlds, involving structural adjustment programmes that created the conditions for the free operation of capital within and across borders and the harmonisation of accumulation conditions worldwide. Through neo-liberalism the world has increasingly become a *single unified field for global capitalism*. Capital has come to achieve a new-found global mobility in a double sense, in that the material *and* the political obstacles to its unfettered movement around the world have dramatically come down. As capital became liberated from the nation state and assumed new power relative to labour with the onset of globalisation, states shifted from reproducing Keynesian social structures of accumulation to servicing the general needs of the new patterns of global accumulation.

A transnational production and financial system

Since the 1970s, the emergence of globally mobile transnational capital increasingly divorced from specific countries has facilitated the *globalisation of production* (I include services here); the fragmentation and decentralisation of complex production processes, the worldwide dispersal of the different segments in these chains, and their functional integration into vast global chains of production and distribution. World production is thus reorganised into new transnational, or global, circuits of accumulation through which values move instantaneously. National economies have been reorganised and reinserted as component elements of this new global production and financial system (on the anatomy of this system, see inter alia, McMichael, 1996; Dicken, 2003), which is a qualitatively distinct world economic structure from that of previous epochs, when each country had a distinct national economy linked externally to one another through trade and financial flows. This is a shift from international market integration to global productive integration. I have referred to this distinction elsewhere as between a *world economy* – in which nation states are linked to each other via trade and financial flows – and a *global economy* – in which the production process itself becomes globally integrated (Robinson, 2003, 2004). At the same time an integrated global financial system has replaced the national bank-dominated financial systems of the earlier period. Global financial flows since the 1980s are qualitatively different from the international financial flows of the earlier period.

Globalisation refers to a process characterised by relatively novel articulations of social power which were not available in earlier historical periods. The increasingly total mobility achieved by capital has allowed it to search out around the world the most favourable conditions for different phases of globalised production, including the cheapest labour, the most favourable institutional environment (e.g. low taxes) and regulatory conditions (e.g. lax environmental and labour laws), a stable social environment, and so on. Transnational capital is the *hegemonic fraction* of capital on a world scale in the sense that it imposes its direction on the global economy and it shapes the character of production and social life everywhere. Although real power and control still remains rigidly hierarchical and has actually become more concentrated under globalisation, the actual organisational form of economic activity is characterised by decentralised webs of horizontally interlocked networks in distinction to the old centralised hierarchies based on vertical integration. The rise of the global economy has been founded on the phenomenal spread since the late 1970s of diverse new economic arrangements associated with the transition from the Fordist regime of accumulation to new post-Fordist *flexible* regimes. Subcontracting and outsourcing have become basic organisational features of economic activity worldwide. In the earlier epochs of capitalism firms tended to organise entire sequences of economic production, distribution and service from within. The *maquiladora* (offshore) factories that are the epitome of the 'global assembly line' are based on this type of subcontracting network, although the phenomenon has long since spread to just about all sectors of the world economy.

Subcontracting and outsourcing, along with a host of other new economic arrangements have resulted in the creation of vast transnational production chains and complex webs of vertical and horizontal integration patterns across the globe. The concepts of flexible accumulation and network structure capture the organisational form of globalised circuits (on this network structure, see, in particular, Castells, 2000). Global production and service chains or networks are *global* in character, in that accumulation is embedded in *global* markets, involves *global* enterprise organisation and sets of *global* capital–labour relations, especially deregulated and casualised labour pools worldwide. Transnational capital, as organised into the giant TNCs, coordinates these vast chains, incorporating numerous agents and social groups into complex global networks. Competition in the new global economy dictates that firms must establish global as opposed to national or regional markets, and that other economic agents must move beyond local markets if they are to remain viable.

Global capitalism and transnationally oriented elites

Epochal changes in the system of world capitalism have had transformative effects on the world as a whole and on each region integrated in, or rearticulated to, the system. Earlier epochs of world capitalism have had major implications for each country and region of the former Third World, which have gone through successive waves of ever-deeper integration into the system. With each new integration or reintegration there has been a corresponding fundamental change in social and class structures and the leading economic activities around which social classes and groups have exercised collective agency. The epoch of corporate capitalism that preceded globalisation saw a deeper integration of Africa, Asia and Latin America into world capitalism, including a major expansion of exports in most cases and the rise of new industrial, commercial and financial elites and new middle and working classes. The groups came together in multi-class populist and corporatist projects that sought development through import-substitution industrialisation and modernisation. Each phase of historical change in the world capitalist system builds on preceding ones and retains important elements from them. Global capitalism is now having a similar transformative effect on every country and region of the world. Developing countries have been experiencing a transition to a new model of economy and society as they become reinserted into the emerging global stage of world capitalism.

As transnational capital integrates the world into new globalised circuits of accumulation it has broken down national and regional autonomies, including the earlier pre-globalisation models of capitalist development and the social forces that sustained these models. Through internal adjustment and rearticulation to the emerging global economy and society, local productive apparatuses and social structures in each region are transformed, and different regions acquire new profiles in the emerging global division of labour. Integration into the emergent global system is the causal structural dynamic that underlies the events we have witnessed in nations and regions all around the world over the past few decades. We want to pay particularly close attention to changes in the economic structure because they provide the material basis for related processes of change in practices and institutions, politics, class structure, and for inquiry into the theme of elites and development.

The remoulding of each national and regional economy creates an array of contradictions between the old and new forms of accumulation. What sets a region off from other parts of the global economy in much of the development literature is uneven geographic development and distinct participation in an international division of labour. I suggest, however, that more determinant (of causal priority) in conceptualising regions within the larger unity of the emerging global economy and society than uneven accumulation, while still important, is the distinct configurations of social forces and of institutions that arise from these configurations. If we are to properly understand the role of local and regional economies and social and class structures they must be studied from the perspective of their point of insertion into global accumulation rather than their relationship to a particular national market or state structure.

Transnational class formation in the developing countries is a major dimension of capitalist globalisation. As global capitalism penetrates new spheres and subjects them to the logic of transnational accumulation, pre-globalisation classes such as peasantries and artisans tend to disappear, replaced by new dominant and subordinate class groups linked to the global economy. We have generally seen in developing countries: the rise of new dominant groups and capitalist fractions tied to the global economy; the downward mobility – or proletarianisation – of older middle classes and professional strata and the rise of new middle and professional strata; proletarianisation of peasants and artisans and the rise of new urban and rural working classes linked to transnational production processes; the working class itself become flexibilised and informalised; and the appearance of an expanding mass of supernumeraries. A global working class has emerged that runs the factories, offices and farms of the global economy, a stratified and heterogeneous class, to be sure, with numerous hierarchies and cleavages internal to it – gender, ethnicity, nationality, and so on.

Here I want to focus on elites. The TCC is composed of the owners and managers of the TNCs and the private transnational financial institutions that drive the global economy (Sklair, 2002; Robinson, 2004). The TCC is a class group grounded in global markets and circuits of accumulation. The globally integrated production and financial system underscores the increasing interpenetration on multiple levels of capital in all parts of the world, organised around transnational capital and the giant TNCs. It is increasingly difficult to separate local circuits of production and distribution from the globalised circuits that dictate the terms and patterns of accumulation worldwide, even when surface appearance gives the (misleading) impression that local capitals retain their autonomy. There are of course still local and national capitalists, and there will be for a long time to come. But they must 'delocalise' and link to transnational capital if they are to survive. Territorially restricted capital cannot compete with its transnationally mobile counterpart. As the global circuit of capital subsumes through numerous mechanisms and arrangements these local circuits, local capitalists who manage these circuits become swept up into the process of transnational class formation.

I have been writing about this process of transnational class formation and the rise of a TCC since the late 1990s (inter alia, Robinson, 1996, 2003, 2004).

The topic has become part of a collective research agenda and the empirical evidence demonstrating the transnationalisation of leading capitalist groups is now considerable (for a sampling, see Sklair, 2002; Kentor, 2005). With the rise of transnational production chains and circuits of accumulation, transnationally oriented capitalists in each country shift their horizons from national markets to global markets. Different phases of production, as they become broken down into component phases that are detachable and dispersed around the world, can be doled out to distinct economic agents through chains of subcontracting, outsourcing and other forms of association. These agents become integrated organically into new globalised circuits, so that they are 'denationalised', in the material if not the cultural sense, and become transnational agents. The vast multi-layered networks of outsourcing, subcontracting, collaboration and so on, increasingly link local and national agents to global networks and structures. The TCC has increasingly exhibited a global political action capacity and placed itself on the world scene as a coherent actor. In the same way as business groups organise to orient national policy planning groups and lobby national governments, transnational business groups have become a powerful lobby in many countries around the world pushing for a shift in state policies towards promotion of the group interests of those integrated into transnational circuits.

The composition of capitalist classes and elites in developing countries is altered by capitalist globalisation. The spread of transnational circuits of accumulation present elites in developing countries with new opportunities to pursue their class and group interests by reinserting local economic activity that they manage as segments of globalised circuits. Other groups whose reproduction was tied to domestic accumulation may lose out if they are unable to transnationalise their local activity. In my detailed case study on Central America (Robinson, 2003) I have shown how local elites who previously strived to build up national circuits of accumulation were confronted from the 1980s on with a situation in which these circuits were no longer viable *and* in which restructuring and integration into globalised circuits became a profitable option. Hence their class and group interests shifted from national development to participation in new global markets and production and service sequences. The restructuring and globalisation of local production processes do bring about new opportunities for upward mobility among some sectors of the national population. But these benefits of global integration, as I shall argue below, do not constitute development in the traditional sense. As these processes have unfolded there have been ongoing struggles in recent decades between ascendant transnational and descendant national fractions of dominant groups and these struggles often form the backdrop to national political and ideological dynamics. Transnational fractions of local capitalist classes and bureaucratic elites vied for state power and in most countries won government in the 1980s and 1990s, or at least came to capture 'commanding heights' of state policy-making via key ministries such as foreign, finance, and central banks. In many developing countries transnational fractions utilised local states to latch their countries on to the train of capitalist globalisation.

National and global accumulation and the state

Here there is a contradictory logic between national and global accumulation. On the one side are the only national fractions of dominant groups whose interests lie in national accumulation and traditional national regulatory and protectionist mechanisms. On the other are transnational groups tied to new globalised circuits of accumulation. Their interests lie in an expanding global economy. There is a tension between nation-centric class interests and those groups who develop new relationships linked to transnationalised accumulation. As conflicts arise between descending forms of national production and rising forms of globalised capital, local and national struggles should be seen as simultaneously global and internal. Transnational fractions, as they have captured governments around the world, or come to positions in which they can influence and redirect state policies, have utilised national state apparatuses to advance globalisation, pursue economic restructuring, and to dismantle the old nation state social welfare and developmentalist projects. While pursuing the neo-liberal model at home they have also pursued worldwide market liberalisation and projects of regional and global economic integration. They have promoted a supranational infrastructure of the global economy.

Transnationally oriented capitalists and state managers in developing countries have pursued a switch from 'inward oriented development', or accumulation around national markets such as the import-substitution industrialisation (ISI) models that predominated in many Third World regions in the middle part of the twentieth century, to 'outward-oriented development' involving export-promotion strategies and a deeper integration of national economies into the global economy. This switch involves the emergence of new economic activities and structures of production in each country and region integrating into the global economy (Robinson, 2002, 2003). These new activities generally imply local participation in globalised circuits of accumulation, or in global production and service chains. As I have shown in great detail for Latin America (Robinson, 2008), these activities include *maquiladora* assembly operations and other forms of transnational industrial subcontracting, transnational corporate agribusiness, transnational banking and other financial services, transnational services such as call centres, software production, data processing, tourism and leisure, and so forth, as well as, very importantly, the transnationalisation of the retail sector, or what I call Walmartisation, along with the supply systems that stock retail. The new dominant sectors of accumulation in the developing world are, in sum, increasingly integrated into global accumulation circuits in myriad ways.

It is important to explore the relationship between transnationally oriented capitalist and business groups and elites in the state and the political system. As new transnational circuits of accumulation became dominant there were powerful pressures on state managers to promote these circuits locally – that is, promoting an environment friendly to transnational capital. Elites found that the reproduction of their status becomes linked to the new global accumulation strategy. Restructuring gave an immanent class bias to agents of the external sector. These agents tended to fuse with political managers of the neo-liberal state and in the latter decades of the twentieth century began to coalesce gradually, in a process chequered with contradictions and conflict, into a transnationalised fraction of the national elite that promote and manage new globalised circuits of accumulation. At the helm of transnational fractions of the elite we generally find a politicised leadership and a technocratic cadre steeped in neo-liberal ideology and economics and sharing a familiarity with the world of academic think tanks, world-class universities and international financial institutions.

What were developmentalist states in the earlier epoch became neo-liberal states under globalisation. These neo-liberal national states have functioned to serve *global* (over local) capital accumulation, including a shift in the subsidies that states provide, away from social reproduction and from internal economic agents and towards transnational capital. These neo-liberal states have performed three essential services: (1) adopting fiscal, monetary and trade policies that assure macroeconomic stability and the free movement of capital; (2) providing the basic infrastructure necessary for global economic activity (air and sea ports, communications networks, educational systems, etc.); and (3) providing social order, that is, stability, which requires sustaining instruments of social control, coercive and ideological apparatuses. When transnational elites speak of 'governance' they are referring to these functions and the capacity to fulfil them.

However, there are other conditions that transnational capitalists and elites require for the functioning and reproduction of global capitalism. National states are ill equipped to organise a supranational unification of macroeconomic policies, create a unified field for transnational capital to operate, impose transnational trade regimes, supranational 'transparency', and so forth. The construction of a supranational legal and regulatory system for the global economy in recent years has been the task of sets of transnational institutions whose policy prescriptions and actions have been synchronised with those of neo-liberal national states that have been captured by local transnationally oriented forces. There is a new transnational institutionality, a new transnational configuration of power, but this is a very incomplete, contradictory and open-ended process. A TNS apparatus is not the same as a 'global government', which does not exist. Transnational institutions attempt to coordinate global capitalism and impose capitalist domination beyond national borders. We can conceptualise a TNS apparatus as a loose network comprised of inter- and supranational political and economic institutions *together with* national state apparatuses that have been penetrated and transformed by transnational forces, and has not yet (and may never) acquired any centralised form. The TNS played a key role in imposing the neo-liberal model on the old Third World and therefore in reinforcing a new capital–labour relation. The IMF, for example, by conditioning its lending on a deregulation and flexibilisation of local labour markets, as it has often done, is imposing the new capital–labour relation on the particular country and in the process fundamentally transforming local labour markets and class and power relations.

Transnational elites set about to penetrate and restructure national states, directly, through diverse political-diplomatic and other ties between national states and TNS apparatuses and functionaries, and indirectly, through the impositions of transnational capital via its institutional agents (IMF, World Bank, etc.) and the structural power that global capital exercises over nation states. Local transnational nuclei, or pools, have liaised with the transnational elite as 'in-country' counterparts through a shared outlook and interest in new economic activities and through diverse external political, cultural and ideological ties. These nuclei sought in recent decades to advance the transnational agenda by capturing key state apparatuses and ministries, by the hegemony they were expected to achieve in civil society, and by the power they wielded through their preponderance in the local economy and the material and ideological resources accrued through external linkages. Hence it is not that nation states become irrelevant or powerless vis-à-vis transnational capital and its global institutions. Rather, power as the ability to issue commands and have them obeyed, or more precisely, the ability to shape social structures, shifts from social groups and classes with interests in national accumulation to those whose interests lie in new global circuits of accumulation.

Although they do not disappear, national states experience dramatic fracturing and restructuring. As globalisation proceeds, internal social cohesion declines along with national economic integration. The neo-liberal state retains essential powers to facilitate globalisation but it loses the ability to harmonise conflicting social interests within a country, to realise the historic function of sustaining the internal unity of nationally conceived social formation, and to achieve legitimacy. Unable to resolve the contradictory problems of legitimacy and capital accumulation, local states opt simply for abandoning whole sectors of national populations. In many instances, they no longer bothered to try to attain legitimacy among the marginalised and supernumeraries, who are isolated and contained in new ways, or subject to repressive social control measures (such as, for example, the mass incarceration of African Americans in the United States or 'social cleansing' in several Latin American countries). A fundamental contradiction in the global capitalist system is a globalising economy within a nation state based political system. A TNS apparatus is incipient and unable to regulate global capitalism or to ameliorate many of its crisis tendencies.

Power did shift in many countries from nationally oriented dominant groups to these emerging transnationally oriented groups. However, the crisis that exploded in 2008 with the collapse of the global financial system has exacerbated crises of legitimacy in many countries around the world and seriously undermined the ability of transnational elites to reproduce their authority. Global elites have been scrambling since the Asian crisis of 1997–8 to develop more effective transnational state apparatuses, or institutions and mechanisms that allow for transnational coordination and supervision. These efforts have intensified since the collapse of 2008. In March 2009, for instance, the Chinese government called for the creation of a new global reserve currency to replace the dominant dollar – a super-currency made up of a basket of national currencies and controlled by the IMF.

From a geographical to a social conception of development

As capitalism globalises, the twenty-first century is witness to new forms of poverty and wealth, and new configurations of power and domination. Class, racial and gender inequalities have in many respects been aggravated by globalisation and new social cleavages are emerging. One major new axis of inequality is between citizen and non-citizen in the face of a massive upsurge in transnational migration and the increasing use around the world of ethnic immigrant labour pools. Yet the dominant discourse on global inequality and development is still territorial, that is, inequality among nations in a world system. In the dominant development discourse what 'develops' is a nation state. But global society appears to be increasingly stratified less along national and territorial lines than across transnational social and class lines (Cox, 1987; Hoogvelt, 1997; Robinson, 1998, 2002, 2003). Certain forms of conceptualising the North–South divide obscure our view of social hierarchies and inequalities across nations and regions. Hurricane Katrina ravaged New Orleans in 2005, for instance, lifting the veil of race, class, poverty and inequality in the United States. The storm disproportionately devastated poor black communities who lacked the resources to take protection and whose Third World social conditions became apparent. A United Nations report released in the immediate aftermath of the hurricane observed that the infant mortality rate in the United States had been rising for the previous five years and was the same as for Malaysia, that black children were twice as likely as whites to die before their first birthday, and that blacks in Washington, DC had a higher infant death rate than people in the Indian state of Kerala (UNDP, 2005).

Clearly we need to rethink the categories of North and South and, indeed, the very concept of development. A sociology of national development is no longer tenable. In earlier epochs core and periphery referred to specific territories and the populations that resided therein. The centre–periphery division of labour created by modern colonialism reflected a particular spatial configuration in the law of uneven development which is becoming transformed by globalisation. The transnational geographic dispersal of the full range of world production processes suggests that core and peripheral production activities are less geographically bounded than previously, while new financial circuits allow wealth to be moved around the world instantaneously through cyberspace just as easily as it is generated, so that exactly *where* wealth is produced becomes less important for the issue of development.

While the global South is increasingly dispersed across the planet so too is the global North. Rapid economic growth in India and China have created hundreds of millions of new middle-class consumers integrated into the global cornucopia even as it has thrown other hundreds of millions into destitution. Globalisation fragments locally and integrates select strands of the population globally. The cohesive structures of nations and their civil societies disintegrate as populations become divided into 'core' and 'peripheral' labour pools and as local economic expansion results in the advancement of some (delocalised) groups and deepening poverty for others. We find an affluent 'developed' population, including a privileged sector among segmented labour markets linked to knowledge-intensive, professional and managerial activities and high consumption exists alongside a super-exploited secondary segment of flexibilised labour and a mass of supernumeraries constituting an 'underdeveloped' population within the same national borders. This social bifurcation seems to be a worldwide phenomenon, explained in part by the inability of national states to capture and redirect surpluses through interventionist mechanisms that were viable in the nation state phase of capitalism.

The great geographic core–periphery divide that gave rise to development studies is a product of the colonial and imperialist era in world capitalism and is gradually eroding, not because the periphery is 'catching up', but because of the shift from an *inter*national to a global division of labour and the tendency for a downward levelling of wages and the general conditions of labour. The international division of labour has gone through successive transformations in the history of world capitalism. For many, the most recent permutation involves the shift in manufacturing from North to South, so that in the 'new international division of labor' (Frobel et al., 1980) the North specialises in high-skilled and better-paid labour supplying advanced services and technology to the world market while the South provides low-skilled and lower paid labour for global manufacturing and primary commodity supply. But this analysis, as Freeman observes, has become increasingly obsolete due to the massive investments that the large populous developing countries are making in human capital. China and India are producing millions of college graduates capable of doing the same work as the college graduates of the United States, Japan or Europe – at much lower pay. The huge number of highly educated workers in India and China threatens to undo the traditional pattern of trade between advanced and less developed countries. Historically, advanced countries have innovated high-tech products that require high-wage educated workers and extensive R&D, while developing countries specialise in old manufacturing products. The reason for this was that the advanced countries had a near monopoly on scientists and engineers and other highly educated workers. As China, India and other developing countries have increased their number of university graduates, this monopoly on high-tech innovative capacity has diminished. Today, most major multinationals have R&D centres in China or India, so that the locus of technological advance may shift.

There remain very real regional distinctions in the form of productive participation in the global economy. But processes of uneven accumulation increasingly unfold in accordance with a social and not a national logic. Different levels of social development adhere from the very sites of social productive activity, that is, from *social*, not geographic, space. Moreover, privileged groups have an increasing ability to manipulate space so as to create enclaves and insulate themselves through novel mechanisms of social control and new technologies for the built environment. The persistence, and in fact *growth*, of the North–South divide remains important for its theoretical and practical political implications. What is up for debate is whether the divide is something innate to world capitalism or a particular spatial configuration of uneven capitalist development during a particular historic phase of world capitalism, and whether tendencies towards the self-reproduction of this configuration are increasingly offset by counter-tendencies emanating from the nature and dynamic of global capital accumulation.

To explain the movement of values between different 'nodes' in globalised production, clearly we need to move beyond nation state centric approaches and apply a theory of value to transformations in world spatial and institutional structures (the nation state being the central spatial and institutional structure in the hitherto history of world capitalism). The notion of net social gain or loss used by development economists has little meaning if measured, as it traditionally is, in national terms, or even in geographic terms. The distribution of social costs and gains must be conceived in transnational social terms, not in terms of the nation state vis-à-vis the world economy, but transnationally as social groups vis-à-vis other social groups in a global society. Development should be reconceived not as a national phenomenon, in which what 'develops' is a nation, but in terms of developed, underdeveloped and intermediate population groups occupying contradictory or unstable locations in a transnational environment.

Conclusions: elites, development and social reproduction in the globalisation age

Under the emergent global social structure of accumulation the social reproduction of labour in each country becomes less important for accumulation as the output of each nation and region is exported to the global level. The transnational model of accumulation being implemented since the 1980s does not require an inclusionary social base and is inherently polarising. Socio-economic exclusion is immanent to the model since accumulation does not depend on a domestic market or internal social reproduction. To phrase it another way, there is a contradiction between the class function of the neo-liberal states and their legitimation function. For neo-liberal elites, successful integration into the global economy became predicated on the erosion of labour's income, the withdrawal of the social wage, the transfer of the costs of social reproduction from the public sector to individual families, a weakening of trade unions and workers movements, and the suppression of popular political demands. Hence, in the logic of global capitalism, the cheapening of labour and its social disenfranchisement by the neo-liberal state became conditions for 'development'. The very drive by local elites to create conditions to attract transnational capital has been what thrusts majorities into poverty and inequality.

At the core of what seemed to be emerging global social structures of accumulation was a new deregulated capital–labour relation based on the casualisation of labour associated with post-Fordist flexible accumulation, new systems of labour control and diverse contingent categories of labour. Workers in the global economy were themselves under these flexible arrangements increasingly treated as a subcontracted component rather than a fixture internal to employer organisations. In the Keynesian–Fordist order, the labour supply and the workforce needed to be stable, which lent itself to more regulated and protected capital–labour relations, whereas in global capitalism labour is reduced to an input like any other, meaning that it needs to be totally flexible, available in large numbers that can be tapped, added to the mix, shifted and dispensed with at will. Labour is increasingly only a naked commodity, no longer embedded in relations of reciprocity rooted in social and political communities that were historically institutionalised in nation states.

The decline of ISI industries and domestic market enterprises disorganised and reduced the old working class that tended to labour under Fordist arrangements, including unionisation and corporatist relations with the state and employers. This fractionation often has political implications, as the declining group is more likely to belong to trade unions, to be influenced by a corporatist legacy, and to agitate for the preservation or restoration of the old labour regime and its benefits. It is also more likely to be male. The new workers faced a flexible and informalised labour regime. In many developing countries there has been a contraction of middle classes and professional strata that had developed through public sector employment and government civil service in the face of the dismantling of public sectors, privatisations and the downsizing of states. At the same time, restructuring involves the rise of new middle and professional strata who may have the opportunity to participate in global consumption patterns, frequent modern shopping malls, communicate through mobile phones, visit Internet cafés, and so on. These strata may form a social base for neo-liberal regimes and become incorporated into the global capitalist bloc.

Added to income polarisation is the dramatic deterioration in social conditions as a result of austerity measures that have drastically reduced and privatised health, education and other social programmes. Popular classes whose social reproduction is dependent on a social wage (public sector) have faced a social crisis, while privileged middle and upper classes become exclusive consumers of social services channelled through private networks. Here we see the need to reconceive development in transnational social rather than geographic terms. The pattern under globalisation is not merely 'growth without redistribution' but the simultaneous growth of wealth and of poverty as two sides of the same coin. Global capitalism generates downward mobility for most at the same time that it opens up new opportunities for some middle-class and professional strata as the redistributive role of the nation state recedes and global market forces become less mediated by state structures as they mould the prospects for downward and upward mobility.

In conclusion, the first few decades of globalisation involved a change in the correlation of class forces worldwide away from nationally organised popular classes and towards the transnational capitalist class and local economic and political elites tied to transnational capital. The elimination of the domestic market as a strategic factor in accumulation had important implications for class relations, social movements and the struggle over development. By removing the domestic market and popular class consumption from the accumulation imperative, restructuring helped bring about the demise of the populist class alliances between broad majorities and nationally based ruling classes that characterised the pre-globalisation model of accumulation. Later on, popular classes – themselves caught up in a process of reconfiguration and transnationalisation – stepped up their resistance and the hegemony of the transnational elite began to crack. The crisis that hit the global economy in 2008 with the collapse of the financial system had been building for some time and is rooted in the structural contradictions of global capitalism alluded to here.

Stepping back in perspective, the problematic of development in the South is ultimately the same as that of social polarisation and over-accumulation in the global economy as a whole. Sustaining dynamic capitalist growth, beyond reining in global financial markets and shifting from speculative to productive investment, would require a redistribution of income and wealth to generate an expanding demand of the popular majority. This is a very old problem that has been debated for decades: how to create effective demand that could fuel capitalist growth. The ISI model was unable to achieve this on the basis of protected national and regional markets; the neo-liberal model has been unable to achieve this on the basis of insertion into global markets.

Seen from the logic of global capitalism the problem leads to political quagmire: how to bring about a renewed redistributive component without affecting the class interests of the dominant groups, or how to do so through the political apparatuses of national states whose direct power has diminished considerably relative to the structural power of transnational capital. This is a dilemma for the global system as a whole. The pressures to bring about a shift in the structure of distribution – both of income and of property – and the need for a more interventionist state to bring this about, is one side of the equation in the constellation of social and political forces that seemed to be coming together in the early twenty-first century to contest the neo-liberal order. Political, economic and academic elites began to look for alternative formulas to address the global economic crisis and at the same time to prevent – or at least better manage – social and political unrest. In my own view, the struggle for development is a struggle for social justice and must involve a measure of transnational social governance over the process of global production and reproduction as the first step in effecting a radical worldwide redistribution of wealth and power downward to poor majorities.

References

Aglietta, M. (1979) *A Theory of Capitalist Regulation* (London: Verso).

Castells, M. (2000) *The Rise of the Network Society*, vol. 1 (2nd edn.) (Oxford: Blackwell).

Cox, R. W. (1987) *Production, Power, and World Order: Social Forces in the Making of History* (New York: Columbia University Press).

Dicken, P. (2003) *Global Shift* (4th edn.) (London and New York: Guilford Press).

Esteva, G. (1991) 'Development'. In W. Sachs (ed.), *The Development Dictionary: A Guide to Knowledge as Power* (London: Zed).

Freeman, R. (2005) 'China, India and the Doubling of the Global Labor Force: Who Pays the Price of Globalization?', *The Globalist*, 3 June, posted at *Japan Focus*, 26 August, http://www.japanfocus.org/article.asp?id=377 (accessed 13 October 2005).

Frobel, F., Heinrichs, J. and Kreye, O. (1980) *The New International Division of Labour* [first published in German in 1977] (Cambridge: Cambridge University Press).

Hoogvelt, A. (1997) *Globalization and the Post-Colonial World: The New Political Economy of Development* (Baltimore: Johns Hopkins University Press).

Kentor, J. (2005) 'The Growth of Transnational Corporate Networks, 1962 to 1998', *Journal of World-Systems Research*, 11(2): 262–86.

Kotz, D. M., McDonough, T. and Reich, M. (eds.) (1994) *Social Structures of Accumulation: The Political Economy of Growth and Crisis* (Cambridge: Cambridge University Press).

McMichael, P. (1996) *Development and Social Change: A Global Perspective* (Thousand Oaks, CA: Pine Forge).

Prashad, V. (2007) *The Darker Nations: A People's History of the Third World* (New York: New Press).

Robinson, W. I. (1996) *Promoting Polyarchy: Globalization, U.S. Intervention, and Hegemony* (Cambridge: Cambridge University Press).

Robinson, W. I. (1998) 'Beyond Nation State Paradigms: Globalization, Sociology, and the Challenge of Transnational Studies', *Sociological Forum*, 13(4): 561–94.

Robinson, W. I. (2002) 'Remapping Development in Light of Globalization: From a Territorial to a Social Cartography', *Third World Quarterly*, 23(6): 1047–71.

Robinson, W. I. (2003) *Transnational Conflicts: Central America, Social Change, and Globalization* (London: Verso).

Robinson, W. I. (2004) *A Theory of Global Capitalism: Production, Class, and State in a Transnational World* (Baltimore: Johns Hopkins University Press).

Robinson, W. I. (2008) *Latin America and Global Capitalism: A Critical Globalization Perspective* (Baltimore: Johns Hopkins University Press).

Sklair, L. (2002) *Globalization: Capitalism and Its Alternatives* (New York: Oxford University Press).

United Nations Development Programme (UNDP) (2005) *Human Development Report* (New York: Oxford University Press/UNDP).

4
Panopticism, Elites and the Deinstitutionalisation of the Civic

Arthur Sementelli

This chapter explores the peculiar phenomena associated with elites and the desire to be under surveillance. That is often understood as part of a broader desire to protect themselves and their possessions from harm, loss, etc. More specifically, the chapter focuses on surveillance as part of the 'Fortress America' movement that emerged as a topic of scholarly discussion from the neo-classical book by Blakely and Snyder (1997) examining gated communities in the USA. Specifically, there are two ideas emerging from this exercise, which have not made it to the forefront of discussions of elites and elite theory. The first involves the application of design strategies in gated communities that reflect Bentham's (1995) concept of the panopticon. Briefly, the panopticon traditionally has been employed in the construction of hospitals and prisons. Oddly, these same panopticon designs have both in part and in total become commonplace in gated communities throughout the USA across multiple socio-economic strata. The second idea concerns the privatisation and com-modification of the civic in general, along with an associated privatisation and commodification of public goods and services in particular. Both observations can be tied explicitly to our contemporary understating of elites and their associated trappings as part of a broader desire to buy 'the good life'.

Understanding how the applications of Bentham's (1995) panopticon shifted from being a primarily negative image of imprisonment and surveillance to one perceived as being positive, and even desirable in certain circumstances can help us understand the privatisation and commodification of the civic and the neighbourhood. By understanding the logic of these phenomena, we might then better understand an aspect of elites and elite theory, as well as the forces, the desires and the 'wants' that drive people to emulate them, or more appropriately to acquire the images and trappings of elites through specific purchasing decisions (Rindfleisch et al., 2000).

One 'trapping' or 'display' of relative wealth that is easy to see is the home. It is often said that homes are one of the most expensive purchases anyone might make. Gated communities in particular, adopt elements of Bentham's (1995) panopticon while representing a commodified, image-laden, privatised quest to obtain the hyper-real simulacrum (Baudrillard, 2000) of the good life. Gated communities represent a sort of nostalgic image or perspective of civic life in general and neighbourhoods in particular. However, in gated communities, these constructs are both fabricated and exclusionary; they look like neighbourhoods without being *actual* neighbourhoods. In practice, these ersatz neighbourhoods are sold not simply as homes, but as bundled packages of images and amenities. As such, people can be persuaded to use, consume and finally sell a house and its associated package of images (ideally for a profit). This makes a house in a gated community not simply an expression of relative wealth, but also a commodity that can *display* the potential or possibility of wealth, an association with prosperity, and at least some of the trappings of the elite since gated communities are designed to exclude non-residents.

In practice, however, particularly in contemporary US markets, this potential as a display has been weighed and found wanting. Yet the image, the package and the amenities often continue to sell, albeit at drastically reduced value and far slower than brokers might hope. It becomes important to ask, what might cause such irrational behaviour? Has the civic become so denatured that people seek the false security of surveillance? Does the notion of somehow aping the behaviour of socio-economic elites act as a mechanism to foster false consciousness through individual purchasing decisions? One might argue that this is an ultimate expression of commodity fetishism (Marx, 1867/1984). Understanding these phenomena becomes a key tool to begin unpacking how we view contemporary elites, their trappings and their images, as well as the fascination that others have with them. It might further help us begin to decipher a more troubling phenomenon, the deinstitutionalisation and commodification of civil society.

Overview

Blakely and Snyder (1997) wrote the now neo-classical piece *Fortress America: Gated Communities in the United States*. The book offers a recent historical account of the development of gated communities. Gated communities are a specific sort of planned residential community with strictly controlled access for pedestrians, bicycles and cars. Currently, these gated communities vary from high security guarded models, to those that simply landscape to reduce automotive and possibly deter pedestrian traffic. Most if not all of these communities charge residents fees for maintenance, which include several items normally handled by cities and counties including street cleaning, rubbish collection, security, landscaping, snow removal and recreation services (Blakely and Snyder, 1997: 25). Regardless of the current implementation, all gated community designs share an origin within the design of retirement and resort areas (Blakely and Snyder, 1997: 5) built using elements of Bentham's (1995) panopticon design as a mechanism to exclude or limit access to the properties by non-residents. There is often a false sense that these designed neighbourhoods can somehow lead to improved security by deterring criminal behaviour through control over access and traffic combined with surveillance.

The growth and mainstream acceptance, at least regionally, of the concept of planned communities as normal is in truth one step in a process that deinstitutionalises the civic elements in a society. By creating these disconnected, gated, 'islands' of exclusion, it becomes easier to privatise the amenities within said geographic area while reducing the delivery of public goods. Such movement allows for the further commodification and sale of the trappings of wealth as an alternative to maintaining neighbourhoods and municipalities specifically, and a civil society more generally. Other side effects of this phenomenon include decreased reliance on public services by all but those in abject poverty, a duplication of services in some areas, and an increase in the value placed on individuality and exclusion over community and engagement.

By artificially drawing boundaries among 'residents' and non-residents, preventing outsiders from entering the development becomes a priority service issue. There is an increased need for observation and control over access as a consequence. As alluded to earlier, a number of the models for these planned communities bear stark resemblances to the panopticon design, a prison 'blueprint' offered by Bentham (1995). Consider the common cul-de-sac, one of the simplest models for a planned community. If one places Bentham's famous drawing of the panopticon next to the standard layout of a cul-de-sac, we find they are functionally identical. Culs-de-sac in particular, and gated communities more generally consciously or unconsciously might foster a feeling of invisible omniscience (Lang, 2004) and protection, but from what?

The panopticon design was employed as a model for prison design and construction to observe inmates. Bentham argued this design allowed one to obtain power over individuals through surveillance, thereby maintaining order. Foucault (1977, 1994) and others began to expand the discussions of the panopticon design, crafting discussions that were focused not only on the design of prisons, but also other institutions such as hospitals. Gated communities represent a curious difference, what some might even call a shift in application. One aspect of the phenomenon of gated communities often relying on a panopticon design involves a shift towards observation as a mechanism to keep people *out* rather than as a mechanism to keep people *inside*. Embracing such a design with a history of removing power, of controlling and observing residents, leads us to ask the following question. Why would wealthy, powerful elites be so inclined to surrender privacy and control? At least initially one might argue that security might trump privacy. However, there is more at work, and it takes the form of the commodification and sale of life as well as the establishment of control over one's private life.

'With the spread of homeowner associations, more and more Americans can set their own taxes in the form of assessments, use them for services they choose, and restrict those benefits to themselves and their immediate neighbors' (Blakely and Snyder, 1997: 24–5). Contemporary gated communities go so far as to hire a management company to handle the day-to-day operations of service provision, analogous to a city administrator, but with one notable difference. The management firm almost always maintains control over surveillance, and is charged with the maintenance of the community's homogeneity (often through architectural rules and standards), while maintaining the control points (private physical devices, e.g. gates) (Blakely and Snyder, 1997: 28).

Gated communities have been remarkably popular throughout the USA and worldwide. They tend to be most prevalent in the southern USA, particularly Texas, Florida and certain other states including Arkansas. Elements of these prison/hospital style designs appear nationally and internationally as specific communities and include security checkpoints at their entry both in the USA and abroad as a means to exclude, maintain security and maintain status. The literature, however, illustrates how this purchased security is often just a false perception (Wilson-Doenges, 2000; Low, 2001; Grant and Mittelsteadt, 2004). Recent census data further illustrate that in practice gated communities' 'status' and exclusivity images have become muddied by the fact more renters and minorities have gained access to these areas perceived to be 'exclusive' (Sanchez et al., 2005, using data from the American Housing Survey (AHS)). Additionally, the research presented by Sanchez et al. (2005) seems to support Somers' (2008) argument that market approaches to community have in practice begun to erode the civic, to exclude, and to undermine governance generally.

New leisure class

After the Second World War there was an unprecedented expansion of the American middle class (Blakely and Snyder, 1997). Real wealth increased well into the 1970s and there was an expansion of both savings and real wages. As disposable income increased, there was an increased desire for certain status items to differentiate the burgeoning middle class. As such, there was a push for home and automobile ownership. Home ownership, in particular, was subsidised heavily by the government, since it was envisioned as a tool to maintain communities, stability, citizenship and control (Rose, 2000). Emergent literature has also begun to link regulation, surveillance and control at the individual level to an application of governmentality (Francombe, 2010). One might argue these links are mechanisms to control mainstream society, not elites. As such, there is a continued interest among elites along with those who desire to be elites (or at least to enjoy the trappings and images associated with them) to uncover ways to separate themselves from mass society (Mills, 1956/2000) and to gain at least some of their associated trappings including exclusive homes with restricted access. Consequently, attention then turned towards one particular status item: the gated community.

The development and expansion of gated communities throughout the USA, particularly from the 1980s into the present created a market for a certain type of 'turnkey' approach to living. The homes eventually shared many common designs and characteristics making them only partially differentiated, commodified products. Differentiation in this case became a function of the 'lifestyle' and the amenities as much as the design elements incorporated into the construction of the properties. The USA in particular experienced a shift away from home ownership in the classic sense towards ownership of *community* (Blakely and Snyder, 1997: 63).

The ownership of a community, in this case, is rather different from the sort of 'ownership' one might take as a function of being a good steward of resources (Sementelli, 2007). This notion of ownership is not for something held in usufruct, but instead a market good or service. As such, these 'communities' are not communities at all. They are instead *commodities* that can be bought, sold, used, consumed and traded. This creates an expectation that home ownership in gated communities can be understood as investments and status items, and the services associated with them are part of the 'entertainment' or amenities associated with ownership. Rather than neighbours, there are members who are not citizens, but residents. Such a change represents another illustration of a broader movement towards the deinstitutionalisation of the civic.

The commodification and deinstitutionalisation continued, as developers began to realise they could segment the markets to sell to the 'top fifth' (Blakely and Snyder, 1997: 81) as well as the very wealthy. These less expensive enclaves could be sold just as their more expensive counterparts, with lifestyle 'perks' that included guards or concierge services. By the 1990s the segmentation of these commodified living communities expanded to the point where the features associated with the expensive communities trickled down into the construction and maintenance of public housing projects, including the inclusion of fences, guards and in some cases direct observation (Blakely and Snyder, 1997: 102–3).

Modes of life: four models of planned communities

There are several different models of planned community. This section examines four of the most common types: prestige, lifestyle, security and purpose design. Prestige communities are targeted to people of elite status and designed with certain amenities and access in mind. Though often architecturally simple, they are purported to 'protect and secure' a place on the social ladder. These prestige communities often resemble subdivisions and are most often enclaves for both the affluent and powerful. Just below the surface, without much attention to design, they create and reinforce an ersatz homogeneous neighbourhood enhanced by control and surveillance (Blakely and Snyder, 1997: 41).

A second type is the lifestyle community. Historically, there have been any number of 'lifestyle' communities, and they continue to gain popularity, especially in the USA as the population ages. These include retirement communities, assisted living communities, country clubs and other themed homogeneous 'neighbourhoods' of seemingly like-minded people. Retirement communities in particular have developed niche marketing such as limiting the number of people under 50 who can live there as well as the age and number of children allowed on the premises. This is often in addition to sets of rules regarding lawns, parking and pet ownership. These rules are typically used as mechanisms to maintain or shape the experience of the 'themed' community.

As the apparent value of Bentham's (1995) work re-emerged, we find that the security (or at least perceived security) associated with his designs has pervaded numerous segments of housing markets. Currently, you can find gates being used to control traffic and sometimes as tools to 'control crime' (Blakely and Snyder, 1997). As gates appear in everything from exclusive real estate to public housing, one must begin to question who is being kept out and who is being kept in? The panopticon, by design, is a tool to keep prisoners in and under control, raising questions about why anyone would willingly adopt such a model as a free person.

There is a fourth type of community: the purpose designed community. Historically, there have been numerous purpose designed communities in both the USA and abroad. Current implementations include the worker compounds in the Middle East, often built by the oil industry for their non-Arabic workers to help them to better 'get along' in unfamiliar surroundings. These communities often look a great deal like suburban America, and even have similar services to their US counterparts. Such a community evokes Baudrillard's (2000) account of Disneyland, where the community acts as a sort of image of a neighbourhood, though it has been fabricated out of context.

Other examples of these purpose designed communities are not quite as cheerful as the ersatz suburbs in the Middle East. One might also argue that the company town or 'mill town' housing projects can also be understood as purpose designed communities (Crawford, 1995). Such communities were also seen as all-purpose, functional mechanisms to enable the workers to more effectively transition between work and home life. Arguably, mill or company towns share much more in common with Bentham's (1995) intended application of panopticism than some current examples might. However, it is not much of a leap from the design of a company town to panopticon or country club. They each have a large facility at the centre with amenities or activity areas that in the case of company towns and country clubs include parks, cultural events and concert venues. So, we are left with the idea that purpose designed communities and the broader 'themed' country club lifestyle communities discussed earlier bear certain family resemblances to each other (Wittgenstein, 1953).

Regardless of the type or model of the gated community, in most if not all of the cases they tend to share some remarkable similarities with Bentham's (1995) panopticon and the contemporary technologies associated with it, including surveillance devices, guards and physical barriers to control traffic. Each of these communities also tends to share another common characteristic. There is a certain privatised element in the implementation of each, separating it in some ways from the municipality or public structure it often inhabits. Historically, if a company were to cut back or go out of business, the company town would be devastated. When a lifestyle, prestige or even purpose designed community experiences economic changes, they too can be devastated by the process. Unlike real neighbourhoods, these ersatz communities do not have the same sort of access to public goods and services because both their rights and access are restricted within the confines of the planned community and its rules *by design*, limiting the degree to which the public sector might intervene.

Given the substantial risks involved with embracing these planned, ersatz communities, what might be their attraction? What drives someone to forgo existing public services that are currently tax subsidised to move into an area that often charges additional fees for the same goods and services a person or family has access to? A key to understanding this is the notion of disposable or discretionary income. As one gains greater access to disposable or discretionary income, opportunities arise to use said resources to acquire prestige items. Although an inexpensive digital watch will tell the time, people still tend to choose a Rolex or some other prestige branded watch over the functionality of a cheap digital one. It remains a function of symbolic display rather than practicality.

Form over function: quest for imagery

At least part of the logic for this cluster of odd-seeming economically or socially irrational choices involves some understanding of value. If we consider the intrinsic value of these decisions, meaning the value a gated community has in its own right, then they can be understood as poor economic choices. Residents often pay for two or more sets of services, and their quality except in the cases of some prestige and lifestyle communities are often inferior to their public sector counterparts. These arrangements tend to be economically inefficient, with additional maintenance and architectural restrictions, as well as rules for access, landscaping and even vehicles creating additional costs for residents. Overall, it often becomes easy to question the economic value of these communities relative to the prices charged for them.

If one instead considers the *extrinsic* value of these communities, or the value based on association with something else, something interesting occurs. These communities often have the images of elites, of elite life, and elite behaviour associated with them, at least implicitly. To understand rationally why one might choose one of these communities, it becomes important to see the extrinsic symbolic value of them. They are commodified, routinised, process- and image-laden mechanisms to engage in a societal level spectacle (Debord, 1967/1995) of elitism, wealth and celebrity. Understanding gated communities as anything else typically leads to frustration and confusion.

Simply having the possibility of these images, these proxies of the elite are not enough. To function as a market good they need to demonstrate a demand for the good or service. To be commoditised and profitable, the extrinsic values of these planned communities need to be sold *without* the buyer realising that they lack a certain qualitative distinction from their counterparts in the public sector (e.g. prisons, public housing, etc.). The *belief* in the extrinsic value of these purchases arguably is what helps to maintain the value of these communities to a targeted audience. In essence, it is the *idea* or image of living in a planned community, rather than the community itself that has the value. That difference drives the decision to purchase in a gated community.

Privatisation

By commodifying housing, segmenting the market and increasing opportunities to live within gated communities, we find that the environment becomes amenable for extending the privatisation of public services. Such movement exacerbates the fragmentation of communities, leading to a 'loss of connection and social contract' (Blakely and Snyder, 1997: 139). People begin seeing themselves as tax*payers* rather than citizens (ibid.). As a tax*payer*, or more importantly, a *customer*, we find that movement to gated communities, and to privatised enclaves, represents a choice to avoid civic engagement and participation at some level. It is a choice to make purchases of goods and services to maintain a personal quality of life:

> 'I took care of my responsibility, I'm safe in here, I've got my guard gate; I've paid my [homeowner association] dues, and I'm responsible for my streets. Therefore, I have no responsibility for the commonweal, because you take care of your own.' (Blakely and Snyder, 1997: 140)

The statement above illustrates a sort of civic fiction that has become the norm for many of the people who became property owners in these gated communities. As each of these communities represents a segment of the market, there is the potential for the service expectation to not be met in reality. To compensate for this disparity, we find these private communities often turn to the public sector to purchase certain goods and services. In many cases, particularly in Florida, gated communities have hired off-duty county Sheriffs' deputies for private security. In communities for the elderly, we find there is a continued reliance on public services including 911 emergency services, emergency medical technicians and sometimes public fire protection.

In times of shrinking budgets, however, we find that municipalities in particular can also cleave to models of privatisation as both political and economic tools. In practice, many have begun or have expanded their adoption of fee for services schemes as well as other pay for use approaches for the provision of public services. In many cases, emergency calls in several states that require an ambulance often result in the person receiving a bill charging them for services rendered. In some US cities, residents discover that they also receive a second bill to cover mileage to the hospital to offset gasoline expenses.

There are limits to these privatised enclaves. *Public* streets cannot be blocked. Developers and municipalities cannot easily craft fully privatised enclaves wholly independent of some municipality, some county, or some state. The communities, however, can be redesigned and monitored (Blakely and Snyder, 1997: 158). This redesign and surveillance creates the boundaries for the enclave. It establishes the island within a municipality. The creation of these virtual islands, virtual enclaves and ersatz 'communities' erodes the civic (Somers, 2008) while it simultaneously helps to perpetuate the myth that the private sector *always* does 'it' better. This belief is based on the erroneous idea that 'free' market solutions can always work in *non-market* situations. Taking the most basic position that government need only get involved at the point of market failure and to protect commerce (Smith, 1776/1977), we find there are substantial and practical limits for the solutions offered as common practices in each sector.

The problem of course, is that 'the market' itself is an idealised myth. Under the best of circumstances, the idealised 'free market' offered by Smith (1776/1977) and others is best understood as a thought experiment. As such, the language, processes and beliefs remain susceptible to the practices of spectacle, both political and otherwise (Debord, 1967/1995; Edelman, 1988). Furthermore, based on a neo-classical interpretation of Smith's work, government *must* become heavily involved in the economy to correct the seemingly endless stream of market imperfections, though by doing so governments create their own imperfections in the case of dead weight losses (e.g. taxes and fees), as well as mechanisms to capture certain externalities (e.g. health and safety standards).

The commodification and privatisation of the community 'experience' offers an escape from the realities of economy and society. It is often based on belief, on image, and sometimes on nostalgia (Rindfleisch et al., 2000). Nostalgia, in this sense, is defined as a certain type of consumer behaviour, something that drives the choice for one product over another. In the case of commodified private spaces, it can be argued that these choices represent a desire to recapture or at least buy some part of the idealised Disneyland approach to community (Baudrillard, 2000) that seems to have been 'lost' over the past several years. One might argue instead that such a thing has never been lost, but is instead mythic.

The myth of community

The notions of community, of *civitas* and democracy have in many cases been exposed as contemporary myth. Democracy, with its basis in mutuality and collective citizenship, has joined the myth of community in the dust bin. Rather than a community and a city, we instead have privatised, planned clusters of property based on notions of exclusion rather than connection. The ability to join these exclusive groups, however, has been distilled into a single factor, that is the *ability to pay*. As such, there is no longer simply an 'elite' community. Instead, there are prestige communities, with people who fancy themselves as being a part of some specific socio-economic group. In practice, we find there is nothing to prevent a grifter, a hustler or criminal from entering the community as long as they have the *ability to pay*.

In recent years, there has been little to prevent the same grifters, hustlers and criminals from *selling* properties in these 'prestige' communities either. Benefiting from specific regulatory loopholes, multitudes of self-styled real estate brokers and loan officers packaged and sold the image of this 'American' dream of a lifestyle to both investors and families. One consequence of this commodification of 'lifestyle' in the USA at least has been the collapse and devaluation of the entire housing market. Granted there are areas hit more severely than others, such as California, Nevada and Florida. It is likely no coincidence these states also hold Disneyland, Hollywood, Disneyworld and Las Vegas, which are four relatively popular 'fantasy' lifestyle destinations for adults. In some cases, the gated communities are on the same property as Disneyland for example. This proximity enables people to choose to live in the magic kingdom, or at least in a condominium that is walking distance from it.

Elites and elite theory

The commodification of community has served to better identify the social and economic divisions in the USA. Despite the collapse of the housing market, there are still certain areas within the USA that are well out of the reach of many who would embrace the trappings of the elites. In a peculiar turn of events, we find instead that those in the mobile middle class, in many cases have found themselves sharing their gated community lifestyle with people on public assistance rather than the power elites. Scholars have argued for decades that the middle class and lower upper class have sought to flee poverty. The irony in this case is that the collapse of the housing market has left few options to the person who owns multiple properties. At some point they decide if they need to rent the property or face foreclosure, and the one place with numerous available tenants in need of housing is the federal 'section 8' housing assistance programme which caters to indigent members communities in the USA.

The quest to buy the trappings of elitism, in the end, leads to a fractured community. The collapse of an identifiable middle class and an increase in both poverty and wealth create certain challenges for society writ large. If the wealthy (or at least those who do not perceive themselves as poor) choose to 'opt out' of citizenship by embracing these ersatz communities within municipalities, there is an increased potential for revenue shortfalls, for broad-based reduction in services, and an overall reduction in many of the goods and services we identify with municipalities. These choices compound their influence, typically reinforcing the choice to opt out by more individuals, exacerbating the problem further.

Turning the lens inward

There is a well-established link between community and crime. Specifically, there has been substantial research on the effect of social cohesion on crime (Sampson et al., 1997). Consider first that gated communities tend to foster a culture of fear (Low, 2001) rather than a culture of cohesion. Combine this with a disconnect among individuals and their municipalities (Blakely and Snyder, 1997: 140). Then add the loss of resources and services associated with the privatisation of communities. One might easily argue that fear (e.g. 'white flight' as described by Avila, 2005) can lead to the decision to live in an elective prison of sorts, specifically a gated community, with guards, gates, an ersatz community, and even a false sense of security.

It is important to recall that the panopticon, by design, was not developed as a tool to keep people out. It was instead used to keep people in. Such is the backward logic of contemporary society. As people shun the civic and democratic choice in favour of ersatz communities with 'condo commandos' (Bowman et al., 2006: 145) that are often more restrictive and far less democratic in practice than the most invasive municipal agents, we find that individuals continue to flock to gated communities. Contemporary research does not necessarily support the image of elite communities (Sanchez et al., 2005), but instead appears to support a post-modern movement towards the designs common in the old company towns (Crawford, 1995). People continue to choose these developments, these gated communities over traditional civic structures such as neighbourhoods, boroughs and other geographically localised areas. The question this chapter has attempted to answer is why this is the case.

The argument for why this keeps happening of course is multi-faceted. However, I have suggested there are certain common themes that drive the move to panopticon designs. First, there is a culture of fear. Second, there is a belief in the marketisation of the civic. Third, there is a belief more generally that people can, in truth, purchase 'the good life' and live to a great extent the lives of elites. Such beliefs reflect a general shift towards a spectator society (Lippmann, 2008), and further support Dewey's argument that a rational, logical democratic public is largely a fantasy in contemporary society (Bybee, 1999). Ironically, this image of the elite existence, the good life, in practice is expressed as little more than an exclusive prison (Bentham, 1995), sometimes populated by renters (Sanchez et. al., 2005). In most cases it fails to reflect the exclusivity and elite status the image is purported to convey.

Commonly understood as a mechanism for the conspicuous display of relative wealth and status, the purchase of the image of the good life has in many cases resulted in certain unforeseen consequences. The first is the commodification and privatisation of the images of community, captured at least in part by the creation of these homogeneous enclaves of residents. The second is the marketisation and commodification of neighbourhood and community, along with the economic consequences often associated with fluctuations in partially differentiated items that often lose value as interest wanes in the item in question. A third consequence is a reduced reliance on public goods and services, combined with a reduction in willingness to pay for public services duplicated by the ersatz community. This can lead to greater socio-economic disparities, while eroding the already fading notions of contemporary civil society. In the end, these consequences create a greater demand for security (real or imagined), for surveillance, and for the ability to pay for your slice of 'the good life'. This in turn creates a situation that leads free individuals to choose to forfeit rights, choices and privacy willingly as part of a greater desire to gain an element of elite status, or at least to imagine it.

References

Avila, E. (2005) *Popular Culture in the Age of White Flight: Fear and Fantasy in Suburban Los Angeles* (Berkeley: University of California Press).

Baudrillard, J. (2000) *Simulacra and Simulation* (Ann Arbor, MI: University of Michigan Press).

Bentham, J. (1995) *The Panopticon Writings*, ed. M. Bozovic (London: Verso), 29–95.

Blakely, E. and Snyder, M. (1997) *Fortress America: Gated Communities in the United States* (Washington, DC: Brookings Institution Press).

Bowman, J., West, J. and Gertz, S. (2006) 'Florida's Service First: Radical Reform in the Sunshine State'. In J. Kellough and L. Nigro (eds.), *Civil Service Reform in the States* (Albany, NY: SUNY Press), 145–70.

Bybee, C. (1999) 'Can Democracy Survive in the Post-Factual Age? A Return to the Lippmann–Dewey Debate About the Politics of News', *Journalism and Communication Monographs*, 1(1): 29–62.

Crawford, M. (1995) *Building the Workingman's Paradise: The Design of American Company Towns* (New York: Verso).

Debord, G. (1967/1995) *The Society of the Spectacle*, trans. D. Nicholson-Smith (New York: Zone Books).

Edelman, M. (1988) *Constructing the Political Spectacle* (Chicago: University of Chicago Press).

Foucault, M. (1977) *Discipline and Punish: The Birth of the Prison* (New York: Pantheon).

Foucault, M. (1994) *The Birth of the Clinic: An Archaeology of Medical Perception* (New York: Vintage Books).

Francombe, J. (2010) 'I Cheer, You Cheer, We Cheer': Physical Technologies and the Normalized Body', *Television & New Media*, 11(5): 350–66.

Grant, J. and Mittelsteadt, L. (2004) 'Types of Gated Communities', *Environment and Planning B: Planning and Design*, 31(6): 913–30.

Lang, S. (2004) 'The Impact of Video Systems on Architecture'. Dissertation submitted to the Swiss Federal Institute of Technology, Zurich.

Lippmann, W. (2008) *The Phantom Public* (New Brunswick, CT: Transaction Publishers).

Low, S. (2001) 'The Edge and the Center: Gated Communities and the Discourse of Urban Fear', *American Anthropologist*, 103(1): 45–58.

Marx, K. (1867/1984) *Capital [Das Kapital]*, trans. S. Moore and E. Aveling, ed. F. Engels (Chicago: Encyclopedia Britannica, Inc.).

Mills, C. (1956/2000) *The Power Elite* (Oxford: Oxford University Press).

Rindfleisch, A., Freeman, D. and Burroughs, J. (2000) 'Nostalgia, Materialism, and Product Preference: An Initial Inquiry'. In S. J. Hoch and R. J. Meyer (eds.), *Advances in Consumer Research*, vol. 27 (Provo, UT: Association for Consumer Research), 36–41.

Rose, N. (2000) 'Community, Citizenship, and the Third Way', *American Behavioral Scientist*, 43(9): 1395–1411.

Sampson, R., Raudenbush, S. and Earls, F. (1997) 'Neighborhoods and Violent Crime: A Multilevel Study of Collective Efficacy', *Science*, 15(277): 918–24.

Sanchez, T., Lang, R. and Dhavale, D. (2005) Security versus status? a first look at the census's gated community data *Journal of Planning Education and Research* 24 (3) 281–291.

Sementelli, A. (2007) 'Managing Blurred Environments: How Usufruct Can Help Address Postmodern Conditions', *Administration and Society*, 38(6): 709–28.

Smith, A. (1776 [1977]) *An Inquiry into the Nature and Causes of the Wealth of Nations* (Chicago: University of Chicago Press).

Somers, M. (2008) 'Imperiled Citizenship and the Market (Critical Essay)', *The Hedgehog Review*, 10(3): 80–92.

Sugrue, T. (2005) *The Origins of the Urban Crisis: Race and Inequality in Postwar Detroit* (Princeton: Princeton University Press).

Wilson-Doenges, G. (2000) 'An Exploration of Sense of Community and Fear of Crime in Gated Communities', *Environment and Behavior*, 32(5): 597–611.

Wittgenstein, L. (1953) *Philosophical Investigations* (Oxford: Blackwell).

5
The Creation of Shared Understanding: Political and Economic Consensus and the Role of the Market in Transformational Policy Discourse

Ian N. Richardson, Andrew P. Kakabadse and Nada K. Kakabadse

Exploring contributions in the policy science, political economy and power literatures, this theoretical chapter proposes that a fundamental effect of structural economic and political interactions within, and between, polyarchies – or liberal democracies – has potentially far-reaching consequences related to the capacity for societal change. Furthermore, it argues that the creation of shared understanding between economic and political elites is critical to a comprehension of how structural determinants are purposed by political activity at the pre-agenda phase of the policy process. It is against this consensual backdrop, and the discursive and deliberative narrowness that it produces, that transformational political change exists largely beyond the capacity of policy-makers or the collective will of ordinary citizens; instead it is, almost exclusively, a function of the invisible hand of market forces. In the absence of a global regulatory framework, the long-term consequences of shared understanding between today's political and economic elites could have profound implications for tomorrow's global citizens.

Responses to the question of how public policy is initiated have evolved in recent years from explanations rooted in notions of objective identification and rational decision-making to post-positivist explorations of how issues are defined for the purposes of policy intervention. The latter have been accompanied by a wealth of interest in policy agendas and, specifically, the intersubjective manner in which problems are framed prior to the more formal processes of policy formation and change. This interest is, in turn, related to notions of power and, more fundamentally, the ongoing debate concerning structure and agency in political decision-making. Despite considerable scholarly activity in the area, there remain profound conceptual questions concerning the origins of policy initiation and, importantly, the boundaries – physical or otherwise – of the policy process. This chapter seeks to explore one aspect of the debate: namely the role played by a shared understanding of the objectives of public policy emanating from the politics/market relationship within, and increasingly between, polyarchal societies. It is argued that a shared understanding between political and economic elites reinforces and lends political purpose to existing structural norms and may, where necessary, represent a deliberate attempt to redefine structural tolerances for the purposes of facilitating more dynamic political change.

The requirement for dynamic change stems from a paradoxical market-driven imperative that is enshrined in liberal democracies: namely that they should provide political and economic stability. Such systems, frequently characterised as being in a state of equilibrium, manifest an inherent resistance to change and a policy process bound by incrementalism, checks and balances, and a myriad of countervailing processes and relationships that defy satisfactory explanation. Against the backdrop of such a deep-rooted model of intransigence, the market functions within a largely predictable – and satisfactory – regulatory framework; content, where able, to influence the direction and detail of government policy. The extent of this ability, however, is governed by factors that serve to protect the overall stability of existing structured socio-economic arrangements. In order to facilitate change that calls into question these existing modes of governance, a new shared understanding of political objectives must first be created and structural norms must be reinterpreted and defined for the purposes of supporting a revised political and economic agenda.

This theoretical perspective challenges a prevailingly reactive theme in the policy sciences literature concerning political inputs and the identification of problems. It suggests that political agenda-setting, far from representing the beginning of the formal policy process, is a function of prior political processes embedded in the articulation – and not just interpretation – of structural and normative conditions.

Theoretical perspectives on policy initiation and change

There exists, in the policy process literature, an overwhelming conception of inputs as external stimulants to the policy or political process; within such a model the process of policy-making is presented, on the whole, as distinct from the demands that are placed upon it. Part of the reason for this may lie with a longstanding theoretical distinction between political activity and public administration in the policy sciences arena (see Wilson, 1941; Goodnow, 1900; White, 1926); but another possible explanation rests with the apparent longevity of ideas expounded in early decision- and system-based depictions of the policy process. Harold Lasswell's (1956, 1963) decision process, for instance, which has inspired volumous iterations (Jones, 1970; Mack, 1971; Anderson, 1975; May and Wildavsky, 1978; Brewer and deLeon, 1983; Howlett and Ramesh, 1995; Norton, 2005), presents a lineal, staged and cumulative depiction of decision activity which takes, as its starting point, an intelligence gathering phase where information pertinent to the decision is collected and prepared. David Easton's (1957) model of input/output exchanges, on the other hand, presents an open policy process conceived as an extension of an overall system of influences; 'analytically separated' but, fundamentally, exposed to other social systems in which it is embedded (Easton, 1966). Exogenous environmental systems such as ecology, economy, culture, social structure and demographics all shape the demands placed upon the political system (Easton, 1957); in essence, inputs are subject to the mediating effects of system-based determinants before being converted into policy outputs which are, in turn, passed back to neighbouring environmental systems (see also the work of Straayer, 1971; Simmons et al., 1974).

These early theoretical approaches have been complemented by a wide number of alternative theories of the policy process focused less upon general systemic devices and more upon the role of structural determinism (Hofferbert, 1974; Simeon, 1976), institutionalism (Kiser and Ostrom, 1982; Skocpol, 1992; Immergut, 1998) and collective ideational constraints (Hall, 1992; Goldstein and Keohane, 1993; Legro, 2000; Jenkins and Eckert, 2000), subsystem activity (Sabatier, 1988; Sabatier and Jenkins-Smith, 1993; Baumgartner and Jones, 1993), and post-positivist theories concerning the role of individual agency (Kingdon, 1984; Hawkesworth, 1988; Rochefort and Cobb, 1993; Fischer and Forester, 1993; Dryzek, 1993; Hays, 1994; Roe, 1994; Danziger, 1995; Campbell, 1998). Collectively, these contrasting views provide a comprehensive sense of the complex issues that have divided and tormented policy process scholars over recent years. Assertions related to the existence and proximity of system boundaries have, in anything other than textbook devices, given way to a broader and more interrelated sense of the system and environmental whole. As with system theory developments in other fields, the role of the environment is seen as central to an understanding of adaptation (see the early contribution of Emery and Trist, 1965). Systems are viewed as largely incapable of self-generated transformational change; the extent of adaptability to environmental turbulence is a function of ability to learn and to perform in line with changing exogenous contingencies (Terreberry, 1968).

Theories concerning the initiation of policy have evolved from straightforward descriptions centred upon collective and objective consensus concerning problems and issues into a more complex debate regarding the intersubjective nature in which issues are defined, framed and, subsequently, managed within the agenda-setting process. Staged depictions of the policy process, with inputs entering at one end and leaving at the other as policy outputs, have been superseded by a multi-dimensional depiction in which inputs can enter the process anywhere – and at any time. The only bar is the extent to which the input can be sufficiently well purposed for the stated scope and objectives of the policy domain. Likewise, the only meaningful obstacle to the promotion of inputs onto the wider political agenda is not an intractable sense of what needs to be done but, instead, an ever-shifting attempt to define political inputs in terms of structural and normative requirements that are, themselves, the subject of interpretation, definition and articulation. The demand for more radical, system-wide, transformational change, given the enormous structural, institutional and normative resistance it is likely to encounter, requires a type of political activity capable of subtly redefining the very substance of these pre-agenda structural and normative patterns. Such activity requires a sustained imperative and the long-term commitment of substantial resources; only the market is capable of such a conscious or unconscious undertaking.

Politics and markets

In Charles Lindblom's seminal work *Politics and Markets* (1977), the common origins of polyarchy and market, as systems of popular control, are cited as a chief reason for the two to be linked together: 'the association between liberal constitutional polyarchy and market is clearly no historical accident. Polyarchies were established to win and protect certain liberties: private property, free enterprise, free contract, and occupational choice. Polyarchy also served the more diffuse aspirations of those elites that established it. For both the specific liberties, and for the exercise of self-help, markets in which the options can be exercised are required' (Lindblom, 1977: 164). Historically, polyarchal societies have been characterised by favourable measures of economic and social development and provide the setting for the conception of the modern dynamic pluralist state (Dahl, 1989); furthermore, and fundamentally entwined with our understanding of such development, markets are part of the very fabric of the constitution of the modern capitalist nation state and contemporary world order (Cerny, 1990). Against a backdrop of international capital flows, and the setting of the price of money across borders, the allocation of all goods in society is subject to the disciplines of the global financial marketplace; in short, this financial system represents the infrastructure of the infrastructure (Cerny, 1994).

The development of globalisation has brought with it an intense pressure to reconcile political and economic tensions related to domestic and international policy; this has led to a rescaling of traditional governance systems (Brenner, 1998), the increasing dominance of private authority in areas such as international finance (Pauly, 2002) and the proactive participation of neo-liberal institutions shaping relations between state and market in the contemporary era (O'Riain, 2000). In short, the state's traditional boundaries have been under attack from the politics of market organisation (White, 1993) and politics, everywhere, is now market driven (Leys, 2003). The interrelationship of economic and political activity is, more than ever, critical to a consideration of social mechanisms and systems: in the words of Lindblom (1977: 8) 'much of politics is economics and most of economics is politics'.

Despite strong pluralist convictions, Lindblom (1988) was keen to highlight the role played by 'advantaged segments of society' in narrowing diversity of opinion and discussion in order to protect their advantages from slow erosion. These concerns for the discursive foundations of democracy, despite the obvious absence of a class dimension, hint at a process similar to that of Gramsci's 'cultural hegemony' (Gramsci, 1971), where the scope for ideological political conflict is, in effect, limited at source. The presence of the market control paradigm, for instance, hardwired into the structural consciousness of polyarchal systems of governance, ensures that the scope of political discursiveness is guided by the dictates of certain inalienable constructs. The extent of the pervasiveness of these constructs is evidenced not only in terms of limited political debate and decisional incrementalism (Lindblom, 1959; Braybrooke and Lindblom, 1963) but also contrasting beliefs related to the distinction between public and private affairs (Drucker, 1962; Nigro and Nigro, 1973; Sharkansky, 1979). Seen in this way, the development of the meta-narrative of neo-liberal microeconomics, the silent 'grand theory' governing contemporary reason (Van Der Pijl, 2005), has profound implications for the diversity of political opinion in liberal democracies.

In all accounts of the liberal democratic model, it is clear that the notion of separated spheres of economic and political activity is, by and large, discounted: the various interpretations of the relationship between politics and markets reflect a substantial agreement over the structurally advantaged position of business. Even if the relationship is far from static and stable (Vogel, 1983), and the role of the state – and state actors – has been significantly underestimated (Nordlinger, 1983; Mann, 1984; Skocpol, 1985; Weir and Skocpol, 1985), we are still some way from the pluralist depiction of community power in which political and economic processes are considered to have a high degree of autonomy (Finer, 1958; Dahl, 1961). Furthermore, it is difficult to escape the conclusion that control of resources lies at the heart of conceptions of the state and notions of coercion and power in the policy-making process. A contribution from the organisational theory field, resource dependency theory (Pfeffer and Salancik, 1978), suggests that organisations are comprised of internal and external coalitions that emerge from social exchanges – for the purpose of influencing and controlling behaviour (Ulrich and Barney, 1984); external organisational links are essentially power relationships based upon exchange resources. External demands are constantly placed on the organisation but it responds most acutely to those upon which it is most dependent for resources and survival. Where organisations are dependent for stability upon one another, mutual interdependencies can lead to increased coordination and mutual control over each other's resources. Clarence Stone (1989), for instance, suggests that, as a consequence of mutual interdependency, economic and political elites form coalitions or regimes; the broad direction-setting nature of such activity distinguishing it from the 'retail politics' of lobbying and policy networks (Stone, 2005). In a system where boundaries are vague, where the distinction between governmental and quasi-governmental activity is blurred, where a structural relationship between economy and state is hardwired into the system of governance, and where non-state actors play a significant role in providing information, expertise and support to those in positions of political power; a huge array of political resource interdependencies have, no doubt, been established. Furthermore, the resulting mode of governance – characterised by incrementalism rather than dynamic change – ensures that the interests of the market are preserved at every turn and the potential for surprises limited.

The extent of economic determinism is, of course, a fundamental question; and its relevance is more acute given the advent of globalisation and the lack of a coherent global regulatory framework. The polyarchal nation state, structurally dependent upon its domestic business interests, now finds itself subsumed within a global and structurally interconnected neo-liberal market paradigm. Within such a paradigm, the alternative to conformity is politically unthinkable; and the processes that have shaped the development of the new world order can only accelerate. Domestically, the demands placed upon government are increasingly influenced by international considerations; and market demands have assumed greater, and more urgent, primacy. Fundamental and rapid change cannot be brought about, however, without the ongoing and willing participation of the sovereign state; a participation that cannot be provided unless governments maintain their legitimacy in the face of structural and normative resistance to change. The market's unique ability to facilitate change in these structural and normative tolerances plays a critical role in securing such legitimacy.

Power relations and policy initiation

For the most part, depictions of political power portray a classic Weberian relationship with the emphasis on one party realising its own will even 'against the resistance of others' (Weber, 1962); within such a conception, the powerful are, unsurprisingly, 'those who are able to realize their will even if others resist it' (Mills, 1956: 9). While Weber's conception of power does not preclude willing consent in the relationship, it does imply the capacity for coercive power based, ultimately, on domination of the subject. This presentation of power as 'power over' underpins practically all empirical contributions on political influence in the policy sciences field although there are marked differences in the form that this coercion can take. Steven Lukes' (Lukes, 1974) typology of the three dimensions of power is a useful mechanism for demonstrating a fundamental distinction drawn between decisional and non-decisional exercises of power as domination in the political sphere. Furthermore, utilising the typology as a metaphor for a hierarchy of system-wide exercises of power provides a crucial insight into the nature of political influences and, specifically, the relationship between politics and markets in polyarchies.

The first dimension of power is that typified by pluralists with their emphasis upon actual, rather than potential, power; and a focus on observable behaviour (Dahl, 1957, 1961; Polsby, 1963). In empirical terms, the unit of analysis is the decision situation and exercises of power are a product of conflict of interests over political preferences. Despite recognising the resource advantages of business (Dahl, 1961; Truman, 1971), and viewing resource availability as a primary determinant of influence, pluralists have tended to view business as part of a much broader depiction of interest group politics; and, in terms of empirical inquiry, political theory has focused primarily on the wider role of groups within society. For the most part, the role of business has been ignored (Hart, 2004) and, it has been argued, the study of corporation activity is essential to a complete understanding of political influence (Salisbury, 1984; Baumgartner and Leech, 1998). The tendency to view business political influence as interest group pressure has led to a curious paradox: at a time when interest group proliferation is seen to have destabilised the policy-making system and weakened the overall impact of interest groups (Salisbury et al., 1990), the overall influence of business and market interests in political affairs appears to have accelerated substantially (Gais et al., 1984; Calhoun, 1992; Crenson and Ginsberg, 2002; Leys, 2003). Moreover, the pluralist approach requires a conflict of interest but, given discrete lobbying practices, an enormous volume of policy activity goes uncontested (Baumgartner and Leech, 2001). Scholarly efforts have, in the main, been directed towards examining these more coercive and observable demonstrations of power; more discrete activities have, for the most part, been overlooked or discounted.

A major criticism of this conception of power, levelled by Lukes (1974), is that it assumes the bias of the system under observation; in other words, it is blind to control of the political agenda. Lukes (1974) defines, therefore, a second dimension of power based upon the earlier work of Bachrach and Baratz (1962) which drew attention to the exercises of power that may have already determined the observable instances of control which represent the pluralist view of power. Adopting Schattschneider's (1975: 69) belief that 'organization is the mobilization of bias' and his view that 'some issues are organized into politics while others are organized out', Bachrach and Baratz went further: 'power is also exercised when *A* devotes his energies to creating or reinforcing social and political values and institutional practices that limit the scope of the political process to public consideration of only those issues which are comparatively innocuous to *A*' (1962: 948). In doing so, they introduce the concept of non-decision-making; a means by which demands for change 'can be suffocated before they are even voiced; or kept covert; or killed before they gain access to the relevant decision-making arena; or, failing all these things, maimed or destroyed in the decision implementing stage of the policy process' (1970: 44). The most obvious exercise of such an activity in the political sphere is that of agenda-setting; where the agenda takes on a strategic form since it is grounded in matters outside of the policies at hand and beyond the more immediate scope of policy-makers (Mouw and Mackuen, 1992). Like the constitutional-choice decisions found in Kiser and Ostrom's institutional approach (1982), such pre-decisional activities are of critical importance in determining the decisions that will, ultimately, be made down the line (Cobb and Elder, 1971; Long and Rose-Ackerman, 1986).

Following McCombs and Shaw's (1972) seminal study of the relationship between public and media agendas, a good deal of attention has been focused on correlations between levels of saliency in different domains and, in particular, between media, public, and policy agendas (Rogers and Dearing, 1988). Since there is evidence to support the contention that media agendas, and the activities of the media, have an influence on the policy agenda (Gilberg et al., 1980; Cook et al., 1983; Wanta et al., 1989) and also the public agenda (McCombs and Shaw, 1972; Funkhouser, 1973; Iyengar and Kinder, 1987), the role of the media must be considered in any discussion of power relations and policy initiation. Relative saliency on the media agenda is central to the formation of the public agenda which, consequently, influences the activities of policy-makers (Dearing and Rogers, 1996). Closer analysis of the concentrated ownership of media assets and, furthermore, the actual sources of media stories provides evidence that the commercial imperative and information dependency of the media results in an inherent bias to the selection and depiction of events; a bias that informs the public agenda and serves the needs of corporations, politicians and bureaucrats alike (Gandy, 1982; Herman and Chomsky, 2002). Furthermore, the growth and role of public policy research institutes or think tanks (Weaver, 1989; McGann, 1992) and an analysis of the supply of technical and professional policy expertise at all levels of government (Brint, 1990) suggest both an agenda-setting role and a degree of informal capture by professional experts. Ultimately, all information is mediated in some way but the extent to which the dynamics of political decision-making are being defined by information bias has potentially profound implications for the shape and tenor of policy debate.

To these first two dimensions of power, Lukes (1974) adds a third: 'A may exercise power over B by getting him to do what he does not want to do, but he also exercises power over him by influencing, shaping or determining his very wants. Indeed, is it not the supreme exercise of power to get another or others to have the desires you want them to have?' (1974: 27). The notion of latent conflict is central to this approach; created by a contradiction between the interests of those who exercise power and the real interests of those who are dominated. Reminiscent, again, of Gramsci's hegemony (1971), the third-dimensional form of power might best, within the macro context of political influence, be seen as operating at the level of ideological or normative predisposition; at work somewhere within, and between, the structural determinants of society and the issue definition and agenda-setting activities of the policy process.

The use of Lukes' (1974) typology to describe the macro interactions between those inside and outside of the formal state policy apparatus is, of course, simply one application of the framework; it is important to stress that the various dimensions might be found operating at all levels of government and in all social interactions. The use of the typology as a hierarchal framework for understanding such macro level political influence does, however, raise one very important line of inquiry related to the strategic options available to those seeking dynamic change. If, as has been suggested, a fundamental market-driven requirement for economic and political stability results in a political process that is highly resistant to demands for transformational change, what happens when it's the market that demands the change?

Attempting to introduce radical policy initiatives at the level of regime politics (C. N. Stone, 1989) is unlikely to yield results since the definition of the issue is predefined, there are dominant existing coalitions informing debate, and significant institutional constraints governing the scope and substance of policy discussions. This is not to suggest that significant gains or losses are not achievable; simply that the scope of such gains or losses is largely defined by pre-existing terms of reference. Likewise, attempting to introduce a radical policy departure at the agenda-setting level requires a sizeable shift in perceptions of a given issue. Agenda-setting is, itself, a function of institutional patterns and a prevailing discourse surrounding the attractiveness and political feasibility of new proposals. This political discourse 'delineates the accepted boundaries of state action … and defines the context in which many issues will be understood' (Hall, 1993: 289). Of course, actors may seek to exercise power in pursuit of their desire to see proposals appear on the policy agenda but unless such proposals are framed within existing structural parameters, and promote a particular problem definition, causal interpretation, moral evaluation and remedy (Entman, 1993), it is unlikely that they will be able to enter, or survive, the policy process. Change that requires a more fundamental punctuation can only take place at the structural level; structural determinants must be reinterpreted, redefined and reinforced, in order to influence the ideological predisposition and normative values of those charged with consideration of political agendas. Moreover, these structural amendments must be transmitted throughout society in order that policy-makers retain essential legitimacy.

Critical to the comprehension of how structural determinants are purposed by political activity at the pre-agenda stage of the policy process is the creation of shared understanding. Distinct from the constructivist description of the definition of issues (Blumer, 1971), their attendant causal stories (D. A. Stone, 1989), and coherent systems of normative and cognitive elements that define 'world views' (Surel, 2000: 496), this kind of shared understanding relates to the shared structural assumptions that underpin the very foundations of public policy activity. These assumptions relate to, among other things: the role that the state sees for itself in the pursuance of its duties; the nature of the relationship that exists between politics and markets; and conditions that lead to the overall betterment of society. The understanding is shared because it is the product of a dialogue resulting from the mutual resource interdependency, albeit heavily skewed, of three dominant groups: the economic, political and media elites.

The consequences of this shared understanding for the scope of policy-making are far-reaching; ultimately, 'governments operate within the bounds of the conventional wisdom of their elites ... [and] cannot operate if policymakers stop to consider first principles' (Wallace, 2004: 281). Given that shared understanding concerning these first principles is the foundation upon which the discursive parameters of polyarchies are based, it is essential to recognise the role played by it in regulating demands for transformational change. Such change may not always be initiated by the elite, but it will, out of necessity, always require its support if it is to find its way onto the policy agenda. Likewise, the development of shared understanding concerning the need for radical change represents a structural shift that will, in time, facilitate access to the policy agenda in both political and societal terms. While such power is not absolute, it is both discrete and effective. Formal and informal communities of political, economic and media elites – ably supported by administrative, professional and academic elites – meeting at the national, international and transnational level are, ultimately, responsible for the creation of an ongoing, and subtly evolving, referential for policy-makers; a referential that acts as a normative, cognitive and linguistic straitjacket, defining the discursive limitations of policy-making.

Conclusion

Transformational change takes time but, more importantly, the requirement for it must enter into collective consciousness at the level of shared understanding between elite groups. Shared understanding is by no means assured and there exists conflict within elites, as well as between them, but when it is created and starts to act as a structural referential within the policy process, the homogeneity of the economic, political and media elite – and, critically, the role of the economic elite in crafting such homogeneity – has profound implications for the discursive and deliberative parameters of policy-making. In short, when the market wants transformational change, it seeks to affect the structural tolerances that prevent it from taking place. When the call for change emerges elsewhere, the market deploys its resources in order to protect existing socio-economic arrangements.

The considerable resource advantages of business ensure that it is, by far and away, the dominant player in day-to-day political activity; its considerable lobbying activities, the interweaving of business and state affairs, and the more direct dependencies of the state – and political parties – on business support, have created a model of 'regime politics' (C. N. Stone, 1989) that is more accessible to commercial interests than the individual or collective citizenry. Furthermore, this access places business at the heart of processes that influence the prioritisation of policy proposals; and this coupled with a significant media dependency on business – for revenue, access and patronage – enables market interests to raise considerable awareness and saliency for political issues. Most significantly of all, however, are those efforts that pave the way for more radical transformations of society; efforts that go largely unnoticed and result in the gradual reshaping of policy objectives.

The extent to which market interests are responsible for the creation of such shared understanding at the elite level is unclear; it seems reasonable to suggest, however, that the resource advantages that wield so much influence elsewhere in the policy process are, at least, a prominent feature of elite interactions. To date, little empirical work has been conducted on the nature of these interactions; scholarly analysis of the dependencies and power relations among elite groups must become a priority for those concerned with the structural parameters of policy-making. And, while the study of elite groups remains an enormously difficult pursuit, especially where political sensitivities are likely to be encountered, its significance to consideration of societal and political change means that scholars must endeavour to find ways of delivering empirical evidence. If more acceptable methodological approaches continue to meet with resistance or fail to deliver meaningful data, scholars must consider alternative methods such as the covert penetration of formal and informal networks.

Finally, it is worth noting the consequence of a policy process that – at the normative and cognitive level – systematically filters issues and initiatives in the way suggested. In their paper 'Problem Definition, Agenda Access, and Policy Choice', Rochefort and Cobb (1993) ask whether, 'given the tendency of the political system repeatedly to define its issues along certain conceptual lines, are there aspects of reality which for some reason are systematically screened out that could, if deliberately incorporated, improve regime performance?' (1993: 69). Their question, of course, presupposes a utilitarian view of the state's function; any response is contingent upon how one views the fundamental purpose of the regime and, more importantly, in whose interest's one believes it should be run.

References

Anderson, J. E. (1975) *Public Policy Making* (New York: Praeger).
Bachrach, P. and Baratz, M. S. (1962) 'The Two Faces of Power', *American Political Science Review*, 56(4): 947–52.

Bachrach, P. and Baratz, M. S. (1970) *Power and Poverty: Theory and Practice* (New York: Oxford University Press).

Baumgartner, F. R. and Jones, B. D. (1993) *Agendas and Instability in American Politics* (Chicago: University of Chicago Press).

Baumgartner, F. R. and Leech, B. L. (1998) *Basic Interests: The Importance of Groups in Politics and Political Science* (Princeton: Princeton University Press).

Baumgartner, F. R. and Leech, B. L. (2001) 'Interest Niches and Policy Bandwagons: Patterns of Interest Group Involvement in National Politics', *Journal of Politics*, 63(4): 1191–1213.

Blumer, H. (1971) 'Social Problems as Collective Behaviour', *Social Problems*, 18(3): 298–306.

Braybrooke, D. and Lindblom, C. E. (1963) *A Strategy of Decision: Policy Evaluation as a Social Process* (New York: Free Press).

Brenner, R. (1998) 'The Economics of Global Turbulence', *New Left Review*, 229(1).

Brewer, G. D. and deLeon, P. (1983) *The Foundations of Policy Analysis* (Homewood, IL: Dorsey Press).

Brint, S. (1990) 'Rethinking the Policy Influence of Experts: From General Characterizations to Analysis of Variation', *Sociological Forum*, 5(3): 361–85.

Calhoun, C. (1992) 'Introduction'. In C. Calhoun (ed.), *Habermas and the Public Sphere* (Cambridge, MA: MIT Press).

Campbell, J. L. (1998) 'Institutional Analysis and the Role of Ideas in Political Economy', *Theory and Society*, 27(3): 377–409.

Cerny, P. G. (1990) *The Changing Architecture of Politics: Structure, Agency and the Future of the State* (London and Thousand Oaks, CA: Sage).

Cerny, P. G. (1994) 'The Infrastructure of the Infrastructure? Toward "Embedded Financial Orthodoxy" in the International Political Economy'. In R. P. Palan and B. Gills (eds.), *Transcending the State–Global Divide: A Neo-Structuralist Agenda in International Relations* (Boulder, CO: Lynne Rienner), 223–49.

Cobb, R. W. and Elder, C. D. (1971) 'The Politics of Agenda-Building: An Alternative Perspective for Modern Democratic Theory', *Journal of Politics*, 33(4): 892–915.

Cook, F. L., Tyler, T. R., Goetz, E. G., Gordon, M. T., Protess, D., Leff, D. and Molotch, H. L. (1983) 'Media and Agenda Setting: Effects on the Public, Interest Group Leaders, Policy Makers, and Policy', *Public Opinion Quarterly*, 47(1): 16–35.

Crenson, M. A. and Ginsberg, B. (2002) *Downsizing Democracy: How America Sidelined its Citizens and Privatized its Public* (Baltimore, MD: John Hopkins University Press).

Dahl, R. A. (1957) 'The Concept of Power', *Behavioral Science*, 2(3): 201–14.

Dahl, R. A. (1961) *Who Governs? Democracy and Power in an American City* (New Haven, CT: Yale University Press).

Dahl, R. A. (1989) *Democracy and its Critics* (London: Yale University Press).

Danziger, M. (1995) 'Policy Analysis Postmodernized: Some Political and Pedagogical Ramifications', *Policy Studies Journal*, 23(3): 435–50.

Dearing, J. W. and Rogers, E. M. (1996) *Communications Concepts 6: Agenda-Setting* (Thousand Oaks, CA: Sage).

Drucker, P. F. (1962) 'Big Business and Public Policy', *Business and Society*, 3(1): 4–13.

Dryzek, J. S. (1993) 'Policy Analysis and Planning: From Science to Argument'. In F. Fischer and J. Forester (eds.), *The Argumentative Turn in Policy Analysis and Planning* (Durham, NC and London: Duke University Press), 213–32.

Easton, D. (1957) 'An Approach to the Analysis of Political Systems', *World Politics*, 9(3): 383–400.

Easton, D. (1966) 'Categories for the Systems Analysis of Politics'. In D. Easton (ed.), *Varieties of Political Theory* (Englewood Cliffs, NJ: Prentice-Hall), 143–54.

Emery, F. E. and Trist, E. L. (1965) 'The Causal Texture of Organizational Environments', *Human Relations*, 18: 21–31.

Entman, R. M. (1993) 'Framing: Toward a Clarification of a Fractured Paradigm', *Journal of Communication*, 43(4): 51–8.

Finer, S. E. (1958) *Anonymous Empire: A Study of the Lobby in Great Britain* (London: Pall Mall Press).

Fischer, F. and Forester, J. (1993) 'Editors' Introduction'. In F. Fischer and J. Forester (eds.), *The Argumentative Turn in Policy Analysis and Planning* (Durham, NC: Duke University Press), 1–17.

Funkhouser, G. R. (1973) 'The Issues of the Sixties: An Exploratory Study in the Dynamics of Public Opinion', *Public Opinion Quarterly*, 37(1): 62–75.

Gais, T. L., Peterson, M. A. and Walker, J. L. (1984) 'Interest Groups, Iron Triangles and Representative Institutions in American National Government', *British Journal of Political Science*, 14(2): 161–85.

Gandy, O. H. J. (1982) *Beyond Agenda Setting: Information Subsidies and Public Policy* (Norwood, NJ: Ablex Publishing).

Gilberg, S., Eyal, C., McCombs, M. and Nicholas, D. (1980) 'The State of the Union Address and the Press Agenda', *Journalism Quarterly*, 57: 584–8.

Goldstein, J. and Keohane, R. O. (1993) 'Ideas and Foreign Policy: An Analytical Framework'. In J. Goldstein, and R. O. Keohane (eds.), *Ideas and Foreign Policy: Beliefs, Institutions, and Political Change* (Ithaca, NY: Cornell University Press), 3–30.

Goodnow, F. J. (1900) *Politics and Administration* (New York: Macmillan).

Gramsci, A. (1971) *Selections from the Prison Notebooks* (London: Lawrence & Wishart).

Hall, P. A. (1992) 'The Movement from Keynesianism to Monetarism: Institutional Analysis and British Economic Policy in the 1970s'. In S. Steinmo, K. Thelen and F. Longstreth (eds.), *Structuring Politics: Historical Institutionalism in Comparative Analysis* (Cambridge: Cambridge University Press), 90–113.

Hall, P. A. (1993) 'Policy Paradigms, Social Learning and the State: The Case of Economic Policymaking in Britain', *Comparative Politics*, 25(3): 275–96.

Hart, D. M. (2004) '"Business" is Not an Interest Group: On the Study of Companies in American National Politics', *Annual Review of Political Science*, 7: 47–69.

Hawkesworth, M. E. (1988) *Theoretical Issues in Policy Analysis* (Albany, NY: State University of New York Press).

Hays, S. (1994) 'Structure and Agency and the Sticky Problem of Culture', *Sociological Theory*, 12(1): 57–72.

Herman, E. S. and Chomsky, N. (2002) *Manufacturing Consent: The Political Economy of the Mass Media* (New York: Pantheon Books).

Hofferbert, R. I. (1974) *The Study of Public Policy* (Indianapolis: Bobbs-Merrill).

Howlett, M. and Ramesh, M. (1995) *Studying Public Policy: Policy Cycles and Policy Subsystems* (Toronto: Oxford University Press).

Immergut, E. M. (1998) 'The Theoretical Core of the New Institutionalism', *Politics and Society*, 26(1): 5–34.

Iyengar, S. and Kinder, D. R. (1987) *News that Matters: Television and American Opinion* (Chicago: University of Chicago Press).

Jenkins, J. C. and Eckert, C. M. (2000) 'The Right Turn in Economic Policy: Business Elites and the New Conservative Economics', *Sociological Forum*, 15(2): 307–38.

Jones, C. (1970) *An Introduction to the Study of Public Policy* (Belmont, CA: Wadsworth).

Kingdon, J. W. (1984) *Agendas, Alternatives, and Public Policies* (Boston: Little, Brown).

Kiser, L. L. and Ostrom, E. (1982) 'The Three Worlds of Action: A Metatheoretical Synthesis of Institutional Approaches'. In E. Ostrom (ed.), *Strategies of Political Inquiry* (Beverly Hills, CA: Sage), 179–222.

Lasswell, H. D. (1956) *The Decision Process* (College Park, MD: Bureau of Governmental Research).

Lasswell, H. D. (1963) 'The Decision Process: Seven Categories of Functional Analysis'. In N. Polsby, R. Dentler and P. Smith (eds.), *Politics and Social Life* (Boston: Houghton Mifflin).

Legro, J. W. (2000) 'The Transformation of Policy Ideas', *American Journal of Political Science*, 44(3): 419–32.

Leys, C. (2003) *Market Driven Politics: Neo-Liberal Democracy and the Public Interest* (London: Verso).

Lindblom, C. E. (1959) 'The Science of "Muddling Through"', *Public Administration Review*, 19(2): 79–88.

Lindblom, C. E. (1977) *Politics and Markets* (New York: Basic Books).

Lindblom C. E. (1988) 'Introduction'. In C. E. Lindblom, *Democracy and Market System* (Oslo: Norwegian University Press).

Long, C. and Rose-Ackerman, S. (1986) 'Winning the Contest by Agenda Manipulation', *Journal of Policy Analysis and Management*, 2(1): 123–5.

Lukes, S. (1974) *Power: A Radical View* (London: Macmillan).

Mack, R. (1971) *Planning and Uncertainty* (New York: John Wiley).

Mann, M. (1984) 'The Autonomous Power of the State: Its Origins, Mechanisms, and Results', *European Archive of Sociology*, 25: 185–212.

May, J. and Wildavsky, A. (eds.) (1978) *The Policy Cycle* (Beverly Hills, CA: Sage).

McCombs, M. E. and Shaw, D. L. (1972) 'The Agenda-Setting Function of Mass Media', *Public Opinion Quarterly*, 36(2): 176–87.

McGann, J. G. (1992) 'Academics to Ideologues: A Brief History of the Public Policy Research Industry', *PS: Political Science and Politics*, 25(4): 733–40.

Mills, C. W. (1956) *The Power Elite* (New York: Oxford University Press).

Mouw, C. J. and Mackuen, M. B. (1992) 'The Strategic Agenda in Legislative Politics', *American Political Science Review*, 86(1): 87–105.

Nigro, F. A. and Nigro, L. G. (1973) *Modern Public Administration* (3rd edn.) (New York: Harper & Row).

Nordlinger, E. A. (1983) *On the Autonomy of the Democratic State* (Cambridge, MA: Harvard University Press).

Norton, P. (2005) *Parliament in British Politics* (Basingstoke: Palgrave Macmillan).

O'Riain, S. (2000) 'States and Markets in an Era of Globalization', *Annual Review of Sociology*, 26: 187–213.

Pauly, L. (2002) 'Global Finance, Political Authority, and the Problem of Legitimation'. In R. B. Hall and T. J. Biersteker (eds.), *The Emergence of Private Authority in Global Governance* (Cambridge: Cambridge University Press), 76–90.

Pfeffer, J. and Salancik, G. R. (1978) *The External Control of Organizations: A Resource Dependence Perspective* (New York: Harper & Row).

Polsby, N. W. (1963) *Community Power and Political Theory: A Further Look at the Problems of Evidence and Inference* (New Haven: Yale University Press).

Rochefort, D. A. and Cobb, R. W. (1993) 'Problem Definition, Agenda Access, and Policy Choice', *Policy Studies Journal*, 21(1): 56–71.

Roe, E. (1994) *Narrative Policy Analysis: Theory and Practice* (Durham, NC: Duke University Press).

Rogers, E. M. and Dearing, J. W. (1988) 'Agenda-Setting Research: Where has it Been, Where is it Going?' In J. Anderson (ed.), *Communication Yearbook*, vol. 11 (Beverley Hills, CA: Sage), 555–94.

Sabatier, P. A. (1988) 'An Advocacy Coalition Framework of Policy Change and the Role of Policy-Oriented Learning Therein', *Policy Sciences*, 21(2–3): 129–68.

Sabatier, P. A. and Jenkins-Smith, H. C. (1993) *Policy Change and Learning: An Advocacy Coalition Approach* (Boulder: Westview Press).

Salisbury, R. H. (1984) 'Interest Representation: The Dominance of Institutions', *American Political Science Review*, 78(1): 64–76.

Salisbury, R. H., Heinz, J. P., Laumann, E. O. and Nelson, R. L. (1990) 'The Paradox of Interest Groups in Washington: More Groups, Less Clout'. In A. King (ed.), *The New American Political System* (2nd edn.) (Washington: American Enterprise Institute Press), 203–29.

Schattschneider, E. E. (1975) *Semi-Sovereign People: A Realist's View of Democracy in America* (Hinsdale, IL: Dryden Press).

Sharkansky, I. (1979) *Wither the State? Politics and Public Enterprise in Three Countries* (Chatham, NJ: Chatham House).

Simeon, R. (1976) 'Studying Public Policy', *Canadian Journal of Political Science*, 9(4): 548–80.

Simmons, R. H., Davis, B. W., Chapman, R. J. K. and Sager, D. D. (1974) 'Policy Flow Analysis: A Conceptual Model for Comparative Public Policy Research', *The Western Political Quarterly*, 27(3): 457–68.

Skocpol, T. (1985) 'Bringing the State Back In: Strategies of Analysis in Current Research'. In P. Evans, D. Rueschemeyer and T. Skocpol (eds.), *Bringing the State Back In* (Cambridge: Cambridge University Press), 3–43.

Skocpol, T. (1992) *Protecting Soldiers and Mothers: The Political Origins of Social Policy in the United States* (Cambridge, MA: Belknap Press of Harvard University Press).

Stone, C. N. (1989) *Regime Politics: Governing Atlanta, 1946–1988* (Lawrence, KA: University Press of Kansas).

Stone, C. N. (2005) 'Looking Back to Look Forward: Reflections on Urban Regime Analysis', *Urban Affairs Review*, 40(3): 309–41.

Stone, D. A. (1989) 'Causal Stories and the Formation of Policy Agendas', *Political Science Quarterly*, 104(2): 281–300.

Straayer, J. A. (1971) 'The American Policy Process and the Problems of Poverty and the Ghetto', *The Western Political Quarterly*, 24(1): 45–51.

Surel, Y. (2000) 'The Role of Cognitive and Normative Frames in Policy-Making', *Journal of European Public Policy*, 7(4): 495–512.

Terreberry, S. (1968) 'The Evolution of Organizational Environments', *Administrative Science Quarterly*, 12(4): 590–613.

Truman, D. B. (1971) *The Governmental Process: Political Interests and Public Opinion* (2nd edn.) (New York: Alfred A. Knopf).

Ulrich, D. and Barney, J. B. (1984) 'Perspectives in Organisations: Resource Dependence, Efficiency, and Population', *Academy of Management Review*, 9(3): 471–81.

Van Der Pijl, K. (2005) 'Gramsci and Left Managerialism', *Critical Review of International Social and Political Philosophy*, 8(4): 499–511.

Vogel, D. (1983) 'The Power of Business in America: A Re-appraisal', *British Journal of Political Science*, 13(1): 19–43.

Wallace, W. (2004) 'Afterword: Soft Power, Global Agendas'. In D. Stone and A. Denham (eds.), *Think Tank Traditions: Policy Research and the Politics of Ideas* (Manchester: Manchester University Press), 281–90.

Wanta, W., Stephenson, M. A., Van Slyke Turk, J. and McCombs, M. E. (1989) 'How the President's State of the Union Talk Influenced News Media Agendas', *Journalism Quarterly*, 66(3): 537–41.

Weaver, R. K. (1989) 'The Changing World of Think Tanks', *PS: Political Science and Politics*, 22(3): 563–78.

Weber, M. (1962) *Basic Concepts in Sociology* (London: Peter Owen).

Weir, M. and Skocpol, T. (1985) 'State Structures and the Possibilities for "Keynesian" Responses to the Great Depression in Sweden, Britain, and the United States'. In P. B. Evans, D. Rueschemeyer and T. Skocpol (eds.), *Bringing the State Back In* (Cambridge: Cambridge University Press), 107–66.

White, L. (1926) *Introduction to the Study of Public Administration* (New York: Macmillan).

White, G. (1993) 'Towards a Political Analysis of Markets', *IDS Bulletin*, 24(3): 4–11.

Wilson, W. (1941) 'The Study of Administration', *Political Science Quarterly*, 56(4): 481–506.

6
The Precession of Simulacra: Elites in the Post-Industrial Society

Arthur Sementelli

The study of elites and elite theory has pervaded the literature of a number of different disciplines including sociology, anthropology, economics and others. Historically, there have been any number of reasons why one might be identified or considered to be a member of the elites. Being identified as an elite typically carried with it specific rights, rules and obligations. As such, there were implicit or explicit associations and judgements regarding the fitness of their decision-making and actions (Veblen, 1934). There were established expectations and responsibilities regarding their roles in political processes (Lippmann, 2008), as well as in concepts of philanthropy, a sense of duty within the concept of noblesse oblige (Skiffington, 1991) and within both ancient and contemporary regimes (Bottomore, 1993). Such breadth and depth of involvement helps justify why one might argue that elites and elite theory need reconsideration in our contemporary discourses and processes.

The assumption that elites and elite theory need not be considered in contemporary social, economic and political systems remains short-sighted. In truth, examining elites and elite theory has never been more important given broad shifts towards a post-modern or at least post-industrial society. As post-modernity makes increasing inroads in our thoughts, beliefs and day-to-day experiences, we find that notions of what it means to be elite are in a state of flux. One category of elite in particular, the celebrity, has experienced deep changes. Notions of what makes a person a celebrity have changed markedly to reflect this trend. We have added terms such as 'mogul' to our contemporary vocabulary to better identify what Mills (1956/2000) formerly referred to simply as the 'very rich'. The use of the term 'mogul' does not supersede the use of Mills' (1956/2000) concept of the very rich. In contemporary society, within the vernacular, all moguls are not equal. We instead have media moguls, Internet moguls and powerful business icons who have both celebrity and wealth. Consequently, the mogul is in practice something 'more' than simply the new very wealthy. In many cases, there are aspects of celebrity associated with being a mogul. This illustrates but one example of the emergent complexity around elite theory.

The language and experiences that shape how we communicate our understanding of elites has in many ways become another meme (Dawkins, 1976), but not necessarily just *anything* (Miller, 2002: 36) at all, acting as a unit of cultural transmission. This is not to say that hollow, or empty memes do not exist; what I am saying instead is that in the case of elites and elitism, there are certain residues (Pareto, 1963) of meaning often understood as sentiments (Bottomore, 1993). These residues have some bit of substance, something that identifies them as elite, though they might not match one's historical understanding of what it means to be elite. In some cases, one might then argue that these residues do not necessarily *embody* the elite, but could instead be better understood as a part of what it means to be elite, or possibly part of the *trappings* of said elites. As such, these trappings, or more generally these residues can become commodified and ultimately *sold* (Baudrillard, 1998) or at least possessed. The moderately wealthy (but not necessarily *elite*) and others in certain circumstances might attempt to buy these residues or trappings of elites as a way to eventually embody the elites themselves, or more simply to *own* elitism by owning the images, ideas and symbols of existing elites.

Consequently, there is a real possibility that the concept of 'elite' itself has become transmogrified from its historical roots, identified as a small dominant group in a society into an ever-increasing, yet dilute group. In each case, these contemporary 'elites' continue to hold at least some of the trappings or symbols of 'the' elite (those historically identified as such). Contemporary elites may not be part of a traditional/historical elite group since they are neither necessarily dominant nor are they necessarily part of a top tier of the social, economic or political strata. Instead, they might be the situational celebrities (e.g. 'Joe the Plumber') or 'stars' from 'reality' television, or any individual or group of individuals who stumble upon their fifteen minutes of fame by some strange twist of circumstance. It becomes easier to make the case that at least in some circumstances, in contemporary society there are *temporary* or symbolic elites. To begin understanding how these new forms differ, one must first consider the more conventional understanding of elites and elite theory.

What it means conventionally to be an 'elite' has been catalogued effectively by Mills (1956/2000) and others. This broad base of multi-disciplinary research provides an excellent foundation to understand what it means to be a part of the 'elites' in contemporary society. If we use Mills (1956/2000) and Bottomore (1993) together we can conceptualise contemporary 'elites' generally and power elites in particular to include those people who have some sort of 'celebrity' along with the more traditional groups such as corporate officials and chief executives as well as members of the ruling class including political actors and members of the military. One must also realise these categories are by no means mutually exclusive as military professionals, CEOs and celebrities become political actors and vice versa.

Consider the peculiar case of *symbolic* elites, who do not explicitly fit into the groups offered by Mills (1956/2000), Bottomore (1993) and others. Mills (1956/2000) provides the broadest framework for consideration by including celebrities. His understanding of celebrity does not describe people who are recognised currently as a celebrity in many realms. With alarming frequency, celebrities are identified as persons known for their 'well-knownness' (Boorstin, 1992: 47). This creates an interesting situation where fame can be fabricated, but in many ways, remains associated with some notion or implied link to 'greatness' (Boorstin, 1992: 47). This process of fabrication represents a departure from Mills (1956/2000: 72), who stated that the *actions* of celebrities had *value*. In contrast, Boorstin (1992) conceives of situations where celebrities' image or name are more valued than their actions. Celebrity has in some cases become a synthetic phenomenon, greatness has been divested from it, and it can be mass produced, branded and sold (Boorstin, 1992: 48, 49). Some, in practice, have indeed become famous for simply being famous.

Given Boorstin's (1992) argument, it becomes possible to reconsider celebrity, in particular, and elite theory more generally as existing as a part of a broader post-modern turn (Lyotard, 1999). Our understanding of what it means to be elite or celebrity then becomes tied explicitly to its associated images. This association can be represented and expressed as a precession of simulacra (Baudrillard, 2000) from what is historically understood as an elite towards these fluid, synthetic (Boorstin, 1992), fame-based 'elites' that emerge or are crafted as part of some sort of spectacle (Debord, 1967/1995) or event. The emergence of such a synthetic elite or celebrity, of course, can have a profound impact on aspects of a post-industrial society, and inevitably provides us with clues as to the current state of both elites and civil society.

A faithful copy of elite theory

The first phase of the image, according to Baudrillard (2000: 6), reflects a profound reality. It is in practice a good appearance. He refers to images as representations of a *sacramental order*. Such a description has specific religious roots. Monks, for example, wore a tonsure to represent their status in the church. Priests within the Catholic Church can still have their status and position identified by their vestments and associated hats. Cardinals typically wear a red cap, while the pope typically wears a large diamond-shaped one, and parish priests remain unadorned. In each case, the symbols (tonsure, vestments and hat) each reflect the position faithfully. In the case of elites, symbols often refer to their trappings as well as their obligations and duties (Skiffington, 1991) that identify them as members of the elite.

Much of the classical and neo-classical literature on elites and elite theory tends to focus on some sort of ruling class, some power elite, or at the very least some member of the intelligentsia (Bottomore, 1993). Historical accounts identify the sorts of images, trappings, duties and obligations associated with elite individuals. Consider medieval Europe, where elites had crests, land, wealth and an obligation to protect their fiefdoms. Contemporary arguments about the power elite, in contrast, tend to emphasise the legitimate and illegitimate roles elites might undertake. These more modern discussions consistently inform the literature on citizenship and democracy. One of the best examples of this comes from the Dewey–Lippmann debates. Lippmann, in particular, had a consistent tone that pervaded his work, supporting notions of a ruling or power elite. From Lippmann's (2008) perspective, these represented an *informed and educated* elite group that might be charged with the task of bringing order to the messy elements of democracy.

As the public moves from a civil society (a public) towards what Mills (1956/2000) argued to be a mass society, there is a nearly inevitable shift away from pluralism towards elitism. This idea of a mass society reflects 'the assumed need for experts to decide delicate and intricate issues', the 'irrationality of the man in the street' and the 'socially conditioned nature of what was once assumed to be autonomous reason' (Mills, 1956/2000: 300–1). Mills' position, in many ways, echoes the work of Lippmann (2008) who challenged the belief in virtues associated with majority rule during a series of debates with Dewey along with a number of other assumptions about the state of civil society in the early twentieth century. As one begins to question virtue itself, and virtue in the context of democracy or more generally, it can create opportunities to uncover hidden, often denatured imagery that stands in contradistinction with the 'sacramental orders' (Baudrillard, 2000: 6) revealed in phase one.

We need only look at contemporary discussions of citizenship and democracy to uncover where we are questioning virtue in both areas. There are any number of scholars and practitioners bemoaning the state of citizenship, some remaining concerned about the continued infantilisation (Berlant, 1993) of the public through the manipulation of imagery and discourses. This manipulation, particularly in US contemporary politics (Ewen, 1990) has become significantly more ritualised (Goffman, 1967) along with a greater focus on the spectacle (Debord, 1967/1995; Edelman, 1988) of dissent. Despite this, some scholars still cling to the 'sacramental order' of democracy, believing in the ideals, processes and systems of both governance and citizenship (Box, 1998; King and Stivers, 1998).

A perversion of elite theory

The second phase of the image, according to Baudrillard (2000: 6) is an image that masks and denatures a profound reality. It was originally described as something with an evil appearance that is 'the order of maleficence', something that corrupts or is harmful. Contemporary applications might include unflattering caricatures, revealed failings and a degeneration or loss of the trappings, obligations and duties associated with being elite.

In the context of the Catholic Church, the simplest examples would be the defrocked or disgraced clergymen who retain their position. In the case of elites and elite theory there are multiple examples that emerge from sociology and economics, helping to make the case that examples of the second phase exist with alarming regularity.

Perversions of elite theory are historically easy to document. Veblen's (1934) *The Theory of the Leisure Class* and his (1964) *The Instinct of Workmanship* can provide a foundation for the examination of phase two in practice. Veblen and others examined the possibility of deterioration as well as progress through the lens of blind drift (Jennings and Waller, 1994; Abel and Sementelli, 2003). Elites in particular had the possibility of forming a specific sort of leisure class, one that not only consumes, but at the same time might fail to undertake their historical, social and status-based duties (Veblen, 1934) associated with the position. Veblen also claimed these behaviours could become detrimental to society as certain classes or cultures might over time degenerate into lesser forms by shifting their focus towards more ceremonial values, and away from technical values (Tilman, 1972). In essence, they become part of what Veblen more generally identified as 'imbecile institutions' (Veblen, 1934; Knoedler et al., 2007), moving away from productive action towards symbolic, ceremonial actions.

Veblen's (1934) work represents an early attempt to distinguish between what he called technical and ceremonial values. The emergence of technical values (e.g. economic growth and expansion) can eventually undermine the ceremonial (Tilman, 1973) leading to the sort of economic egalitarianism promised by free markets. Such a shift can cause any number of problems for elites within a 'predatory' institutional system (Tilman, 1973). If the dominant institutional system is successful it can, in turn, lead to the development of a closed society (Tilman, 1972). In practice, such a closed society, according to Veblen, would be expressed through the stagnation or degeneration of existing institutions, meaning that positive change (or progress) was not happening. Instead, there is some potential for institutional ossification (Veblen, 1934), which might ultimately lead to the wholesale decay or collapse of said institution over an extended period of time.

In practice, these ossified institutions often attempt to shore up their position through a broader adoption and application of existing or adapted ceremonial values and systems. This represents a 'perversion of reality' (Baudrillard, 2000) as these purported socio-economic 'elites' shift away from a productive, contributory, 'high thinking' (Veblen, 1934: 24) position in society (e.g. one focusing on noblesse oblige, charity, economic growth) towards a predatory one. In this predatory state, 'elites' exist as a distortion of the high-thinking 'noble' individuals described in phase one, effectively illustrating the denatured, masked images of what it means to be an elite in phase two.

This stagnation or ossification of elites and institutions can create situations where cosmopolites and their progeny might no longer produce anything, but rather can *abstain* wholly from the technical processes of labour while maintaining rates of conspicuous consumption. They become engrossed with the maintenance of a leisurely lifestyle often through the application of their wealth (Veblen, 1934). Upon abstention, such individuals might choose to embrace the realms of 'government, war, sports, and devout observances' (Veblen 1934: 26). In each case, there is no increase in wealth by productive effort; instead, there is a further shift towards leisure, consumption, sloth and *ceremony.*

At this stage, in contemporary society we see examples of this behaviour in political circles where wealthy businessmen use their resources, name and, most importantly, their image as tools to gain political power and prominence with varying degrees of success. Arguably, Silvio Berlusconi would be one of the most successful examples of this phenomenon. Rick Scott was elected governor of Florida and currently enjoys an approval rating of roughly 32% up from a low of 29% in May of 2011. Carly Fiorina gained support during the primary elections, but was defeated in the general election.

A common thread among these examples is that economic elites shifted their efforts away from the technical, from what Veblen (1964) might argue is the productive role of elites towards more ceremonial, consumptive, processes often described as political (Edelman, 1988) or social (Debord, 1967/1995) spectacles. These shifts often are nominally related to some development or event. One might argue that the frequency of these 'events' supports the claim that they are instead pseudo events (Boorstin, 1992) used simply as tools to gain ceremonial advantage for the individual in question, yet they can still be identified or described as one of the power elites discussed by Mills (1956/2000).

An absence of elites

In contemporary society, especially in the USA we find there are any number of attempts to try to fabricate elites from essentially nothing. In this case, such a process embodies the third phase of Baudrillard's (2000) progression of simulacra. There is in truth an absence, or at least a dearth, of what Mills (1956/2000), Bottomore (1993) and others identify as 'elites'. Consequently media, politics and other cultural outlets attempt to fill these gaps with hollow images, fabricating elites from the ether (Boorstin, 1992). Consider Mills' (1956/2000) category of the celebrity. What it means to be a celebrity has changed considerably from the 'Names that need no further identification' (Mills, 1956/2000: 71–2), to someone who has in effect achieved their '15 minutes of fame' (Warhol, 1968) or someone 'known' for being well known (Boorstin, 1992). In many cases, cultural institutions including the media create celebrities, who can in certain situations begin to act like elites. Their relative 'clout' is a function of which *tier* or level of recognition they have and the value associated with it. These celebrity 'elites' can range from the more historically 'legitimate' (e.g. multi-generational celebrity or elite families, talented performers, etc.) to those wholly crafted for mass consumption (e.g. the cast of *Survivor* or *Big Brother*). Additionally, some gain celebrity and thereby temporary 'elite' status by chance, offering some element of socially or politically useful imagery ('Joe the Plumber'). Most, if not all of these people could not be linked to the notion of celebrity or elite without substantial aid from the media and mass culture.

In practice, we find that many of these fabricated elites (Boorstin, 1992) embrace the trappings of the image, and often attempt to wield power associated with the elite position by either lending or 'selling' themselves to some cause, idea or goal. The contractor Joe Wurzelbacher ('Joe the Plumber') has parlayed his celebrity into a career as a motivational speaker. The process by which someone might transform from being an underemployed construction contractor into a motivational speaker illustrates the power of this hollow image in practice.

The important question in this section involves the why and how such phenomena happen. Lacan (1996; Fink, 1995), in particular, discusses the lack of order, the lack of structure and the lack of 'meaning' in the day-to-day lived existence of people. As some people struggle with life and lack of meaning, they clutch at the scant meaning that can frame their existence within a mass culture. As things become increasingly relative, the notions of elite, of celebrity and of fame and their relation to society become far more malleable as the link between the sign (celebrity) and the exegesis (the process) becomes less clear and less formalised (Fink, 1995; Lacan, 1996).

The notion of mass culture or mass society as examined by both Mills (1956/2000) and Lippmann (2008) was employed to help make sense of this day-to-day lack of order, this lack of structure, and seemingly incommensurable sets of ideas and images by creating a space for the production of commodified though hollow elites. Early work by Bottomore (1993) considered this as well. Using the work of Karl Mannheim, Bottomore focused on the need to reconcile democracy and economy, or more appropriately what Veblen (1934) described more broadly as the ceremonial and technical. Bottomore concluded that such a process demanded a new mode of elite selection because 'what changes most of all in the course of democratization is the *distance* between the élite and the rank-and-file' (Karl Mannheim, quoted in Bottomore, 1993: 113, italics added). Additionally, Mannheim argues that the 'democratic élite has a mass background' (quoted in Bottomore, 1993: 88). In essence, he alludes to the possibility of fabricated, commodified elites (Boorstin, 1992).

It becomes easy to envision a process in contemporary society where the creation of elites from a mass background can become a process or possibly a device used as a tool for control, a mechanism to reinforce the 'predatory' status of some (Tilman, 1973). This possibility for the creation of mechanisms of control is, in practice, similar to what has been argued by some critics of civil democracy (Herman and Chomsky, 2002; Chomsky, 2003; Lippmann, 2008). If one accepts the argument that there exists a group of people who carry on executive functions, and another that make up a 'bewildered herd' (Chomsky, 2003: 16), we can extrapolate that an easy way to maintain order within the 'bewildered herd' might be to create control mechanisms from within the herd itself. Maintaining control over these 'spectators' (Lippmann, 2008) becomes a simpler practice. You need only create an empty image, a hero, a celebrity, or a person of note using the media or other ceremonial processes. That image might be distributed, sold or promoted as a mechanism for other members of the mass society to reconcile or at least cope with the lack of meaning in day-to-day life.

In contemporary society, this could mean that a subgroup of 'traditional' elites (though more likely elites that fit within phase two as described earlier), meaning the power elites can guide or create an image or series of images of 'mass' elites. Such images might be created from someone who emerges from mass society, and creates an urge for the bewildered herd to utter the phrase 'We want you to be our leader' (Chomsky, 2003: 16). The result, of course, is that we maintain and reinforce this hollow image of democracy. Thus satisfied, the masses then sink back into their spectator role (Lippmann, 2008).

At this juncture, we are left with at least two hollow images: 'elites' and 'democracy'. In both cases, they mask the absence of a profound reality; democracy becomes a copy with no original, claiming to represent something (democratic values and participation) that does not exist. It is in many ways consistent with Baudrillard's (2000) notion of an order of sorcery since these 'crafted' elites, in practice, often act as phase one elites might. They might dress, act and behave very much like more traditional elites. Sometimes, they might even begin to offer opinions regarding the nature of democracy. At this stage of the precession of simulacra, mass society and culture continues to see and believe that there is participative democracy, and that elites among them represent their interests even though their primary role is that of spectator, and their 'elites' are in truth fabricated and commodified (Boorstin, 1992).

Simulacra

The fourth phase, which might best embody notions of elites in a post-industrial society is linked to Baudrillard's (2000) notion of a pure simulation. In practice, it describes a simulacrum with no relationship to any reality whatsoever. Signs merely reflect other signs unhinged from references. In this sense, notions of elites change one more time. They can arguably emerge from anywhere, and can be linked to anything. Elites become both accessible and unhinged. They are multiplied and destroyed, as the only thing necessary to become an elite is the identifier or moniker. With a contemporary immersion in media, to become a celebrity, and thereby an elite, requires simply exposure to media. In practice, it is the embodiment of the notion of 'fifteen minutes of fame' (Warhol, 1968).

The movement from an absence of elites to elites as pure simulacra has a number of effects. Some of these might best be described as unintended. As these elites are simulacra, they are only elite as long as people believe it to be the case. Realising this we discover a shift away from phase three where 'elites' might be created as mechanisms to maintain and develop power and control over a mass society. Instead, it is the *spectators* (Lippmann, 2008) in many cases who become empowered to create, determine and otherwise develop these simulacra.

From a critical theory perspective, the shift from an absence to simulacra ultimately represents a return of power to the spectator. The spectator in this case changes from being spectator to being a 'consumer' (Baudrillard, 1998) of these simulacra, meaning that these simulacra only have power or value as long as the mass culture or mass society believe it to be. If the consumer or spectator does not 'buy' or buy into the idea of the person as an elite, then put simply, they are not elites. If the consumer or spectator, however, buys into the idea of the person as elite, then they are in effect elite, albeit a simulacrum.

The notion of elite as simulacrum offers a great deal of power, yet it is not always wielded. Mass society has the power to create, to craft or to elevate any number of people to the status of elite regardless of their background. It might be a function of some odd or unique talent, a peculiar moment of happenstance, or even the choreographed development of a public image. The progression of simulacra does not in this case always begin at phase one and end at phase four. Instead, we find that in the case of elites, the creation of simulacra continues alongside the development of more traditional examples such as the very rich (Berlusconi), those perceived as rich (Trump) and even the American socialites and their children.

One might argue that the particular case of celebrity as described by Mills (1956/2000), Boorstin (1992) and others remains most susceptible to the creation of simulacra, as it tends to require very few 'resources' relative to the creation of other elites, such as wealthy businessmen, military leaders and the very rich. As celebrity and elites more generally can be crafted any number of ways, we find that in a post-industrial society being born into an elite class or category is sometimes not enough. In practice, we find cases where more 'traditional' elites (executives, the wealthy and corporate elites) increasingly embrace the practice of recreating themselves as simulacra.

Consider as an example Donald Trump, an American business magnate who has experienced multiple instances where his elite status has been branded and rebranded, resulting in multiple images being commonly associated with him. Originally best described as a commercial real estate developer, Trump has transformed into a television personality and in some instances a political commentator. Unlike some elites in similar positions, Trump has used his influence, his elite status, to attempt to shape policy, to shape perception, and in many ways to shape mass society. The elite *simulacrum* known as Donald Trump situationally has become more powerful than Donald Trump, the commercial developer. He can wield a great deal of power and influence, sometimes beyond what one might expect from those embodying more traditional, more historic roles of elites in the USA and globally.

Consider next the example of celebrities who are famous for 'being famous' (Boorstin, 1992). Being famous in a post-industrial society affords opportunities if not social spaces for the creation of elite simulacra. In certain circumstances, many or at least some of these individuals as simulacra have been able to parlay their celebrity into something that resembles real power and influence. In practice, this has been wielded to achieve specific ends (Gabler, 1995). Gabler (1995), in particular, offered the example of gossip columnist Walter Winchell, who wielded his celebrity to alter social, economic and political life, though many would be left wondering why and how this was the case given the peculiarity of his circumstances.

The movement towards creating celebrity from the state of being famous allows for the multiplication of elite simulacra, for rebranding, and for reconsideration of existing notions of elite, often with little or sometimes wholly without substance to justify the image of elite, or of celebrity. Currently, there are numerous 'pseudo celebrities' populating mass culture in America. Their fame is merely a function of taste, of choices, of age, and possibly of gender. Yet these pseudo celebrities, these elite simulacra, can and often do wield influence for good or for ill.

Post-industrial civil society

In Lippmann's book, *The Phantom Public*, originally published in the 1920s, he crafted a scathing critique of both democracy and of civil society in America. Nearly a century later, it appears that Lippmann was prescient. In contemporary governance in particular, there is little support for Dewey's notion of civic virtue based on educated, omnicompetent individuals. As we experience a post-modern turn, as we move forward as a post-industrial society, many elements of Lippmann's critique continue to ring true.

His proposed solutions, however, which were often linked to *elite* control over democratic processes, appears to ring hollow, as many of the 'elites' that might be tasked with the process of governing fall into Baudrillard's (2000) second, third and fourth phases of the image. In practice, these contemporary 'elites' are not faithful copies of the competent intellectual

(Bottomore, 1993), the war hero or the competent executive identified by Mills (1956/2000), Lippmann and others who 'ought' to be guiding the mass society of spectators towards some positive end.

Instead, we find our contemporary elites are often anti-intellectual, as described and understood by Hofstadter (1966) and developed by Jacoby (2009). In the USA in particular, political actors often take pride in making rash, snap decisions without proper reflection, consideration or deliberation. This rise in anti-intellectualism, combined with the broader associated trend towards the removal of intellectuals, competent managers and professional administrators from political and managerial decision processes, creates further opportunities for the unfettered manipulation of images and ideas, even if they make little sense.

The traditional power elites (or ruling elites) typically born into social circles in Europe, with obligations to professionalism associated with their station, do not exist in the USA. Instead, American 'power' elites, the pool of available political decision-makers in the best cases are a cross-section of mediocre actors (Ronald Reagan, Arnold Schwarzenegger), professional wrestlers (Jesse Ventura) and comedians (Al Franken). In the worst case, they have been associated with fraud (Rick Scott), with prostitution scandals (Eliot Spitzer), the potential abuse of position to create hostile work environments (Mark Foley), as well as solicitation (Senator Larry Craig, Ted Haggard) and drug abuse (Ted Haggard).

Consequently, Lippmann's (2008) idealised solution – placing decision-making in the hands of what is understood to be the US power elite (Mills, 1956/2000) – would be disastrous in practice given the combination of social factors, environmental factors and the movement towards anti-intellectualism. The 'benefit' of having agents acting on behalf of the bystanders or spectators, requires these insiders or agents to have requisite sets of skills, knowledge and training to undertake the process of governing. In practice, we find that similar to Lippmann's (2008) conception of the public, these actors, these agents, these insiders are also incapable of deciding rational courses of action either as part of day-to-day experiences or as a reaction to crises.

What is left, for good or ill, is a mass society of spectators that is highly populist. It is populist in the sense that only the broadest, most persuasive groups of individuals, only the most powerful prevailing communities of interest (Abel and Sementelli, 2007) can influence civic action. In this society of spectators, inertia itself remains the most powerful force balancing the interests of the powerful against the needs of society. The choice to act no longer reflects any need to be rational or real. In practice, it needs only to be persuasive, imaginable or believable. As such, invitations to action can be conveyed by some sort of elite (simulacrum or otherwise), and success becomes measured as a function of the products or policies associated with that person or group of persons (Zimmerman and Ayoob, 2004). Success also reflects the acceptance of the commodified image (Baudrillard, 1998), and of the spectacle associated with actions (Debord, 1967/1995).

In the case of civil society, the phenomenon of elites and Baudrillard's (2000) progression of simulacra in many ways has opened a space for a highly egalitarian approach to governance. Contemporary elites in many cases are only power elites as long as their 'brand' continues to sell to the mass culture or mass society. It might take only a single media faux pas, a single indiscretion, or some other misstep to wholly destroy the influence of someone identified as elite. Ironically, in certain cases infamy, or the same faux pas, indiscretions and missteps might be used to create or elevate someone to elite status as well.

As I close this chapter, it remains important to realise that elites in a post-industrial society include the odd, unbalanced, partially fabricated, partially inherited, and always fluctuating group of simulacra and people. Examining Baudrillard's (2000) precession of simulacra reveals the existence of examples in each phase. Their relative influence over social and political processes remains in flux. In an odd twist, it is the society of spectators and the culture of inertia that ultimately balance the ambitions of the powerful in practice. This stands in sharp relief when held against the classical notion that ambition must be pitted against ambition.

In some cases, power elites remain elite only as long as a large enough group in a mass society is willing to 'buy' or support their brand. As tastes shift, the population of elites can as well. In practice, this can lead to a proliferation of multiple 'imbecile institutions' populated with former elites and their associated trappings and left to fade into obscurity unless they can reimagine themselves into something that might be understood to be elite once more. The success of this reimagining, however, remains in the hands of the spectators, of the mass society, who ultimately what might best be described as *customers* driving the creation and maintenance of what it means to be elite in a post-industrial society.

References

Abel, C. F. and Sementelli, A. (2003) *Evolutionary Critical Theory and its Role in Public Affairs* (Armonk, NY: M. E. Sharpe).

Abel, C. F. and Sementelli, A. (2007) *Justice in Public Administration* (Tuscaloosa, AL: University of Alabama Press).

Baudrillard, J. (1998) *The Consumer Society* (Thousand Oaks, CA: Sage).

Baudrillard, J. (2000) *Simulacra and Simulation* (Ann Arbor, MI: University of Michigan Press).

Berlant, L. (1993) 'The Theory of Infantile Citizenship', *Public Culture*, 5(3): 395–410.

Boorstin, D. (1992) *The Image: A Guide to Pseudo-Events in America* (New York: Vintage).

Bottomore, T. (1993) *Elites and Society* (2nd edn.) (London: Routledge).

Box, R. (1998) *Citizen Governance: Leading American Communities into the 21st Century* (Thousand Oaks, CA: Sage).

Chomsky, N. (2003) *Media Control: The Spectacular Achievements of Propaganda* (2nd edn.) (New York: Seven Stories Press).

Dawkins, R. (1976) *The Selfish Gene* (New York: Oxford University Press).

Debord, G. (1967/1995) *The Society of the Spectacle*, trans. D. Nicholson-Smith (New York: Zone Books).

Edelman, M. (1988) *Constructing the Political Spectacle* (Chicago: University of Chicago Press).

Ewen, S. (1990) *All Consuming Images: The Politics of Style in Contemporary Culture* (New York: Basic Books).

Fink, B. (1995) *The Lacanian Subject: Between Language and Jouissance* (Princeton, NJ: Princeton University Press).

Gabler, N. (1995) *Winchell: Gossip, Power, and the Culture of Celebrity* (New York: Vintage).

Goffman, E. (1967) *Interaction Ritual: Essays on Face-to Face Behavior* (New York: Pantheon Books).

Herman, E. and Chomsky, N. (2002) *Manufacturing Consent: The Political Economy of the Mass Media* (New York: Pantheon Books).

Hofstadter, R. (1966) *Anti-Intellectualism in American Life* (New York: Vintage).

Jacoby, S. (2009) *The Age of American Unreason* (New York: Vintage).

Jennings, A. and Waller, W. (1994) 'Evolutionary Economics and Cultural Hermeneutics: Veblen, Cultural Relativism, and Blind Drift', *Journal of Economic Issues*, 28(4): 997–1030.

King, C. and Stivers, C. (1998) *Government is Us: Public Administration in an Anti-Government Era* (Thousand Oaks, CA: Sage).

Knoedler, J., Prasch, R. and Champlin, D. (2007) *Thorstein Veblen and the Revival of Free Market Capitalism* (Northampton, MA: Edward Elgar).

Lacan, J. (1996) *Écrits*, trans. B. Fink (New York: W. W. Norton).

Lippmann, W. (2008) *The Phantom Public* (New Brunswick, CT: Transaction Publishers).

Lyotard, J. (1999) *The Postmodern Condition: A Report on Knowledge*, trans. G. Bennington and B. Massumi (Minneapolis, MN: University of Minnesota Press).

Miller, H. (2002) *Postmodern Public Policy* (Albany, NY: State University of New York Press).

Mills, C. (1956/2000) *The Power Elite*. (Oxford: Oxford University Press).

Pareto, V. (1963) *A Treatise on General Sociology* (New York: Dover).

Skiffington, K. (1991) 'Noblesse Oblige: A Strategy for Local Boundary Making', *Ethnology*, 30(3): 265–77.

Tilman, R. (1972) 'Veblen's Ideal Political Economy and its Critics', *American Journal of Economics and Sociology*, 31(3): 307–17.

Tilman, R. (1973) 'Thorstein Veblen: Incrementalist and Utopian', *American Journal of Economics and Sociology*, 32(2): 155–70.

Veblen, T. (1934) *The Theory of the Leisure Class* (New York: Random House).

Veblen, T. (1964) *The Instinct of Workmanship* (New York: Augustus Kelley).

Warhol photo exhibition, Stockholm, 1968: Kaplan, J. (ed.), *Bartlett's Familiar Quotations*, 16th edn. (Boston: Little, Brown, 1992), 758: 17.

Zimmerman, J. and Ayoob, E. (2004) *The Role of Products in Consumer–Celebrity Relationships*. Human–Computer Interaction Institute, Paper 235 (http://repository. cmu.edu/hcii/235).

7
Social Value Creation by Elites

Philip Sugarman

Introduction

It is human nature to be ambivalent about successful and privileged people. We often take a negative view of some elite groups, whilst also sharing positive narratives about particular individuals, who are nevertheless usually also members of elites. These contradictory tendencies can be discerned in the evolution of academic thought.

The socio-political study of elites in society has developed from a critique of power, and has contributed to popular beliefs about 'the establishment', 'the ruling class' and 'the military–industrial complex'. Elite theory has evolved as political culture has changed, but academic work on the contribution of elites specifically within organisations remains sparse. However, students of commercial and social enterprise do often study the examples of individual leaders in successful ventures.

It is important to recognise that organisations are often led by people from diverse elites, whose creative interaction develops new social structures, ideas and identities. The author, who is not a sociologist, offers a case example of the interaction of elites, and believes that a transparent discourse about how empowered groups bring value should be a feature of a mature and open society.

A view of elite theory

What do we mean when we talk about elites? Most often, in connection with political and social influence, wealth and worldly comforts, and access to education and health care, we imply a small group of people with disproportionate power, privilege and protection in our society. Such perceived groups are commonly criticised and stereotyped. However, in other contexts, such as elite individuals in sport, art, philanthropy and entrepreneurship, a more positive response is often evoked, with appreciation and celebration of excellence and personal achievement. A moot point seems to be whether individuals' success is attributed to their own contribution and merit, or to their social background and connections, or to selfish motives or practices. However, this will always be a complex judgement, one that is rarely exercised without personal bias. So it seems true that it is human nature to sometimes take a decidedly negative view of the successful and privileged, and at others times to take an equally positive view.

The deep ambivalence we all have about those luckier than ourselves is seen at its most stark and distasteful in the fate of the famous at the hands of pundits, and occasionally, of mobs. These natural tendencies are very prominent in contemporary media, which is rightly criticised for building up and tearing down celebrities, from powerful political leaders to hapless talent contest winners. Sometimes the psychological pressure of elite or celebrity status seems to be causal of the self-destructive behaviour so common amongst those in the public eye, exemplified particularly by artists and entertainers.

These profound tensions can also be discerned in the more cerebral perspectives in the modern world. Amongst these are sociology and politics, both often styled as 'critical' disciplines, which name Karl Marx amongst their founders. Marx led of course the most radical critique of the wealthy and dominant social class (Marx and Engels, 1848). Ideas on elites were subsequently elaborated by the so-called classical elite theorists (e.g. Michels, 1915; Pareto, 1915; Mosca, 1923) who broadly agreed that income and power in a population were not distributed randomly, nor even largely according to talent or merit. They delineated in more detail a narrow political class, perpetuated by advantages such as inherited wealth and family connections, functioning as an oligarchy controlling money, knowledge and preferment. To some extent, unlike the revolutionary Marx, they regarded this arrangement as inevitable.

Following the rise of the Nazi state in Europe and its fall after a cataclysmic war, newly critical theorists such as Mills (1956) discerned a broad political, economic and military power elite, later dubbed the 'military–industrial complex'. Various mechanisms were seen to funnel control to a self-serving group, corrupting modern democracy at both local and national levels. Such ideas have evolved as elites have changed, to describe ever wider decision-making groups across management, administration and political circles, who carry influence through specialist knowledge. These include industrial executives, scientists, economists, political advisers and lobbyists (see e.g. Putnam, 1976). Modern thinkers continue to be concerned with elites, and the risk they pose to society (e.g. Femia, 2001).

To the lay reader such socio-political thinking about the role of elites in society seems fundamentally value-laden, with its currency greatest amongst certain intellectual groups, whose vision of the world and technical language is unrepresentative of wider society. These 'elite theorists' are themselves mostly members of an elite academic group, an irony that is no doubt not lost on them. It would seem likely that any stream of thought that was once part of an anti-establishment 'movement', pressing for change, may later become incorporated into 'the establishment', as the two sides to political discourse were dubbed by the poet Emerson (Milder, 1999). Perhaps in Marxist terms there is a historical dialectic between the ruling elite and its critics.

A recent review in the area by John Higley of the University of Texas at Austin shows both how far thinking on elite theory has come, but also how it still struggles, with palpable discomfort, to fully reconcile its critical origins with an acceptance of the positive contribution of elites:

> Elite theory teaches, in other words, that a mature and experienced advocate of democracy must always settle for a political order that is considerably less than ideal.

> Elite theory rejects the fashionable but fatuous notion that the most desirable political system is one in which the divergent interests of a population are clearly represented and forcefully articulated at the elite level.

> [N]ot a few persons holding elite positions in post-industrial conditions see themselves as one of a kind with non-elites, among whom they frequently have intimate personal associates ... [which may] ... help ensure that elite persons are better able to determine measures that at least partially assuage non-elite discontents and aspirations. (Higley, 2008)

Partial assuagement of discontent is hardly a ringing endorsement of democratic political progress, and leaves this reader feeling the field is reaching across the void – from being a movement to accepting the establishment view. Do these grudging statements of the obvious and inevitable suggest we are at end of the road for critical elite theory? Perhaps there is a way forward. Farazmand (2002) reviews the gap between political and organisational theories. Whilst recent elite theory focuses on inter-organisational activity, it does not examine the role of elites within organisations.

It is also true that organisational theories, more oriented towards the rationalities of effectiveness, typically don't examine the role of elites either. Elites as groups are rarely highlighted for MBA students in their studies, but individual business leaders are a central topic of both lecturers' anecdotes and textbook case studies. Business leaders' insights are also the stuff of popular management books. Some of the most influential and serious management volumes of all time do focus on the importance of people in successful companies. However, the lessons to be learned are about the individual features and company features which bring success by merit, rather than by the exercise of influence and activity as members of a wider group (e.g. Peters and Waterman, 1982).

Students of management who come to work in organisations of any kind will nevertheless find that elite individuals and groups within the organisation are a topic of 'water cooler' conversation. They will also discover that whilst positive official discourse about diverse, disempowered groups (such as the disabled, ethnic minorities and women) has become commonplace in most organisations, a similar open dialogue about more empowered groups remains somehow frowned upon. In short, in a mature and largely open society, people in organisations often still whisper about those in power.

The positive role of elites in value-creating organisations

The interaction between elites can take many forms, and has been the subject of theoretical analysis, but studies of elites within organisations are rare (Farazmand, 2002). We appear to have limited information about how those in positions of power and privilege work together positively to develop institutions. Clearly in any field of human endeavour such bodies can be the substance of new social structures and affiliations, professional identities and value-creating ideas. Possibly great value in economic and human terms can be traced to leadership and innovation, which occurs in the shrouded confines of influential organisations across government, commercial and not-for-profit sectors in every country.

There is literature examining the different kinds of individual leadership contribution that occur at the foundation of, for example, international institutional arrangements (Young, 1991). However, political science is in its relative infancy in taking a developmental approach, being philosophically disinclined to chart the complex interplay of structure and agency, ignoring how individual leaders and elite groups create organisational success (Leftwich, 2010).

Speculation cannot be a sufficient basis for a measured understanding of the positive role of elites in organisations. How can we grasp the processes by which organisations are very often established and led, the crucial inter-actions of varied elites and individuals, and how the bodies may continue to function as the venue for their creative interplay? It may be worthwhile to begin with an anecdotal, narrative approach. I therefore set out below some observations on a large, long-standing charitable hospital in the UK, intimately connected with different elite social groups over a long period of time. It is intended to demonstrate the value created by the interaction of such social and professional elites, and the values they bring, in the creation and development of a social enterprise with benefit to the wider community. The form of the case study is to deliberately convey both some elements of very local context, and draw lessons which may be more 'time-less', and applicable in other settings across our evolving global society.

Enlightened institutions

Society in England two hundred years ago had been moving for some time towards a widening concern for the rights and sufferings of human beings. In a time of increasing circulation of letters, books and ideas, there were numerous examples of the identifiable elite groups of the time taking up causes which can be seen as part of a social enlightenment, and a precursor to modern humanitarianism. Whilst the philosophy of the Enlightenment may have been generated by philosophers and radicals in the newly fashionable coffee houses of capital cities, the social roll out of this trend depended on members of the landed families, i.e. the aristocracy and gentry, professions such as lawyers, doctors and the clergy, newly emerging industrialists and leaders in trade, and the educated class in general (see e.g. Outram, 1995; Fitzpatrick et al., 2004).

Elite groups have continued this work over a long period, identifiable in present-day philanthropy. Long-standing religious traditions of charity and good work were developed in the industrial age into a modern activity of founding sustainable institutions, and creating permanent social change to improve the lives of the people. Most celebrated now are the movements against the slave trade, for prison reform, for the rights of women, and for widening of the democratic political franchise. Of course all of these have yet more to achieve across the world.

Whilst it is easy to identify psychological and social reasons for any individual to pursue good causes, high-minded people can champion such causes with remarkable selfless vigour. It is hard to deny, for example, that the eventual success in the abolition of the slave trade must be partly ascribed to the individual persistence of a number of campaigners such as William Wilberforce, the moral force of their arguments, and the consciences of those they influenced. In short there is a role in human history for altruistic ideas, which can exist over and above the interests of privileged groups.

At a local level the Enlightenment fuelled the growth of important charitable and social institutions, such as the general hospitals which developed in English towns and cities. It took longer, however, for the oppressive stigma of madness inherited from the Middle Ages to be sufficiently dispelled, and for a more enlightened approach to appear towards mental illness. Institutional provision for care of the mentally ill was therefore very limited before the end of the seventeenth century, after which the widespread development of private madhouses brought a series of scandals over abusive and exploitative practices. In consequence, from the end of the eighteenth century a stream of legislation in England and Wales was enacted to regulate proper care and treatment (Jones, 1955).

In England in 1806 the Home Secretary in the government in London, in charge of internal affairs for the country, was the second Earl Spencer, head of the influential dynasty based at Althorp House in Northamptonshire (see Spencer, 1998; interestingly his famous descendant, the late Princess Diana, visited St Andrew's Hospital in Northampton in 1983 to open a new women's unit, Spencer House). Earl Spencer set up an inquiry into the situation of 'the criminal and pauper lunatics of England'. He championed a new law which became the County Asylums Act 1808. This seminal social intervention allowed and encouraged public funds to be used for building the institutions then known as lunatic asylums. At that time the concept of 'asylum' was one with positive connotations of safety, protection and care, developed from religious establishments and infirmaries which traditionally offered protection and care for vulnerable people. However, the cost of such building projects was considerable, and the English counties were reluctant to find the finances from local rates (taxation). Eventually Parliament in 1845 passed another Act to make the provision of county mental hospitals compulsory, and also to mandate key standards such as a resident Medical Practitioner.

St Andrew's Hospital, Northampton

Northamptonshire is a county strategically placed in the heart of England, close enough to London for influence, but with a continuing rural culture of landed estates, less affected by the industrial revolution and urbanisation than other counties. The good and the great of Northamptonshire had for years supported the General Infirmary at Northampton. In 1789 the development of a 'lunatic wing' was first mooted, and donations to the fledgling fund began in 1804 (Foss and Trick, 1989). By 1814 a group of Trustees including the future 3rd Earl Spencer were administering a public appeal, but it made limited progress towards the large sums needed. However, in 1828, at a meeting at the George Inn in Northampton, Sir William Wake Bt. of Courteenhall announced that subscribers to the Northamptonshire Yeomanry, following the end of the Napoleonic wars, had agreed to contribute their surplus monies to the fund. At £6,000 this met half the cost of the project, and galvanised further fundraising with the fulsome support of the prestigious families of the county. Sir William's family name can be traced back to tenth-century Normandy knights, with a long-standing link also claimed to the outlaw Hereward the Wake (Gordon, 1992). The Wakes were one of several local families involved by this time, whose active contribution continues to this day, including the Robinsons of Cranford (the Robinson Baronetcy of London), the Comptons (Marquesses of Northampton, based at Castle Ashby), the Smyths of Little Houghton, and the Fitzroys (Dukes of Grafton).

Building commenced in 1836 on land once owned by the Cluniac Priory of St Andrew. The Priory of St Andrew had been founded after the Norman Conquest under the patronage of the 1st Earl of Northampton Simon de St. Liz, linked with Northampton Castle, local hospitals and an early university (Serjeantson and Adkins, 1906), foreshadowing St Andrew's future links with the National Health Service (NHS) and with the University of Northampton.

It was a matter of great local pride that the hospital was to be erected not through the rates (local taxes), but by charitable public subscription. The laying of the foundation stone in 1836 was preceded by a service in All Saints Church, and a parade from the George Inn to the site on the south-east of Northampton. This procession, accompanied by large crowds, included not only the mayor and sheriffs, bands and banners, but also various Lodges carrying a rich variety of Masonic symbols and objects. Earl Spencer duly declared in the Name of the Great Architect of the Universe that the stone was properly laid. Of course the Masons more than any other organisation bring together *par excellence* the common high ideals and aspirations of varied groups, and attract the adverse attention of those concerned over controlling elites. The activities of Masonic Lodges internationally very much embody the ideals of the Enlightenment, as well as a rather British approach to governance, in which elites work together for positive social ends (Jacob, 2006). In this way aspirant members of the local community were drawn into an important social project. In addition, those who had given more than £20 to the fund became founding Governors of the Hospital. Donations to the hospital from this group continued for many years, supporting the care of 'pauper', i.e. non-fee-paying, residents. The landed gentry and successful local figures have had continuing prominence as Governors of the Hospital, presided over by the Sovereign's official representative in the county, in the honorary role of President of the Hospital.

The building was designed by George Wallet, previously of the famous Bethlem hospital in London. The hospital opened in 1838, dedicated to offering humane care to the mentally ill, and was probably the first institution explicitly founded on the principle of 'Moral Treatment' (Yorston and Haw, 2004), led by Medical Superintendent Dr Thomas Prichard. Moral Treatment was the leading idea of the time in mental health care, a way of describing a general calming regime, a psychological approach, with minimal use of physical and chemical forms of restraint and sedation. This had its origin in the Enlightenment movement to 'liberate the mentally ill from their chains', which had begun in Paris under Pinel in the eighteenth century, and been developed at the Retreat in York.

Reminiscent of a large country house, St Andrew's has always had a prominent reputation in mental health care (see Foss and Trick, 1989; Hall, 2009). Its design from the start embodied a principle which could be characterised as the 'therapeutic value of the picaresque', expressing still relevant beliefs that space, light and scenic views can benefit mental health. The original architecture is appreciated by patients even today, who enjoy fine panelling and ceilings, wide corridors, well-lit lounges and pleasant views, as well as Sir Gilbert Scott's 1863 chapel set in the 120-acre grounds – Scott is better known for the grand hotel front at St Pancras Station in London, as well as the Albert Memorial.

Whilst having much in common with a handful other charitable hospitals, St Andrew's has uniquely endured an array of legal and social changes over 170 years. Its success can be attributed to the combination of the involvement of elites – certainly the prominent echelons of the local community, but also successful figures in the developing profession of psychiatry. Following the original building and regime instigated by Wallett and Prichard, notable superintendents included the remarkable Dr Joseph Bayley, who for forty-seven years to 1912 stewarded the hospital to a national pre-eminent position. At his death the local newspaper commented that he transformed St Andrew's 'into a lordly mansion set in the midst of one of the prettiest parts of the midlands. Its extensive grounds have been likened to those of Warwick Castle' (Foss and Trick, 1989: 205).

The hospital originally provided a programme of treatment both to fee-paying private patients, and to the wider population of mental illness sufferers unable to pay for their care. Amongst the latter was St Andrew's best-known resident, John Clare, England's greatest rural poet, who was Northamptonshire-born. His fame helped attract a later elite clientele including musicians and artists, and aristocratic patients (Sugarman, 2009).

The importance of the environment for recovery continued to be matched by therapeutic developments. In the twentieth century the formidable superintendent Dr Daniel Rambaut, a former Irish Rugby International, robustly pursued modern treatments, and became President of the Royal Medico-Psychological Association (RMPA). His successor, Dr Thomas Tennent, previously deputy superintendent at the Maudsley Hospital, successfully led post-war negotiations on behalf of charitable mental hospitals to stay out of the new state-run National Health Service (NHS), and also became President of the RMPA, shortly before it transformed into the Royal College of Psychiatrists. Under their guidance St Andrew's Hospital became a major centre for the training of mental health professionals, especially in Occupational Therapy.

In the hundred years until the introduction of the NHS in 1948, the charitable mental hospitals had offered a standard of care and treatment significantly superior to the public asylums, and from the twentieth century a number of them were clearly concerned to provide the best facilities and treatments available (Hall, 2009). A leading historian of the mental hospital era commented in the *British Medical Journal*:

> The reputation of St Andrew's rests just as much on its therapeutic excellence as it does on its coincidental facilities. Since its inception, inspired by a succession of brilliant and innovative medical superintendents, the hospital has spearheaded some of the most important developments in psychiatry in England and it would, in fact, be fair to claim that the history of St Andrew's is, broadly speaking, the history of British psychiatry. (Rollin, 1990)

St Andrew's was one of only four Registered Psychiatric Hospitals exempted from joining the NHS, maintaining its charitable status, and now only St Andrew's and the smaller Retreat in York remain in the charity sector. Both avoided the stigma of becoming run down which attached to the hospitals taken over, run down and eventually closed by the NHS.

Since 1948 an increasing number of patients have been funded by the NHS, and St Andrew's in Northampton is by far the UK's largest mental health facility. Services in other sites in England bring the Charity's total provision for patients to over 1000 places, with 'St Andrew's Healthcare' now the largest charitable provider of any kind to the NHS, and the UK's largest mental health charity.

Over the last thirty years the Charity has become the country's leading specialist provider of secure care, managing individuals with challenging behaviour for whom the NHS does not have provision or capacity. Innovative specialist services for men, women, adolescents and older people span the range of mental illness: learning disability, autism, brain injury and dementia. Many new buildings have enabled the Charity to expand and provide several national specialist services. A new adolescent facility was opened by the Prince of Wales in 2000 and a major new building for men, William Wake House, opened in 2010.

The Charity has entered the twenty-first century as a thriving social enterprise developing new forms of care, at the cutting edge of a £1bn independent sector providing outsourced care for the NHS. The origins of some of St Andrew's main competitors can be traced to key individuals – including some elite professionals – leaving the Charity to work with commercial backers to roll out service ideas for wider benefit. This has left the Charity with a competitive challenge to which it has been able to respond.

St Andrew's has found its answer by developing into a more entrepreneurial trading entity, incorporating in a timely way modern business values and knowledge into its governing structure. Working closely with the Charities Commission, St Andrew's re-enforced this new culture by becoming in 2004 the first UK charity with a 'Unitary Board' – a commercial-style Board upholding the charity principle of voluntarism. The Court of Governors elects Trustees as unpaid non-executives, to work closely with a professional Executive team who also have Trustee status.

The prestige of the Charity's history and Governors has helped attract Governors with substantial commercial board experience, including 'FTSE 100' and similar size privately owned companies, as well as smaller enterprises. As a result the Executive team has gained strength from the injection of business experience as well as health-care knowledge. This has given the Charity the confidence to invest £200m successfully in new facilities over a decade, and give more people the opportunity to enjoy enhanced lives.

It is important to understand the key interaction between social elites – landed, business and professional. This of course happens in formal exchanges across the Board table, but more importantly in trusting relationships built up over time. Ceremonial events such as the opening of buildings, formal and informal meals, and mentoring relationships are an integral part of the network within which knowledge is shared and innovation emerges.

The attraction of emerging elites into already prestigious institutions, which are open to change, with the resulting interactions, exemplifies exactly how the influence of elites brings enduring value and success to similar social institutions. It has enabled a strong position for this Charity, able to innovate and compete and to further fulfil its charitable mission to benefit the public (Sugarman, 2010a). Charities in this mould may have a major role in efficient public provision, in the aftermath of the credit crunch and the era of public debt (Sugarman, 2010b). It represents a modern incarnation of charitable philanthropy and social enterprise, with the record to put itself forward as a model for the future.

Conclusion

The values of the Enlightenment have been enacted in social reforming institutions for many years, led by members of various elites. The example of St Andrew's shows how the input of elites can create a continuing record of innovation, combining the best values of charity, professional and business practice into enlightened provision, in the particular field of mental health. Whilst such organisational and social structures are hardly unique, they still need to be transparently described, understood and accepted as the medium for value-creation by elites.

The process by which elites build a shared narrative and common purpose in institutions is a key facet of social leadership, under-investigated by the relevant academic communities. It is a normal human process which can be seen to occur in institutions small and large, from local to global, and is deserving of our attention. A positive and inclusive appreciation of the contribution of elites is not only a key to value creation in business and social networking, but also an emerging feature of contemporary culture which political theorists would do well to recognise. It is hoped that such an understanding of the mechanisms of elites in social enterprise can leverage the potential of elites to contribute to wider society.

Note

Enquiries about the history of St Andrew's should be addressed to: The Archives Manager, St Andrew's Healthcare, St Andrew's Hospital, Billing Road, Northampton, UK, NN1 5DG.

References

Farazmand, A. (2002) 'Elite Theory of Organization: Building a Normative Foundation'. In A. Farazmand, *Modern Organizations: Theory and Practice*. (London: Praeger), 97–132.
Femia, J. (2001) *Against the Masses: Varieties of Anti-democratic Thought since the French Revolution* (Oxford: Oxford University Press).
Fitzpatrick, M., Jones, P., Knellwolf, C. and McCalman, I. (eds.) (2004) *The Enlightenment World* (London: Routledge).

Foss, A. and Trick, K. (1989) *St Andrew's Hospital, Northampton: The first 150 Years (1838–1988)* (Cambridge: Granta).

Gordon, P. (1992) *The Wakes of Northamptonshire: A Family History* (Northampton: Northamptonshire County Council).

Hall, J. N. (2009) 'The Registered (Mental) Hospitals in England from c.1920 to 1960: The Case of St Andrew's Hospital, Northampton', MA dissertation, Oxford Brookes University.

Higley, J. (2008) 'Elite Theory in Political Sociology'. Paper presented at the International Political Science Association conference on New Theoretical and Regional Perspectives, Montreal (see http://montreal2008.ipsa.org).

Jacob, M. (2006) *The Origins of Freemasonry: Facts & Fictions* (Philadelphia: University of Pennsylvania Press).

Jones, K. (1955) *Lunacy, Law, and Conscience, 1744–1845: The Social History of the Care of the Insane* (London: Routledge & Kegan Paul).

Leftwich, A. (2010) 'Beyond Institutions: Rethinking the Role of Leaders, Elites and Coalitions in the Institutional Formation of Developmental States and Strategies', *Forum for Developmental Studies*, 7: 93–111.

Marx, K. and Engels, F. (1848) *Manifest der Kommunistischen Partei* (London: Communistischer Arbeiter-bildungsverein).

Michels, R. (1915) *Political Parties. A Sociological Study of the Oligarchical Tendencies of Modern Democracies* (New York: Collier Books).

Milder, R. (1999) 'The Radical Emerson'. In J. Porte and S. Morris (eds.), *The Cambridge Companion to Ralph Waldo Emerson* (New York: Cambridge University Press), 49–75.

Mills, C. W. (1956) *The Power Elite* (Oxford: Oxford University Press).

Mosca, G. (1923) *The Ruling Class* (New York: McGraw-Hill).

Outram, D. (1995) *The Enlightenment* (Cambridge: Cambridge University Press).

Pareto, V. (1915) *The Mind and Society: A Treatise on General Sociology* (New York: Dover).

Peters, T. J. and Waterman, R. H. (1982) *In Search of Excellence: Lessons from Americas Best Run Companies* (New York: Harper & Row).

Putnam, R. D. (1976) *The Comparative Study of Political Elites* (New Jersey: Prentice-Hall).

Rollin, H. (1990) 'Lordly Mansion', *British Medical Journal*, 300: 1213.

Serjeantson, R. M. and Adkins, W. R. D. (1906) 'Houses of Cluniac Monks: The Priory of St Andrew, Northampton'. In *The Victoria History of the County of Northampton: Volume 2*, 102–9 (http://www.british-history.ac.uk/report.aspx?compid=40225, accessed 25 August 2010).

Spencer, C. (1998) *Althorp: The Story of an English House* (London: Viking).

Sugarman, P. (2009) 'History of the Charity' (http://www.stah.org/about-us/charity-history.html, accessed 25 August 2010).

Sugarman, P. (2010a) 'Charity governance' (http://www.knowledgepeers.com/networks/553/portfolio.html#t311, accessed 25 August 2010).

Sugarman, P. (2010b) 'On Charity's Big Chance', *Health Service Journal* (Sept.): 12.

Yorston, G. and Haw, C. (2004) 'Thomas Prichard and the Non-restraint Movement at the Northampton Asylum', *Psychiatric Bulletin*, 28: 140–2.

Young, O. (1991) 'Political Leadership and Regime Formation: On the Development of Institutions in International Society', *International Organization*, 45: 281–308.

8
Elitism, Class and the Democratic Deficit: Founding Themes of the American Republic

Kalu N. Kalu

The founding fathers of the American republic had an Aristotelian moment, a subtle experience drawn generally from their aristocratic backgrounds and from the simple fact that their view of government was shaped by the need to have a system that safeguarded the individualistic values of the Protestant work ethic on the one hand, but on the other, also recognised the class-based nature of social and economic organisation. To the extent that wealth and education represent a socially elevating criterion, they were also seen as necessary for accomplishing all matters of state interest. In fundamental ways, this also could have shaped their preference for 'representative democracy' over 'direct democracy' or what they called 'rule of the rabble'. The justification for these sentiments has persisted in the annals of American government in such a way that despite its acclaimed democratic credentials, the nation's elites always rule both in matters of legislative policy making or in the workings of the free-market system. Even when we consider the formation and control of political parties (an essential tool for political participation and interest articulation in liberal democracies), we also find that Robert Michels' hypothesis concerning the 'iron law of oligarchy' still resonates in terms of who leads American political parties and who decides what issues or policies are important or not, and in whose interest they serve. In the end, this work argues that the kind of democratic pluralism so much revered in liberal democracies serves essentially as a 'legitimating' force for narrow elite rule devoid of popular consent.

Philosophical idealism and heritage

In his much acclaimed book, *The Rise of American Democracy: Jefferson to Lincoln*, Sean Wilentz (2005) discusses the era after the American revolution, when the ideal of democracy remained contentious, and the Jeffersonians and Federalists clashed over the role of ordinary citizens in government. With a healthy dose of scepticism, he opined that as the revolutionary War of Independence cooled, the new American republic might easily have hardened into rule by an aristocracy; but instead, the electoral franchise expanded and the 'democratic' creed transformed every aspect of American society:

> The conflict between the Federalists and the Jeffersonian Democrats was a conflict between the followers of Hobbes (strong government) and the followers of Locke (weak government), between those whose greatest fear was anarchy and those who feared tyranny as man's most terrible political fate. Hence the issue over the extent of powers which government ought to exercise involved a judgment regarding the nature of man and how man would behave in the absence of strong governmental restraints. (Grimes, 1983: 129)

Nonetheless, it is safe to point out that the democratic ethos did not pervade American society in one big 'swoop', but it was a process that unfolded incrementally, casting its cultural vignette over a large expanse of land and society for more than a century after the civil war. As Wilentz (2005) carefully points out, the build up to the civil war was a battle over democracy between the South's 'master race' localism and the egalitarian nationalism of Lincoln's Republicans, which in itself meant that region, culture and identity were uppermost in the minds of most Americans more than any other moral imperative drawn from the democratic ideal. It took the passage of a few constitutional amendments to initiate the process of change in the direction that we witness today as a democracy. First was the passage of the 13th Amendment of 1865 (the emancipation proclamation) that ended slavery, second was the passage of the 14th Amendment of 1868 (equal treatment under the law), and the 15th Amendment of 1870 (the right to vote irrespective of race). It took until the passage of the 19th Amendment in 1920 to constitutionally guarantee women suffrage or the right to vote. These series of milestones – including the *Plessy* v.. *Ferguson* case of 1896 (separate but equal doctrine), the *Brown* v. *Board of Education* of 1954, the Civil Rights Act of 1964 and the Voting Rights Act of 1965 – all helped to shape America's receptivity and political conflicts over the mean-ing and role of democracy in the republic.

But the question arises as to who made these policies or decision possible, and what were the underlying convictions that drove them. To the extent that the founding theme of the American republic was not anchored on direct democracy, the basis for making public policy choices could not therefore be said to represent the overwhelming interest of the public at large. If the idea of representative democracy is that the people elected to public offices would make policies on behalf of the citizens and their constituencies, it then sug-gests that the framework of government in the American state would, for all practical purposes, continue to reinforce the class-based nature of political representation and the elevation of a few (those elected to representative offices) to elite status. From this vantage point, 'elite ideologies serve in the macro level processes of class-based legitimation – a practice that creates a belief on the part of a large majority of the populace that institutionalized inequality in the distribution of primary resources – such as power, wealth, and prestige – is essentially right and reasonable' (Della Fave, 1980: 955).

E. O. Wright (1996) argues that class analysis continues to make sense of inequalities such as those that divide industrial societies, and in fundamental ways, sees class as a significant and sometimes powerful determinant of many aspects of social life. Because 'class boundaries, especially the property boundary, continue to constitute real barriers in people's lives; inequalities in the distribution of capital assets continue to have real consequences for material interest; capitalist firms continue to face the problem of extracting labor effort from non-owning employees; and class location continues to have real, if variable, impacts on individual subjectivities' (Wright, 1996: 711). But in the absence of such overt and identifiable manifestations of class and socio-economic distinctions, 'there are many indicators that people in the upper classes are active agents in the process of reproducing class-based lifestyles that have a positive effect for elites and a negative effect for those in other classes' (Kendall, 2005: 14). Because many of these manifestations and 'boundary maintenance activities' are rather subtle and esoteric, they escape much public scrutiny and hence become taken for granted – even as they continue to have a powerful impact on the evolving socio-political and economic policies.

The spoils system (or patronage politics) which characterised much of the later Jacksonian era of American public service (1828–83) came to an end following the passage of the Pendleton Act in 1883 and the consequent attempt to improve the management, efficiency and responsiveness of government at the federal as well as the state levels. This Herculean revolution coincided with an increasing call for the rationalisation of government and support for the economic interests of the professional class and occupational guilds. As a result of this, Mitchell Langbert (2008) argues that the earliest American reform took the form of an alliance between narrow professional interests and the evolving character of governmental and administrative rationalisation:

> Hence the impulse toward a rudimentary form of social democracy came in part from the fixation on professional problems, as opposed to equalitarian impulses. As the pattern of government programs that combined rationalization with social welfare began to take root with the passage of the Pendleton Act, the professions (generally upper socioeconomic status) began to gain in power, prestige, and access to resources. As American elites, both in business and the professions, found that they had much at stake in state largess, the ensuing political debate became increasingly a debate among elite economic interests (business and professions). (Langbert, 2008: 3)

This is a process that continues to shape American domestic and foreign policy interests to this day.

State and religion: isolating the moral constraint

While the American founding fathers had a healthy appreciation and understanding of the key precepts of Puritan Calvinism and its corollary in Judaeo-Christendom, one would therefore assume that such religious ethos and doctrinaire attitude would find itself as the focal point as well as the normative underpinning of life in the new republic and also in the consequent constitutional framework. But this was not the case in terms of the American state, since the founding fathers opted for state autonomy as reflected in the passage of the First Amendment to the US Constitution in 1791. (The rest of the Bill of Rights comprising the first ten amendments to the US Constitution was also passed in 1791.) There were two watershed events that could possibly have informed the thinking of the founding fathers regarding state autonomy and the separation of church and state in political governance (not necessarily in individual moral beliefs) assuming that we can absolutely separate individual actions from their personal sentiments and judgements.

The Treaty of Westphalia (1648) brought an end to the Thirty Years War which had drowned Europe in bloody battles over religion. The treaty also affirmed the principles of state sovereignty and equality and enshrined the benefit of 'advantage of the other' (the common good) in the statecraft of sovereign nations. It affirmed the principle that state authority is different and also supreme to any other including that of the church, especially in matters concerning the affairs of society and governance, including of course, war and peace. For the founding fathers of the American republic, this treaty served as a secular justification for the 'separation of church and state' – an essential ingredient, taken in light of the European experience in peaceful coexistence. But they also remained cognizant of the fact that in Calvinist thought:

> the church performed a crucial and all important function – its preoccupation with things of the spirit – the hoped for grace of redemption, as well as the validity of individual claims to salvation – hence the church could not risk the possible corruption that might come with partnership or alliance with the secular state. Because Calvinism presupposed two societies (one secular, the other ecclesiastical), there could be no union of church and state in a single monarch. And even though these societies might, in fact, inhabit the same territory; they were under separate government jurisdictions. (Grimes, 1983: 9–10)

The founding fathers knew that the art of politics and political gamesmanship cannot, in the absolute sense of the term, exclude the kind of amoral sentiments that we often associate with individual behaviour under specific circumstances. They aimed, therefore, to build a new republic in which the measure of a man's wealth would be determined, more or less, by who he is and what he has done on earth. And consistent with the precepts of the Protestant work ethic, a man's worth can be measured, therefore, by his earthly activities and rewards. Their consequent embrace of individualism and the Lockean ideal regarding the labour theory of value and ownership, and a repudiation of his argument regarding the 'commons' created a dilemma for the founding fathers. Since essentially all or most of them were property owners and of aristocratic bearing either by birth or through education, it was important for them that their status and property interests be protected. And to do this, it was expedient to shed much of the ecclesiastical precepts of the church and the moral imperative of being 'commanded' to share what one has laboured unto oneself. To the extent that worldly possession was a virtue unto itself, the Lockean requirement of forfeiting one's property to the 'commons' above and beyond one's immediate needs was a proposition that ran counter to the founding father's inclination for wealth and private ownership.

Locke argued that:

> though the things of nature are given in common, yet man, by being master of himself, and the proprietor of his own person and the actions or labor of it, had still in himself the great foundation of property; and that which made up the great part of what he applied to the support or comfort of his being, when invention and arts had improved the conveniences of life, was perfectly his own, and did not belong in common with others. (Skoble and Machan, 1999: 191)

But Locke goes further to suggest that property ownership and the right it confers extends only so far as to satisfy one's needs without denying the others their own right to share in the benefits:

> No man's labor could subdue or appropriate all, nor could his enjoyment consume more than a small part; so that it was impossible for any man, this way to intrench upon the right of another, or acquire to himself a property, to the prejudice of his neighbor who would still have room for as good, and as large a possession [after the other had taken out his] as before it was appropriated from the commons. (Skoble and Machan, 1999: 187)

It is this latter aspect of the Lockean labour theory of value that the founding fathers rejected simply because it would have been contrary to their belief in the right to property and the social status and entitlement that go with it.

It is evident that in the series of debates that ensued during the revolutionary period, neither Thomas Jefferson nor the other signers of the

Declaration of Independence were in any way opposed to the right of property. While Locke claimed that property ownership was a natural right, Jefferson saw it as a right dependent upon and conditioned by civil society. Jefferson, nonetheless, held the view that the 'most profound right was the goal of human happiness, and for which the acquisition of property might be instrumental in achieving' (Grimes, 1983: 154). In order to avoid having to address the moral conflict between private property and the more egalitarian principle reflected in the Lockean concept of the 'commons', the founding fathers opted for the safer bait of separation of church and state. They were also concerned about being seen to have committed a sin, not to talk of the guilt of having to violate an honoured ecclesiastical tenet – a violation which, consistent with Puritan teachings, would evidently become an obstacle to one's heavenly salvation and redemption. Hence the separation of church and state became a practical expediency for protecting their economic individualism from the moral imperative of religious calling.

Market individualism and elite consensus: upholding the Republican ethos

The year 1776 afforded a propitious opportunity for the founding fathers, following the publication of Adam Smith's *The Wealth of Nations* – for it provided them the philosophical argument to embrace market capitalism, its laissez-faire concept, and certainly its emphasis on private ownership over the argument for the 'commons' which had been central to the Lockean theory of property. It was also a means of granting economic power to the 'people' because it is by their actions that the market would take its cues and, invariably, adjust itself appropriately without any overt governmental intrusion. Because it rewarded private initiative (a worthy virtue though) and also justified a person keeping the fruits of his labour, the free-market system became a dogma that resonated quite well with the propertied class much more than among the poor and the 'plebeians'.

Even though it has often been stated that the market, if left alone, would self-adjust, history has always been the best judge as to the veracity of this economic rule of the game. Nonetheless, historical economic crises, including the later Great Depression and the series of market crashes over the years, are good indicators that the market would surely need a complementary or regulatory power after all. The founders, in the early days, saw that power in state authority. Despite historical claims of state autonomy, the American state has always been a blend of state power and economic corporatism:

> It is a fragmented government completely open to outside agents, and therefore vulnerable to domination through the electoral process and through appointments from the corporate community and policy-planning

network. The movement by members of the corporate leadership group between the private sector and government blurs the line between the corporate community and the state, which does not fit with the idea of state autonomy. (Domhoff, 2005: 5)

It is true that a 'business system could not survive without some degree of market regulation by the government. Hence and contrary to assertions about markets being "free", markets are historically constructed institutions dependent upon governmentally sanctioned enforcement of property and contract rights' (Domhoff, 2010: 174).

The founding fathers never really opted for an absolute free-market system unimpeded by the regulatory power of the state. While the state was viewed as a sovereign authority, its relative autonomy was only seen as a potentiality rather than in the absolute sense of the term. In his *Federalist* argument, it was Alexander Hamilton's contention that 'political power flowed from economic sources and that a firm political union of the states required an underlying and unifying economic system; thus recognizing the importance of economic power to politics, he sought to strengthen the national government by identifying it with the interests of the major economic groups' (Grimes, 1983: 136). He held the view that 'for the national government to act contrary to the interests of the major business groups would disrupt the political system, for the national government, like all government, was dependent upon the support of these same groups' (Grimes, 1983: 136). Although the logic of the free market operates on the assumption that individuals can enter and exit the market of their free will and choice, it can also be argued that the structure that undergirds the very process of entry and exit is, more often than not, anchored in elite interests and protection. As the structure endures over time, it becomes the lens through which social and economic policy is framed and implemented, hence resulting in continuing social inequality regarding economic and political opportunity. Sooner than later, economic power transcends political power as the lines of demarcation between the political and economic estates becomes further blurred.

Drawing from this, one therefore comes to an understanding of the type of mindset that informed the thinking of the founding fathers, at a time when the nation was still trying to establish an economic doctrine for wealth creation and ownership. But while this worked in the interest of the corporate and economic elites (power elite), it also meant that public policies would be framed around those issues that mattered most to this group, even if it meant the exclusion of other equally competing interests. The operational mechanisms of the 'power elite', therefore, offer a mirror through which class and institutional interests come together to shape a more holistic framework of power in the American state. 'In concert with the large banks and corporations in the corporate community, the foundations, think tanks, and policy-discussion groups in the policy-planning network, extra-governmental institutions provide the organizational basis for the exercise of power on behalf of the owners of all large income-producing properties' (Domhoff, 2010: 115), hence 'leaders of these institutions have an economic stake in preserving the governmental rules and regulations that maintain current wealth and income distributions' (Domhoff, 2010: 115).

The American elite often seems less a collection of persons than of corporate entities, which are in great part created and spoken of as standard variants of 'personality' types (Mills, 1956: 15), resting upon the similarity of its personnel, their official and personal relations, their social and psychological affinities (Mills, 1956: 278), as well as 'the reciprocal attraction among the fraternity of the successful' (Mills, 1956: 281). In the broad sense of the term, they share a common interest in sustaining a semblance of control (or rather influence) on the processes of legislative, economic and public policy-making. Regarding economic policy, one example of the ways in which wealth and income distribution are sustained in favour of the elite stratum is the policy of privatisation. 'Privatization of public utilities means that only those who have money can bid for such facilities; and while a sizeable proportion of the citizens are poor and less disposed, they are not generally able to bid or buy shares in such public utilities' (Kalu, 2009: 209). And so one finds that in mainstream liberal economies such as the United States, privatisation programmes rarely spread the wealth or improve the economic circumstances of the average citizen; they essentially secure and protect the economic commonwealth that has always existed between big business and political elites. Rather than the 'trickle-down' effect and associated investment synergies that could be derived from it, privatisation is a conversion process in which public wealth is potentially transferred to those who could afford to participate in the scheme – and these are mostly the wealthy, as opposed to the poor.

The welfare state: a necessary expedient?

The passage of the Social Security Act of 1934 during the presidency of Franklin D. Roosevelt helped to mitigate much of the Depression era economic problems both for society and state. While that, in itself, could be construed as a reluctant admission of the failure and inability of the market system to spread the wealth and to sustain vibrant economic growth and development, it represented one of the earliest attempts at bringing to bear the role of state power and presidential activism to address fundamental social and economic problems. By providing for unemployment insurance, pension benefits and other civic and social benefits, the Act became a central policy element in the New Deal programme. The consequent Social Security Act of 1965 which formed the authorising legislation for President Lyndon Johnson's Great Society programme established a set of public health insurance schemes in the form of Medicare and Medicaid, as well as other needs-based and/or in-kind benefits programmes. It was also an expedient way of accommodating the failure of the market to self-correct, as well as a recognition that changing lifestyles due to industrialisation, population and demographic shifts, and cultural change in the American socio-political firmament demanded a firmer governmental response if political order and social stability were to be maintained.

While these could be construed as 'expedient' policies, largely reactionary and framed in their orientation to assuage the series of economic fallouts, they invariably exposed fundamental weaknesses in the free-market system to address emerging issues of rising expectations and increased social stratification based on wealth, education and prosperity. Nonetheless, there are two broad tendencies that seem to evolve from the welfare state: 'first, a tendency to crowd out democratic possibilities; and second, a tendency to undercut the kind of community on which it nonetheless depends – and it is these institutional developments that may begin to account for the sense of powerlessness that the welfare state fails to address and in some ways doubtless deepens' (Avineri and De-Shalit, 1992: 27–8). Hence it remains a 'striking feature of the welfare state that it offers a powerful promise of individual rights, and also demands of its citizens a high measure of mutual engagement; but the self-image that attends the rights cannot sustain the engagement' (Avineri and De-Shalit, 1992: 28). The welfare state may be necessary as well as expedient, but it still begs the question: To what extent does it serve to bridge existing economic asymmetry or the dynamics of distributive politics within liberal economies? Why do most Americans continue to be alienated from their government, a government that seemingly operates on the very system (representative democracy) that the people, by their popular consent and vote, have legitimised?

A concluding postscript

There are four ways (though not exclusively) through which individuals attain elite status: education, wealth, family and the professions. Because access to these four factors is not evenly distributed in the wider society, it therefore creates a structural inequality that essentially trumps all consequent efforts at addressing income inequality by way of liberal public policies and/or social engineering. Education and wealth, as essential as they are, are equally crucial in creating economic access as well as political opportunity. But it is by unearthing the underlying philosophy and the founding theme of the society that we can begin to understand why these structural inequalities continue to exist and will likely, in all probability, endure for the foreseeable future.

Habitually, Americans seem to take the desirability of democracy for granted without questioning changes or adaptations in the underlying assumptions.

There is a continuing reluctance to make the stark distinction between political rights and the efficacy of their expression in the public space. This enduring disposition stems from the simple fact that over the years they have been confronted with a persistent argument that democracy fosters an ideal condition for individual freedom, a platform for accommodating the public will (public space) in the fostering the deliberative consensus critical to public policy-making and execution. When citizens see the democratic process as a *fait accompli*, democracy, invariably, becomes its own legitimising force without any further critical analysis and judgement on its civic and political efficacy – especially on the all-important issue of pluralism and inclusiveness. Robert Dahl (1982: 1) makes the point that: 'the problem of pluralist democracy, or democratic pluralism, is only one aspect of a general dilemma in political life, that of autonomy or control'. He asks the question: how can we justify the conclusion that even in a fully democratic system some organisations would be entitled to a certain range of autonomy vis-à-vis the demos (people) and its representatives? This is based on the essential premise in which 'to affirm that the democratic process is desirable is to assert that citizens must possess all the rights necessary to that process; and if a body of citizens were to deprive any citizen of any fundamental right necessary to the democratic process, then by its own action it would violate the criteria of the democratic process' (Dahl, 1982: 49).

As William Domhoff (2005: 6) argues, the jury is still out as to who controls the American state. Is it elected officials, appointed officials, and career employees, or the corporate community that finances the elected officials and supplies many of the appointees, or the American public through political parties, elections, interest groups, lobbying and the force of public opinion? Whatever the answer may be, there seems to be an enduring consensus, supported by numerous studies, that in the American political-economic system 'the wealth distribution has been extremely concentrated throughout American history with the top 1 percent owning 40–50 percent of marketable wealth' (Domhoff, 2010: 11). Hence if history is any guide, and if the past can be construed as prologue, it is important to understand the role of elitism and class in the practice and exercise of democracy so as to find ways of mitigating its more deleterious effects.

References

Avineri, S. and De-Shalit, A. (eds.) (1992) *Communitarianism and Individualism* (New York: Oxford University Press).
Dahl, R. A. (1982) *Dilemmas of Pluralist Democracy: Autonomy vs. Control* (New Haven, CT: Yale University Press).
Della Fave, L. R. (1980) 'The Meek Shall Not Inherit the Earth: Self Evaluation and the Legitimacy of Stratification', *American Sociological Review*, 45: 955–71.
Domhoff, G. W. (2005) 'Theories of Power: Alternative Theoretical Views' (http://sociology.ucsc.edu/whorulesamerica/theory/alternative_theories.html, accessed 25 October 2010).

Domhoff, G. W. (2010) *Who Rules America? Challenges to Corporate and Class Dominance* (New York: McGraw-Hill).

Grimes, A. P. (1983) *American Political Thought* (Lanham, MD: University Press of America).

Kalu, K. N. (2009) *State Power, Autarchy, and Political Conquest in Nigerian Federalism* (Lanham, MD: Rowman & Littlefield).

Kendall, D. (2006) 'Class in the United States: Not Only Alive but Reproducing', *Research in Social Stratification and Mobility*, 24(1): 1–16.

Langbert, M. (2008) 'Elitism in American History' (http://mitchell-langbert.blogspot. com/2008/07/elitism-in-american-history.html, accessed 25 October 2010).

Mills, C. W. (1956) *The Power Elite* (Oxford: Oxford University Press).

Skoble, A. J. and Machan, T. R. (eds.) (1999) *Political Philosophy: Essential Selections*. (Upper Saddle River, NJ: Prentice Hall).

Wilentz, S. (2005) *The Rise of American Democracy: Jefferson to Lincoln*. (New York: W. W. Norton).

Wright, E. O. (1996) 'The Continuing Significance of Class Analysis: Comments', *Theory and Society*, 25: 693–716.

9

New Turkish Business Elites: Resources, Networks, Boundaries and Mobility

Sibel Yamak, Ali Ergur, Artun Ünsal, Mustafa Özbilgin and Elif Ünal Çoker

In this chapter, we explain how the new Turkish corporate elites mobilise their varied resources in order to seek integration into the business community through their international, national and local networks. Our findings show that intensive use of economic, social and cultural resources accounts for the success of Turkish elites in navigating their way from local settings to international fluency. We draw upon the relational sociology of Bourdieu and the network theory of Granovetter in order to frame the theoretical background of our study. We have three main findings: First, local and international networks are more accessible to new business elites than national networks. In order to access national networks new business elites require higher levels of economic capital. Second, new business elites in Turkey do not have elite tastes. In fact, our study demonstrates that the new elites have common rather than refined tastes. This may be explained by the fact that they have only recently joined elites. Third, education has been exceptionally instrumental in allowing new elites to access elite status in Turkey. The significance of education in allowing for class mobility cannot be overstated in the case of Turkey.

Turkey is an interesting country in which to study new elites. As a rapidly developing country, new business elites are considered economic pioneers, who are responsible for the significant growth in the financial scope and geographic reach of Turkish businesses in local, national and international settings. The Turkish example is important as Turkish businesses' willingness to integrate with the global economy contrasts strikingly with the common resentment against internationalisation by business elites of the old Europe. Furthermore, we demonstrate in this chapter that the routes, trajectories and requirements of capital for access to elite status in Turkey differ from those in advanced economies.

The centrality of networks in explaining socio-economic phenomena was first underlined by Mark Granovetter. Granovetter tried to transcend an old debate on the institutionalisation of autonomous relations in an economic process, especially that espoused by Karl Polanyi (1944), who asserted that either exchanges were auto-regulated in autonomous systems or individuals were highly embedded into the exchange process. Granovetter rejected this polarised conception of economic activity, and instead, his framing of economic activity allowed wider scope for the individual in the decision-making on the redistribution of resources. Yet, he offered a balanced point of view when he discussed the distinction between the concepts of over- and under-socialised individuals. Human behaviour, particularly when it is manifested in economic relations, is not bounded only in terms of instrumental rationality, but also of sociability, approval, status and power (Granovetter, 1985: 506). Thus, Granovetter constructs an instrumental flexibility for the conception of economic behaviour neither totally determined by institutions nor the expression of a boundless free will (Steiner, 2002: 30–4). Therefore, embeddedness is not conceptually rejected as such, but it is conceived as instrumental for understanding multi-purpose economic behaviours of individuals. Personal interest cannot be considered as the only guideline for individuals to act economically. Instead, he argued that individuals draw on a mixture of economic and social motivations (Granovetter, 2008: 227). Ronald S. Burt has made an important contribution to network theory, which was initiated by Granovetter, developing the notion of *structural holes* for measuring the efficiency of a set of relationships. According to Burt, a structural hole is a functional discontinuity in a given network system, which multiplies and varies the possible connections. Burt (2005: 18) insists on the importance of a social focus through which social capital is proliferated, and directed to more rewarding opportunities. Nevertheless, such a porous network conception seems to be a consequence of development in network managing capacity.

Particularly since the 1990s Turkey presents an interesting case in which modernisation has facilitated access of relatively local firms to the global market (Kazgan, 1994). This phenomenon places the Turkish model, where kinship is also based on being from the same geographical origin or from the same ideologically driven association, close to *the strength of weak ties* conception of Granovetter when he asserts that weak ties function in a community as *bridges* with which individuals form new relationships (Granovetter, 1973: 1375). In the case of Turkey, the interplay of kinship relationships and business relationships presents a combination of entirely structured relationships and the operation of personal interest in the business world. The relative lack of correlation between possession of economic capital and the tendencies to develop international network relationships in our study can be considered as an indication confirming the importance of *weak ties*. *Weak ties* emerge from only individual education, and are not a function of a business tradition or possession of considerable amount of economic capital that offer to the social capital owner a series of possibilities to bridge different types of networks, in that case from local and limited background to an exclusively international level networking.

Granovetter points out that only the weak ties that offer bridges between network segments can function as a cohesive force (Granovetter, 1983: 229). We explore the significance of education as a weak tie in the Turkish context in our study. Consequently, as Granovetter (1983: 208) underlined, 'only bridging weak ties are of special value to individuals; the significance of weak ties is that they are far more likely to be bridges than are strong ties'. This seems to be typically the case of most of the functionally set, ad hoc relationships in and through the globally coalescing networks, from Internet-driven ties to international capitalistic alliances.

The network theory developed by Granovetter challenged both self-centred theories and structural approaches, while trying to fuse their contradicting assumptions. However, Pierre Bourdieu's theory of culture and capital provides us with rich possibilities for conceptualising Turkish business elites' transformation, which, beside the network connections, has significant cultural implications. According to Bourdieu, power is diffused throughout cultural products and their uses by sufficiently motivated actors to establish their own domination over other individuals and groups. Studying Bourdieusian concepts of different forms of capital and the field allows a reading of organisations as webs of social, economic and cultural relations which share power and resources among their members (Ozbilgin and Tatli, 2005). Social action is thus conditioned in more or less determined sets of rules of the *art of domination*. These are called *fields* (*champs*). Individuals, though they are agents with free will, are submitted to a process of domination, which then creates a series of multiple strategies of distinction; three of these are the most relevant ones here: diet, presentation and culture (Bourdieu, 1979: 204–5). This is why we tried to depict some practices of Turkish business elites, related to their use of cultural tools. The refined tastes of business elites in Turkey commonly involve sporting activities as horse riding, golf, sailing and cultural activities such as collecting art work and antiques (see, for example, Kıraç, 2006; Eczacıbaşı, 2010). Culture as an autonomous battlefield has been conceptualised by Bourdieu as a form of capital.

The concept of capital as a Marxist notion has long been regarded merely as an economic concept. Nevertheless, Bourdieu asserts that there exist in fact, beside the well-known economic capital, two other types which determine social action: social and cultural capital. Both are socially conditioned in fields where the individual is inserted through class ties and especially education (Bourdieu and Passeron, 1970). As the notion of social capital manifested a wide range of theoretical uses, it also resulted in a certain conceptual ambiguity. James Coleman (1988) is one of the thinkers who tried to clarify the notion of social capital, while defining it by its functions. Coleman argues that it is not a unique entity, but a plurality of entities that have two elements in common: their dependence on structural characteristics and their function as catalyst for certain actions of individuals (Coleman, 1988: 98). Social capital is constituted in a variety of ways, from formal school origin, especially university as a cultural system, capable of creating and attributing identities to its members (Considine, 2006) to clan associations (Wong, 2007). This is also done at the high-school level in the Turkish context (Yamak, 1998). We explore the significance of social capital in the access to different levels of business networks. We investigate the social ties granted by specific alumni affiliations as well as place of birth and residence.

As for cultural capital, Bourdieu asserts that it is an instrument of power at individual level under a form of a set of intellectual qualifications produced by the familial environment and the school system (Bourdieu, 1979). The very quality of persistence of culture through its potential to become a myth, a fabrication, a mystification (Sahlins, 1999: 403) helps also to explain its conversion into a socially determined asset. In a globally managed economic order, business interaction has become, as never before, a fluent and culturally supported process, in which cultural capital not only plays a major part but gradually increases its variety. Basic factors such as education and foreign language acquisition (Ward, 2009) function as propelling effects in actual global business practices. Indeed, globalisation had a deep impact on the reconfiguration of cooperative models and their diffusion throughout cultures of the world (Rivera, 2004). We explore cultural capital as a resource for accessing local, national and international networks.

The aim of this study is thus to examine how individual members of the new corporate elite in Turkey mobilise their varied forms of resources, or as Bourdieu would call them, economic, social and cultural forms of capital, in order to realise the elite's ambitions to attain and hold on to certain positions of power and influence in business society in Turkey and internationally.

Methodology

Drawing upon the view that 'elites are those groups that hold or exercise domination within a society or within a particular area of life' (Scott, 2008: 32) we have defined business elites as the leading executive figures (such as chairperson, vice-chairperson and CEO) of the business groups whose affiliates are listed among the largest companies in Turkey. This definition is also consistent with previous studies which perceive the corporate elite as 'a configuration of capitalists (major shareholders and top executives) and organic intellectuals occupying positions of ultimate authority within leading corporations' (Carroll, 2008: 47).

We gathered a triangulated qualitative data set, including interviews, non-participant observation and documentary searches (Eisenhardt, 1989) during this study. We developed our semi-structured questionnaire based on literature and feedback from audiences of our presentations and pre-testing. A total of 60 open-ended interviews were conducted with key informants with executive roles such as CEO, chair or vice-chair of the board in each company. Respondents were assured that their responses would be kept strictly confidential and they would only be used for scientific research. Interviews lasted typically two to three hours, of which 58 were audio-taped. Only in two cases were we not allowed to tape and we took detailed notes during the interview instead. Field notes were taken independently by each researcher on the observations. A wide range of archival documentary materials were collected regarding each interviewee and his/her company. Since in this chapter our focus is on the integration of the new elites into the business community, we have used the data of the elites whose companies made their first appearances among the largest enterprises after the adoption of liberalisation policy in Turkey in 1980. Thus, a total of 30 interviews were used in this research.

The data were collected starting from October 2009 to October 2010. We have checked non-response bias in two ways. First we have contrasted earlier respondents with the later ones. Second, we have also contrasted non-respondents with the respondents on key dimensions such as total sales, export ratio and geographical location of their companies. No significant difference was detected between the contrasted groups of respondents.

Multiple correspondence analysis (MCA) is conducted to analyse the data. It can be considered as a generalisation of simple correspondence analysis. The aim of MCA is to explore the relationships between three or more categorical variables and to discover the underlying pattern via a visual map (Greenacre and Blasius, 2006). The similarities and the differences of the variables are summarised in this map where they facilitate the interpretation. In this context, MCA can be regarded as a powerful method due to its visualisation feature.

Variables

The abbreviations of the variables that are used in the figures are presented in parenthesis for each variable.

Integration with the business community is assessed at three levels namely international, national and local:

- International integration: This is a dummy variable taking the value of 1 (Int:Yes) if the person is a member of international business associations and 0 otherwise (Int:No).
- National integration: This is a dummy variable taking the value of 1 (Nat:Yes) if the person is a member of nationwide business associations and 0 otherwise (Nat:No).
- Local integration: This is a dummy variable taking the value of 1 (Loc:Yes) if the person is a member of regional or smaller district based business associations and 0 otherwise (Loc:No).

Economic capital, which is highly emphasised by Marx (1956) and less so by Bourdieu, is investigated by three different variables: total sales of the holding company, family capital (Marx, 1956) and total foreign sales of the holding:

- Total sales of the holding: Four categories of total sales are identified. The first one includes the companies with total sales less than or equal to 100 million US dollars (Sales < 1). The second group comprises those with total sales more than 100 million up to 500 million US dollars (Sales:10). In the third group total sales ranges from more than 500 million and up to one billion (Sales:50) and finally holdings whose sales exceed one billion US dollars (Sales > 1) constitute the fourth group.
- Family capital: This is a dummy variable taking the value of 1 (Family:Yes) if the person is a member of a wealthy family and 0 otherwise (Family:No).
- Total foreign sales: We have also wanted to check the origin of sales in terms of different markets which may insulate the company from the economic and political inconsistencies of the local market. There are three categories for this variable. 'Export oriented companies' are the ones which export more than 50% of their production (Export:Export). 'Locally oriented' companies export less than 50% of their production (Export:Local). Finally, 'no export' indicates the firms which do not export at all (Export:No).

Social capital is another capital stressed by Bourdieu (1979). It is assessed by birth place (Urry, 1995), the city where the elite lives (Castells, 1998), age (Rahikainen, 2001), continuity of the business (Sennett, 1998) and high school type (Yamak, 1998).

- Birth place: This is assessed along three categories which are the largest three cities, Istanbul, Ankara and Izmir (Birth:I&A&I), other cities (Birth: Other) and villages (Birth:Village).
- The city where the elite lives: his is assessed along two categories which are the largest three cities (City: I&A&I) and other cities (City:Other).
- Age: This is a grouping of birth decade of the person: the 1920s (Age:20s), 1930s (Age:30s), 1940s (Age:40s), 1950s (Age:50s), 1960s (Age:60s), 1970s (Age:70s).
- Continuity of the business: This is a dummy variable taking the value of 1 (Business:Yes) if the person's family had a similar business in the past and 0 otherwise (Business:No).
- High school type: This is a dummy variable taking the value of 1 (High:Yes) if the person is graduated from a prestigious high school in Turkey and 0 otherwise (High:No).

Cultural capital is very much emphasised by Bourdieu (1979) in explaining domination. In this study, it is assessed by sports habits (Bourdieu, 1979), cuisine preferences (Bourdieu, 1979), painting and antiques collection (Bourdieu, 1979), education level (Bourdieu, and Passeron, 1970) and foreign languages mastered by the elite (Ward, 2009).

Table 9.1   Distributive characteristics of participants

Business association	N	Gender		Top management position in the association
		F	M	
International	3	0	3	3
National	17	2	15	9
Local	11	1	10	7

- Sports habits: We have used Bourdieu's classification of elite and non-elite sports.
- Cuisine preferences: We differentiated between international and Turkish cuisine preferences.
- Painting collection: We have checked whether the person is a painting collector or not.
- Antiques collection: We have checked whether the person is an antiques collector or not.
- Education level: This indicates the last diploma obtained by the individual. It is assessed along six dimensions, namely primary school (Edu:1), secondary school (Edu:2), high school (Edu:3), bachelor (Edu:4), master (Edu:5) and PhD (Edu:6).
- Foreign languages: This variable indicates the number of languages (other than Turkish) that the person knows. (No:1) signifies one foreign language, (No:2) two foreign languages, (No:3) three foreign languages and so on. (No:0) implies that the person does not know any foreign language.

Distributive characteristics of the participants are presented in Table 9.1. The members of international, national and local business associations are respectively 3, 17 and 11. In our sample, there is no female participant in the international associations. There are 2 and 1 female members in national and local business organisations respectively. The participants with an international membership are also actively involved in the top management of these associations. More than half of the participants hold a top management position in national and local business organisations. While there are overlaps in international and national memberships, none of the international association members are affiliated with local organisations. While almost half of local business associations' members in our study are also affiliated with the national networks, none of them are present at international level. Only three of the national business network members are present at international level.

Results

We find that the new elites in Turkey are integrated across the larger business community at the international, national and local level. We had participants from these three different levels in our study with distinct configurations of member characteristics in terms of their capital at all three levels.

Our first finding is that local and international networks are more accessible to new business elites than national networks. In order to access national networks new business elites require higher levels of economic capital. Our second finding is related to cultural capital. We observe that new business elites in Turkey do not have elite tastes. Their tastes are rather common. This may be explained by the fact that they have only recently joined elites. However, the second dimension of cultural capital measured in terms of education and foreign language acquisition provides interesting insights. It appears that education and mastering foreign languages have been instrumental in allowing access to elite status in Turkey.

The findings suggest that there is an association between economic, social and to a certain extent cultural capital of the new elites and their integration with the business community at international, national and local level. Unfortunately the results for some variables of the cultural capital do not indicate a particular pattern. Hence, we have only included in the figures cultural variables displaying a sensible grouping, namely education level and foreign languages. So, no differentiation is observed along the variables assessing tastes such as diet and sports preferences or arts collection. Therefore, one of the interesting findings of the study is that elites who are members of different levels of business association do not display differences along some of the forms of cultural capital involving sporting habits, diet preferences and habits of collecting paintings and antiques. Those are variables directly related to the tastes of the individual. However, new elites do differ along other forms of cultural capital such as education level and foreign languages. So, it is also worth noting that their differentiation along education and foreign language knowledge is not reflected in their tastes. Even if the new elites possess a higher education level and they master several languages, these cultural assets are not necessarily accompanied by so-called 'refined tastes'.

In the following section we present the major findings of multiple correspondence analysis in relation to international business association members (Figure 9.1). These are the characteristics (as assessed by the capitals) of the international business association affiliated participants.

International business association membership

Figure 9.1 displays the findings in relation to international business association membership and the economic, social and cultural capital of the new elites. International business association affiliation is observed only in three cases among new elites. However, all three hold top executive roles in these institutions. It is also interesting to note that all three individuals who are integrated into international business associations have spent long years abroad, namely in Germany. Two of them even took their university degree there. Therefore, residing in a foreign country for a long time appears to be an important factor for international association membership. This residence appears also to motivate self-identification with the culture of the host country. The affiliates of international business organisations in our sample seem to identify themselves more with German culture.

> 'I am involved with business associations more in Germany than in Turkey ... I have found many German–Turkish Business Associations ... I have also established and institutionalised many Turkish–German congresses.'

One other member has claimed that he is not a Turk in business life since his work values are more aligned with foreigners which makes it hard to become part of any collaboration and social affiliation in Turkey. The youngest member of this category also maintained that he feels 'more like German'. Among these three participants being German is associated with punctuality, precision and professionalism.

Affiliation with an international business association seems to be at the top of a presumed hierarchy of business associations. The quote of a member affiliated with international business organisations delineates the potential reach and power of these members:

> 'I work in close cooperation with German top political persons and act as a liaison to promote the links between them and their Turkish counterparts.'

Economic capital

Given the small number of international association members, this group seems to be quite varied in terms of their positions. Findings indicate with a pattern of absence of family wealth among international association members that economic capital is not a must to become integrated into international business networks. This seems to support the importance of weak ties in the globalisation process.

Social capital

The findings regarding social capital are consistent with the above results. The most striking finding is about intergenerational business continuity within the immediate family. New business elites with international business institution membership are likely to be entrepreneurs since they have not inherited their businesses from their family. They have started their own businesses. In two cases the families never did possess a business. This means that they did not benefit from the social ties of a previous business owned by their family. In fact, when we go back to the database, we observe that two persons had parents who were not previously involved in any business either in the same sector or in a different one. In only one case the father

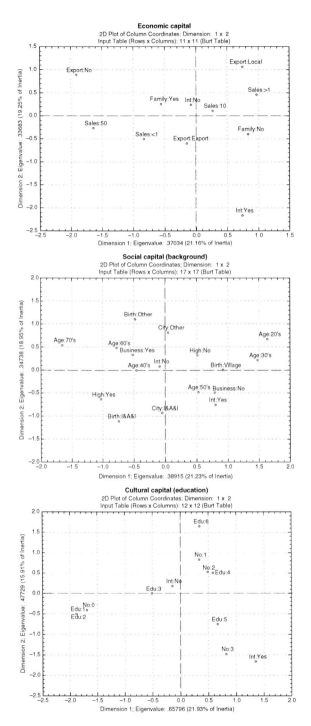

Figure 9.1 International business association membership and the capital possessed by the elite

was also an entrepreneur. However, the person we interviewed had started his own business and had not pursued the work of his father: 'I wanted to prove that I was capable of founding my own business.'

On the other hand, it is also worth noting that new business elite members who are not affiliated with an international organization are closely associated with business continuity which appears to be an important differentiating factor between the members and non-members.

Although we could not detect a connection with birth place, new business elites with international business institution membership are likely to have been born around the 1950s. No association could be detected with graduation from the prestigious high schools, meaning that they do not benefit from the social networks of these schools.

Cultural capital

Again no difference could be detected in terms of tastes. However, there are significant differences between international versus local and national network members along the cultural dimensions related to education. Strong associations are observed between international association membership and education level. Education facilitates new business elites to access international business networks. Members of the new business elite, who are integrated with the international business community, have higher educational qualifications than traditional business elites. All persons in this category (new business elites that are connected with international networks) are university graduates. This group is also associated with a master's degree. Similarly, they speak three languages, scoring on the average higher than those who are not affiliated with international associations.

Turkish business people, especially those with a high degree of education, develop the ability to link themselves to these structurally weak, but fluently bridging ties to the international level, through business associations.

In the following section we present the major findings of multiple correspondence analysis in relation to national business association members (Figure 9.2). These are the characteristics (the capital) of the national business association affiliated participants.

National business association membership

Figure 9.2 displays the findings in relation to national business association membership and economic, social and cultural capital of the new elite. Members of national business associations (17 persons) constitute the largest group of whom more than half hold top executive roles in those organisations.

In Turkey, national level associations are very active in creating industrial policies and lobbying thus negotiating with the ministers and other government officials. As several of the new elite members in our sample have put it, 'such organizations at national level are among the best and most effective occasions to approach government officials'. To establish links with the state

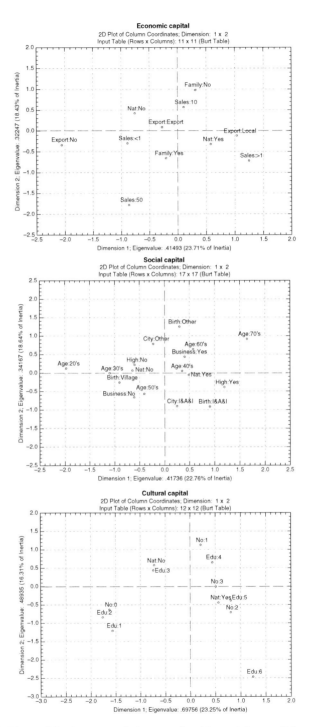

Figure 9.2 National business association membership and the capital possessed by the elite

is an important act in the Turkish business system since the national level organisations are influential actors which could act as creditor, competitor or regulator in business life and could protect the companies from foreign competition (Bugra, 1994). Therefore to become integrated to national level business institutions may also be interpreted as a key act to develop and protect the business. Such an affiliation with its potential of supplying critical resources and links may also necessitate a threshold level of characteristics on the part of the business elite. We may expect business people to have a specific bundle of economic, social and cultural capital in becoming integrated into the national level business organisations and thus to display both strong and weak ties.

Economic capital

National business association membership seems to be related to larger sales scores. Therefore the new elites with a national membership are likely to come from the largest companies, thus possessing considerable economic power. This economic capital is also associated with the level of exports. In the national network category, there may be more people who own companies with mainly Turkish market orientation exporting less than 50% of their production.

Social capital

Findings point to a limited association between membership of national business organisations and social capital. New elite members who are affiliated with national business associations are likely to have business continuity. This means that there is a business tradition in the family which may provide them social links to the business community.

They are likely to be born between the 1940s and 1960s. They seem to be relatively younger than the non-members. An older member of the elite claimed: 'We send youngsters to the associations. It requires too much activity and I am old now.'

It is also interesting to note that new elites who are not members of national business associations tend to be born in villages around the 1930s. It appears that birth place and time are differentiating factors between members and non-members. Being born in a village appears among the factors that may limit social networks and related social capital to access the national level business organisations.

Cultural capital

While no difference could be detected along the factor of tastes, significant differences are observed along the cultural dimensions related to education among elites affiliated with national business organisations and those who are not. Affiliated ones are likely to have a master's degree and to be able to speak two to three foreign languages. Again, the non-members are associated with a high school degree.

In the following section we present the major findings of multiple correspondence analysis in relation to local business association members (Figure 9.3). These are the characteristics (the capital) of the local business association affiliated participants.

Local business association membership

Figure 9.3 displays the findings in relation to local business association membership and the economic, social and cultural capital of the new elite.

Local level business organisation affiliation appears to be at the lower end of the hierarchy. A limited number of forms of capital may be associated with local business organisation membership. In fact while no economic capital could be associated with it, the associated social and cultural capital appeared to be limited both in number and scope. Local network appears as a first step in becoming integrated into business circles. When we asked one of the locally networked new business elite members why he was not part of the largest national business association he replied that 'It was too big for me.'

Economic capital

There is no significant differentiation in terms of economic capital among the members and non-members of the local business associations.

Social capital

Being born and living in cities other than the largest three are among the major differentiating factors between the members and non-members of the local business organisations. The geographical surrounding constitutes the social capital. While the participants affiliated with the local associations are more likely to come from smaller cities in terms of both birth place and residence, non-members are likely to live in the largest cities.

Cultural capital

Again no difference could be detected along the dimension of tastes. However, there are significant differences along the cultural dimensions related to education. New elite members who are affiliated with local business associations are likely to have an undergraduate degree. They are able to speak one foreign language. Again when we contrast the members and non-members of local business associations we observe that non-members are better educated and they are able to speak several languages. This confirms our view that local business associations which in fact operate at the city or neighbourhood level are at the bottom of the business organisations' hierarchy.

Conclusion

We have shown that the new Turkish corporate elites make intensive use of economic, social and cultural relationships in their way from local to

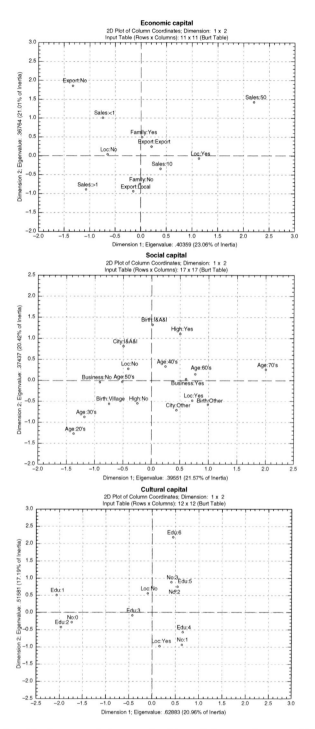

Figure 9.3 Local business association membership and the capital possessed by the elite

international business settings and seek integration into the business community through international, national and local networks. In this study, we explored the constitution of the new Turkish business elites in terms of their varied forms of resources. The findings of the study delineate differences in the overall member characteristics of three types of networks. It is suggested that there is an association between economic, social and to a certain extent cultural forms of capital of the new elite and their integration with the business community at international, national and local level.

Education was an important cultural resource which had significant explanatory power in new business elites' access to international networks. The relative lack of correlation between possession of economic capital and the tendency to develop international network relationships can be considered as an indication confirming the importance of *weak ties* (those issuing from only individual education, and which are not a function of a business tradition or possession of considerable amount of economic capital) that offer to the social capital owner a series of possibilities to bridge different types of networks, in this case from local and limited background to an exclusively international level networking.

We observe that business elites who join international networks are not necessarily those who have a business heritage from their families; on the contrary, they are economically uprooted individuals, having recently ascended in the social pyramid, due to their life opportunities triggered by education. Such a model of social mobility confirms, in a different way, that in a highly fluid world, social and cultural capital may play a crucial part which can even eradicate, in some cases, the predominance of economic capital. Yet when the new elites cannot access the international level, they are limited in their local scale. Again, education determines not only the social function of the individual, but also his or her entire set of networks, which affect, in fact, their access to the international or national level business relationships. As for the largest part of the new business elite who are affiliated with the national associations, though they categorically possess a well set-out economic capital and usually considerably developed social and education-based cultural capital, they tend to act rather at the national scale. Among them, there are a few cases of complete integration in international networks, but these are exceptions. To access international networks seems to be related to social and cultural capital. Furthermore, a previous work life in a foreign country appears to be an important factor in becoming actively involved in international business associations.

Therefore, in Turkey today, new elites seem to benefit from social and cultural capital which seem to be more important than economic capital, which is often taken for granted. Integration with the business networks is associated with educational background which facilitates access to international or large-scale national networks. Education functions as a kind of transition opportunity at the junction of life trajectories of different origins, while accelerating the capability to establish new *bridges* between unconnected networks. The higher the education the wider is the access of business elites from local to international networks. Briefly, education and mastering foreign languages appears to extend network opportunities for the new elite from a local scale to an international scale. It is also worth noting that holding a university diploma and mastering a foreign language seem to be the necessary baseline for every network affiliation. This seems to be the minimum that the members are expected to have in each type of business network. University diploma and foreign language knowledge may even cancel out the disadvantages that the lack of economic capital brings about. One other interesting point is that the new elites' social surrounding in terms of the city of residence or birth is not limited to the largest three cities. Elites originating from other cities are able to join different business networks at international and national level. However, city of residence or birth may also act as a constraining factor. Being from a village may limit access to the national business organisations as seen in Figure 9.2.

One other interesting finding of the study is about tastes. Even if the new elites possess higher education levels and they master several languages, these cultural assets are not necessarily accompanied by so called 'refined tastes' as defined by Bourdieu. They do not seem to collect paintings or antiques as the established elites do. They do not seem to be open to different diet options either.

In Turkey a wide interest in global integration is observed, not only among business elites but also among a significant section of the intellectuals, in explicit contradiction with their counterparts in old Europe, such as the French attitude (Schmidt, 2007: 998). The case of Turkey in the globalisation process offers a variety of particularities, together with similarities with other experiences of emerging countries. Indeed, the new urban dynamism, especially observed in metropolitan peripheries, proves, beside its numerous problems, a potential for global connectivity (Ayata, 2008: 50–1). The progressive establishment of new forms of adaptation to the global market is realised through cultural and ideological syntheses between conservative and modernist historical forces in the secular Turkish context. Though this proves the potentialities that Islam offers (Stone, 2002a: 125), it also displays a clear divergence from non-secular examples of Islamic nations such as the neo-liberal Indonesian experience which is challenged by the preserved local interests (Hadiz and Robison, 2005: 236). Yet, Turkish integration with the world and especially the European economy is not a recent fact; it has strong historical roots that make this relationship continuous (Stone 2002b: 194–8). As a typical indication of the rise of global economic integration, metropolitan areas in Turkey present the scope of a more or less 'fragmented glocal city' (Swyngedouw and Kaïka, 2003: 12), where the business elite is growing due to the advantages of such an articulation of the local and global, and conservatism serves as a protecting tissue against the fast-growing corporate mentality.

In our research, we stress that newly emerging economic elites are still in a phase of constituting rather traditionally defined networks, and thus a set of well-known relationships. But the more they involve themselves in internationally driven business, the more they seem to become integrated in a network of structural holes. Our chapter demonstrates that the new Turkish business elites find it easier to access international networks than national networks. The former are about merit based on education, experience and skills while success in joining national networks may be more related to economic capital as well as religio-national kinship and ideological ties. In a way, internationalisation liberates and gives a renewed lease of life to the human capital of Turkish business elites.

There are several limitations of the study. The first one is the small sample size. The second is the selection of the cultural capital variables in relation to tastes. We could have identified a number of tastes which are unique to the Turkish context instead, and that might have presented us with an altogether different picture.

Acknowledgement

The authors gratefully acknowledge the support provided by Galatasaray University through research funding under grant no. 09.502.003.

References

Ayata, S. (2008) 'Migrants and Changing Urban Periphery: Social Relations, Cultural Diversity and the Public Space in Istanbul's New Neighbourhoods', *International Migration*, 46(3): 27–64.

Bourdieu, P. (1979) *La Distinction: Critique sociale du jugement* (Paris: Minuit).

Bourdieu, P. and Passeron, J.-C. (1970) *La Reproduction : Éléments pour une théorie du système d'enseignement* (Paris: Minuit).

Bugra, A. (1994) *State and Business in Modern Turkey: A Comparative Study* (Albany: State University of New York Press).

Burt, R. S. (2005) *Brokerage and Closure: An Introduction to Social Capital* (Oxford: Oxford University Press).

Carroll, W. K. (2008) 'The Corporate Elite and the Transformation of Finance Capital: A View from Canada'. In M. Savage and K. Williams (eds.), *Remembering Elites* (London: Blackwell), 44–63.

Castells, M. (1998) *The Rise of the Network Society* (New York: Blackwell).

Coleman, J. S. (1988) 'Social Capital in the Creation of Human Capital', *American Journal of Sociology*, 94, Supplement: Organizations and Institutions: Sociological and Economic Approaches to the Analysis of Social Structure: 95–120.

Considine, M. (2006) 'Theorizing the University as a Cultural System: Distinctions, Identities, Emergencies', *Educational Theory*, 56(3): 255–70.

Eczacıbaşı, S. (2010) *Çağrışımlar, Tanıklıklar, Dostluklar* (Istanbul: Remzi).

Eisenhardt, K. M. (1989) 'Building Theories from Case Study Research', *Academy of Management Review*, 14(4): 532–50.

Greenacre, M. and Blasius, J. (2006) *Multiple Correspondence Analysis and Related Methods* (New York: Chapman & Hall).

Granovetter, M. (1973) 'The Strength of Weak Ties', *American Journal of Sociology*, 78(6): 1360–80.

Granovetter, M. (1983) 'The Strength of Weak Ties: A Network Theory Revisited', *Sociological Theory*, 1: 201–33.

Granovetter, M. (1985) 'Economic Action and Social Structure: The Problem of Embededness', *American Journal of Sociology*, 91(3): 481–510.

Granovetter, M. (2008) *Sociologie Économique* (Paris: Seuil).

Hadiz, V. R. and Robison, R. (2005) 'Neo-liberal Reforms and Illiberal Consolidations: The Indonesian Paradox', *Journal of Development Studies*, 41(2): 220–41.

Kazgan, G. (1994) *Yeni Ekonomik Düzende Turkiye'nin Yeri* [The position of Turkey in the new economic order] (Istanbul: Altın Kitaplar Yayınevi).

Kiraç, S. (2006) *Ömrümden Uzun İdeallerim Var* (Istanbul: Suna Inan Kırac Vakfı).

Marx, K. (1956) *Le capital* (Paris: Presses Universitaires de France).

Ozbilgin, M. and Tatli, A. (2005) 'Understanding Bourdieu's Contribution to Organization and Management Studies', *Academy of Management Review*, 30(4): 855–69.

Polanyi, K. (1944) *La Grande Transformation: Aux Origines Politiques et Économiques de Notre Temps* (Paris: Gallimard).

Rahikainen, M. (2001) 'Ageing Men and Women in the Labour Market: Continuity and Change', *Scandinavian Journal of History*, 26: 297–314.

Rivera, W. S. (2004) 'Elites and the Diffusion of Foreign Models in Russia', *Political Studies*, 54: 43–62.

Sahlins, M. (1999) 'Two or Three Things That I Know About Culture', *Journal of the Royal Anthropology Institute*, 5: 399–421.

Schmidt, V. A. (2007) 'Trapped by their Ideas: French Elites' Discourses of European Integration and Globalization', *Journal of European Public Policy*, 14(7): 992–1009.

Scott, J. (2008) 'Taking Stock of Elites: Recognizing Historical Changes'. In M. Savage and K. Williams (eds.), *Remembering Elites* (London: Blackwell), 27–43.

Sennett, R. (1998) *The Corrosion of Character: The Personal Consequences of Work in the New Capitalism* (New York: W. W. Norton).

Steiner, P. (2002) 'Encastrements et sociologie économique'. In Isabelle Huault (ed.), *La construction sociale de l'entreprise* (Colombelles: EMS).

Stone, L. A. (2002a) 'The Islamic Crescent: Islam, Culture and Globalization', *Innovation*, 15(2): 121–31.

Stone, L. A. (2002b) 'Late Ottoman and Modern Turkish Perceptions of Europe: Continuity and Change', *Turkish Studies*, 13(2): 181–99.

Swyngedouw, E. and Kaïka, M. (2003) 'The Making of "Glocal" Urban Modernities: Exploring the Cracks in the Mirror', *City*, 7(1): 5–21.

Urry, J. (1995) *Consuming Places* (London: Routledge).

Ward, J. H. (2009) 'Acquisitions Globalized: The Foreign Language Acquisitions Experience in a Research Library', *Library Resources & Technical Services*, 53(2): 86–93.

Wong, S. (2007) 'Partner or Pariah? Building Social Capital with Clan Associations in Hong Kong', *Chinese Sociology and Anthropology*, 40(1): 54–71.

Yamak, S. (1998) 'Seksenlerden doksanlara Türkiye'deki yönetici elitler: Eğitim durumlarında neler değişti', *Amme İdaresi Dergisi*, 31(4): 65–77.

10
Board Directors as Elites in the Context of International Joint Ventures

Jelena Petrovic, Nada Kakabadse and Andrew Kakabadse

Introduction: IJV board directors as elites

Forbes and Milliken (1999: 493) characterise boards of directors as 'large, elite and episodic decision making groups that face complex tasks pertaining to strategic-issue processing'. From an individual director perspective some scholars have argued that individuals join boards for financial remuneration, prestige and contacts that may prove useful in the future and to promote upper-class cohesion creating a business elite (Useem, 1984; Zajac 1988). For example, according to the reputation hypothesis, entering in the corporate elite has a positive impact on firms' value (Phan et al., 2003). As a group, it is up to the corporate elite to ensure good corporate governance. At the same time, the concentration of corporate control in the hands of relatively small, often homogeneous and closed corporate elites has long been recognised as a democratic difficulty for capitalism.

Throughout the twentieth century, big business in the Western industrialised world has been organised in national business communities whose foundational elements were corporate board 'interlocks', where the corporate elite of directors sit on multiple boards. Within the growing institutional power of financial institutions, corporate elites are often accused of possessing too much, uncontrolled power. According to a political model, firm behaviour responds to the interests and beliefs of the dominant coalition (Kakabadse et al., 2004). However, whilst organisations are ruled by political elites, or dominant coalitions, these elites do not last due to inter-elite conflicts that provide impetus for change (Selznick, 1957; Pareto, 1968; Kakabadse et al., 2004).

Although rules and legislation are used to confine and discipline corporations and the corporate elite, many EU economies endorse a principle-based code of good governance, which leaves room for manoeuvring and flexibility. The dominant, shareholder-oriented form of capitalism promoted the international scope in strategy, finance and operations that underscores the potential importance of the internationalisation of business and finance (i.e. globalisation) and in turn creates corporate directors who are less embedded in national elite networks. The shift from mono-ethnic nationalism to multi-ethnic elite is particularly true in international joint ventures (IJVs).

The role of a board director in an IJV has been considered as important and potentially very complex due to the unique governance requirements of this form of organisation (Shenkar and Zeira, 1992; Carver, 2000; Garrow et al., 2000; Gong et al., 2001; Child and Rodrigues, 2003; Bamford and Ernst, 2005). IJV ownership structure (the division of equity investment in the IJV among the partners, as specified by the IJV contract), directly affects representation on the IJV board in terms of the number of IJV directors the partner company is entitled to appoint relative to the total size of the board (Zeira and Shenkar, 1990; Garrow et al., 2000). IJV board directors are responsible for protecting their parent company's interests in the IJV, which may not always be in accord with interests of the other IJV parent (Shenkar and Zeira, 1992; Garrow et al., 2000; Luo et al., 2001). This combination of the multiple partners' agendas and shared ownership in IJVs points to the complex and potentially problematic nature of an IJV board director's role in comparison to a board director in a more 'traditional' form of organisation.

However, little evidence exists that focuses on the role and contribution of IJV board directors. Such a situation could be explained by the fact that board directors represent elites who, by their very nature, 'establish barriers that set their members apart from the rest of society' (Hertz and Imber, 1993: 3) and as such, could be difficult to access (Groot and Merchant, 2000). Hence, it is perhaps not surprising that research on boards of directors has usually had a low response rate, often lower than 20% (Minichilli et al., 2009). The task of conducting research on elites becomes even more challenging in the international business context (Welch et al., 2002).

Based on qualitative exploratory case studies of board directors from three IJVs, this chapter presents the empirical evidence concerning board directors as elites in the context of IJVs. After a consideration of methodology adopted for the research, the chapter presents the research findings that concern IJV director attributes that derive from their 'elite status' and which have emerged as influencing director role and contribution to board effectiveness. This is followed by an illustration of the learning experience of dealing with board directors as elite informants in international business research. The chapter concludes by discussing the theoretical, practical and methodological implications of the research.

Methodology

Due to the limited amount of existing theory in the area and in response to the call in the literature for researchers to 'get beyond the boardroom door' (Samra-Fredericks, 2000), we adopted an exploratory case study research design. Since the focus of the study was on individual director role (as a part of a wider inquiry into IJV director contribution to board effectiveness), the unit of analysis and therefore the case in this research was the individual IJV board director.

The participants included thirteen board directors – foreign and local representatives – from three Serbian–foreign (two Serbian–German and one Serbian–Italian) joint ventures based in Serbia. The directors are members of a multi-tier board consisting of the Assembly, Managing board, Supervisory board and the CEO. No further details about directors or their respective joint ventures could be disclosed here for confidentiality reasons.

Semi-structured interview was the main data collection method used in this research. This is a useful method of gaining access to business elites in an international context (Welch et al., 2002). Wherever possible, information obtained from an interview was triangulated with other data collection methods/sources of evidence. Informal observation, secondary research of the literature and an examination of documentation (e.g. press releases about directors, their boards and IJVs, and company documents provided by the informants) served in the interest of triangulation to corroborate the evidence from other sources.

A data analysis strategy suggested by Eisenhardt (1989) and Miles and Huberman (1994) was followed in analysing the results of the study. This involved a thematic/conceptual analysis of data for each individual case and then comparison was made of the emerging themes and subthemes from each individual case across cases in search for the themes that 'replicate' across cases.

The use of a qualitative case study approach for this research confirmed the existence of numerous issues associated with conducting qualitative research on elites in the international business context (Vallaster and Koll, 2002; Welch et al., 2002), as will be discussed in more detail later in the chapter.

The next section focuses on the research findings related to director attributes that emerged as influencing director role and contribution, which derive from the director's 'elite status'.

Research findings

Participants' 'elite status'

The previous literature points to certain dimensions that indicate the 'elite status' of research informants, such as a position of high authority in the organisation, considerable industry experience, a broad network of relationships, and functional responsibility in an area which enjoys high status in accordance with corporate values (Hambrick and Finkelstein, 1987; Pettigrew, 1992; Pettigrew and McNulty, 1995; Welch et al., 2002). It could be argued that participants in this research 'score' high regarding each of these dimensions, as all but one director sits on their respective partner company's board and had been previously working together in their respective partner companies. The directors have considerable industry experience and most of them have known other representatives from their company for a long time (some for more than two decades). The participants who are the Serbian partner representatives in their respective IJVs are considered as key experts in law and economy in Serbia, whereas some of the international partner representatives enjoy international reputation in their fields. Details about the participant profile in terms of their 'elite status' are presented in Box 10.1.

Box 10.1: Participants 'elite status'

DIRECTOR 1 represents the Serbian partner on the IJV1 Assembly. Apart from this governance role, she also holds the management role in IJV1. In addition, she is Chairman of the Serbian partner's Assembly. With a background in political studies, she used to work for the Serbian partner company until the IJV creation and has known the other Serbian partner representatives on the IJV1 board for more than 25 years.

DIRECTOR 2 is the Serbian partner's representative on the Supervisory board of IJV1. He is also a member of the Serbian partner company's Managing board. He used to work in the Serbian partner's company as Financial Director until the IJV creation and was involved in the IJV negotiations.

DIRECTOR 3 is CEO in IJV1 and also a member of the Serbian partner's Managing board. He spent most of his life working abroad. Due to his family background and international experience he possesses a broad network of relationships which have been of crucial importance for his role in the IJV negotiations and his selection to the position of the IJV CEO.

DIRECTOR 4 is Vice-Chairman of the Managing board in IJV1 and the Company Solicitor as well. He also holds a role of Vice-Chairman of the Serbian partner's Managing board. He is a writer and a well-known solicitor in Serbia, and generally, a person very much involved in politics. He was actively involved in the IJV negotiations process.

DIRECTOR 5 is Deputy CEO and the German partner representative on the Managing board of IJV1, as well as a member of the German partner's Managing board. He has a strong industry background and has known the other German partner representatives for a number of years.

DIRECTOR 6 is the German partner representative on the Managing board of IJV1. He is also a member of the German partner's Managing board and holds the role of Chief Financial Controller for the German partner's South Eastern European operations as well. Moreover, he is

Chairman of the Managing board of another IJV that the German partner has in Serbia.

DIRECTOR 7 is CEO of IJV2 and the Serbian partner representative on the Managing board of IJV2. Before the IJV creation, he worked in the Serbian partner company for more than 20 years, as Director for Personnel and Legal Matters. As a lawyer by profession, he was involved in writing the IJV contract. He is the only participant who is not a member of his parent company's board.

DIRECTOR 8 is the Italian partner representative on the Managing board of IJV2. He is also Managing board member in another IJV that the Italian partner has in another country, and sits on the Italian partner's Managing board as Director for Strategic Development. Before joining the Italian partner's company, he briefly worked for the Italian university he has his PhD from and then spent seven years working for Confederation of Italian Industry, where he was involved in lobbying with the local governmental authorities in order to make the legislation more favourable for companies. That was where he met DIRECTOR 9 who subsequently 'lured' him to come to work for the Italian partner's company and create business opportunities internationally. Consequently, DIRECTOR 8 played an important role in the IJV negotiations process.

DIRECTOR 9 is the Italian partner's representative and Chairman of the Managing board of IJV2. He is also CEO, Chairman and main shareholder of the Italian partner's company, or, as DIRECTOR 8 comments, he is the 'boss of everything'. In effect, he is the one who set up the Italian partner's company more than 40 years ago. The IJV2 is again primarily a result of his idea and friendship with the Serbian partner's Chairman. Hence he is also the one who, together with the Italian Ambassador in Serbia and the Serbian Minister of International Economic Relations, officially put into operation the IJV's factory, pointing to the possibility that, with the help of the Italian government, other Italian companies will also come to Serbia.

DIRECTOR 10 is CEO and Serbian partner representative on the Managing board of IJV3. In addition, he sits on the Serbian partner's Managing board. Prior to the IJV creation, he used to work in the Serbian partner company as the CEO. Throughout his 20-year career there, he played a key role in developing the company's brand image and competitive position in the market. He was actively involved in the IJV negotiations and has even been considered to be instrumental in establishing IJV3.

DIRECTOR 11 is Chairman of the Supervisory board in IJV3, where he represents the Serbian partner company. He also holds the role of Chairman of the Serbian partner's Supervisory board. He is a renowned economic expert in Serbia and is considered a leading advocate of the privatisation movement. He was the member of the working group involved in making the first Serbian Law on Privatisation. Although DIRECTOR 11's 'main' professional role is that of university professor, he plays a key role in creating cooperation between the country's economists and is Supervisory board member of different companies in Serbia.

DIRECTOR 12 is Chairman of the Managing board in IJV3. He is also the CEO and Chairman of the German partner company's Managing board. Generally, he has enormous experience of being a board member. In the German partner's company Annual Report it is possible to ascertain at least a dozen companies' boards which he sits on. Suffice it to say, he is Chairman of almost half of these boards. He has been involved in the German partner's company business for more than 35 years and seems to be driving alone the most crucial decisions regarding its strategy. He played an active role in the IJV negotiations.

DIRECTOR 13 is the German partner representative on the Managing board in IJV3. He is also Member of the German partner's Managing board. He has more than 15 years' experience in the industry and a board network of relationships internationally.

Source: Compiled by the authors.

The findings showing director attributes that emerged as influencing director role and contribution, which derive from the director's elite status, are presented above. These include IJV board director role in the parent company and in IJV negotiations, education, professional background/experience, reputation and length of relationships.

Role in the partner company and in the IJV negotiations

The findings show that most of the participants sit on their respective parent companies' boards, which confirms the previous literature where most IJV boards of directors were top executives from their parent companies (Salk and Brannen, 2000; Hambrick et al., 2001; Ravasi and Zattoni, 2001; Currall and Inkpen, 2002). The director role in the partner company appears to be a determinant of their role in IJV negotiations. For example, DIRECTOR 11 claims that his role of Chairman of the Serbian' partner's Supervisory board was important for his active role in the IJV negotiations:

'As a member of the Serbian partner's Supervisory board, I had an important role in the IJV negotiations in terms of control of whether what our [Serbian partner company's] Managing board members were doing was in shareholders' interests. Besides the Serbian partner Managing board's suggestions, the Supervisory board members were also giving their opinion regarding the whole IJV concept, including partner selection. In order to be successful in that role, I had to learn the details of the situation. I was working in the team charged with the assessment of various scenarios ... and was completely satisfied that, by the creation of the IJV, the shareholders' interests were not jeopardised. Consequently, the Serbian partner's Assembly made a decision to accept the German partner as the strategic partner for the IJV.' (DIRECTOR 11)

Another example is DIRECTOR 1, who claims that, from the Serbian partner's side, she had almost a decisive role concerning the IJV creation, because of the role she holds on the parent company's board:

'I had a very important role in negotiations – in terms of whether to enter the IJV at all. When I convinced myself that the IJV was a good idea, then, as the Serbian partner's Assembly Chairman, I had to convince the Serbian partner's shareholders about that as well ... I must have made a good case for the IJV, because at the Assembly meeting, the Serbian company's shareholders unanimously accepted the decision to endorse the Serbian partner representatives to continue negotiations with the German partner.' (DIRECTOR 1)

Director role in IJV negotiations further had an impact on their selection for the IJV board director role. For example, given his role in the IJV negotiations and driving of the IJV vision, DIRECTOR 12 considers it 'natural' that he, as opposed to someone else, holds the role of the IJV Managing board Chairman. He also points out that the Serbian partner representatives are very happy that he remains Chairman:

'Last week, when we had a board meeting, my role should have been transferred to the Serbian partner's Chairman, because the IJV contract stipulates that the Chairman's tenure is two years. However, the Serbian partner representatives suggested that we change the IJV contract, so that I remain as Chairman! I think they were right in suggesting that, because I gave the basic ideas regarding the IJV vision ... I had a vision and was looking for a partner who would correspond to it. I chose the Serbian partner because they had the same objective as us [the German partner company].' (DIRECTOR 12)

DIRECTOR 10 also claims that his leading role in negotiations meant that it was expected that he take on the role of the IJV CEO:

'I was one of the initiators for everything that has happened regarding the IJV since the moment I met DIRECTOR 12 and our talks started ... Also, when we were negotiating the IJV agreement, it was expected that I become the IJV CEO. Therefore, when we signed IJV contract, I knew I would be taking role of the CEO.' (DIRECTOR 10)

Generally, most of the participants were involved in negotiations as prospective IJV board directors. This is in line with the previous literature (Kanter, 1994; Currall and Inkpen, 2002; Luo, 2002; Adobor, 2004) where IJVs are seen as frequently resulting from personal rapport and shared vision between the partner companies' leaders and other senior executives.

Reputation

The findings show that director reputation has also been important for their role in negotiations. DIRECTOR 4 claims that owing to his reputation, he had an opportunity to influence the IJV vision, ownership structure and even the Supervisory board composition:

> 'As a reputable lawyer, I was invited to participate in the negotiations process, so I was one of the people who negotiated the IJV agreement with the German partner ... I also insisted that my friend be appointed as a member of the Supervisory board, because he could be of great help if there were a redundancy situation in the IJV ... We negotiated a 50/50 governance structure and agreed with the Germans on the IJV goal.' (DIRECTOR 4)

The findings also show that director reputation influences their role selection. For example, DIRECTOR 4 claims that he was appointed as the Serbian partner representative on the IJV Managing board primarily because of his political reputation, whereas the choice of DIRECTOR 3 for the role of CEO seems to be directly influenced by both his professional reputation and personal background:

> 'I have been "recommended" to be the IJV Managing board member based on my political background and reputation.' (DIRECTOR 4)

> 'Since DIRECTOR 3 enjoys respect as our colleague and descendant of the Serbian partner company's founder, the German partner insisted that he be the IJV CEO. This could be seen as their respect of the Serbian partner's tradition and of a founder of such an old company.' (DIRECTOR 1)

Moreover, IJV board directors' reputation is seen as driving their motivation, which, in turn, 'implies' trust:

> 'People sitting on the IJV board are all highly reputable experts and are thus genuinely interested in the IJV success. I believe that this implies the presence of a high level of trust between them; otherwise, they wouldn't be sitting there.' (DIRECTOR 2)

These results are in line with the view in the previous literature (Langevoort, 2001) that director contribution is expected to be driven by their reputation.

Education and professional background/experience

The IJV board director's education and professional background/expertise emerged as factors influencing their contribution, both in terms of director behaviour (for example, a tendency to rely on formal contract appears to be driven by the director's legal professional background) and in terms of a director's knowledge of business and competence-based trust.

DIRECTOR 1 points to the significance of her education and previous experience for her effective contribution in terms of her good preparation and her ability to have an impact on the Assembly's decisions:

> 'I have a background in political studies and used to work for a while in a solicitor's office, so they say I have some sort of "solicitor's cleverness" – I can prepare the argument very well, so, perhaps, that makes me be more convincing.' (DIRECTOR 1)

DIRECTOR 8 also points out that his education is particularly important for his role:

> 'My PhD thesis was on game theory and rational decision-making. Although I don't think that this theory really has a practical application in business, still, this background is important for me, since in the first part of decision-making and defining the alternatives, a rational, scientific approach is essential.' (DIRECTOR 8)

Generally, the directors see their education and professional background as important for their successful contribution:

> 'Ideally, people on the board should all have higher education and possess expert knowledge, for example, in economy. It is not a coincidence that I have a degree in economics.' (DIRECTOR 2)

> 'Given the situation in the country, the success of these companies is a result of extremely good people who lead them, which is, in turn, a result their excellent education and knowledge of business.' (DIRECTOR 11)

The results also point to the link between directors' different professional backgrounds/expertise and education and the existence of different views on the IJV board, which further impact board interactions:

> 'Since the board consists of people with different professional backgrounds, there is always a possibility that some of them would have different views and ideas about a particular decision and consequently try to influence and modify it.' (DIRECTOR 2)

Generally, the above findings support the previous literature where an individual's education and professional background are seen as conferring the individual with certain information and mindset (Forbes and Milliken, 1999; Hambrick et al., 2001; Li and Hambrick, 2005) and, in a boardroom context, affecting an individual board director's ability to influence board decision-making (Ingley and Van der Walt, 2003; Sherwin, 2003).

Length of relationships

The findings also show that length of relationships with others is directly related to the reputation and trust that other directors have in the director's competence. This is in turn related to the directors' role in the partner company, their involvement in IJV negotiations, their selection for the role on the IJV board, as well as their ability to impact board decisions.

For example, DIRECTOR 1 argues that both her professional respect and length of relationships with other Serbian partner representatives have been very important for trust that the Serbian partner representatives on the IJV board have in her decisions:

> 'I had been working in the Serbian partner company for 25 years, have known many people there and have had very good relationships with them. So, to be "modest", I can say I enjoy respect in my profession. I think it contributes to trust that others have in my decisions.' (DIRECTOR 1)

For DIRECTOR 10, other directors' trust in his competence, based on both expertise and length of relationships, appears to be very important for his successful contribution:

> 'The person who appoints an expert to a position needs to be an expert himself. But the essential question is, whether you have confidence in people. I have been lucky to be working with the Serbian partner's Chairman for 25 years. DIRECTOR 12 has also been in this business for over 30 years. For all these years, the basis for everything was trust and complete openness.' (DIRECTOR 10)

DIRECTOR 7 argues that his previous experience of working in the Serbian partner's company and, thus, the length of relationships with the Serbian partner's Chairman and the other Serbian partner representative on the IJV Managing board, helps him a lot in preparing the boardroom agenda. He simply 'knows' their expectations about strategic decisions:

> 'Performing my role perhaps seems complicated and difficult, but it isn't, because I was working in the Serbian partner company for 21 years.

I've known the Serbian partner's Chairman and the other Serbian partner representative for such a long time. So I simply know how they think, what they want and how.' (DIRECTOR 7)

Similarly, the length of relationships between DIRECTOR 11 and other directors and their mutual trust and respect based on their professional backgrounds also facilitate his contribution:

> 'Given that I've been Chairman of the Serbian partner's Supervisory board for five years and I've been holding the same role in the IJV since the beginning of its operation, I've had a great pleasure and honour to work with DIRECTOR 10 and the Serbian partner's Chairman. We've known each other for a long time and we've learned about each other through work. So, our trust has been developed on a professional basis and respect, which enormously facilitates my contribution ... DIRECTOR 10 and the Serbian partner's Chairman are really business elite and represent a great motivating factor to me.' (DIRECTOR 11)

The role that length of relationships plays in developing IJV board directors' interpersonal trust represents an important implication for this research, given that the corporate governance literature shows that board members' familiarity with each other is likely to lead to higher levels of cohesiveness and, possibly, to better use of their knowledge and skills (Forbes and Milliken, 1999).

Summary

The research findings presented above point to director role in the partner company and their reputation as determinants of their role in IJV negotiations. Director role in IJV negotiations, again together with their reputation, further impacts on their selection for the IJV board director role. The results also show that length of relationships with other directors directly concerns their reputation and impacts on trust in their competence. Finally, the IJV board director's education and professional background/expertise emerged as factors influencing director contribution, particularly regarding their knowledge, trust and motivation. Figure 10.1 summarises these findings and illustrates the impact of IJV director 'elite status' on their role and contribution.

Conducting research on elites in the IJV context: reflection and learning

The study shows that conducting research on elites in the IJV context involves a number of issues, staring from gaining access to elites through the issues regarding the use of the interview protocol, time, openness, confidentiality and culture.

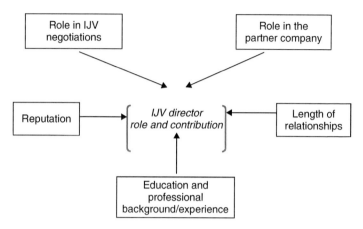

Figure 10.1   Impact of IJV director 'elite status' on their role and contribution
Source: Compiled by the authors.

Gaining access

Whilst the issue of gaining access to elites in complex organisations such as IJVs did have some influence on the number and selection of cases in this research, the study also supports the notion in the literature (Welch et al., 2002) that, to gain access to elites, it is important to know others that the elites know. For example, 'a friend of a friend' was the access facilitator (AF) for IJV1, as he had known some of the board directors there for years. Knowing well the internal relationships within IJV1, the AF helped enormously in creating the 'sampling strategy' for this research. For example, the AF recommended that the first interview be with a member of the Assembly (DIRECTOR 1) who could help in both gaining access to other directors as well as providing clearer picture of IJV1. Then, the idea was to talk to a member of the Supervisory board (DIRECTOR 2). This person could, further, facilitate access to the CEO (DIRECTOR 3). The AF would enable access to the Vice-Chairman of the Managing board (DIRECTOR 4) as well, who would also facilitate access to the CEO. Finally, the CEO could help in contacting his Deputy (DIRECTOR 5), who could in turn facilitate access to other German partner representatives on the IJV board (e.g. DIRECTOR 6). Needless to say, this strategy worked very well.

In similar vein, gaining access to board directors of IJV2 and IJV3 was through personal contacts with CEOs from both IJVs (DIRECTOR 7 and DIRECTOR 10 respectively). After interviews were conducted with both CEOs, each of them then facilitated access to other board directors in their respective IJVs (DIRECTOR 8, DIRECTOR 9, DIRECTOR 11, DIRECTOR 12 and DIRECTOR 13). This confirms Yeung's (1995) notion that sometimes decisions on access may only be made at an elite level.

Use of interview protocol and interview themes/questions

Welch et al. (2002) suggest that, as opposed to non-elites, elite interviewees are more likely to use the interview protocol as an initial orientation to select and order their responses, but would not consult the list of questions during the interview. This is because they are much more confident in making a judgement on which issues were most relevant to the researcher's study. In this research, this was the case with a majority of informants. For example, DIRECTOR 3 and DIRECTOR 5 preferred to summarise some of the questions into a story, allowing for just a few interruptions on the part of the researcher. On the other hand, DIRECTOR 10 seemed to have decided on what was important to talk about and it took the researcher some patience and effort to steer the conversation in the direction she wanted. DIRECTOR 11 was even more 'direct' in this respect, by saying, 'Let me tell you the story I think is relevant for your research and then you can ask me the questions.' DIRECTOR 12 provided a more 'rational' explanation for not 'adhering' to the interview questions: 'You'll understand my experience from running an IJV better if I gave you examples than if I only answered the list of questions.' Probably the most extreme example was DIRECTOR 7, who said: 'The Western literature regarding boards and IJVs is definitely mystified! I looked at your questions and thought I'd be able to answer them all in just one sentence!'

Still, most of the participants explicitly stated that the interview was very interesting and made supportive comments such as 'That's a very good question'. For example, DIRECTOR 6 argued that the questions helped him clarify certain things, whilst for DIRECTOR 8, the interview was 'a good opportunity to exchange opinions' and also recall his time of working at the university.

The above described experience shows that it really an 'art' to try to elicit the information from elites and cover the interview questions/themes. For that, preventing the 'danger' of the elite participants talking only about what they regarded as important, and, at the same time, being flexible in allowing them to open up new perspectives, was important. As a result, each of the directors has provided information that has considerably enriched the information gathered in this study.

Time

Another issue concerns the time needed to get the interviews from the elite. For example, setting up an interview with DIRECTOR 5 took almost three months due to his extremely busy schedule and the fact that he was not always in Serbia but was travelling to Germany. The usual reply was either he was not in the country or he should be booked three weeks in advance.

Yet, it was not possible to book the interview with him in advance because 'he deals with things as they come'. Finally, an agreement for the interview with DIRECTOR 5 was made primarily owing to good rapport created with DIRECTOR 3's secretary, as well as DIRECTOR 3's personal recommendation. Setting up the interviews with the German partner representatives from IJV3 board (DIRECTOR 12 and DIRECTOR 13) also took several months due to their busy schedule.

On the other hand, once the interview was set up, the degree of enthusiasm with which most of the directors participated was notable. For example, meeting DIRECTOR 1 and DIRECTOR 2 in their office in IJV1 was very pleasant experience as the atmosphere there was very welcoming. Another example is DIRECTOR 12, who even cancelled the meeting he was supposed to have after the interview, in order to devote more time to the interview.

Openness and confidentiality

The research topic and its perceived sensitivity among elites can be critical for their openness (Welch et al., 2002). Elites may answer questions in a guarded fashion because of fears that their comments may be used against them, like DIRECTOR 4, whose concerns about anonymity might be very real. This further leads to the ethical issue in this research in that the informants can easily be recognised.

To exemplify this, generally, it was very difficult to persuade DIRECTOR 4 to participate in the research. He was very cautious so it proved necessary that the AF and DIRECTOR 4's friend join the interview. It became apparent later that the reason for DIRECTOR 4's reluctance to be interviewed and for bringing someone with him was his concern regarding confidentiality. This is probably best exemplified through his direct warning: 'Since this conversation is recorded, I hope you are not going to abuse the information provided here in any way. For that reason I have brought two friends of mine here, as I am very cautious person.'

In addition, whilst DIRECTOR 6 easily agreed on the interview, his first sentence at the start of the interview was, nevertheless, 'Please don't mention my name!' DIRECTOR 10 also showed some concern about confidentiality, as he explicitly noted that some of the documents he prepared for the research were 'internal'. Moreover, the presence of his personal assistant and brand manager at the interview could also be seen as indicators of this concern. Hence it was important to reassure DIRECTOR 10 that the documents and information would be treated strictly confidentially and that, for any publication, he would be asked for permission.

On the other hand, in contrast to Groot and Merchant (2000), who were unable to get a copy of IJV contract from any of the IJVs they studied because the contract seemed to contain some elements that were highly confidential, access to documentation in all three IJVs was not an issue. In fact, the participants prepared, without even being asked for it, the IJV contract

(DIRECTOR 3, DIRECTOR 7 and DIRECTOR 10) and some other important documents, such as the Supervisory board agenda (DIRECTOR 2), presentation slides for the board meeting (DIRECTOR 8 and DIRECTOR 10), and even a paper about the IJV written by one of the participants (DIRECTOR 10). Whether or not the reason for this is that IJV contracts and other documents seem not to have many 'too confidential' elements, this reflects willingness on the part of the informants to help with the research. Moreover, none of the participants asked the researcher to sign any official secrecy agreement nor did the researcher encounter any reluctance concerning the taping of the interviews. The latter seemed even encouraged ('goes without saying').

Moreover, the directors were sometimes too open, which raised an ethical question of what information to divulge and whether some information could be used at all for the study. In fact, some of the director comments were so frank they have been unusable. This confirms Welch et al.'s (2002) view that a high degree of elite openness in providing information does not necessarily equate to a high level of usefulness.

Culture

It can be argued that one really needs to be from a particular country to manage to 'elicit' some information from elites in that country. Knowledge of the culture and mindset of the people being approached and interviewed is crucial here. This research experience shows that in Serbia it is necessary to create a good rapport with everyone, including the secretaries of the key people. Once the 'right' access facilitator is found, and information on director mobile phone numbers obtained (again, a 'normal' thing in Serbia), the situation becomes much easier.

Conclusion

Based on qualitative exploratory case studies of board directors from three IJVs, the chapter presented the empirical evidence concerning board directors as elites in the context of IJVs, with a focus on IJV director attributes that derive from the director's 'elite status' and emerged as influencing director role and contribution to board effectiveness. These characteristics include IJV board director role in IJV negotiations, role in the parent company, education, professional background/experience, reputation and length of relationships.

The chapter holds theoretical, practical and methodological implications. It provides evidence regarding the aspects of IJV board director role and contribution that have been largely under-researched and thus contributes to the literature on corporate elites, role and IJVs. Practically, the discussion points to the importance of taking into account director reputation, education and professional background/experience, length of their relationships, role in the parent company and IJV negotiations for their role and contribution.

The study also shows that conducting research on elites in the IJV context involves a number of issues, starting from gaining access to elites through the issues regarding the use of the interview protocol, time, openness, confidentiality and culture.

References

Adobor, H. (2004) 'High Performance Management of Shared-Managed Joint Venture Teams: Contextual and Socio-Dynamic Factors', *Team Performance Management*, 10(3–4): 65–76.

Bamford, J. and Ernst, D. (2005) 'Governing Joint Ventures', *McKinsey Quarterly*, 15: 12–16.

Carver, J. (2000) 'The Opportunity for Re-inventing Corporate Governance in Joint Venture Companies', *Corporate Governance*, 8(1): 75–80.

Child, J. and Rodrigues, S. B. (2003) 'Corporate Governance and New Organizational Forms: Issues of Double and Multiple Agency', *Journal of Management and Governance*, 7(4), 337–60.

Currall, S. C. and Inkpen, A. C. (2002) 'A Multilevel Approach to Trust in Joint Ventures', *Journal of International Business Studies*, 33(3): 479–95.

Eisenhardt, K. M. (1989) 'Building Theories from Case Study Research', *Academy of Management Review*, 14(4): 532–550.

Forbes, D. P. and Milliken, F. J. (1999) 'Cognition and Corporate Governance: Understanding Boards of Directors as Strategic-Decision Making Groups', *Academy of Management Review*, 24(3): 489–505.

Garrow, V., Devine, M., Hirsh, W. and Holbeche, L. (2000) *Strategic Alliances: Getting the People Bit Right* (Horsham: Roffey Park Institute).

Gong, Y., Shenkar, O., Luo, Y. and Nyaw, M.-K. (2001) 'Role Conflict and Ambiguity of CEOs in International Joint Ventures: A Transaction Cost Perspective', *Journal of Applied Psychology*, 86(4): 764–73.

Groot, T. L. C. M. and Merchant, K. A. (2000) 'Control of International Joint Ventures', *Accounting, Organizations and Society*, 25(6): 579–607.

Hambrick, D. C. and Finkelstein, S. (1987) 'Managerial Discretion: A Bridge between Polar Views of Organisational Outcomes', *Research in Organizational Behavior*, 9: 369–406.

Hambrick, D. C., Li, J., Xin, K. and Tsui, A. (2001) 'Compositional Gaps and Downward Spirals in International Joint Venture Management Groups', *Strategic Management Journal*, 22(11): 1033–53.

Hertz, R. and Imber, J. B. (1993) 'Fieldwork in Elite Settings', *Journal of Contemporary Ethnography*, 22(1): 3–6.

Ingley, C. B. and Van der Walt, N. T. (2003) 'Board Configuration: Building Better Boards', *Corporate Governance*, 3(4): 5–17.

Kakabadse, N., Kakabadse, A. and Kouzmin, A. (2004) 'Directors' Remuneration: The Need for a Geo-political Perspective', *Personnel Review*, 33(5): 561–82.

Kanter, R. M. (1994) 'Collaborative Advantage: The Art of Alliances', *Harvard Business Review*, 72(4): 96–108.

Langevoort, D. C. (2001) 'The Human Nature of Corporate Boards: Law, Norms, and the Unintended Consequences of Independence and Accountability', *Georgetown Law Journal*, 89(4): 797–832.

Li, J. and Hambrick, D. C. (2005) 'Factional Groups: A New Vantage on Demographic Faultlines, Conflict, and Disintegration in Work Teams', *Academy of Management Journal*, 48(5): 794–813.

Luo, Y. (2002) 'Stimulation Exchange in International Joint Ventures: An Attachment-Based View', *Journal of International Business Studies*, 33(1): 169–81.

Luo, Y., Shenkar, O. and Nyaw, M.-K. (2001) 'A Dual-Parent Perspective on Control and Performance in International Joint Ventures: Lessons from a Developing Economy', *Journal of International Business Studies*, 32(1), 41–58.

Miles, M. B. and Huberman, A. M. (1994) *Qualitative Data Analysis* (2nd edn.) (Thousand Oaks: Sage).

Minichilli, A., Zattoni, A. and Zona, F. (2009) 'Making Boards Effective: An Empirical Examination of Board Task Performance', *British Journal of Management*, 20(1): 55–74.

Pareto, V. (1968) *The Rise and Fall of the Elites* (New Jersey: Bedminster Press).

Pettigrew, A. M. (1992) 'On Studying Managerial Elites', *Strategic Management Journal*, 13 (Special issue): 163–82.

Pettigrew, A. M. and McNulty, T. (1995) 'Power and Influence in and around the Boardroom', *Human Relations*, 48(8): 845–73.

Phan, P. H., Lee, S. H. and Lau, S. C. (2003) 'The Performance Impact of Interlocking Directorates: The Director of Singapore', *Journal of Managerial Issues*, 15: 338–52.

Ravasi, D. and Zattoni, A. (2001) *Ownership Structure and the Strategic Decision Process: A Comparative Case Study*. SDA Bocconi Research Division Working Paper, No. 01-46. Available from the Social Science Research Network (SSRN) Electronic Paper Collection: http://ssrn.com/abstract=278238 (accessed 24 October 2005).

Salk, J. E. and Brannen, M. Y. (2000) 'National Culture, Networks, and Individual Influence in a Multinational Management Team', *Academy of Management Journal*, 43(2): 191–202.

Samra-Fredericks, D. (2000) 'Doing "Boards-in-Action" Research: An Ethnographic Approach for the Capture and Analysis of Directors' and Senior Managers' Interactive Routines', *Corporate Governance: An International Review*, 8(3): 244–57.

Selznick, P. H. (1957) *Leadership and Administration* (New York: Harper & Row).

Shenkar, O. and Zeira, Y. (1992) 'Role Conflict and Role Ambiguity of Chief Executive Officers in International Joint Ventures', *Journal of International Business Studies*, 23(1): 55–75.

Sherwin, L. (2003) 'Building an Effective Board', *Bank Accounting and Finance*, 16(5): 22–8.

Useem, M. (1984) *The Inner Circle* (New York: Oxford University Press).

Vallaster, C. and Koll, O. (2002) 'Participatory Group Observation: A Tool to Analyze Strategic Decision Making', *Qualitative Market Research: An International Journal*, 5(1): 40–57.

Welch, C., Marschan-Piekkari, R., Penttinen, H. and Tahvanainen, M. (2002) 'Corporate Elites as Informants in Qualitative International Business Research', *International Business Review*, 11(5), 611–28.

Yeung, W. H. (1995) 'Qualitative Personal Interviews in International Business Research: Some Lessons from a Study of Hong Kong Transnational Corporations', *International Business Review*, 4(3), 313–39.

Zajac, E. J. (1988) 'Interlocking Directorates as an Interorganizational Strategy', *Academy of Management Journal*, 31: 428–38.

Zeira, Y. and Shenkar, O. (1990) 'Interactive and Specific Parent Characteristics: Implications for Management and Human Resources in International Joint Ventures', *Management International Review*, 30 (Special issue): 7–22.

11
Joining the Global Elites: Dilemmas for China in Reforming its Systems of Scientific and Technological Innovation

Shaowei He and Richard Sanders

Introduction

China presents us with many puzzles. Is it a developed or still developing economy, is it capitalist or communist, planned or market-led? Many of these puzzles find resonance in the country's latest scheme to attract global scientific elites for not only does the initiative represent China's strategy to reform its national innovation system, but it also offers a lens through which to understand this huge and dynamic country and an opportunity to confront the puzzles within it.

The transition of the Chinese economy and its systems of innovation

China has maintained very rapid economic growth and development over the last three decades; indeed the scale and speed of economic growth, at approximately 9% per annum since 1980, is nothing short of heroic (it must be remembered that the only country in modern times to achieve anything close to such rates of GDP growth – Japan between the 1950s and 1970s – has a population one-tenth the size of China's). Economic reforms, including the launch of the 'open door' policy in the early 1980s and the accession of China to the World Trade Organization in 2001 have paved the way for this extraordinary performance and the country has now re-emerged – after many centuries – as a major power in the world economy. In purchasing power parity (PPP) terms, China is now the second largest economy in the world and not only a major destination for foreign direct investment but also a source as Chinese companies export increasing amounts of capital abroad. Although GDP per capita is still low compared to the OECD average, recent economic growth in China has nonetheless allowed more of the world's population to escape poverty than at any other time in human history.

Underlying China's impressive achievement has been a fundamental and ongoing reform of all aspects of the society and in particular of the economic system itself. In contrast to the 'big-bang' model adopted by the economies of the former Soviet Union and Eastern Europe in the 1990s, China has taken a gradual, pragmatic and experimental approach to reform ('crossing the river by feeling the stones'), leading to the parallel existence of a planned and a market economy. While some observers argue that this gradual approach has focused on changes at the microeconomic level, delaying reforms in the macroeconomic environment (OECD, 2008a), the overall scale, scope and success of the reforms in achieving material economic progress are undeniable.

In parallel to China's economic reforms has been a modernisation strategy which emphasises science and technology and enlarging the innovative capacity of Chinese industry. Thus, China is not satisfied with merely becoming the (low-tech) 'workshop of the world'. In practice, when the Chinese leaders called for reforms to modernise the country as early as the mid-1970s – 'the four modernisations' – they specifically referred to the modernisation of industry, agriculture, national defence and *science and technology*. Since then, great efforts have been undertaken to reform the educational system not only to supply the required skills but also to foster students' creativity. A range of initiatives have been set up to encourage firms in acquiring and absorbing imported technologies. Meanwhile, reforms have also been made to strengthen cooperation between the science and technology community and the industrial sector by 'breaking the vertical separation of the old R&D and production systems under the planned economy and stimulating market-based relationships between the two sectors' (OECD, 2008a: 426). In 1995, the authorities launched a strategy of 'revitalising the country with science, technology and education' (*kejiao xing guo*), attaching great importance to the role of science and technology in stimulating growth and development.

More recent years have seen an increasing pace in the mobilisation of resources to further upgrade China's innovation capacity. Apart from continuously seeking better access to global knowledge and technologies, China has focused on becoming part of what has been seen as a new global knowledge-based elite network based on science and technology, to include ICT and biotechnology.

Thanks to the government's rapid, decades-long commitment to research and development (R&D) expenditure, China's R&D intensity – R&D expenditure as a share of GDP – reached 1.42% in 2006, up from 0.7% in 1998. Indeed, since 1999, China's spending on R&D has increased by more than 20% each year (Wilsdon and Keeley, 2007). As a result of the market-oriented reforms, industry has begun to play a major role in the R&D system. In addition to the rapid increase in R&D expenditure, China has become home to the world's second largest stock of science and technology personnel, second only to the United States (OECD, 2008b). Attracted by the quality of human resources for science and technology and the massive Chinese market, there has been a strong increase in R&D investment by foreign firms in the last decade there.

Science and technology outputs have also grown, although sometimes not at the same pace as inputs. China has become a large exporter of high technology products. It has jumped from thirteenth place in the mid-1990s to fourth place in terms of share of world total publications (CREST, 2007). Table 11.1 illustrates some of the important achievements China has made over the last fifteen years.

Indeed such is the pace of China's progress in upgrading its innovation capacity that the OECD (2008a) has ranked the country as the second largest R&D spender in terms of purchasing power parity, just behind the USA. Commentators have begun to consider whether or not China is destined to become the next scientific superpower (e.g. Wilsdon and Keeley, 2007).

Although the transition and upgrading of the Chinese economy and its innovation system has been impressive, there remain tremendous challenges facing the country. In particular, it has been pointed out that it is extremely difficult to maintain *sustainable* development with its current growth model based as it is on 'a combination of low-cost manufacturing, imported technology and substantial flows of foreign investment' (Wilsdon and Keeley, 2007). Major challenges include income inequality between urban and rural areas and also between the western and eastern parts of the country,

Table 11.1   China's science and technology inputs and outputs

	Quantity	Year
% GDP spent on R&D	0.7%	1998
	1.42%	2006
S&T workforce	2.25 million scientists and engineers	2004
Enrolment in tertiary education	15 million	2004
Number of colleges and universities	1,731	2004
Number of scientific publications (in the Science Citation Index – SCI)	13,500	1995
	46,000	2004
Share of world citations	0.92%	1995
	3.78%	2004
Applications for invention patents	130,000	2005
Growth rate of invention patent applications	23% annually since 2000	2005
Inflows of foreign direct investment	$72.6 billion	2005
Multinational R&D centres in China	750	2005

Source: Adapted from Wilsdon and Keeley (2007).

fundamental demographic shifts owing to a rapidly ageing population and environmental and ecological challenges caused by rapid economic growth, industrialisation and urbanisation (OECD 2008a).

With regard to China's system of scientific and technological innovation, universities have been struggling with a dramatic expansion of students, with considerable concern about the mismatch between the quality of the graduates and the skills demanded in the labour market. In addition, despite a rapid increase of R&D investment in the business sector, R&D expenditure as a share of value-added remains low (CREST, 2007). Partly because of this, China is still unhealthily reliant on foreign technologies. Indeed, a large share of China's high-tech export is based simply on the assembly of imported high-tech components. It is reported, furthermore, that only 0.03% of Chinese firms own the intellectual property rights (IPR) of the core technologies they use (Wilsdon and Keeley, 2007).

The Chinese authorities are well aware of the challenge of making the country's future development economically, socially and ecologically sustainable, and of achieving a more balanced pattern of development. They acknowledge, in particular, that developing innovation capacity can significantly help to escape from the 'low-end path' of development characterised by intensive use of low-skilled labour and natural resources and the low level of technological capabilities so characteristic of the early years of reform. They have taken steps, through pushing concepts such as 'the harmonious society' and 'the innovative economy', to shift towards a new development model and to achieve greater social, ecological and environmental sustainability.

The internationalisation of innovation and the search for global scientific elites

To many observers, globalisation in the last several decades has involved developing countries, particularly Asian economies, building up their industrial production capacities rapidly while innovation activities have remained concentrated in OECD countries. This is beginning to change. Indeed, in recent years, the world has experienced an increasing trend towards the internationalisation of science, technology and innovation, manifested by the rapidly growing volume of cross-border technology transfer, joint generation of knowledge to include international co-publications and co-patenting activities, offshoring of corporate R&D activities and increased mobility of science and technology personnel, all increasingly involving developing countries (see, for example, OECD, 2008b).

Increased mobility of such personnel is part of the process of the internationalisation of innovation. The movement of highly skilled people has intensified as economic activity becomes ever more globalised. Moreover, the growing emphasis of knowledge means that countries across the world have a greater appetite for highly skilled specialists who are able to understand, access and exploit knowledge and consequently contribute to innovation and economic prosperity.

It is no surprise therefore, although less well-reported than the competition for raw materials and capital, that there has also been increasing competition between countries and between firms for highly skilled people. Against the background of the internationalisation of innovation, many countries have set up schemes to attract top scientists and researchers and encourage international mobility of highly skilled people. The European Union Scientific and Technological Research Committee reported that the majority of its member states have national policy measures in place to enhance the mobility of researchers through governmental funds (CREST, 2007). Finland, for example, launched a new funding programme to recruit foreign top researchers in 2005. Similar polices have been found in other countries (OECD 2008b, 2008c).

Developing countries such as China and India have recently joined the developed world to include the USA, the EU, Japan, Canada and Australia in chasing highly skilled people (Wyckoff and Schapper, 2005). China, in particular, has scaled up its efforts recently and has targeted the large pool of talent amongst the more than one million mainland Chinese who have travelled abroad to study and work. China has recognised that the networks maintained by repatriates with their former host country can be vital to knowledge creation and transmission. Using examples from India, China, Malaysia and Chinese Taipei, research has shown that highly skilled repatriates have played a key role in developing high-technology sectors in these countries (Saxenian, 2006; Lazonick, 2007).

In the 1990s, there were a number of high-profile schemes initiated in China by some of the key science and technology institutions for returnees. For example, the Ministry of Education launched the Chung Kong scholarship in 1998 to encourage overseas Chinese scholars to return to China, funded by a Hong Kong billionaire. In the following ten years, 115 universities participated and recruited 1,308 professors from overseas, 38 of whom have become academicians of either the Chinese Academy of Science (CAS) or the Chinese Academy of Engineering (CAE). Meanwhile the CAS itself initiated the 'One Hundred Talent Programme' in 1994 which offered promising scientists under the age of forty-five 2 million RMB (approximately £200,000) in the form of research funding, equipment expenditure and housing benefit in order to lure them back to China. This scheme funded more than 1,300 highly skilled returnees, among whom 20 have become Academicians of the CAS. The National Natural Science Fund's 'Distinguished Young Scholars' offered similar incentives to overseas Chinese scientists who were willing to return. There have been other smaller-scale programmes from various science and technology institutions. Moreover, provincial and regional government have also introduced their own initiatives to encourage the return of overseas scholars and graduates.

While there have been some successful initiatives in the past, the Chinese authorities' efforts to lure back repatriates have intensified in recent years. Incentives offered to returnees now include low-interest loans and high salaries, government subsidies, tax deductions, IPR incentives and priority employment for spouses and education enrolment for children (CREST, 2007; OECD, 2008a). Highly skilled returnees are also exempt from the household registration system – the *hukou* – and therefore are able to choose to live and work wherever they like.

Despite the lucrative incentives, however, the results of these initiatives to date appear to be rather mixed. On the plus side, according to the Ministry of Education, 77% of the presidents of Chinese universities, 84% of the academicians at the CAS and 75% of the academicians at the CAE have overseas study and/or work experience. But while the government schemes mentioned above have attracted some top scientists back from abroad, the number of returnees still falls short of what is needed (OECD, 2008a). Indeed, the Communist Party's Central Personnel Department, in charge of policy-making and the implementation of senior level human resource management, has admitted that the quantity and quality of the returnees is still far from meeting the future needs of China. In particular, the country is still short of top scientists who are able to make scientific breakthroughs in key areas. Meanwhile, among those who have returned, it is claimed that some were merely opportunists pursuing windfall benefits.

Looking at the broader picture, it has been reported that, altogether, about 319,700 overseas gradates have returned between 1978 and 2007. However, this still means that about 75% of the over one million Chinese who have studied or are studying abroad have not returned home. The number of returnees falls short of what would be needed to significantly reduce the current and prospective shortages of certain types of skills (OECD, 2008a). It is widely assumed that those who remain overseas include many of the best and brightest (Cao, 2007; Wilsdon and Keeley, 2007). And some of the latest news suggests that things are not getting any better. It is reported that since 1985, Tsinghua University and Beijing University, the two most prestigious universities in China, have seen, respectively, 80% and 76% of their science graduates leaving for the United States. In 2006, they became the top two suppliers of PhD students in the USA, surpassing University of California at Berkeley.

China has certainly felt the pain of this brain drain and the urgency to lure back more expatriates has become ever more acute in the context of the authorities' push for innovation. The Chinese government plans to raise R&D intensity from 1.42% of GDP in 2005 to 2% in 2010 and 2.5% in 2020. However, there remains a great deal of tension between the push for innovation and the capacity of the system to deliver it. The OECD estimates that China needs an additional 2.6 million researchers over and above the numbers in 2005 in order to meet the target of 2.5% R&D intensity by 2020 and that there will be a large gap even if the current level of growth in the absolute number of researchers is maintained (OECD, 2008a). Recognising that the country lacks scientific leadership and that its national innovation system is intimately embedded in global networks and flows of knowledge, capital and talent, the Chinese authorities have now decided to launch a new flagship initiative to attract top scientists from overseas. Acknowledging that innovation plays a key role in future sustainable development, China has stepped up its efforts in human capital formation and in the enhancement of its capabilities in science, technology and innovation. Thus, one of the most recent and striking schemes has been a flagship initiative called the 'One Thousand Talents Scheme' with the aim of attracting global scientific elites – and particularly those of Chinese origin – back to China.

The One Thousand Talents Scheme and global scientific elites

Chinese leaders since the inception of the People's Republic in 1949 have always displayed a strong commitment to science and technology. However, their beliefs in the power of science and technology to deliver social and economic progress have become ever stronger as more and more of its current leaders have been trained in science and technology subjects. With the acknowledgement of the challenges to securing sustainable development and a strong faith in science, technology and innovation to help China overcome these challenges, the State Council, on 9 February 2006, outlined the Medium to Long Term National Plan for the Development of Science and Technology (2006–20). The overarching aim of the plan is to boost the country's innovation capacity to sustain economic growth and development and at the same time to provide technological solutions to social and environment challenges. Apart from reform programmes in intellectual property rights, scientific institutions and industrial innovations, the Plan identifies a number of key science and technology priorities and aims to increase China's spending on science to 2% of its GDP in 2010 and 2.5% in 2020, by which time the country will have become an 'innovation-oriented economy'.

Following up the Medium to Long Term Plan, the Central Organisation Department of the Chinese Communist Party launched the 'One Thousand Global Talents Scheme' to help China make the transition from the 'workshop of the world' to an 'innovation-orientated economy'. The scheme represents China's latest effort in a global hunt for top-notch talents and plans to recruit 2,000 talents of any nationality (but particularly targeting overseas Chinese) in the next five to ten years. Candidates will normally be under 55 years old and hold an overseas doctorate degree. They should also fulfil one of the following criteria: (1) have an academic title equivalent to professor in internationally renowned universities and research institutions; (2) work as a senior manager or professional within a well-known international company or finance institution; (3) have developed technologies and patents and established their own businesses abroad; or (4) have other highly innovative or entrepreneurial talents.

According to the scheme, there are four recruitment routes:

1. Via national key innovation projects: talents via this platform will be recruited for the national key scientific projects specified in the Medium to Long Term National Plan for the Development of Science and Technology (2006–20) and another two key national basic research projects called 863 and 975 projects. The Ministry of Science and Technology will administer the candidate application and evaluation processes.
2. Via key scientific subjects and laboratories: these are to recruit talents for universities and key national scientific laboratories, which are administered by the Ministry of Education and Ministry of Science and Technology respectively.
3. Via enterprises (with an emphasis on state-owned enterprises) and finance institutions. The processes are administered by the State-owned Assets Supervision and Administration Commission and the People's Bank of China respectively.
4. Via high-tech parks: these are to attract returnees to set up businesses in various types of high-tech parks. The process is administered by the Ministry of Science and Technology and Ministry of Human Resources.

Since it was launched in early 2009, the scheme has recruited 825 talented individuals. It is noticeable that, although the scheme has a focus on Chinese expatriates, it does not exclude top talents of non-Chinese origin. Indeed, among the latest list of 163 recruited talents, 104 hold foreign passports and 3 are of non-Chinese origin.

It is easy to find close links between the scheme and the Medium to Long Term National Plan for the Development of Science and Technology (2006–20). The scheme is viewed as a strategic action to transform China into an 'innovation-oriented country'. There is a strong emphasis that the scheme should serve the national science and technology objectives and that it should recruit 'strategic scientists' and science and technology leadership to help bring forward breakthroughs in key scientific areas and develop high-tech industries.

It is a high-profile flagship scheme in at least two senses. Firstly, it targets global scientific talents who are able to achieve scientific breakthroughs and offer scientific leadership as mentioned above. Secondly, the scheme offers global competitive financial incentives including a 1 million RMB relocation package on top of normal salaries, research funding, *hukou* exemptions and preferential visa policies and medical services for the talents and their relatives.

Arguably, the recruited top talents are joining a prestigious group of scientific elites, giving them enormous power in the elaboration and orientation of science and innovation policies in China. Firstly, they are offered the title of National Prestigious Professor, giving them very high social status. Secondly, they are able to access many resources not available to the general scientific public. For example, many of them are offered senior management roles in universities, research institutions, state-owned enterprises and finance institutions. Some are also able to take leadership roles in key national scientific projects. Last but not the least, they are connected to the Communist Party leadership via the Party's Central Talents Coordinating Group, which coordinates national policy-making in the human resources area and is headed by the CCP's powerful Central Personnel Department. The latest manifestation of this is the Party's invitation to 70 scientific elite personnel associated with this scheme to enjoy a week's holiday at Beidaihe, a traditional tourist resort for the Party leadership. During their stay, three members of the Politburo of the Party's Central Committee (which includes the most powerful twenty-five people in China) including Xi Jinping, the likely successor of current Chinese President, Hu Jintao, paid them a visit and held conversations with them.

Continuing challenges

It is reported that since the launch of the scheme, more than 100,000 expatriates returned to China in 2009 alone. It seems that this high-profile project has had a rippling effect. However, there are still significant challenges for the Chinese authorities to identify and recruit the right candidates and for the recruited scientific elites to achieve significant scientific breakthroughs and offer scientific leadership and consequently to boost China's innovation capacity.

Challenge 1: Innovation takes more than investment

According to Wilsdon and Keeley (2007: 61) 'China has a focused and strategic approach to science and innovation policy, which is being supported by dramatic increases in funding at every level, and in the overall share of GDP devoted to R&D.' Mobilising resources is obviously one of the strengths of the Chinese innovation system. The 'One Thousand Talents Scheme' is timely as most of the developed countries are hit by the financial crisis and cutting education and research budgets. China, in contrast, continues to invest in science and technology and is now able to offer talents globally competitive salaries. However, there is still the question as to whether China is able to lure the 'best and brightest' Chinese who are still overseas and allow those who have returned to flourish. This depends not only on investment in 'hardware' and infrastructure for innovation, but also on improvements in 'software' and the culture for innovation, particularly with respect to the environment, entrepreneurship, creative culture and wider political reform (Leadbeater and Wilsdon, 2007; Wilsdon and Keeley, 2007; OECD, 2008b). However, there are worrying signs in this regard.

Firstly, it is widely accepted that innovation and creativity depends on openness and the freedom to debate and disagree. The Chinese education system, however, despite recent reforms still encourages largely passive learning. More worrying to some observers is the fact that the Chinese authorities seem to be tightening censorship of the media and the Internet, illustrated, for example, in the recent battles between China and Google over the control of the Internet and information. To many, the excessive efforts by the Chinese authorities to tighten censorship is in direct conflict with its desire to encourage science and innovation, with the practice of restricting access to the Internet and information having negative repercussions in the longer term.

Secondly, there has been a widespread campaign across Chinese universities and research organisations for more international publications, especially in journals included in the SCI. However, it could be argued that scientific institutions in China place more emphasis on quantity rather than quality, evaluating and rewarding their scientists accordingly. As spending on R&D has increased, so have the society's expectations for the scientists.

No doubt elite membership of the 'One Thousand Talents Scheme' is 'a stepping stone for controlling resources and for gaining material privileges' (Cao, 2010), but the talents recruited via the scheme will soon face mounting pressure on 'visible' outcomes. The increasing incidence of academic fraud and corruption in recent years testifies to this mounting pressure for 'visible' outcomes and quantity, associated with an erosion of Chinese traditional values and ethics. The most notorious example in recent years involved Jin Chen, Dean of the Microelectronics School at Shanghai Jiaotong University, who claimed to have developed a groundbreaking microchip and subsequently received over £7.5 million in research grants. Dr Chen was highly praised by the top Chinese leadership for his alleged technological breakthrough, which was found later to have been fraudulent, based as it was on reusing Motorola's chips, from which he had simply erased the original logo and to which he had added that of his own company.

Unfortunately, the case of Dr Chen is only the tip of the iceberg of academic misconduct in China. According to the Chinese Association for Science and Technology, more than 55% of Chinese scientists who responded to its recent survey indicated that they knew colleagues who were involved in academic misconduct cases including plagiarism and fraud. More worryingly, more than 30% of the respondents were sympathetic to the offenders.

There is therefore a question as to whether the scientific elites recruited via the 'One Thousand Talents Scheme' are able to transplant the norms and values of the world's learning centres of innovation, to which they have long been exposed, to an environment so different from those centres. Apart from the cultural shock in dealing with the established hierarchy in the established innovation community, they will find themselves in a less open, more closely knit and more quantity and materially driven society. Because of this there have already been warnings that without further reform in China towards a more transparent, open and autonomous innovation system, the recruited 'One Thousand Talents' could soon flee from China again to whence they had been recruited.

Challenge 2: Political problems

According to Leadbeater and Wilsdon (2007), China is attempting an authoritarian modernisation combining markets and Communist rule. It is not difficult to find evidence of this nor is it difficult to find evidence of the influence of the ubiquitous shadow of politics on the implementation of the 'One Thousand Talents Scheme'. The fact that the Communist Party's Central Personnel Department is in charge of the scheme is closely in line with the Party's basic principle of 'the Party controlling human resources'. Li Yuanchao, Head of the Central Personnel Department and one of the members of the Party Politburo of the Central Committee, sees the scheme as his own initiative and wants it to work well at least partly if not entirely so that he will be in an advantageous position in the forthcoming leadership reshuffle in 2012.

Since the launch of the scheme in early 2009, many provincial and regional governments have developed their own talent initiatives in line with the central scheme, as required by the Party and the central government. The Governors and Party Generals in the provinces and regions also have an interest in recruiting as many talents as possible, with the aim of winning the support of Li Yuanchao in their own political ascendancy bids.

With so much politics at stake, it is no wonder that we have witnessed such enthusiasm for the scheme, yet so much politically inspired enthusiasm may well be ultimately detrimental to it and to the Chinese innovation system more generally. For example, this enthusiasm has led to an almost unseemly rush for global scientific talents with the scheme being viewed as a political task. Consequently, there is a risk that some will be (have been?) recruited without much assessment. By the end of 2009, the scheme had already recruited 326 people. However, there is criticism over the rigour of the evaluation process with some organisations being preoccupied with meeting targets rather than with ensuring that the recruits have the appropriate expertise. It was reported that the second round of recruitments of the scheme, for example, took less than three months from application to the end result and that candidates were evaluated only on the basis of their application forms and without an interview process.

Another problem with such overt political involvement is that it may, in the end, stifle innovation. Many of the recruited talents will be put in important positions such as school deans or heads of research institutions. Some of them may even rise to positions at ministerial level, as did Wang Gang who worked for Audi in Germany for fifteen years before returning in 2004 and becoming, as he is today, Minister of Science and Technology. Indeed, as Xi Jinping emphasised when he visited Beidaihe recently, the recruited talents will be offered key positions, will participate in key decision-making, and lead key scientific subjects. And associated with these administrative and management roles come *political* opportunities. No doubt some will become members of the Chinese Communist Party or be selected as deputies to the National People's Congress (NPC) or members of the Chinese People's Political Consultative Conference (CPPCC), the country's highest legislative body and political consultation organisation. Apart from the requirement that they attend annual sessions, this will give them the opportunity to be included in the nation's political process, involving them in decision-making, legislation and consultation and advisory work.

The disadvantage for the scientific elites of taking administrative, management and political roles is that they have to spend a great deal of time looking after *guanxi* (relationships) internally and externally and therefore have little time for research and innovation, as illustrated in Cao and Suttmeier's (2001) study on Chinese scientific elites. In addition, many have argued that the privileges enjoyed by these elites discourage innovation and encourage poor scientific practices. It is true that scientific elites have enormous power in the elaboration and orientation of science and innovation polices in China. The Medium to Long Term National Plan for the Development of Science and Technology (2006–20), for example, is partly a result of a two-year consultation with more than 2,000 scientists, and in the past they have managed to persuade the authorities to increase spending on science and technology development (Cao, 2007). However, the privileges the scientific elites enjoy mean that they risk losing a degree of autonomy and independence and become more obedient to authority, with implications detrimental to science and innovation.

Challenge 3: Open innovation vs. techno-nationalism

Corresponding to the fact that more firms are embracing 'open' innovation approaches and actively cooperating with actors outside the firm to gain access to new knowledge and commercialise their own knowledge, the internationalisation of innovation continues to accelerate and spread to an increasing number of countries. According to OECD (2008b), there have been significant increases in cross-border R&D and international cooperation in scientific research and publication. In addition, multinational companies (MNCs) increasingly seek to source technology internationally and tap into centres of increasingly multi-disciplinary knowledge worldwide. Also, it has become evident that a few emerging countries have become increasingly incorporated within the global innovation networks in recent years.

Increasing international mobility of workers and, in particular, of highly skilled science and technology workers, is one of the prominent features of internationalised innovation. Those involved spread their knowledge to colleagues when they move and there are also knowledge spillovers to others in the same location not only because of geographical proximity and social relationships but also through a 'community of practices' (Gertler, 2003) bound together by shared experiences and expertise.

Arguably China has seen some benefits as MNCs establish their R&D centres in the country. In particular, the increasing number of returnees from the West in recent years suggests that the brain drain in one period may well become the source of 'brain regain' at a later date (OECD, 2008c). Indeed, as stocks of repatriated scientists and engineers return in increasing numbers, one may wonder whether China is starting to see a wave of 'brain circulation' of the sort that South Korea experienced in an earlier period. This 'brain circulation' represents a complex and decentralised two-way flow of skills, capital and technology between different economies. Economic geographer Anna Lee Saxenian has recorded how the circulation of skilled workers from the Chinese diaspora has contributed to the development of high-tech industries and regions in China, transforming local institutions and improving local information exchanges there, while at the same time maintaining their social and professional ties to the science and technology communities in Silicon Valley (Saxenian, 2005).

There are, however, concerns over China's Medium to Long Term National Plan for the Development of Science and Technology (2006–20). Because of the Plan's emphasis on 'independent innovation' (*zizhu chuangxin*) and China's policy in promoting key firms as 'national champions', there is some concern that China risks becoming overly inward-looking in relation to science and technology, impeding international collaborative innovation (e.g. Leadbeater and Wilsdon, 2007). One may even trace the origins of this back to Mao's self-reliance policies of the 1960s. Without a clear definition of 'independence' in the context of internationalised innovation, some observers wonder whether the implications of 'independent innovation' might include reduction in support for international collaboration (Wilsdon and Keeley, 2007).

However, speculation over 'independent innovation' may merely indicate a misunderstanding of China's policy and a mistranslation of *zizhu chuangxin*, which, as far as we are concerned, involves Chinese institutions and scientists merely playing a much more active and leading role in innovation instead of being passive recipients of imported technology. In addition, China is sufficiently aware of its diasporas' foreign relationships for it to benefit from brain circulation. Therefore, we suspect the emphasis on *zizhu chuangxin* does not necessarily involve China in withdrawing from the global innovation network.

Conclusion

China has been through a remarkable transition journey over the last three decades. There has been significant economic growth and improvement in living standards. The reforms cannot be turned back and the market is now playing an extremely important role in every corner of the economy. China is now a much more open country and people enjoy a much larger degree of freedom. On the other hand, the country is still ruled by the Communist Party and is faced with the formidable challenge of making its development more socially, economically and environmentally sustainable.

It seems that the Chinese authorities increasingly resort to science and innovation to face up to the country's challenges as evident in its Medium to Long Term National Plan for the Development of Science and Technology (2006–20). Following up the Plan the high-profile 'One Thousand Talents Scheme' aims to attract global scientific elites to contribute to the country's science and technology development, with a particular focus on luring back top scientists of Chinese origin. The scheme itself reflects the transition of the Chinese innovation system to a more open one on the one hand and, on the other, represents China's latest effort to boost its innovation capacity, taking advantage of the internationalisation of innovation and large pool of overseas Chinese talents.

With China's huge spending power and the opportunities its outstanding economic growth brings, the scheme seems to be working well with more than 800 high-level scientists and professionals since early 2009 having been lured back to China as a result of the scheme. No doubt China has an advantage in mobilising resources and the returnees will help to energise and orchestrate innovation in China. However, whether this 'brain circulation' is a permanent feature and whether the transition of the Chinese innovation system is successful will depend on a number of factors beyond mere investment of financial resources. In particular, to enable global scientific elites to transplant the norms and values of the world's learning centres of innovation to China, the Chinese innovation system needs to become more transparent, open and autonomous. In addition, there is a strong argument for the Chinese authorities to free global scientific elites from tight political control and to grant them a greater degree of independence and autonomy. Moreover, the Chinese need to clear the doubts around its emphasis on *zizhu chuangxin* and convince their foreign partners that they fully embrace the global innovation network and encourage international cooperation.

China is increasingly important in the global economy and it could have a disproportionate impact on the global innovation network in the long term. The future of its efforts in attracting global scientific elites will send a signal as to the direction of the country's future transition.

References

Cao, C. (2007) 'Chinese Scientific Elites and their Political and Social Role', *Modern China Studies*, 1.

Cao, C. (2010) 'A Climate for Misconduct'. Available at: http://roomfordebate. blogs.nytimes.com/2010/01/18/will-china-achieve-science-supremacy/ (accessed 26 August 2010).

Cao, C. and Suttmeier, R. P. (2001) 'China's New Scientific Elite: Distinguished Young Scientists, the Research Environment and Hopes for Chinese Science', *China Quarterly*, 168: 960–84.

CREST (2007) 'Internationalisation of R&D – Facing the Challenge of Globalisation: Approaches to a Proactive International Policy in S&T'. Available at http://ec.europa.eu/invest-in-research/pdf/download_en/report_international.pdf (accessed 20 August 2010).

Gertler, M. (2003) 'Tacit Knowledge and the Economic Geography of Context, or the Undefinable Tacitness of Being (There)', *Journal of Economic Geography*, 3: 75–99.

Lazonick, W. (2007) 'Foreign Direct Investment, Transnational Migration, and Indigenous Innovation in the Globalisation of High-tech Labour'. Revised version of paper presented at the International Forum of Comparative Political Economy of Globalisation, 1–3 September 2006, Remin University of China, Beijing.

Leadbeater, C. and Wilsdon, J. (2007) *The Atlas of Ideas: How Asian Innovation Can Benefit Us All* (London: Demos).

OECD (2008a) *OECD Review of Innovation Policy: China* (Paris: OECD).

OECD (2008b) *OECD Science, Technology and Industry Outlook* (Paris: OECD).

OECD (2008c) *The Global Competition for Talent* (Paris: OECD).

Saxenian, A.-L. (2005) 'From Brain Drain to Brain Circulation: Transnational Communities and Regional Upgrading in India and China', *Studies in Comparative International Development*, 40(2): 35–61.

Saxenian, A.-L. (2006) *The New Argonauts* (Cambridge, MA: Harvard University Press).

Wilsdon, J. and Keeley, J. (2007) 'China: The Next Science Superpower?' *Demos* [online]. Available at www.demos.co.uk (accessed 28 August 2010).

Wyckoff, A. and Schapper, M. (2005) 'The Changing Dynamics of the Global Market for the Highly Skilled'. Available at http://www.advancingknowledge.com/drafts/Wyckoff-Version%20Feb%2028%20-%20Global_HRST_7-Jan_Draft.doc (accessed 16 August 2010).

12
Strategising from the Perspective of Global Elites

Robert Galavan

'You just don't have some whizz kid off in a room doing complicated stuff and hey presto it's like a circus and out rolls your strategy.' (Kevin Toland)

Introduction

The concept of strategy or strategising is central to many aspects of management practice today. The concept has evolved as a field of study from its early base in business policy formulation, moved through strategic analysis and strategic planning, and on to the more action-oriented strategic management that links formulation and implementation. It then swings from an outward-facing perspective to a more inward-looking one that considers strategic assets, competences and capabilities as building blocks in a more uncertain world. Learning organisations, core competences, open innovation and Blue Ocean strategy are among the many frameworks managers have applied to the strategy problem in a rapidly changing world. Strategy is big business and the quest for the next breakthrough goes on.

Rather than get caught up in the chase for the next idea or search for the holy grail of strategy I have taken the opportunity in this chapter to consider important issues in strategy as described by global elite strategists, each from different industries and with different experiences. What they all have in common are successful track records in globally competitive businesses. They all have a focus on making strategy work, because their job depends on it.

I conducted interviews with four executives and what follows is a synthesis of their thinking, framed by my own biases. Where you spot important insights thank the elites, where it falls down blame me.

The four are very different characters and yet what emerged from the conversations was a view of strategy with amazing similarity in concept, albeit different in context and application.

Each of the participants brought a perspective, insight and personality unique to them. Kevin Toland is Chief Executive and President of Glanbia

USA and Global Nutritionals, part of a multi-billion Euro food business headquartered in Ireland (Kevin works and lives in the USA). Prior to joining Glanbia Kevin worked in the drinks industry in Europe and held positions with Coca-Cola bottlers in Russia. Kevin could be described as a rapid-fire machine gun, although that might unfairly frame him as somewhat less than precise, which he isn't. Kevin is the type of executive that could run through 25 strategic objectives with you in 25 minutes and instantly know to hone in on the one you were hoping he would gloss over. Kevin knows the second of the participants, Ned Sullivan, quite well. Kevin worked for Ned when Ned was CEO of Glanbia PLC. Ned described Kevin as a 'great contrarian' in the strategic debates and as a valuable counter to the 'research based process oriented people'.

Ned Sullivan is currently Chairman of a food business and a telecommunications company, Eircom, formerly Ireland's national carrier. He has also chaired businesses as diverse as banking and building. He was formerly CEO of Avonmore Waterford, which became Glanbia PLC. Ned also has the distinction of being the man who brought Baileys Irish Cream to the world (now one of the top global brands). He went on to develop his career in Grand Metropolitan both in Europe and as President of Asia-Pacific operations.

Peter Robbins is an independent innovation consultant, and was previously Global Director of Innovation Excellence at GlaxoSmithKline. Peter has a rich history in the pharmaceutical industry, but his later times at GSK focused on consumer health-care products. His experience working to help teams innovate and strategise in this very complex arena brought wonderful insights. Finally, I chatted with Jim O'Hara, Vice-President of Intel's global Technology Manufacturing Group and General Manager of Intel's Irish operations. Jim has been with Intel in Ireland since 1991 and oversaw development from its first fabrication plant and on through the billions of dollars in investment that have followed. Jim has high-technology manufacturing in his bloodstream and the experience of a player from a world-leading highly capital-intensive business in the IT sector nicely rounds out the group.

For such diverse characters bringing very different industry and personal perspectives one would expect very diverging views. Indeed there were differences, for example, some talked of the teasing out of strategy and the evolving dialogue where others describe more blunt exchanges. But behind the different manifestations, they all talked in some shape or form about the importance of the strategic conversation, the engagement of people in challenge and dialogue, and the need for focus and flexibility.

Simultaneously managing complexity and simplicity

'Beyond the hill of complexity lies simplicity.' (Ned Sullivan)

One of the many fascinating insights from the conversations was the ability of each of these global elites to deal with the complexity of strategy, but at the same time not be bound by it. When somebody tells you that a phenomenon that is manifestly complex, is actually quite simple, there are two possible explanations. One, they have not grasped the full impact of the situation they face or two, they understand the complexities very well, but realise that if they are to get others to engage they must simplify it (without losing its essence). Elite leaders in these situations have the capacity to absorb complexity and its underlying uncertainty, and from the morass, extract simple coherent principles.

At the product level Ned Sullivan described the almost torturous process of iteration after iteration while developing the Baileys brand – now one of the world's leading liqueurs – concluding that developing the Baileys brand was simple 'although it didn't seem simple at the time'.

> 'But we eventually realised that it was blindingly simple in a way and we come back to the core of what the brand was or what makes the brand tick, which was that it tastes great to most people.'

The detailed work that follows the simple principles is then actually fairly straightforward because while the principles are complicated, in the sense that they take time and detail to work through, they are not all that complex, they have underlying principles that guide the decision-making through the other levels. As Ned described it, once the core of the brand had been simplified the job was then to

> '... get out of our own way and make the brand available through distribution, make it appealing through advertising, make it contemporary, keep it relevant and stuff like keeping the pricing and packaging right. I wouldn't say it was straightforward, but once we'd kind of got the formula, if you like, it was more just about hard work to implement it.'

Clarity and focus with flexibility

> 'So where are you off to, where's the hill, how quickly do you want to climb it, and what are you prepared to do to climb it. It's all very ordinary, unsophisticated stuff. All the sophisticated analysis and the scenarios and the evaluation and the thinking to me are really the tools of achieving simple clear answers to those first couple of questions.' (Kevin Toland)

Over and over again in the interviews the job of making strategy simple kept coming up. Simple but not simplistic, and not simple in a way that resolves issues beyond thought processes, but simple in a way that allows you to get to the next level of thinking and to keep on thinking.

'It's not that this is easy, it is just that beyond the hard and complex work you need to arrive at clarity. Simplicity is a key thing from the leader, they need to be able to ask simple, penetrating questions ... through that simple insatiable curiosity they're learning and also continually challenging and building the management team's capability.' (Kevin Toland)

This search for simplicity is in some ways a search for meaning: at the product level a search for the brand DNA as Peter Robbins described it. Similarly Ned Sullivan described the search for 'what makes the brand tick' and the hunt for the 'truth that emerges about the brand'. So do the relatively narrow issues involved in brand translate to the business and corporate levels? One can answer yes and no to this. Certainly the complexity of the corporate strategy has greater breadth and depth but, at the same time, the need to simplify the challenges to a level that can be grasped and communicated does not diminish.

While brand strategy varies along the lines of pricing, customer perceptions, uniqueness, channels, availability and the like, corporate strategy varies along lines of market opportunities, core competencies and strategic orientation. These higher-order variables are collected in what Peter Robbins described as a cathedral built on strategic pillars. The principles are the same though, the simplicity and the focus at one level removes complexity and uncertainty at the next. While it takes time to get to the required level of clarity, once it is there people say 'That's obvious ... but that's the challenge, it has got to be so clear and so compelling' (Ned Sullivan).

Reaching this level of clarity allows people to get on board with the strategy, quicker and with less investment of time and energy. The energy goes towards making things happen, rather than figuring out what it's all about. Equally it allows people to stay on board when difficult times come along. When shocks hit the firm, if the core of the strategy, the nature of the beast in other words, is robust enough, it creates a steadying hand.

'If you are sailing along at high speed and suddenly in the race you come up to Cape Horn or somewhere and you hit a squall, you don't suddenly say, "Oh sugar should we be in a boat? Should we be in the sea? Should we be in the race?" All that it really means you hunker down hard and you may go a bit sideways for a while but, your job is to minimise the sort of drift and maximise your momentum forward to your destination anyway.' (Kevin Toland)

So while the timing, the tactics of the race and the route to the end point are all up for discussion, the notion that you are in a particular race to win isn't. At the same time we live in quite a volatile world and moving out further on strategic horizons it becomes more difficult to predict market demands. Even in this context though there are things we can know; in fact Kevin belittles the proposition that 'there is no point in thinking where you want to go because who knows what the future holds' as absurd. In one of his businesses he simplifies it to a question of 'will people be eating cheese in 5, 10 or 50 years'. Once you have a sense of an answer to that question it is easier to focus on the subsets. How are the supply chains evolving and where should we be deeper or shallower? Are we in the right market segments? Are we selling cheese as a product and should we be selling it as a product plus service – incorporating logistics handling and risk management?

> 'Once the firm has clarity on what it's trying to achieve, earthquakes creating cracks in the system present both challenges and opportunity. It is our job to understand the pace of these changes, the risks and the opportunities, and where and how we sit in relation to them.' (Kevin Toland)

Kevin went on to explain that unlike many business that have spent two years saying how bad the crisis is

> 'We quietly cracked on, hit our plan and continued with our growth. Because we had clarity, we were able to say here is where we will slow things down, here is where we will hold costs, here is where we will preserve investment, even if a little thinner than intended, and as the storm clears we will come out of it stronger. We will have adapted but kept the key talent and our competitive advantage and we will have accelerated it relative to others.'

Clarity and focus are also about building solid platforms for harnessing opportunities. Jim O'Hara talked briefly about mobile applications and the way they took off in unexpected ways. How, nevertheless, Intel was able to respond with the Centrino technology that was already being developed, not specifically for the applications it was used in but as a solid core platform from which they believed opportunities would emerge.

   Viewed through the eyes of these global leaders, clarity and focus can both reduce uncertainty and at the same time through the pursuit of excellence provide flexibility and opportunity. Setting targets and objectives plays an important part in this so that organisations' goals are 'clear and transparent' (Peter Robbins). Yet always built into the discussion is the ability to incorporate flexibility with clarity. Perhaps one of the revealing characteristics of the global elite strategists is their unquestioned ability to live, perhaps even thrive, on these ambiguities.

> 'The process is relentless, it's very focused and it has to be pretty ruthless in terms of squashing deviations from the strategy once it's determined, but at the same time being open to the necessary evolutions of it.' (Ned Sullivan)

Peter Robbins, who worked closely with the businesses within GSK's consumer division, talked extensively about the ability to translate higher-level objectives into everyday work for the business teams. He noted that 'in order to get people to coalesce around a vision, you have to be able to interpret it in a way that relates to their local activity'. Strategy is about getting all the little arrows to line up with the intended direction of the big one. Through properly interpreting the big focus in the context of the smaller ones, you allow people to align themselves. This translation goes right through budgeting, functions and shared services.

> 'The real task of the strategist is to ensure that all the little domains and fiefdoms are switched on and coming along with the overall group, delivering in a kind of orchestral symphony. Every initiative must be questioned to ensure that it clearly connects to the strategic pillars.' (Peter Robbins)

Creativity and analysis

The past couple of decades have seen an explosion in business interest in innovation. This interest has been helpful in some ways: it has raised the profile of the challenges that need to be addressed and it has encouraged firms to engage with innovation as an essential process of business – one that needs to be understood and managed. It has, however, also created confusion, with creativity and invention being mistakenly touted as somehow equivalent to innovation. They are of course not the same thing. In the business world creativity is an important component, but most businesses don't suffer from lack of ideas. They suffer from the inability to sort the good ideas from the bad. There is a tongue-in-cheek saying in marketing circles that only 10% of advertising is effective, the problem is trying to figure out which 10%.

Innovating strategically therefore requires a balance, or perhaps a tension between the creativity that generates ideas and the rigorous analysis that informs resource allocation. It is perhaps on this latter dimension that I saw the most significant differences in responses across industries, driven to a large extent by the nature of their risk and in particular the initial and sunk capital costs. In an organisation like Intel the development of a new product often precedes the emergence of the market, requires extensive R&D, and sinks capital in dedicated plant and equipment.

Perhaps part of the issue I am highlighting here is driven by the risk of a disconnect between those who create ideas and those who must make judgements to commit capital and implement actions. I am reminded of reports of one of the creative guru Edward de Bono's suggestions to the British Foreign Office that they should send Marmite to help solve the Arab–Israeli conflict. The logic, with some technical merit, is that there is a lack of zinc in the local diet (caused by yeast-free unleavened bread). Lack of zinc makes men irritable and belligerent. Marmite, which contains zinc, might therefore make them less irritable and peace could break out. The idea is genuinely creative, radical, outside the box and a whole host of other clichés. One wonders, however, if de Bono was in charge of the Foreign Office's limited resources would this suggestion be implemented? Somehow it strikes me that the tension between creativity and the resource allocation analysis is missing here. We have creativity disconnected from the analysis of the situation. Creativity of thought has few direct loss-inducing consequences, poor resource allocation has many. Those working in such roles must endeavour to close the gap.

In our conversation Jim O'Hara emphasised the testing of ideas more than the creation of them. I certainly never got the sense that this was because there was any lack of ideas, but more a value that this capital-intensive business placed on the rigorous analysis and challenge of each and every idea. He talked about a 'more action oriented' approach to strategy than planning implies. An approach where executives are 'challenged to come up with hypotheses', the hypotheses are built up and knocked down until eventually 'some are chosen and become part of the on-going strategy'.

The problem with any situation where ideas are challenged is of course the risk that people present only safe ideas. A common line one hears in response to this issue is that firms make it okay for people to fail and so encourage risk-taking. What nonsense! It's never okay to fail, it is certainly acceptable to recognise that failure will happen, but that's not the same as making it okay to fail. Years ago as a quality manager I was trained in the concept of acceptable quality levels (AQLs). AQL was a perversion of the word 'quality'. What it in fact meant was that there was a certain amount of faulty product that it was okay to produce. So in the minds of staff, the acceptable quality level became the acceptable junk level. The proponents argued that failure is a fact of life and so we should acknowledge and control it. But making it okay, which is what AQLs did, is not the same as acknowledging it happens. My retort was a bit cruel, but to the effect that if a nurse was about to handle your newborn child, what AQL would you set for dropping babies? Unfortunately I am sure that occasionally babies do get dropped, I recognise that, but that's not the same as saying it is okay.

So how do global elites deal with such issues? Jim described his approach in Intel where a culture of informed risk taking is developed, a culture that expects and even demands innovation:

> 'We don't expect people just to do what's prescribed, we expect them to go beyond that ... They won't get dinged for coming up with an initiative that ultimately fails in itself. They will get dinged if they haven't set up the work, the experiments, and so on correctly.' (Jim O'Hara)

In a slightly different vein, perhaps as Ned Sullivan's background is in somewhat less capital-intensive businesses or at least businesses without the huge upfront sunk capital costs of Intel, Ned discussed the strategy process noting:

> 'It's researched based, it's creative, it's creative tension, it's arguments, it's going down blind alleys sometimes and making huge mistakes at times, but recognise them as quickly as you can and back out of them as quickly as you can.'

Perhaps in this context we can allow failure to run a little further because it is possible to do some backing out. Not that failure is necessarily more acceptable, but that it's just not as expensive.

What struck me in the conversations was the fluidity with which they moved from creative thinking, through analysis and on to implementation. It certainly appears that these global elites move easily across academic constructs of creative strategy formulation and implementation without much regard for the distinction. These are not separate phases of a process that lead to outcomes, but elements of a cycle that iterates as meaning is unpicked from data that is collected on the journey. Strategy is creativity, strategy is analysis, strategy is implementation; all simultaneously orchestrated. This is not to say that strategy is so tightly defined that there is no room for opportunity or chance. Kevin Toland put it eloquently when he said

> 'There may be accidents in strategy it's just that it can't all be accidental.'

Evolution and time

> 'I think strategy is an agonising birth process that partly mobilises and taps into the wisdom of the organisation as it evolves. It is also partly a more formal process where people get into a room and they get some external people who do an analysis and they show them worldwide comparators and all that. So it's a bit of both and you have to have both I think.' (Ned Sullivan)

Ned paints an interesting picture here of the formal planning and informal emergent aspects of strategy development. It's not planned or emergent, it's planned *and* emergent. All of the interviewees, at some point, came around to the strategic conversation. It was described as difficult, challenging, agonising and time consuming – a process that took place on aeroplanes, in bars and chatting over coffee. Through iteration after iteration, building on experience as more was learned the process honed the strategy down tighter and tighter.

Once the core of the strategy has been honed the attention shifts. A management team can only focus in depth on a small subset of the business activities at one time. So when one is satisfied they move on to put more effort into other aspects in a cycle that eventually revolves back around to a review of the strategic principles. As progress is achieved some aspects get simpler but at the same time get harder. For example Ned described setting a target in the early 1980s for Baileys to become the biggest liqueur brand in the world. 'Lo and behold, by about 1990 or 1991 or so we were the biggest liqueur brand in the world – the challenge then is, now what?'

It was interesting to hear that while formal strategy planning sessions played a role, there was little belief that strategy emerged from them. These global elites seemed quite comfortable that one can't know all one needs to know at once and that pressing for answers where they are not ready to come will not deliver good strategy. So while annual cycles of strategy and budgeting played a role in all their lives, there was an explicit recognition that you can't say we are going to start 'doing strategy in March, and by May we will have a strategy' (Ned Sullivan). Rather strategy was seen as a process of evolution, emergence and iteration. A process that could take many years. By taking the time to develop the strategy, by revisiting difficult questions, through diligent process and good research the strategy becomes woven into the fabric of the organisation, 'to a certain extent by osmosis'. The process is punctuated, but not defined by strategic plans and annual budgets.

> 'I can remember in a number of companies that kind of agonising period you know you haven't got it and yet it's tantalisingly close – you just can't kind of put your finger on it. Then it emerges and you've got it.' (Ned Sullivan).

This sense of giving it the time it needs was echoed by Kevin Toland who reminded me of the importance of being patient. 'You can always do something you want to do a day late, it's very hard to undo something if you're a day early.'

Kevin went on to describe the traditional annual strategy process as a kind of time-bound health check. However, he was advocating a more discursive approach than the checkbox health-care one. An approach where the unresolved questions are unearthed and picked at over time. He said that rather than rush to solutions or get a poor answer because it fits with the process timeline, we need to come back to the issue in time when we can get the right answer. Jim O'Hara added a twist to this and advocated a process

> 'where you're always looking for opportunities rather than planning for a particular outcome. I call it like "Pacmaning" your way into the future. So the big problem about strategic planning is you tend to look at an end point and then you plan to get to that end point and the problem is in doing so you miss a whole range of other opportunities that you're not geared up to look for. So strategic action is more appropriate, a regular

process of strategic action and a regular process of possibility, discovering and testing those possibilities.' (Jim O'Hara)

Getting real engagement

'These days strategy is much more active, it's much more focused, it's much more real, it's much more … you know people are serious about it and there's always consequences. If you put up a hypothesis and you can't defend it there's implications for your own career so there's a lot more skin in the game these days than there probably was years ago.' (Jim O'Hara)

The skin in the game, as Jim describes it, captures the fact that strategy at these elite levels is not an abstract game. It is real time, difficult, uncertain, and most of all it matters. It matters because these elites have a passion to give leadership and it matters because there are consequences for them and their organisations. This should and does lead to vigorous debates – debates with real stakes, real challenges, real uncertainty. But out of the process of debate must emerge action if any strategy is to be implemented. Real debate comes from real differences of opinion. Opinions that matter to those that own them and yet to be successful everybody must support the outcome. Jim described a process, probably more than a process actually, a cultural value maybe of 'disagree and commit'. A 'value of openness and debate, but of finality and clarity and then strong leadership'.

A similar engagement, perhaps not as explicitly framed, was expressed by Peter Robbins. Peter described a perceived shift in the approach to strategy. A shift from a more secretive hierarchical orientation to one that sought to be inclusive. A process of greater transparency and of engagement that ensured people engaged with the priorities. 'The more contemporary approaches are about including people and it's more about teams.'

As Kevin reflected on the growth in Glanbia and the introduction of new managers he described the importance of making time to 'get to know' the key managers, noting that it was 'important to tell them some of the folksy stuff about how we think, how we developed and the sort of culture and freedom we give people'.

This folksy, engaged, debate intensive approach is a far cry from the clinical application of strategy tools from the traditional MBA programme. In the world of global elite strategists the tools are given, analytical capacity is assumed, and excellence in the application is expected. It is only beyond these standards that the global elite find competitive advantage. Kevin put it well when he said

'I went to school in England for a couple of years and you've got to do the 11 plus to get into grammar school. So everyone that's in grammar school has the 11 plus but not everyone is the same. So if you're hiring someone from a good strategy house they've all got their 11 plus in strategy, funnily enough what makes the better ones stand out for my money is two characteristics, one is an insatiable curiosity, insatiable, simple curiosity as opposed to complex curiosity, and the second thing that actually makes the good ones stand out is a bit of humility.'

The final analysis

In the final analysis it appears that strategy for global elites is much less about analysis than we might have thought. Rigour, testing, challenging, analysing, creativity, leadership, commitment, passion, and even humility are all in the global elite strategists' make-up. The strategy challenge for the global elite is not a race; it is a process, it has few right answers but many evolving ones. It is a tension of creativity and feet on the ground grind. It is at the same time planned and emergent. It is perhaps the ability to believe passionately in all of these opposing concepts that sets global elites apart.

13
Leadership Skills of the Political Elites: The Case of Ohio

Thomas Sigel

In the 1953 smash Broadway musical, *Wonderful Town*, with music by Leonard Bernstein and lyrics by Betty Comden and Adolph Green, the two main characters, Ruth and Eileen, leave Columbus, Ohio, for the big city of New York in pursuit of excitement and establishing new careers. At one point, they lament in the song 'Ohio', made famous by Rosalind Russell and Edith Adams, why they ever left Ohio. Little did they know that in this same year, the Buckeye State, once at the forefront of business and industry, would enter a period of economic and political decline. Once touted as 'The Heart of it All', Ohio's leadership has flailed, causing the state to tailspin into mediocrity.

A native Ohioan, I have spent the majority of my adult career in Europe. I always said that one day I would return to my roots. In spring 2007 I did indeed come home, and much to my shock I encountered an alien landscape. I had remembered from my childhood that Ohio had been a diverse place: a vibrant agricultural bread-basket, a forerunner in the industrial revolution with coal, iron ore, rubber and steel and automobile production. Certainly, by the 1960s and 1970s, many manufacturing industries began to close, partly due to competition, but also because businesses shifted to more service-oriented positions (Ohio History Central: An Online Encyclopedia of Ohio History, 2010).

In an attempt to find out what happened, I turned to a pre-eminent authority on Ohio politics. From our discussion and referring to an article, 'Democracy in Ohio: Problems and Prospects' (Asher et al., 2008) which appeared in *Democratic Renewal: A Call to Action from America's Heartland* (Redfield, 2008) I set out to speak with as many Ohio public leaders as possible to answer the following questions:

1. How do you define a successful leader?
2. How has Ohio gone from being an influential state in all sectors – business, education, political leadership – to a floundering state with an economic and brain drain?

3. Ohio's democracy and state government face serious challenges, including public corruption, a flagging economy and relatively low levels of educational attainment. What can effective leaders do to turn this around?
4. A hallmark of Ohio's political culture is the major political parties' success in using public offices to serve their own partisan interests. I would be interested on your thoughts on this and what you feel needs to happen to change this.

Connecting with Ohio political leaders was a frustrating process. These political elites profess to represent the voice of their constituents both on a state and national level, yet many have no interest in engaging on a substantive level. Of course, the challenge of reaching any political figure is to get beyond the gatekeeper. Whilst websites and political literature encourage the 'people' to contact their congressmen and senators, once I connected, the gatekeeper probed deeper to find out why I wanted to meet the leader. After either hesitation or word that they would be in touch, I was told that he/she was not available. In one instance I made many phone calls and sent numerous emails to a leading senator's office. I had no return phone call or email acknowledgement. In this instance, I knew this politician's driver, so I typed a brief note for the driver to hand to the senator. About two weeks later I received the following email from his Deputy State Director:

From: X
Sent: 14 October 2009 17:43
To: 'tsigel@xxx.com
Subject: A message from Senator X's office

Mr. Sigel,
X forwarded your email about your request for an interview with Senator X. Unfortunately I am unable to schedule an interview. Senator X is spending a tremendous amount of time and energy in Washington working on health care reform and climate change legislation. Therefore, his schedule is booked solid for the foreseeable future. I am sorry we cannot accommodate your request, but I hope you understand just how challenging and demanding these times are for the senator. Please accept my apologies.

In another instance, I tried to line up an appointment with a long-serving local state representative. After finally breaking through the barrier, his aide scheduled a meeting, only to cancel it, reschedule, cancel again and then never return my phone calls or messages. I had absolutely no apology. With the imminent deadline of this chapter, I contacted this office again to no avail – complete silence – not even the courtesy to say that the politician was unable to meet with me or answer my questions.

To no surprise, the interviews I did manage to secure were through mentioning a familiar name and indicating that individual X or Y suggested I contact them. In some instances, I used the strategy of, 'X, who recently supported your campaign with a fundraising event, suggested I give you a call.' This yielded some success. This is the spin I used to try to clinch an interview:

> 'I have been asked to write a book chapter on Ohio political leadership in a contributed book. This is a great opportunity to give Ohio some global exposure and take a critical look at the leadership crisis in Ohio. You can see the list of contributors below and their proposed topics. I am gathering data, doing research and conducting interviews between now and mid-August. I know that you are busy, but it would be super to have your feedback on the following questions. I have already interviewed U, V, W, X, Y, Z. I'd love to get a good cross section of Republican and Democratic responses/feedback, as well as thoughts from journalists and academics.'

Interestingly, in some cases, the fact that I had mentioned that X had participated served as an impetus for another person to participate, especially when they recognised that I had interviewed somebody holding a different political perspective. Underscoring to them that I wanted to obtain a good cross-section of Republican and Democratic responses/feedback helped garner participation.

In the end, I managed to interview five Republicans and four Democrats, along with a seasoned academic and a journalist who spent 34 years covering Ohio politics. Before examining the participants' responses, let's first examine Ohio's political landscape in the context of its history.

Ohio's political landscape

Few states, if any, can match Ohio's historic balance – a balance of interests that rested in large part on geography, which in turn helped determine economic development. Both geography and economic opportunity helped determine settlement patterns. Geography shaped the agricultural–industrial balance that developed in the late nineteenth and early twentieth centuries. Whilst remaining among the most productive agriculture states, Ohio was also in the forefront of the industrial surge. The balance between farm and factory was reflected in a balance between rural dwellers and urban dwellers (Knepper, 2007: 2).

By the late nineteenth century, industrialisation boomed as coal, oil and iron ore became important businesses. Factories started manufacturing rubber and steel products, and then in the beginning of the twentieth century, automobile production emerged.

As a result of industrialisation, people started moving to the cities in pursuit of jobs, not only from rural areas of Ohio, but from within the United States and also from abroad. By the 1960s and 1970s, many manufacturing industries began to close, partly because of competition, but also because many businesses relocated to other states and countries (ohiohistorycentral. org). To address this, Ohio businesses, in recent years, have shifted to more service-oriented sectors.

Unlike other states, Ohio has an extraordinary number of cities, many which in their heyday thrived on their successful industrial bases. The 'Big 8' are Akron, Canton, Cincinnati, Cleveland, Columbus, Dayton, Toledo and Youngstown. Because of the influx of many people, politics have had 'an ethno-cultural base, especially strong in the nineteenth and early twentieth centuries. There was also a geographic and economic base to Ohio political behaviour that created an uncommon balance in the state between agricultural and industry, between rural and urban' (Knepper, 2007: 2). The diverse population helped shape Ohio's political behaviour.

For most of its history, Ohio has proven to be a microcosm of government and politics in the rest of the Midwest. It has also served as a political barometer at a national level. More presidents of the United States have come from Ohio than any other state. These eight political leaders are: William Henry Harrison, Whig (9th president); Ulysses S. Grant, Republican (18th president); Rutherford B. Hayes, Republican (19th president); James Garfield, Republican (20th president); Benjamin Harrison, Republican (23rd president); William McKinley, Republican (25th president); William Howard Taft, Republican (27th president); and Warren G. Harding, Republican (29th president). Numerous former state politicians have served Ohio nationally in the US House of Representatives and the US Senate.

Whilst the presidential representation has been exclusively conservative, Ohioans have belonged to every major political party that has ever existed since the state's establishment in 1803. In the early nineteenth century, political wrangling between the Democratic-Republican Party and the Federalist Party almost delayed Ohio's statehood. During the first part of the nineteenth century, Ohioans who desired an industrialised economy favoured the Whig Party, whilst those who wished to remain agricultural generally supported the Democratic Party. By the mid-nineteenth century, many Ohioans favoured the Republican Party, which sought to limit slavery. At this time, those Ohioans who favoured the Democratic Party generally opposed a strong federal government. Class became a major factor in political-party loyalty during the late nineteenth and twentieth centuries, as the working class tended to favour the Democratic Party, whilst the middle and upper classes favoured the Republican Party.

Just as Ohioans' political loyalties have evolved over the years, the state's government has also changed. The Ohio Constitution of 1803 allowed the legislative branch of the Ohio government to dominate the state's governmental structure. Over the first decades of the nineteenth century, the judicial branch established its right to declare legislative actions unconstitutional. The governor served really as a mere figurehead at first, but by the early twentieth century, this office assumed much more power, providing an effective check on the legislative branch (ohiohistorycentral.org).

Definition of a successful political leader

In Bolman and Deal's 'four framework approach' (Bolman and Deal, 1991) they suggest that leaders display leadership behaviours in one of four types of frameworks: Structural, Human Resource, Political or Symbolic. Under the political framework, the authors define an effective leader as 'an advocate, whose leadership style is coalition and building'. In an effective leadership situation, the leader is 'a hustler, whose leadership style is manipulation'. The authors go on to say that political leaders clarify what they want and what they can get; they assess the distribution of power and interests; they build linkages to other stakeholders, use persuasion first, and then use negotiation and coercion only if necessary.

Throughout this chapter, in order to maintain confidentiality of the interviewees, they will be referred to as Academic A, Journalist A and Politicians A, B, C, etc. respectively. Five of the eleven interviewees pinpointed the notions of convincing/influencing and persuasion as key in defining a successful leader. Not surprisingly, none referred to the 'hustler' style of leadership, nor did they use the words 'negotiation' or 'coercion'. Three interviewees expressed the need for clarity to create a vision. Three mentioned integrity, two indicated courage, and two stressed the ability to educate. Other single responses included:

- Humility
- Trust
- Discerning intelligence
- Ability to look outward, not inward
- Lead by example
- Participate
- Openness
- Honesty
- Fairness
- Must be a moderate
- Tenacious
- Confident
- Passionate
- Responsible
- Servant leader
- Engender hope

Without doubt, all the elements that the interviewees mentioned are crucial to effective leadership. Journalist A sums up the definition quite succinctly:

> 'A successful leader has the capacity to influence public opinion and steer it in a direction it might not otherwise go. A successful leader has core integrity and a discerning intelligence as guides. Combining integrity, intelligence and a capacity (perhaps an eloquence) to mold public opinion, that leader can move the populace (electorate) to embrace solutions that otherwise would be unobtainable. The commonplace leader simply follows public opinion, or is immobilized by it. The true leader educates the public to make collective decisions that otherwise would go against the public's selfish interests.'

Whilst effective leadership is necessary to propel the Buckeye State into the twenty-first century, Academic A contends that there is a dearth of leadership in Ohio. He states that leadership should lay out a vision and engender hope, but asks how you harness it. He also suggests that leadership must come not only from statewide business organisations, but also from regional entities such as local chambers of commerce and growth associations.

No stranger to politics, Politician A, currently Assistant to the Vice President of Governmental Relations at a state educational institution, holds a similar view to Academic A regarding a lack of current leadership. During his 32-year legislative career, Politician A served in both the House and Senate and held roles including Majority Whip, Assistant Majority Leader and Minority Leader. He has been a delegate or alternative to several Democratic National Conventions, was an advance man for a presidential vice president, a member of a president's finance council and Ohio chairman of a candidate's presidential campaign.

Politician A states:

> 'There is no leadership in Ohio. Leadership is implementation of a vision whether or not it is yours or not. It is about trying to get votes – trying to persuade. Far too much compromise comes as a result. So what is leadership? The art of persuasion is leadership. God gave us the gift of imagination and curiosity. Also, without passion there will be no leadership. Passion is an ingredient that makes things happen and the ability to persuade. I have watched leadership and the lack of it and have seen smart people who have great ideas, but they become consensus builders, thus mediocre people who play it safe. Putting together efficiencies requires skill levels and a level of passion.'

With politicians having to walk the delicate tightrope of pleasing everybody, effective leadership is indeed a double-edged sword. How is a politician truly able to lead? As a result, leaders in Ohio have strategically had to play more to the middle in order to achieve success. Currently a consultant with a firm specialising in public policy and management strategy, Politician B contends that if you look at state-wide leadership you have to be a moderate to win state-wide.

In the 1990s, Politician B was Director of an Ohio cabinet and also held a high-level financial post. He also served as senior policy adviser to the governor, providing advice on a range of policy issues and major system reforms, including health care, education, tax and fiscal policy.

Politician B comments, 'Successful politicians have to be something of everything without giving up integrity. The governor is going through difficult times. If he gets in trouble politically, it is because he goes off the centrist view.'

Whilst unable to connect directly with Governor Ted Strickland, I was able to have a conversation with a high-ranking spokesperson at the Governor's Residence in Columbus. Politician C noted that politics is about winning and losing in order to get control. 'When a campaign starts you need to be partisan, but when it comes down to effective leadership, it really needs to be about motivation and change and new ways of doing things.' Politician C noted that when in office, effective leadership boils down to working and making progress in a bi-partisan environment. An effective leader, Politician C says, needs to lead with courage, tenaciousness and confidence. Politician C also noted the trust factor stating, 'It is difficult for people to trust a leader.'

Politician D, a younger politician who has had success on the county level as a County Commissioner, remarks that a successful political leader is one of integrity and humility who is able to convince his/her followers to do something they are currently not doing, or to give up something they currently possess in order to secure long-term gain. Politician D entered the race for a congressional district in autumn 2009, but did not succeed in the primary election. Nonetheless, this young, charismatic leader who is fervently religious also touches upon the principle of trust:

> 'The successful leader must have developed a deep enough trust with his/her followers that even though the new direction might be uncomfortable in the beginning, and the path a bit rocky, his/her followers will remain on the new path until they reach a place better than the one they left behind.'

Based upon Politician D's comment, building trust inherently involves Politician A's notion of the art of persuasion, because one must be able to persuade people to trust in order to smooth the rocky path. It also aligns with Bolman and Deal's (1991) definition of a successful leader.

It would also make sense that the art of persuasion embraces an element of educating in order to win not only constituent, but peer support. Currently a high-ranking official, Politician E comments:

> 'It takes courage to be a political leader. One has to take responsibility. This means doing things that are unpopular, but there is the need to include people in the process. This requires educating people on what needs to be done. An effective political leader is a servant leader – serving to empower the people to get more done.'

Thus, in order to persuade and educate, an effective leader must create a vision. Politician F is involved with a committee to ensure that the Ohio Senate has an appropriate venue to promote increased accountability and transparency in the operation of state government offices and agencies. This senator started his political career from the grassroots level and has been a rising conservative star in Ohio politics. Politician F emphasises:

> 'You need clarity to create a vision. Why would you expect people to follow you? Very few people are capable of articulating where they want to take Ohio. When I was [in a certain position] I had a mission statement. It was about the economy. It's about the dollars. If people have good jobs and a good standard of living they really want less government. Good things come from having a vibrant, healthy economy. Business and political leaders must look outward, not inward. Too many leaders have failed to solve Ohio's problems. Ohio needs to fit in.'

Fitting in, however, can be a challenge. Seasoned Politician G, who is involved with the Ohio Elections Commission, and a former member of the Ohio House of Representatives, notes the difficulty. He indicates that the problem is that 'we need leadership by example – providing supporting data, offering pros and cons to an issue and openness to discuss issues'. Politician G goes on to say:

> 'Because of term limits we only have two years to accomplish things, so we need participatory leaders. Before term limits it was easier to get support and move things fairly quickly, but it was not representative. It was top-down management. Today it is bottom-up management, but it is like trying to get 50 frogs in a wheelbarrow. Somebody will say, "I'll vote for your school funding bill if you vote for my issues, but you have to tell everybody else, then 3 frogs jump out. It is a game that has to be played."'

Politician H, who is serving a second term in the Ohio Senate, has been working to improve the educational opportunities for children, provide new economic opportunities for Ohio's economy, improve services for veterans, increase accessibility to children's health insurance, and to criminalise human trafficking, and touches upon Bolman and Deal's (1991) effective leadership component of building linkages to other stakeholders. Politician H explains:

> 'A successful political leader works at trying to accomplish important goals that affect people every day and to sustain goals over time. A leader needs to listen to the people and hear all aspects in order to approach issues and weigh all the facts. A leader must bring stakeholders together. That is how you are most effective. No one person in the state can make things happen at one time. It takes intuitiveness, understanding, listening and influence. There are 99 house members, and 33 senators. As a senator, I need to influence them, the constituents, support and special interest groups. I like to refer to successful leadership as turning a ship. If you turn a ship too quickly it tips over. Leadership is a long term process. You need to make compromises. No one person has the answer. There are different philosophies and principles that we approach, but that's what makes our republic great. As leaders, we must strive to benefit the common good of the republic.'

To benefit the common good of the republic, a former Speaker of the Ohio House, Politician I, believes the strategy for a successful political leader is openness, honesty, fairness. Whilst in office, Politician I advocated welfare reform and played a major role in the deregulation of electricity in Ohio. Politician I was integrally involved with the Republican National Committee in Washington, DC. Politician I also helped direct a historic grassroots effort that enabled President Bush to win Ohio by a decisive margin. Today Politician I continues to devote energies to growing the Party and developing a strong grassroots political organisation.

Certainly, as political leaders, the interviewees provide upbeat, optimistic and perhaps somewhat idealistic responses regarding their notion of an effective political leader. Some sprinkle their responses with a bit of cynicism, i.e. there is no leadership in Ohio, so let us now examine how Ohio has transformed from an influential state in all sectors – business, education, political – to a floundering state with an economic and brain drain.

A floundering state: how to reverse the economic and brain drain

According to Journalist A

> 'factors largely beyond the control of Ohio's public-sector leaders have led the state's decline – a globalising economy, a dramatic shrinkage

of the state's highly-paid, heavy manufacturing jobs, and an exodus of population from most of the state's big cities. The state's leaders actually have responded fairly effectively to these changes, but the positive effects of those responses will take a long time to reveal themselves. The state actually is much friendlier to business, and much more competitive with other states in overall business climate, than it was in the 1960s, 1970s and 1980s.'

Politician D contends that Ohio continues to be an influential state, but the number one factor that has led to many of its economic challenges has been the lack of true leadership within the state government. Politician D explains:

'Consider the performance of those who have recently occupied the office of governor or leadership roles in our state's legislature. Over the last several decades we have elected governors who were managers rather than leaders. They were successful politicians who had been fairly effective when it came to managing public opinion and managing the day-to-day activities of our state government, but when it came to leading change within our state, i.e., designing new economic, social welfare or education policies that would allow our state to compete with other states and countries, they simply did not take action. They tinkered a little with a few of our existing policies and programs, polished them with a little "political spin" and glided to re-election.'

Politician D believes that it is fairly clear why they did not take necessary actions to redirect the state. He feels that they did not want to risk their party's political capital and their majority in the legislature. Politician D continues:

'You see, by now most of us realize that in order to set our state on the right track our state's leaders are going to have to change long-time policies that will impact many people in many different ways. For a politician this means the possibility of upsetting some of their long-time constituents, and possibly jeopardizing their re-election. After all, even though conditions may not be ideal, we as citizens tend to like the status quo. We may say that we want change, but the truth is often we would prefer the security of our current situation. While we may claim that we want to see things be better, the reality is we often do not want to change our lives or our activities – we do not want to give up anything – to make them better. We want a new school building, but we don't want to pay higher taxes to build it. We want a smaller, less bureaucratic government, but we don't want to cut any of the current programs because either we or our friends are currently receiving a benefit from that program. Our most recent governors and legislators were good at managing public opinion, keeping us comfortable enough where we were that we would support their re-election.'

Politician D says that the trouble is the principle 'no pain, no gain' is often true in politics as well. Ohioans relaxed in our 'not too good, but not too bad' state of being until we found ourselves way behind our competition.

Politician E points to poor leadership and home rule for Ohio's decline. Home rule is the power of a constituent part of a state to exercise the state's powers of governance within its own administrative area that the central government devolves to it. Politician E explains that there are so many sectors of government such as county boards, school and library districts that are doing their own thing. Politician E notes that when there is not strong leadership at the top, it is hard to bring the sectors together to manage leadership. 'We can stand to take a look at how government is organised,' Politician E states. 'A strong, effective leader doesn't come along every day. A strong structure can mitigate this and foster better leadership.'

Politician H is quick to defend Ohio's rich agricultural and manufacturing heritage, noting that it was the first state to form out of the Northwest Territory, but acknowledges that because of the economy that the manufacturing base has moved out. 'Jobs have shipped overseas and there is a huge trade deficit which has had an impact,' Politician H explains. 'We now have to look at the strife in our state and need to re-tool and use the same strengths to keep us moving forward.' This politician notes that young people go where the jobs are and that we need to attract young people to return to raise families. Politician H feels that Ohio is still diverse, but emphasises that 'we need to find our strengths again'.

Like Politician H, Politician F also acknowledges Ohio's illustrious past, but admits that the glory is bygone. 'That Ohio was on the leading edge of the agricultural and industrial revolution, but not at the forefront of the technology revolution has hurt us,' states Politician F. 'Ohio is now not necessarily for the better. We need to solve our own problems.' Politician F talks about how Ohio, in the 1990s, had considerable influence nationally, noting that other states looked to its welfare reform and higher education as national models.

The flight of big business out of Ohio has had significant economic impact. Politician F continues, 'In the 50s, 60s and 70s, Ohio had political and economic power – the industrialists. Politicians relied on private sector leaders. This is no longer the case. Ohio needs to become an economic power house again. It is all about money. You had powerful leaders that were produced as a result of that.'

Politician F also points to education. Whilst Ohio has fine educational institutions, this politician says they are entrenched in the past and slow to react. 'We don't need to lead the nation, but we can't be held up because of lack of ability. We need to change the culture in Ohio. Another problem is that we have taxed the goose that lays the golden egg. We have taxed companies out. As a result, people stopped earning and investing here. Ohio needs to work with what it has to strengthen and rebuild.'

Politician C skirts away from factors that have led to decline, but notes that in our current economic climate we need to rethink what we really value. Politician C says, 'We don't have the dollars to sustain what we gave in the past. We must go back to local leadership to think creatively. Our biggest problem is whether or not there will be dollars.'

Politician A more scathingly places the blame on partisanship ideologies coming into political bodies. This politician explains, 'People are passionate about issues – guns, abortion, and gay rights. These have taken such a stronghold that the electorate is responding to these issues. Couple these issues with partisanship and you have deadlock.'

'America loves to throw tea into the ocean,' says Politician A. He feels that the political environment has been taken over by special interest groups – guns, abortion and gay rights. 'People become too passionate about issues. So what if two guys want to hold hands? Who cares?'

Politician A also points to the Republican Party, which he says uses special interest groups to block progress. 'We are a victim of our own ability to move quickly on issues such as tax and education. Ohio is a "wait and see" state.'

Politician A also attributes the decline to the tax problem of the 1960s and 1970s. He explains

'Ohio had its first income tax bill in the 1970s. Other states had created this because of increasing costs, such as Medicare. There are regulatory agencies and expensive government programmes which came about with the shift to income tax. Forty years later we need lower taxes to stimulate the economy. We are all a victim of this. The tax structure in Ohio is unfavorable to business. When locating a plant do you want to come here? The cost of doing business is not good.'

Regarding the current economic woes, Politician A says that Ohio felt the recession early. 'We are an export society. Things got depressed so companies went elsewhere. Other cities are offering more tech opportunities. There are some forces that you can't beat.'

Politician A confesses that he is glad that he is out of government. He says, 'I was responsible for [a certain] bill. It went from what you should and shouldn't do to "now I'm gonna' get you!" I can find corruption on every street corner.'

Academic A stresses that Ohio's political leaders must realise that every year that they defer making key choices and strategic investments, Ohio loses more ground because other states are not standing still even in difficult budgetary times. Ohio is entering this competition at a disadvantage since other states already have a more extensive track record in making investments in their citizens and their economies. As the state creates new programmes and plans, it must not let regional rivalries unduly influence allocation decisions lest scarce resources be spread too thinly with little positive benefit to the state.

Regarding jobs, Academic A acknowledges that this is a major issue for Ohio as the state goes through a wrenching transformation. He explains:

'The context of Ohio is very different than other states. Talking specifically about political leadership, this is not a good time. [Governor] Strickland is criticised for not having leadership. The Speaker of the House [Armond Budish] is not a strong speaker. The Governor will need to be more aggressive and proactive. How does an incumbent run when you have a bad economy? You need to seize opportunities – take some risks to push the discussion of an agenda. Strickland is super cautious, afraid to do anything. The proposed budget is not balanced. The government has never been so bad. We can attribute it to term limits. We are at a stage where people are frustrated by performance of government.'

Academic A was not the only interviewee concerned about term limits. Let's now turn briefly to this overriding issue that has stifled progress and put a damper on effective leadership.

Term limits and the impact of leadership

Cleveland *Plain Dealer* columnist Brent Larkin goes so far as to state in a 27 June 2010 editorial that term limits stifle democracy. He notes that since voters passed the eight-year cap on terms for the Ohio General Assembly in 1992 that this has been bad for state government. 'Term limits make every member of the legislature a lame duck from the moment he or she first walks into the Statehouse. Instead of creating a legislative atmosphere that promotes sound reasoning and statesmanship, term limits have increased divisiveness and instability within the political process.'

Politician G notes that term limits have changed the way Ohio conducts politics. Whereas politicians of the past had 30–40-year terms, the grassroots impetus to create term limits, initiated by the Chamber of Commerce, ensured that politicians no longer have a lifetime career. Politician G notes that holding a political office is now a 'stop on the ride' as leaders aspire to move from local to state and then national office.

Journalist A says that it is incredibly important to eliminate term limits, or to greatly lengthen them: 'The state legislature has declined incredibly in institutional knowledge, political leadership and understanding of the state because of term limits. The legislature has a crowd of preschoolers attempting to grapple with problems needing postgraduate knowledge and experience. The state also badly needs reapportionment and redistricting reform. The problem of noncompetitive elections results in far too many buffoons in elective office.'

Politician I notes that much experience walked out the door with the introduction of term limits. Politician I explains:

> 'It helps to have experienced people around. We must learn from history. Term limits changed the face of political leadership. It caused different dynamics in managing a legislature and managing a caucus. The current Speaker of the House [Armond Budish] is having some problems. There is a talent to managing. Ohio has compelling partisanship. People are not around long enough. Some caucuses have never been in the minority or majority. We need to hone skills – completely different from any other skills we have used. In time of some of the greatest economic problems, it would be good to have more experience.'

Looking back to 1995–6, the second term of Governor Voinovich, Politician I reminisces that there were other state-wide leaders who had worked together. Politician I says, 'It was a natural fit and the economic climate gave us a breather. We had the bipartisan support during that period to accomplish it. The Republicans had not been in the majority for 22 years. We had good working dynamics.'

So what is the solution? Ohioans have supported term limits with the belief that they have fostered good government, arguing that they increase competition and encourage new challenges. Proponents of term limits believe that unlimited terms create a need in the legislature for a seniority system in which mediocre politicians thrive. They also argue that term limits build a 'citizen' legislature made up of real people versus 'career' politicians. They also believe the system breaks ties to special interests and lobbying organisations and will force those interests to reconnect with a type of politician who thinks differently from a career politician – one interested in the causes at stake, not concerned with re-election.

Proponents of term limits feel that with these ordinary people, they will vote on principle and on what is best for the country, rather than trading votes with other legislators or special interests. There is also, perhaps, the naïve belief that term limits will introduce fresh thinking and new ideas. But this happens at the expense of losing seasoned experts. These freshmen politicians need experienced mentors to help break them in to the rigours and demands of the legislature. The public also believes that term limits will create a natural reduction in wasteful spending, as politicians up for re-election often have incentives to obtain Federal spending for 'constituents'.

There is also the perception that term limits encourage lower taxes, smaller government and greater voter participation in elections.

Clearly, term limits have changed the Ohio General Assembly in several ways, including high turnover of members, more competitive campaigns, increased partisanship, a less efficient legislative process and a shift in balance of power in Ohio state government. The suggestion of, perhaps, a 12-year term limit might create a compromise that would satisfy Ohioans and make political leaders happier in their pursuit to effect significant change that would positively benefit the Buckeye State and its citizens.

Term limits, however, are only one of many issues in the bigger picture. Academic A notes that Ohio's democracy and state government face serious challenges, including public corruption, a flagging economy (as interviewees have already mentioned) and relatively low levels of educational attainment. What can effective leaders do to turn this around?

Tackling public corruption

According to Journalist A, Ohio has made progress against corruption and the state is not ignoring it. Journalist A indicates that 'the record of indictments and incarcerations is evident'. The massive federal investigation into public corruption in north-eastern Ohio is impressive. It will have long-term beneficial effects.

Politician D believes that we need to stop wasteful government spending and reduce the size of our state government. This will require strong political leadership. Politician D says that fiscal responsibility must be returned to the state and federal government if we are serious about restoring our state and national economy. He explains:

> 'One of the number one reasons why businesses are afraid to expand in the present climate is because of all the economic uncertainty that exists in Washington today. Business owners understand that the federal government is going to come to them to foot the bill for all of the massive spending that is currently taking place in Washington. In this context, Ohio leaders must work extra hard to create a stable economic situation here in Ohio.'

Politician H, a schoolteacher for nearly 20 years, was astonished when entering politics to see there were no audit tools to monitor fiscal spending. Politician H says, 'Transparency in state government is lacking and tools to measure the effectiveness of our programmes is lacking. Legislators don't have auditing tools to measure public dollars that are pumped into programmes. This leads to waste, fraud and abuse.' Politician H believes we need to look to other states' best practices in legislative auditing in order to create change.

Politician E also points to fiscal responsibility, stating that the government needs to be more careful about how they spend what they get. Politician E says:

> 'Whether one is a Girl Scout troupe leader or a public official, we need to look to how what we do contributes to the betterment to be part of a bigger picture. Good leadership inspires. Look at the 2008 elections. People listened to Barack [Obama] and Hillary [Clinton]. While Hillary had more knowledge and experience, when you looked at Obama, he oozed with charisma. This influences how people react toward a leader. The point is a leader needs to inspire. Look at 9/11, Katrina, and the Gulf oil spill. Responding to these events is to understand that it is about working for the greater good.'

In the 2008 report, *Democracy in Ohio: Problems and Prospects*, the authors also concur. They feel that the state legislature needs to improve transparency to better enable citizens to monitor the legislative process, including committee hearings and the drafting process. They believe that the legislature should have additional hearings to allow public comment when the legislature proposes new amendments.

Politician A stresses that we need leadership. Without it, the demagogues are going to win. Politician A believes that Ohio needs regionalism to clear out much of the chaff. With its 88 counties and major cities that operate more like city states, Politician A makes a good point. Why not streamline efficiencies and bring together mayors, city council members, county commissioners, township trustees, state and federal elected officials, philanthropic organisations, the business community and the plethora of planning associations to implement a programme that will allow Ohio to share and grow together? This would take real leadership to make such a shift. The challenge, however, is incentivising people to join together regionally.

Academic A agrees that there is a challenge. He acknowledges that Ohio has many small to regional cities with jealousies and rivalries. He feels there is a need to consolidate. As an example, he points to too many school districts. The obstacle is that people fear losing local control. Academic A states, 'The charisma and eloquence of leaders should not hide the reality of what is happening now. How do you handle transformation of the economy in a changing world? You need team work and coalition building. Leadership becomes greater, but more difficult.'

A flagging economy

The interviewees all agree that job creation and attracting people and companies to Ohio is the solution to a flagging economy. Politician D believes that we must reduce the corporate tax rate in America if we wish to see Ohio businesses remain competitive with those overseas. Doing so would free up capital that our businesses need in order to expand and would allow them to hire new employees. Politician D also believes we need to address the high energy costs by allowing offshore drilling and drilling on federally owned lands by American-owned oil companies. He also believes that we need to focus our efforts in developing a skilled workforce by supporting technical schools, colleges and universities. Politician D believes that we need to reclaim our culture by restoring traditional values, such as decency, honesty, personal responsibility, integrity and respect. All men and women should be able to agree that these values are necessary in order for a free government, a representative democracy, to survive.

Politician C believes that economic development will come with the next industries: renewable energy, sustainability and repairing past abuses of our environment. Politician C says, 'Ohio needs more creativity and innovation, but politics gets in the way. [The governor] believes that this country's advantage is creativity, innovation and global confidence. It is time to change. We need to create small businesses and get healthcare coverage under control.' Regarding leadership, Politician C says that one person at the top cannot provide leadership to move people forward. 'We cannot be dictated from the top down. Action should begin at the local level.' Politician C believes that we need to show that the state is better positioned and on a growth track to attract people back. If successful, it will lay a greater foundation for a growing economy. It we are not successful, it will continue to feel like a struggling, failing state.

A significant component in getting the economy back on track is education. This is a topic on which the interviewees have strong opinions.

Education

Politician C notes that the Governor has put a huge emphasis on education and educational reform. He has tried to make college more affordable. Politician C says, 'We need to have an educational system that ensures that people are prepared for new types of available jobs.' Politician C believes that we need to find the outstanding schools and find outstanding teachers and make them leaders.

Journalist A indicates that Chancellor Eric Fingerhut is leading an aggressive effort to remould the structure of higher education in Ohio. It is being embraced by public-sector leaders and those in academia. Journalist A believes that the state needs a prestigious, flagship university, and Ohio State University is on the correct path there. Elsewhere, he notes, the state is pursuing a strategy to streamline universities and community colleges to do what they do best, and in the process to greatly reduce inefficient duplication of programmes. This is always a work in progress, but progress is being made. Journalist A feels that Ohio is competitive with any state in its higher-education landscape.

Politician H also believes in streamlining. Politician H says that Ohio has not modernised its education – the system needs to respond to modern needs. This politician states, 'Not everybody needs a 2 or 4 year degree. We need to focus on training people to have skills to build things.' Politician H points to education programmes that have not been effective, for example Workforce Development. In 1998, US Congress passed the Workforce Investment Act to reform federal job training programmes and create a new, comprehensive workforce investment act. The system is supposed to help Americans access the tools they need to manage their careers through information and high quality services, and to help US companies find skilled workers. Politician H notes, 'Workforce Development has done nothing. Government bureaucracies just capture the dollars and do not channel them effectively.'

Like Politician H, Politician A is in favour of educational reform. He would throw out the community colleges and combine them with universities to create a local infusion of talent.

Politician E is also critical of the state of education and notes that the system is fractured. 'Forty percent of students who graduate need remedial training.' That is a sad commentary on the state of education, but it is difficult to progress. Politician E says, 'Change is the enemy.'

Change, indeed, is an enemy which causes individuals to operate within their own microcosms. This leads to deep partisanship which has been, as Academic A notes, a hallmark of Ohio's political culture. Political parties have used public offices to serve their own partisan interests. Why has this been the case and what needs to happen to change this?

Using public office to serve partisan interests

Political leaders often define themselves in terms of a set of beliefs and values which they embrace. These shape their political actions. Politician D says that one term that is rarely used to describe those who are currently elected to serve in public office is 'statesman'. Perhaps that is because many define a statesman as an individual of highest integrity who is willing to take and endure great personal loss in order to serve the best interests of others.

Politician D explains that one of the primary reasons why government spending continues to grow at every level of government is because politicians are trying to secure various blocks of voters by bribing them with government spending or special government programmes catering to special interests rather than to the general population. Both parties are guilty of using state money and programmes to secure votes, but in recent years they do it on a grand scale that the government cannot sustain. Politician D says:

> 'As a county commissioner, I recall a high-ranking political insider describing the situation that particular year this way. He said the legislative leaders at that time basically said "yes" to every single special interest group request for state funding and then implemented a 20% increase in the state sales tax to pay for them. Many would suggest that a true leader would have recognised that not everything could be funded, prioritised and even eliminated some expenses and balanced the budget without going to the taxpayers for more of their hard-earned money.'

Politician D believes the only way to fix the problem is electing men and women who care more about doing the best thing for our state rather than their political party or their own political interests. After all, money will always be a corrupting force in politics, whether in the form of political campaign contributions or earmarked government spending. We just need to find more men and women who can resist the temptation to fall in love with the power of money.

The irony in all of this, Politician D says, is the fact that if our elected officials would start making the tough decisions to set our state on the right course, although some citizens might be a little volatile at first, soon they would see the improvement in the state and give their full support to their elected leaders. Voters are looking for someone whom they feel they can trust even if they don't always agree with them on all of their policies.

Politician C says that we try to be bi-partisan when in office, but when the campaign starts again, we need to be partisan. Politician C worries that the campaign year will usurp necessary precious time to make things happen. Politician C says, 'We do not want to taint the good work that we do.'

Politician H believes that engaging the average citizens and informing them can help lessen partisanship. People need to be informed about issues. Politician H stresses the need for active participation and engagement with the citizens. 'We must put pressure on all the parties to have communities and governments that we pay for.'

Both Politician E and Politician A believe that political parties need to provide services, not wrap themselves up in power. That just doesn't happen any more. Like Politician H, Politician E believes the leader's role is to share information. Politician E says that the more robust and healthy the leadership, the more people participate. Politician A says, 'Political parties now just raise dollars to sell candidates. Neither the Democrats nor Republicans say, "Here is our platform and we mean it." There is more demagoguery than substance. If I am the governor and want to change health care, I have the network – 88 counties. The same goes for income tax. First, I would find out who the enemies are and how to neutralise them and persuade them they are wrong.'

This drives home the point of regionalism once again. Politician E says, 'We are wasting dollars with all those little fiefdoms. People in Ohio are strong, work hard, and have common sense, but we need to bring together their diverse experiences to be progressive and cutting edge. The government needs to empower the people.'

Asher et al. (2008: 85) note that partisanship is not an easy issue to address. They state:

> Governance has focused largely on the spoils of victory, how to reward one's friend, and how to stay in office rather than on overarching policy debates. States with such individualistic politics are more likely to experience graft and corruption, partly because the dominant party sometimes overreaches – especially if it controls all branches of governments and has enjoyed control for a long period of time. Victorious parties and their supporters are rewarded with tangible benefits, such as jobs, contracts, and favorable public policies, while the interests of ordinary citizens may be disregarded.

Certainly, citizens vote for those for whom they think best represent their beliefs. It is human nature for elected officials to march to the beat of their own ideological drum. There may be circumstances where elected officials embrace a position that does not fall under the umbrella of his or her party's platform. However, the role of the elected official should be to serve to the greater good of the constituents and in the case of Ohio, elected officials need to think outside of their narrow silos and work together collaboratively for the better good of the people.

Summary and conclusion

This chapter has examined leadership in Ohio from the perspective of nine political leaders, including five Republicans, four Democrats, an academic and a journalist. Ohio, once at the forefront of business and industry, has entered a period of economic and political decline. Leadership has flailed and the state has slipped into mediocrity. Despite this downturn and all the virtuous comments from the interviewees, there is still very little effective leadership in the Buckeye State. It will take more than their upbeat, optimistic and perhaps somewhat idealistic responses regarding their notions of an effective political leader for Ohio to regain strong leadership. There are no easy answers or short-term solutions.

A step in the right direction, however, would be for leaders to seek practical solutions to specific concerns. That starts with listening to all points of view, and objectively and critically examining situations. This may force leaders into embracing and implementing new ways of doing and thinking which would entail breaking tradition. This could threaten, damage or destroy the networks that these politicians have fought hard to nurture in building their careers – albeit grassroots organisations, associated political groups, economic and business players and constituents. Are these leaders prepared to go out on a limb to truly create effective change, or are they stuck in colloidal suspension in fear of breaking out of the mould?

Next, effective political leaders need to seek practical solutions to specific concerns. In some instances, this would entail putting aside partisan interests, so often a roadblock to progress, to advance Ohio's interests. The parties must work collaboratively to discover common ground.

Political leaders also need to continue working hard to create transparency, root out corruption and act as responsible critics, offering meaningful alternatives. They cannot capitulate to past practices. Change is the enemy that has caused people to work within their own microcosms which has prevented progress.

In order to progress, political leaders will need to become more open-minded. In Jerome Lawrence and Robert Edwin Lee's famous 1955 play, *Inherit the Wind*, which fictionalises the 1925 Scopes 'Monkey' Trial, Matthew Harrison Brady (corresponding to the real-life political leader, Williams Jennings Bryan, who opposed to the teaching of Charles Darwin's theory of evolution in the classroom) turns to Henry Drummond (corresponding to the real-life high-powered lawyer Clarence Darrow) and says, 'Why have you moved away?' Drummond responds by saying, 'Perhaps it is you, my friend, who has moved away by standing still.' Ohio cannot afford to stand still if it intends to adapt to the times and make a successful comeback.

Ohio has seen better days economically and politically, but the state has the resources and the wherewithal to rebound despite these challenging economic times. Political leaders, in conjunction with education, business and industry leaders must collaborate on local, country and state levels. To achieve success, leaders, no matter what political affiliation, need to work openly and honestly to address the crucial issues at stake. At the same time, they need to engage, motivate and educate the populace to become more informed and involved to make Ohio a better place to live. Ohio can once again become 'The Heart of it All'.

References

Academic A (2009) Interview, Columbus, Ohio, 20 August.

Asher, H., Henkener, A., Rosenfield, P., Tokaji, D. and Turcer, C. (2008) 'Democracy in Ohio: Problems and Prospects'. In K. Redfield (ed.), *Democratic Renewal: A Call to Action from America's Heartland* (Midwest Democracy Network), 81–110.

Bolman, L. and Deal, T. (1991) Reframing Organizations: *Artistry, Choice, and Leadership* (San Francisco: Jossey-Bass).

Journalist A (2010) Email, 'Ohio Political Leadership'. Message to Thomas Sigel, sent 29 July, 11:11 (tsigel@sigelpress.com).

Lamis, A. P. and Usher, B. (eds.) (2007) *Ohio Politics* (revised and updated edn.) (Ohio: Kent State University Press).

Knepper, George W. (2007) *Ohio Politics: A Historical Perspective* (Ohio: Kent State University Press).

Larkin, Brent (2010) 'Ohio's Term Limits Stifle Democracy', Sunday, 27 June, 5:30 a.m (www.Cleveland.com).

Ohio History Central (2010) *An Online Encyclopedia of Ohio History* (www.ohiohis torycentral.org), http://www.ohiohistorycentral.org/topic.php?nm= business_and_ industry&rec=6; http://www.ohiohistorycentral.org/topic.php?nm=government_ and_politics&rec=10.

Parker, G., Sisson, R. and Coil, W. R. (2005) *Ohio and the World, 1753–2053: Essays Toward a New History of Ohio* (Columbus: Ohio State University).

Politician A (2010) Telephone interview, Cleveland, Ohio, 30 July.

Politician B (2009) Interview, Columbus, Ohio, 20 August.

Politician C (2009) Interview, Columbus, Ohio, 20 August.

Politician D (2010) Email, 'Ohio Political Leadership'. Message to Thomas Sigel, sent 18 August, 17:02 (tsigel@sigelpress.com).

Politician E (2010) Telephone interview, Columbus, Ohio, 31 August.

Politician F (2010) Interview, Columbus, Ohio, 20 August.

Politician G (2010) Interview, Medina, Ohio, 10 August.

Politician H (2010) Telephone interview, Toledo, Ohio, 31 August.

Politician I (2009) Interview, Columbus, Ohio, 20 August.

Redfield, K. (ed.) (2008). *Democratic Renewal: A Call to Action from America's Heartland* (Midwest Democracy Network).

14

Entrepreneurs as Elites

Peter Lawrence

It is unusual to have a chapter on entrepreneurs in a book about elites.

This does not mean that entrepreneurs are the victim of some cultural bias, but the reasons for their characteristic exclusion from the elite corral are both several and instructive. To start with entrepreneurs appear to lack the historical embeddedness of other elites. The power elite, like the poor, are always with us, even though the composition of this elite has evolved over the centuries from warrior chieftains and then henchmen through divine right kings to elected of representatives organised by party machines. The religious elite have been similarly enduring. An educational elite, likewise, was originally associated with organised religion and now with top universities and with 'learned professions'.

In contrast entrepreneurs seem much more recent. Although we can look back over the centuries and identify a few folk whom we could appropriately label entrepreneurs, these innovators do not get much air time until the industrial revolution in the later eighteenth century in Britain and similarly with the fast developing American economy in the nineteenth century. Yet these mostly inventor-innovator entrepreneurs do not seem to put down roots. This is probably because they are remembered for their inventions and adaptations of machines but these led to the setting up of factories and then to corporations often becoming giant corporations. From Henry Ford to the Ford Motor Company as it were. In short, corporations surpassed and supplanted the entrepreneurs. The corporations dominated business consciousness throughout the twentieth century. It is only in the latter part of the century that governments in Western countries came to recognise the contribution of SMEs (small and medium enterprises) and new business to the creation of employment. The idea also arose that these new businesses might be more innovative, bringing forth new products that were spurned by the more established companies, content with their existing product markets. The outcome: governments in Western countries adopted policies and programmes to support new businesses.

Then in the last decade or so of the twentieth century various factors conjoined to increase competition (Lawrence, 2002). This, together with recessions in the early 1980s and early 1990s, led established companies to slim – downsize, rationalise, restructure, and to institute BPR (business process re-engineering).

While all this was going on the business academics 'gifted' the corporations the idea of core competence, something special that particular companies do better than others, that links their products but is independent of any particular product. An often-quoted example is Honda and petrol engines. 'How many Hondas can you get in a two-car garage?' students on business strategy courses were asked, and the answer is not two (or three if you put two on their side, side by side, and a third on top) but a bigger number that embraces all the Honda products with a petrol engine from outboard motor to snow blower.

'How do you determine your core competence?' came the rhetorical question. Answer: 'Outsource everything you can and what you have left is the core competence.' So 'outsourcing away from core competence' became the norm in the 1990s and is still running its course. This in turn creates extensive opportunities for both SMEs and new companies, to take up the slack in doing for larger companies things they previously did for themselves (we will offer some examples as the present chapter enfolds). The entrepreneur is centre stage at last.

In this way one may make the case for having a chapter on entrepreneurs. But a rather tricky question remains, namely, which entrepreneurs should appear in it?

Perhaps the answer to the question has been clouded by academic research. While a great deal is being published on entrepreneurs and business start-ups in the present time, one line of social science research has been enduring. This is to determine the psychological make-up of the entrepreneur, to answer as fully and as accurately as possible the question: What personality traits does the entrepreneur exhibit? – strong achievement drives, for example, strong desire for independence, dislike of taking orders from others, confident about own decisions and actions, and so on.

Now this is a perfectly legitimate and indeed worthwhile line of enquiry, but there is a catch. Of the many people who fit the profile, who exhibit all or most of the personality traits, not all of them go forth and found companies! The personality trait approach, that is, fails to isolate the population of *de facto* entrepreneurs. Rather it flags up those who in personality terms and particularly in terms of independence drives are the kind of people inclined to set up new businesses, but not all of them actually do so.

There is a further difficulty following on from the trait approach. This is that among the many with the right personality profile who do set up companies, thus as it were, confirming the psychological selection, not all of them succeed. Indeed the high failure rate among newly formed companies is well recognised. Those who try, succeed for a while, then falter and have to disband their companies, are well worth our attention. No doubt much can be learned from their endeavours. Though the learning is likely to be business learning rather than anything psychological. Nonetheless, those who tried but did not make it are not candidates for a chapter on entrepreneurs as elite!

So what we need is a way of isolating at least a sample group of successful entrepreneurs. There is a way of doing this. It is contemporary, it is British, and the data are already published and available to all who wish to pursue them.

Fast Track

Fast Track companies are ones which appear on the *Sunday Times* lists of the fastest growing 100 companies in the UK in a given year, though it is quite common for the same company to appear several years in a row. The *Sunday Times* research operation defines 'fastest growing' in terms of year on year revenue growth. This is not the only way in which success may be measured, but it is credible criterion.

My initiative was to visit and interview the principal founders of 30 of these companies, many of which appeared in more than one annual listing. The selection of companies was opportunistic rather than scientific in that I tended to 'go for' anything that caught my imagination. Having said this I am only aware of two biases. First, these *Sunday Times* lists are light on manufacturing companies, yet I pursued businesses that were 'making something' because I have in a way a manufacturing background and was convinced I would understand them better. But for all my efforts I still only found four of them! Secondly, though this is not a bias of my making, though I approached many Fast Track companies in London none of them granted me an interview. So the sample has turned out to be a tribute to friendly Northerners and Midlanders.

I recognise that the tactic adopted here is ad hoc. But if the goal is to have a plausible elite sample of entrepreneurs, this gets you down the runway and into the air.

The idea of looking at the successful to see what might be different and interesting about them goes back to *In Search of Excellence* in the 1980s (Peters and Waterman, 1982). Here the authors set up a number of financial performance criteria which they projected back over some 20 years to yield a subset of the sturdily successful from among the larger companies of the USA – then they took their sample apart, looking for causes and commonalities. In the present study, of course, the successful have been prequalified and preselected for us by the *Sunday Times* and its backroom research organisation, but the model is the same.

How it started

In the run-up to the millennium I embarked on a stocktaking exercise of the trends and developments of business in the West. The approach was to ask senior representatives of diverse companies what had been changing in their industries and in their particular company over the last few years, and what they expected to happen next. This formula was so absorbing I carried on doing it into the new century, when a colleague drew my attention to the *2000 Sunday Times* list. I was taken with that idea, new to me at that time, and quickly visited seven companies from this list as a finale to my 'millennium study'.

This little sample was made up of:

- A marine outfitter
- A music products retailer
- A civil engineering contractor
- A generics and parallel imports pharmaceutical products wholesaler
- A pub-restaurant chain
- An IT contractor
- A subcontract housebuilder

The 'magnificent seven'

All of these were absorbingly interesting. In every case you could see a reason or usually several interlocking reasons why they had done so well. The founders of the marine outfitter, for instance, used their prior experience in an established company in that industry to reduce costs to their clients, at the same time offering clients across the board services and expertise that would normally be associated with bigger, well-established companies. Some of this expertise, knowledge crossed with the regulatory requirements, also acted as a barrier to possible new entrants. The company cultivated customer relationships more zealously, and rendered superior service at the customer interface.

The music retailer had engineered a simple, low-cost retail format, driven by ingeniously sourced low-cost merchandise, enabling competitive pricing in the shops together with good margins. This formula establishes a reputation for cheapness that facilitates some raising of prices when conditions change, without harming sales!

With the civil engineering contractor there seemed to be lots of factors:

- Focus on 'all the things you can't see' like boilers, air-conditioning, electrical outfitting, and unglamorous structures like internet switching sheds – not so price sensitive, more difficult for the customer to second guess.

- Like the marine outfitter, it offered broader capability, in this case design *and* build, than would normally be the case with same-sized rivals.
- They had resourcefully solved the skills and manpower shortage in the London area where they operated.
- They offered employment management services to other companies.
- They exploited employment law and worker expectation differences to gain contracts in the more regulated EU countries.

The pharmaceuticals wholesaler majored on a price competitive mix dominated by generics and parallel imports. These categories, especially the imports, are subject to severe regulation, and 'qualifying' represents a significant entry barrier. The company had a clear segment focus, singleton pharmacies and smaller groups, which removed it from competition with the big players. It had a very clear picture of the operational and social needs of its customers, dispensers in scattered chemist shops, and met these needs in a way that was both sensible and kindly. In an industry awash with complicated discount and rebate systems, it operated a transparent discount that was deducted from the *initial* price. And like the marine outfitter and the civil engineering contractor it exhibited the image and capability of a larger more established company.

The pub-restaurant chain was founded on a customer segment in terms of class/occupation and life stage, and themed by the physical location of many of the pubs. It had a standardised low cost operational format and employed countless bits of trade know-how to make its offering more appealing (and lucrative). One of its strengths was addressing the needs and preferences of female customers.

The IT contractor had identified a high end, high margin niche, protected by an intangible entry barrier. Most IT contractors work on big numbers and thin margins, and compete on price. But this company is specialising in the top 10% of IT staff, those with management and interpersonal skills. It has taken the trouble to select and 'qualify' this minority, which normal IT contractors do not/cannot do, and this is the entry barrier. The major consultancy and accountancy partnerships can do this selection and offer a comparable service, but their fees are much higher. And at the other end of the chain this company has more discussion with the client organisations, tending in turn to strengthen the relationship, leading to repeat business, and to developing its 'know-how image' in particular industry segments.

Lastly our subcontract housebuilder was amazingly efficient in an industry often regarded as sloppy, overly driven by 'the way we've always done it' and slow to adopt IT. This company's strengths were anticipation (of needs and developments), control, process simplification and heavy IT. The result: the subcontracts from the volume housebuilders, which were expected in the industry to yield margins of 2–3%, came out at 8–9% for our company.

Going back for more

I had been fascinated by this exposure to these Fast Track companies. When I came to write the book on the pattern of business development around the millennium (Lawrence, 2002) I made a disproportionate use of the testimonies of the founders of these seven companies to develop arguments, illustrate points and above all to show how competitive advantage may be constructed.

At the same time I was beguiled by the 'magnificent seven'. There were plenty of answers to the question: Why did they succeed? But no single success formula. Nothing that applied to all of them. But then, I only had seven of them. What would it be like with a larger sample? What generalisations might be possible if you had 20 or even 30 on which to base them?

Both in response to this question and because of the high level of interest and understanding that they offered I resolved to go back for more.

So between the autumn of 2007 and January 2009 I visited another 23 Fast Track companies and their principal founders (or occasionally key lieutenants). These 23 were taken from the 2006 and 2007 *Sunday Times* lists, most of the companies being on both lists. These 23 include four manufacturing companies and another three building/civil engineering firms. The rest are a fascinating mix of service companies (see Table 14.1).

Table 14.1 *Sunday Times* Fast Track companies (2006 and 2007)

1.	**Prohire** Truck hire and maintenance.
2.	**Covion** Facilities infrastructure support (more conventionally, facilities management).
3.	**SPI Materials Ltd.** Manufacturer: Metal (tubular) components, mostly emissions related for auto industry, then components for the chemical and medical industries too.
4.	**AYS** Domiciliary care provider for the old and infirm.
5.	**T-Wall Garages** Car dealerships, principally Vauxhall, added Ford.
6.	**Reflex Labels Ltd.** Manufacturer: Sticky labels, mostly for food industry.
7.	**Widget** Software originator, later distributor for Tom Tom SatNav, with other intellectual property based initiatives, referred to in the interview as 'the 9 dwarves'.

(continued)

Table 14.1 Continued

8.	**Really Useful Products** Manufacturer: Plastic storage boxes.
9.	**Gladedale Holdings Ltd.** Housebuilder.
10.	**McLaren Construction Ltd.** Civil engineering.
11.	**SEH Holding Ltd.** Builder cum civil engineering, some manufacture, some plant hire, some direct sales.
12.	**Encore Personnel Services** Recruitment agency, specialising in providing blue-collar workers, mostly Polish or other Central Europeans.
13.	**Go Interiors** Wholesaler – suspended ceilings and other internal building products.
14.	**99p Stores** Discount retailer, distinctive format, seasonal offerings.
15.	**React Fast** Domestic repairs (plumbing, electrical, locksmith, etc.) via subcontractors, plus a domestic maintenance insurance product, plus fee-based intensive courses (plumbing, electrical, etc.), plus franchising domestic repair operation.
16.	**Esterform Packaging Ltd.** Manufacturer: PET containers and later plastic bottles.
17.	**Parasol Plc** Tax plus services to contracted (freelance) IT professionals, later to other occupational groups.
18.	**Audley Travel** Upmarket private (overseas) travel.
19.	**The Specialist Hire Group** Fork lift truck and crane hire.
20.	**Power On Connections** Taking electrical power from grid to non-domestic users (shopping malls, office complexes) via substations, cable and meters.
21.	**Wind Prospect Group** Wind power generation installations.
22.	**Clipper Logistics Group** Trucking.
23.	**Riverford Organic Vegetables** Production (variously sourced), sale and distribution of boxed organic vegetables, principally to households.

A winning formula?

A larger sample now totalling 30 does indeed facilitate more confident generalisation. Clearer patterns emerge, and some new themes surface, all of which is explored in the pages that follow.

It is probably unrealistic to hope for a single winning formula that applies to every company in the sample. But this larger data set does suggest a looser formula, consisting of three related elements. This formula is the three F's – First, Fast and Focused.

First

Some of the companies were quite literally 'the first' to do something. The founder of Really Useful (plastic storage boxes) told me he was fed up with archiving papers in cardboard boxes, had the idea of a plastic alternative, set up a company to do it, did the design and then produced them first with the manufacturing subcontracted, later with production in-house.

Audley Travel is a personal travel company, which designs and manages individual trips and is the opposite of the package tour with its set departure dates and group travel arrangements. Its founder told me:

'Ten years ago [when he started it] there was nothing like this.'

Power On Connections' work is connecting up new non-residential entities such as shopping malls to the national grid. Once upon a time this could only be done by the regional power companies. Official deregulation occurred in 1996 but not until 2002 did OffGen publish documentation showing new entrants what they had to do to become competitors. Of course you needed Lloyds certification to do this work. Power On was the first company to get it.

But it is important here to understand 'First' in a more diffuse way. That is, almost all the companies did something new, there was some element of originality in what they did or how they did it. They reconfigured the industry in some way, reformulated a service or its delivery, found new applications or new customers or new ways of propagating themselves or they brought together diverse players in a creative way.

Examples will emerge when we look at some of the specifics.

Fast

Going at it hammer and tongs, especially in the early days, was a recurrent theme across the sample. That is to say, conspicuously striving to build up the customer base, market share and revenue.

Really Useful Products, for example, founded the company within weeks of having the idea, racked up sales and production to match, and at the time of the interview was stockpiling produce to ship to the USA.

The founder of Encore Personal Services (a blue-collar worker recruiting agency) after a partnered management buy-out (MBO) that did not work out, losing the stake the vice-chairman insisted he put up, and facing a restraint of competition which kept him out of his newly founded business for six weeks, reminisced:

> 'God, did we sell! We sold like nobody before. In fact we were very success-ful in the first six months, more profitable than at any time.'

Or the principal founder of Esterform, dealing at the beginning in his high-margin, speciality products:

> 'Did this for six months flat out to get cash, I packed bottles during the night and sold by day.'

Or Parasol, whose initial value proposition is to service IT freelancers/ contractors, on the web, with an integrated data and accounting package, for £100, where previously many of these freelancers had paid a higher fee to have their affairs processed by accountants by post! Furthermore, Parasol is a Plc! All quite legal, the capital requirement is only about £50k, the reporting requirements are more stringent but not unbearable, and of course it gives the impression of a big company with an established presence in the industry. The founder ran these two key facts together for me, viz:

> 'Plc x Cheap = Customers!'

Or again the exemplary Power On Connections who spoke in 2008 of 40% growth per year.

Focused

After being first and fast, the next thing is being focused. Again Power On Connections is a good example. They are focused in several ways:

- They don't do this connection work as an adjunct to an existing business; this *is* their business.
- They do the work themselves, there is no subcontracting.
- They focused on the Midlands, only allowing themselves to be drawn into other regions at the request of existing customers.
- They concentrate on retail parks, office developments and industry parks; not housing estates – more precarious, lower-margin, get bossed around by national builders!

Power On is a nice follow-on case, but my 23 companies are awash with examples of this focus, especially in their early days. Reflex Labels concentrates on the food industry via supermarkets; SPI (Materials) Ltd. concentrated on emissions-related parts for the motor industry; 99p Stores on shops with a distinctive function and format; Parasol (management of the employment of contractors) on IT contractors, and got critical mass here before moving on to other professional groups; Encore (recruitment) focused on blue-collar employment and on Polish workers in particular, broadening out to workers from other Eastern European countries; Clipper Logistics started with a fashion-retail focus, and so on.

These three F's – First, Fast and Focused – appear to explain a lot of the success of these Fast Track companies. I have only sought here to give a few illustrations, not to list the lot, though there is a lot that could be listed. But the three F's are not the whole game.

Reconfiguration

Many of our Fast Track companies are adapting to or benefiting from a change in the ways companies organise themselves and industries are configured. Consider first the big picture.

For more than twenty years focus has been the name of the game, and companies have been outsourcing away from core competence. One simple result – companies are less keen to own things just because they need to use them. Enter Prohire, one of our companies, that hires out trucks and manages the maintenance and documentation. And enter The Specialist Hire Group, another one; after all who wants to own a crane and tie up £1m or even fork lift trucks for that matter when they can lease them from Specialist Hire and get free advice on how and when to upgrade the fleet and indeed on what equipment they need for their industrial purpose.

Or consider manpower. No company wants to personally employ a surplus of expensive IT people that it only needs occasionally for major projects or system upgrading. Enter all the IT contractors, including the high end operator reviewed earlier in the discussion of the 'magnificent seven'. A further twist is that these IT contractors want to contract the staff and take the fee but not necessarily manage them in terms of tax and employment contract. Enter Parasol, another of our companies, that provides just that service.

It is the same with manning levels. No one wants to staff up to meet (intermittent) maximum demand. Enter another of our companies Encore Personal Services, providing contract blue-collar workers. Indeed the *Sunday Times* often points out when presenting its list of winners that consultancy and recruitment firms are the most numerous categories.

The same with health care. Because of demographic change there is greater need for care for the elderly. And because of legislation during John Major's premiership (1990–7) much of this provision has to come from the private sector. Enter AYS, another of our companies that is a provider of domiciliary care for the elderly, and in its glory days a great 'taker-over' and successful integrator of other such facilities, often at their request.

But sometimes it goes further than this. The idea that an industry may be reconfigured from within, albeit by an upstart, has gained credence since Southwest Airlines set up originally to offer cheap fares flying the Texas Triangle (Dallas–Houston–San Antonio) and thus became the inspirational model for cheap airlines.

The *Sunday Times* lists also offer examples of this dynamic reconfiguration. One of the stars of the 2007 list, for example, Move-with-us, is an Internet-based estate agency. Parasol (supra) is driving change (reconfiguration) rather than responding to it. Another of our companies, Covion, is a good example.

Covion is what is usually thought of as a facilities management company. My visit was just after the company had been sold to Balfour Beatty.

Now most facilities management providers are system integrators: they front with the client offering the whole range of services which they then subcontract to specialists (cleaners, security staff, electricians, etc.) and put in a small management team at the client organisation.

This system integration will lead providers to bid on price and then drive a hard bargain with their subcontractors. Then when something goes wrong, say the cleaners don't turn up, all you can do is call the subcontractor and ball them out: but this is not the stuff of which *esprit de corps* is made.

Covion are not a system integrator, though they do offer a range of services. They do this by taking relevant service people on to their own staff via the TUPE (transfer of undertakings protection of employment) scheme. This gives, or rather gave, Covion:

- Cost efficiency gains from integrating Covion employees on site, without pretending that everyone can do (all of) everyone else's job.
- Easier integration of Covion employees with the client organisation workforce.
- Customers like the fact that there is no outsourcing.

This is another instance of reconfiguration. It was enough to make Balfour Beatty want to buy them.

My judgement is that reconfiguration, or relating to a non-traditional configuration of players, is an important issue for some thirteen of the 23 companies I visited in the second part of the research.

This stronger version where companies are driving or shaping the change we will call configurational leverage.

Qualifications or experience

There is an intriguing asymmetry regarding qualifications and experience. This is that the depth-relevance of experience prior to starting their business is a constant for the whole sample, but qualifications vary greatly.

First, qualifications. With a sample of 25 (occasioned by meeting/interviewing more than one founder at some companies) the biggest group have qualifications in engineering/science/IT, some degrees – some intermediate qualifications. Then there are four accountants, and another six with non-technical degrees. The subset with university degrees include two Oxford graduates, one with a first, and another star with three A's at 'A' level followed by a first class degree.

That leaves over a quarter of an admittedly modest sample who have variously left school at the statutory leaving age with no qualifications or left a little later with 'O' levels, sometimes just one or two; one had started in the sixth form, but got bored and left.

This group were most interesting. They tended to speak of school as something that did not really impact on them, they sounded impatient to get out and get on. Then when you asked them about their early work experiences they often spoke much more enthusiastically and came across as zealous learners and opportunity exploiters.

But when it comes to experience before founding their companies they all have it. Their wealth of prior experience includes:

- Engaging in the activity that would become the core of their later business; an obvious example is the principal founder of Audley Travel who travelled extensively in Vietnam as soon as it was opened up to the West, and then 'practised' leading small groups there on adventure treks.
- Working for a variety of companies.
- Working for established companies in the same industry, that is, the one they were destined to enter as entrepreneurs.
- Working in other people's start-up companies.
- Having started companies before, which were variously sold, merged or failed.

All this was given a spine of intentionality by the founder of Really Useful Products:

> 'I tried to create my own training programme. I chased experience rather than money.'

Working for established companies in the same industry is particularly valuable. Not only does it afford trade and industry knowledge but they came away knowing where the fat is and how to cut it, what not to do, and in the accounts they gave me the established company experience figures as an incentive to do it better!

Consider as a good example of the benefits of prior experience the principal founder of Esterform Packaging (PET containers and later plastic bottles). By the time he came to found Esterform he had:

- Worked as a lab technician.
- Got a chemistry degree, part-time.
- Worked at a mid-size company, PET Plus.
- Worked for Shell and for Alcan/Pechiney.
- In these earlier roles he had become very familiar with the material (PET), its uses and applications, and with selling it to corporate customers and tweaking it for their needs.
- So he was well connected in the industry before he went solo.
- And he had got to know the two people who were to become his partners – one finance, the other an engineer.

What a hand to play!

Knowledge or know-how

This is probably a false dichotomy. The knowledge and skill acquisition that leads to the award of qualifications, not to mention the personal development entailed, will shade into enabling and doing. Yet when I listened to the entrepreneurs' accounts it was the know-how element that emerged more strongly.

After each company visit when I had been given an account of the business, I would ask myself: Could I do this? The answer was usually no. And what I lacked was not typically something that could be addressed by reading a book or looking it up on the Internet.

I would not know how to go about finding a company in China that could make the bits I wanted to sell in Europe, as did the founder of SPI Materials Ltd. I would not know how to theme a pub-restaurant chain, I would not have dreamed up the retail format of 99p Stores (it is much more than simple discounting). How would you know who out there has some product that would benefit from being stored in a customised PET container (Esterform), know how to frame a grant application to a local authority for a care facility (AYS), know how to identify the contingencies pertaining to a holiday in Bolivia (Audley Travel), or could you come up with a plan to increase selling space by reducing storage space for traders on a retail park (Clipper Logistics)?

In short we know all these companies are successful, by a credible measure. We know these entrepreneurs are uniformly strong on relevant experience, and know-how is strongly implied in their testimonies. This is a consistent picture.

The Trans-Canada Highway or the pub car park?

Several of our companies are niche operators, including the pharmaceuticals wholesaler (singleton chemist shops in three geographic regions) and the high end IT contractor (top 10% of IT staff with proven managerial capability) and the pub-restaurant chain (clear market segment) reviewed under the 'magnificent seven', as well as Audley Travel and Riverford (organic boxed vegetables delivered to households) – this last is approaching nationwide coverage for sure but it is still a niche market.

But this brief listing overlooks the fact that several of the others are exploiting niches where they have the chance. All the builders are: there are types of jobs they like and others they avoid. This idea came out clearly with Ipswich-based SEH Holdings, where, for example, they go for:

- Subcontracts from major housebuilders to do the roads, sewers and foundations; this is a bit less routine than building the house shell, less easy for the contractor to second-guess you.
- Work on brownfield sites, which pose more problems, and not everyone can deal with them.
- Work for well-off summer residents in Aldeburgh; that came to SEH via an acquisition.
- Any assignment where you needed to interface with local government (they have local knowledge).
- Plant hire (usually the prerogative of bigger companies).
- Sea defence work, particular to the East Anglian coast, where local knowledge and reputation are important.
- Conservatories, well known to add value to homes; SEH make them on site, display them in their own showrooms in Chelmsford and Ipswich, sell only to the general public (trade would expect a discount) and SEH do the erection.

So the answer to the question posed in the heading is that you do not want to build the Trans-Canada Highway: you will have to tender, it will be competitive, the contract will be awarded on cost, and every highways administrator from Vancouver to St John's will be able to second guess your costings. But a pub car park in Suffolk: they will want it done on Sunday, it needs to be quick (ready by opening time), there may be drainage problems, a need to liaise with the local authorities on account of temporary road closure or traffic diversion, and the customer may want special materials or a particular finish in keeping with the pub itself (Suffolk has the prettiest pubs in the UK) – more rewarding than those endless miles of tarmac across the wheat fields of Canada.

In short, niches tend to be good news, and a lot of our companies have or include them.

It should be added that I have probably been a bit cavalier with the niche concept, expanding it to embrace the higher margin, better protected bits in more heterogeneous operations.

Reputation

The Fast Track companies are a strategic site for the study of reputation. They demonstrate, that is to say, reputation in the making, and in this they contrast with more established companies. Let us start with the latter.

Larger and more established companies tend to assume they have reputation. This assumption is usually justified: they have been around for some time, they are a presence in the market, they have an established customer base, and so on. But they do not expect their reputation to work dynamically in their favour. They do not expect to make *more* gains from it than they have already. Rather it is 'a given' to be safeguarded, and the corporate fear is that this reputation may be lost by some mischance or misdemeanour.

It is the reverse with the companies studied here. They start from scratch, and appear to build reputation by quality of execution and by service. A very common claim is that they give value for money, are competitive in the marketplace, treat every customer as though they were the first customer or the only customer, majoring on customer service, and so on.

Now while as an outsider you cannot verify this, it has verisimilitude. It is what you would expect newer companies to aim to do, and the likelihood is that a subset which have been rated as highly successful are doing it.

I was struck by this from the outset in the 'magnificent seven' phase. I spent half a day at the marine outfitters listening to stories of resourceful moves to solve problems for client organisations, to simplify their work for them, to aid clients with emergencies, to dig them out of pits where established companies had left them. Or again the pharmaceuticals wholesaler whose principal modus operandi was telephone order taking where the founder urged that staff taking the calls would never tell callers they could not take the order without an order number or a product code or whatever. He concluded referring to the customers:

'If they have a problem, *we* own it.'

This 'can do' spirit was also echoed by McLaren:

'We never say no without having a good look!'

Likewise they relay stories of over-achievement. The founder of Clipper Logistics, for instance, referred to ASDA, giving them six weeks to open a relief warehouse for Christmas but they did it in five days. Outside recognition is important to them. SPI Materials were due to receive a Queen's

Award for international trade, to be presented by the Lord Lieutenant the week after my visit. Covion had already received an Entrepreneur of the Year award. The founder of Really Useful Products was proud of a contract to supply the Bundesbank, won against competition from a Swiss rival. Most of SEH Holdings' friendly acquisitions were the result of people coming to them, or being sent by their accountants, and the same was true of care provider AYS. The Business Development Manager at McLaren Construction told me how just after he had joined McLaren he accompanied a senior to a meeting at Land Securities whose executive at the meeting declared:

'McLaren is the best firm in the business.'

Incidentally all those companies whose operations involved recourse to sub-contractors or suppliers claimed to pay them promptly, contrary to industry norms. This includes GO Interiors, Gladedale, indeed all the builders.

What I think we are seeing here is a symbiotic relationship between quality of execution and service and growing reputation, where the latter in turn serves to enhance business success.

Finally, during the months of the study several companies received the accolade of industry approval by being bought! The ranks include Power On Connections, AYS and Covion, the last having been bought by Balfour Beatty the week before my visit.

There is a twist to the Covion story. My interview had been set for the late afternoon because the founder had been out visiting a client organisation to assure them there would be no adverse change from the takeover and that the founder was staying on transitionally anyway. He concluded:

'People do business with a person not a company.'

No doubt there is some truth in this dictum at all levels of corporate size and substance. But it is likely to be telling at the Fast Track level, and it will be part of the reputational advantage.

Competitive advantage

There is a tendency for competitive advantage to be identified in terms of (if possible) single overriding determinants of success. Business journalists like this, it gives them a better story; business school teachers like it, it facilitates learning and enhances the gain of business case studies. There is much value in this, but I would like to suggest some modifications.

First, there is a measure of dynamic interaction among the three F's (First, Fast, Focused) where the presence of two or three of them has an enhancement effect. Likewise I have suggested a dynamic interaction between quality of execution and reputation. Furthermore a looser dynamic has been posited between prior experience–know-how–quality of execution and overall success.

Second, competitive advantage often seems to be made up of a lot of factors, fitting together nicely. Consider as an example the first company listed, the marine outfitter from the 'magnificent seven':

- Its founders have experience in an established company in the same industry.
- They know there is systematic overcharging.
- They perceive a customer reaction to this, particularly the CRIME (cost reduction scheme) adopted by the oil companies.
- They know how to cut the fat!
- They started as an electrical outfitter, but added mechanical capability via an acquisition (and acquired a set of non-marine customers at the same time).
- They also do design and build, onshore and offshore (the latter being unusual).
- They manage the supply of materials for their customers, doing their own inspection and not relying on the suppliers' quality control.
- They also refrain from 'marking up' the price of supplies such as cables, and passing the mark-up on to the client (common in the industry at the time).
- They are able (qualified) to do Lloyds vessel verification.
- They can do hazardous zone work, for example, electrical work in an underpass with dripping fluids!
- Likewise they offer extreme climate know-how.

The result of all this is that they offer a complete service, unusual for a company of their size, so their clients never need to bring in one of the big outfitters (and get 'ripped off' is the implication).

It is a tightly wound ball of advantage when you put it all together.

Reflecting on entrepreneurialism

We started by suggesting reasons for the usual omission of entrepreneurs from the class of elite groups. These reasons have the further effect of flagging up some of the changes that have occurred in the nature of entrepreneurialism.

Most obviously we have come a long way from Richard Arkwright and his Spinning Jenny! In the early years entrepreneurs were usually inventors, or sometimes their sponsors. These inventor entrepreneurs built or adapted machines, equipment or the means to produce power. This is not 'gone for ever' but it is no longer the norm. And 'inventors' nowadays are likely to be in genetic engineering rather than mechanical engineering.

This is not just a reference to the simple move from manufacturing to services in Western countries, though this transition is clearly evidenced in the *Sunday Times* lists. My examples of entrepreneurs are less likely to be dealing principally with artefacts and tangibles, indeed some of them are scarcely dealing with them at all.

No doubt this reflects the maturity of the UK economy, and that of Western countries generally. All the obvious stuff has already been done; we are now into the subtle, the complicated and the resourceful. This has the effect of 'ramping up' the business rationale of contemporary entrepreneurial endeavour. What kind of businesses they founded, how they were positioned, what adaptive moves they made, how they were developed – these have become key questions.

Thus the companies in my Fast Track sample are variously:

Originating concepts, for example the themed pub-restaurant chain discussed in the 'magnificent seven' where a defined customer group is matched with a milieu, a service offering, and an operational mode to produce something that is consistent across the chain and distinctive in the industry; 99p Stores a retail concept; Audley Travel a recreational travel concept.

Identifying gaps in the market, for instance the IT freelancer provider discussed in the 'magnificent seven'; Riverford Organic providing boxed organic vegetables delivered to homes or Audley Travel arranging customised foreign holidays for professionally successful 30-somethings and affluent 50–60-somethings on either side of the retirement line.

Exploiting opportunities created by government policy or regulatory change, for instance AYS reacting to legislative change in the 1990s requiring the greater part of care for the elderly to come from the private sector, or Wind Prospect Group helping to meet nationally enacted clean energy targets, or Power On Connections being the first private sector to receive regulatory validation.

Engaging in merger and acquisition (M&A) activity to extend their competence and capability, which Esterform do by acquiring a bigger and better production facility to replace the now inadequate original site and acquiring at the same time a new product range; SEH Holdings are another example, adding extras such as plant hire and conservatory manufacture and erection.

Engaging in M&A as a means of growth, for example Gladedale, Reflex Labels, T-Wall Garages; interestingly although year on year revenue growth is what gets a company on to the *Sunday Times* lists, only a minority of my 30 companies had made M&A their principal means of growth.

Picking or preferring particular product-market segments from within an established industry, the 'pub car park' syndrome; the pharmaceuticals wholesaler described in the 'magnificent seven' did this, so do all the builders and civil engineers.

Engaging in creative reconfiguration, for example Covion already discussed, or Wind Prospect Group bringing together available wind farm sites, bank finance, technical feasibility appraisal, planning permission and end-user need.

Resourceful cross-border sourcing, for instance SPI Materials Ltd. sourcing most of its supplies in China, or the music product retailer discussed in the 'magnificent seven' that had ingeniously sourced discounted product from Europe.

Exploiting the established company trend to outsource away from core competence – all the equipment, transport, and facilities providers are doing this including Prohire, The Specialist Hire Group, Covion, Reflex Labels, Parasol Plc, and Clipper Logistics solving logistical problems for fashion retailers.

End play

It has been suggested that entrepreneurs deserve to be counted as elite because of their achievement and impact. But the focus needs to be on those that succeed, while recognising that this exhortation involves horrendous issues of definition and measurement – we have used an ad hoc method here just to get started.

Given the maturity and sophistication of the economies of Western countries successful entrepreneurs will frequently employ resourceful and imaginative strategies in positioning and developing their companies or at least such strategies are implied by what they do. We have sought to surface some of these in the preceding sections. The successful will know how to combine inspiration and implementation, to get a sufficient number of different things right to prevail.

It is by their business behaviour that ye shall know them.

References

Lawrence, P. (2002) *The Change Game* (London: Kogan Page).
Peters, T. and Waterman, R. H. (1982) *In Search of Excellence* (New York: Harper & Row).

15

A Multi-level Understanding of the Careers of Minority Ethnic Elites

Akram Al Ariss, Joana Vassilopoulou, Dimitria Groutsis and Mustafa F. Ozbilgin

Introduction

The purpose of this chapter is to theorise the experience of minority ethnic elites in their host countries. We frame the notion of 'minority ethnic elite' as workers who possess high levels of education and who sometimes are able to gain access to elite forms of professional education and employment. We also demonstrate that the link between their skills and career success is not simply unidirectional as identified by human capital theorists. We adopt a multi-level perspective through which we frame experiences of minority ethnic elites in pursuit of their careers. We identify a gap in and contribute to the literature on careers, which to date, we argue, fails to capture the experiences of minority ethnic elites. In order to capture the experiences of minority ethnic elites, we ask two key questions: First, what are the coping strategies of migrant elites in their efforts to develop their careers? To address this question we draw on findings of a field study examining the career experience of migrant elites in France. Second, we ask how the abilities and skills of ethnic minority elites are undermined across various job criteria by the majority ethnic group. The field study from Germany seeks to explain the experiences of minority ethnic elites in the context of organisational structures. These two studies are presented in this same order. We make a distinction between migrant and minority ethnic workers, as many minority ethnic workers themselves do not have migration experience. Nevertheless, they face similar and sometimes even stronger barriers to labour market entry. The first study uses the term 'migrant' as the participants are drawn from groups who have personally experienced migration, with a focus on migrants from Lebanon to France. However, the second study focuses on minority ethnic workers who were born and educated in Germany. We use the term 'minority ethnic' as an overarching concept to refer to individuals who are not from majority ethnic groups.

By consulting a variety of scholarly repositories, we endeavour to address what we see as weaknesses in the literatures on industrial sociology, migration and self-initiated expatriation by developing a multi-level and relational conceptual model that forges links between the home and host country, majority and minority ethnic labour market contexts, the individual and their requisite human and social capital resources and the elite profession to which they gain entry (Al Ariss and Ozbilgin, 2010; Harvey, 2008). In doing so this model allows us to explain and understand the labour market adaptability in professional contexts of the minority ethnic elites over time. It is to a definition of what constitutes a minority ethnic elite that we now turn.

Who are minority ethnic elites?

There is no one definition of minority ethnic elites. The literature on industrial sociology sheds the light on the nature of elite professions (Muzio et al., 2008). This is helpful in understanding who minority ethnic elites are. A profession is a socially constructed entity, which as a unit translates one order of scarce resources, that is, special knowledge and skills, into another set of resources, such as social and economic rewards. According to Larson (1990) the maintenance of scarcity implies a tendency to monopoly, including a monopoly of expertise in the market and as a corollary monopoly status in the system of labour market stratification. That is, professions are protected in terms of entry and access to qualifications, affording professions elite status when compared to other forms of work and employment. In spite of the 'internationalisation' of professional services and the employment of migrants in various professions (OECD, 2002; Stilwell et al., 2003; Aiken et al., 2004; Forcier et al., 2004; Buchan, 2006), training and professional boundaries remain rooted in the nation state (Allsop et al., 2009). This raises questions about the breadth of the boundaries surrounding the 'community of practice', which according to Brown and Duguid (2001: 203) sees professionals defined as members of an 'organization and members of a larger, dispersed occupational group'. Who is a 'member' though is dependent on who is granted access, and it is to the features of professional entry that we now turn.

Requisite characteristics setting the boundaries of a profession include: a training process centred on a body of knowledge and techniques, a code of ethics which justify self-regulation, a process of registration and a sense of altruism (Larson, 1977; Iredale, 1987: 26; Abbott, 1988; Freidson, 2001). Combined, these features create the 'habitus', or in other words taken-for-granted rules, of the profession (Bourdieu and Passeron, 1977; Atkinson and Delamont, 1990: 105). Conditions of entry though may be subject to change according to pressures from those within, and externally to the occupation pointing to the contextual features of the labour market. For instance, professional schools, professional associations and licensing bodies directly and indirectly influence the demand conditions and therefore who gains access to and who is excluded from the profession. That is, they determine the number of trainees, establish how the 'quality' of candidates is assessed and as a corollary directly influence the supply of candidates into the labour market. These bodies also shape the norms of practice, the culture of the profession and the social organisation of work. In sum, these bodies serve several ends. First, they set a standard of practice in the public interest to protect consumers from unqualified practitioners. Second, they protect those within the occupation from less skilled outsiders, and from a rush of competition at a time of market surplus. Bound to this process of selection is the public image of the profession. In the same vein, an additional component shaping professional boundaries (closure/openness) and professional status is the establishment of a degree of power and prestige (Cullen, 1978: 211).

This position is legitimised through a number of areas. First, state-sponsorship which according to Larson (1977; see also, Allsop et al., 2009) is secured by the political and economic influence of the elite who sponsor it. And, secondly through the socially granted conditions whereby the exclusivity of the profession is dependent on the skill that is 'bought' by the public (Parry and Parry, 1976; Larson, 1977; Witz, 1992: chapter 2; Freidson, 1994). This position is therefore different for different occupations and subject to change over time.

We accept professions as elite forms of work, although not all professions have the same level of elite power and prestige. We also challenge the literature on business elites as it tends to focus on home country nationals and majority ethnic workers and fails to capture the experiences of minority ethnic elites. We explore below a number of assumptions on which the characteristics of minority ethnic elites are predicated (Table 15.1).

It is a challenge for minority ethnic workers to navigate their way through the maze of rules and regulations set by the majority ethnic groups in the host country and subsequently gain access to their chosen profession in

Table 15.1 Characteristics of minority ethnic elites

They may gain access to the host country or majority ethnic labour market jobs in a position commensurate with their skills and qualifications.

They meet the requisite criteria for access to what is historically and socially constructed as an elite profession.

Their integration into/navigation in the labour market is shaped by factors beyond their formal human capital attributes and includes the utilisation of social capital resources.

This group is not migrating in the safe confines of inter-/intra-firm transfer.

They may treat their migration move or their minority ethnic status as a permanent or temporary characteristic.

They migrate to the host country or they are born to parents with migration experience.

a position representative of skills and qualifications. We now turn to the careers of minority ethnic elites in order to understand the interplay of their choices in the context of professional structures in constituting their career outcomes.

Understanding the careers of minority ethnic elites

Careers of skilled persons living and working outside their countries of origin are extensively discussed in the literature on self-initiated expatriation (SIE) (Bozionelos, 2009). SIE is most often described as remaining abroad on a permanent and temporary basis (Tharenou, 2009). This literature is useful in understanding the career experiences of migrants who gain access to prized professions in their host country labour markets. However, the literature on SIE suffers from three inadequacies in accounting for the careers of minority ethnic elites. First, the international career experiences of migrants moving from developing to developed countries are under-researched. Second, this literature remains silent with respect to the significance of ethnicity in accounting for the career experiences of minority ethnic workers. Third, this literature does not sufficiently explore the career barriers imposed on minority ethnic workers. Nor does it explore their respective coping strategies. This section exposes the three gaps in this same order.

A great deal of research focuses on the careers of persons from developed countries undertaking an international experience (Doherty and Dickmann, 2008). For example, Jokinen et al. (2008) discuss the work experiences of professionals from Finland. Nevertheless, migrant elites from less developed countries remain 'an almost hidden aspect of the international labor market' (Jokinen et al., 2008: 979). Frequently, self-initiated expatriates (SIEs) are conceptualised as free agents who can cross organisational and national borders (Myers and Pringle, 2005; Tharenou, 2009). Less focus is attached to the barriers that constrain their career choices (Richardson, 2009). Working abroad is considered helpful for developing work-related and personal skills. For example, Richardson and McKenna (2003) investigate the career experiences of 30 British SIEs (16 women and 14 men) living in New Zealand, Singapore, Turkey and the United Arab Emirates. Their findings suggest that professional experience earned abroad was beneficial for career development.

There is research evidence that ethnic minority groups may be subject to discrimination in organisations (Jehn and Bezrukova, 2004). Ethnicity is understood as socially constructed and includes characteristics such as 'language, history, or ancestry (real or imagined), religion, and styles of dress' (Giddens, 2001: 246). Vance and Paik (2006) recognise that ethnic tensions emerge in societies as the global economy makes it easier for people to travel between countries. Career studies remain underdeveloped with respect to understanding the career experiences of migrant elites from ethnic minorities (Syed, 2008; Al Ariss and Syed, 2011). Berry (2009) suggests that the under-representation of minorities in the international management literature can be explained as resulting from the fact that much of management research is generated by people who are demographically similar to expatriates.

Finally, we know little about how migrant and minority ethnic elites face and cope with barriers to their career development in the host countries. Persons who face legal barriers, e.g. labour regulations imposing restrictions on migrants such as work permits, are known to have strong career constraints (Syed, 2008; Al Ariss and Syed, 2011). Drawing on interviews with 50 SIE New Zealanders, Inkson and Myers (2003) found that when they did not get appropriate visas and work permits, the SIEs worked in jobs that did not suit their qualifications. In addition, organisations and institutions in the host countries could discredit expatriates' human capital, such as by not recognising their academic qualifications and professional experiences. Migrants can also face discrimination in accessing jobs and advancing careers. Legal barriers and discrimination can lead to migrants' underemployment (Carr et al., 2005). Underemployment is defined here as underutilisation of the individuals' skills and expertise. This causes job dissatisfaction and a low level of job involvement (Lee, 2005). Our empirical data explain career experiences in terms of how the experience of professional elites transpires with a cross-comparison by country context and professional group.

In attempting to fill the gaps mentioned above, we now turn to the work of Duberley et al. (2006) and Richardson (2009) as a framework for understanding the career experiences of elite ethnic minorities. These same authors describe the 'modes of engagement' that individuals use in managing structural influences on their career experiences. These studies are presented in this same order. Duberley et al. (2006) examine how public sector research scientists make sense of and seek to develop their careers within their organisational and macro-contextual settings. Their study is based on qualitative interviews conducted with 77 public sector research scientists from the United Kingdom and New Zealand. It suggests that individuals choose orientations, in the forms 'modes of engagement', which can help them to manage contextual influences such as social institutions and structures. Results show that participants either maintained the existing social structures or attempted to transform them. Maintenance, as opposed to change, is a default state rather than a specific strategy, where a person recognises constraints and injustices but does not attempt to change them.

The second paper (Richardson, 2009) investigates the modes of engagement of 74 academics who were pursuing an internationally mobile career – thus engaging in international mobility. The paper draws on qualitative interviews conducted with 30 British academics working in Turkey, Singapore, the United Arab Emirates and New Zealand. It also refers to a further study comprising 44 interviews conducted with 'international faculty' who had moved to Canada for work purposes. Richardson identifies the different structural levels (i.e. scientific, national and institutional contexts) that international academics must navigate. In Canada, for example, the recruitment of international academics is governed by restrictions imposed by governmental agencies. These structural constraints described by Richardson suggest that an international career is characterised by 'seams' (Richardson, 2009: 168) which must be navigated by individuals. Accordingly, some academics adopt a maintenance approach whereas others, opting for change strategies, use transformative approaches in order to advance their careers.

In the next sections we present our methods and empirical and conceptual data drawn from two field studies, one in France and another one in Germany where the position of migrant and minority ethnic elites is surprisingly ignored. The study on France explores how migrant elites coped with the complexities of the French labour market and negotiated their professional status. The second study, in Germany, explores how minority ethnic elites' ambitions to access professions were hampered by structural barriers.

Methods

In France, the field study was made up of qualitative interviews conducted with 18 women and 25 men. Additionally, interviews were conducted with six persons involved in the making and implementation of immigration policies. Furthermore, relevant French immigration policies were analysed. In order to achieve a diverse group of participants, we used a purposeful sampling strategy in selecting interviewees. Participants had lived in Lebanon and worked for at least a few months in France. Their period of residence in France varied from 2 to 39 years. Thirty participants had acquired French citizenship by the time of the interview, while most of the others had only Lebanese citizenship. They had various educational levels, such as Doctoral (11 interviewees), Master's (22 interviewees), Bachelor (nine interviewees), and one participant had only a high school diploma but possessed extensive training and professional experience. All but five of them had done all or part of their studies in France. Participants were either employed in organisations (28 interviewees), entrepreneurs (12 interviewees) or unemployed (three interviewees). Excluding the three participants who were unemployed, interviewees worked in management (22 interviewees), engineering (13 interviewees), medicine (3 interviewees), restaurant (1 interviewee) and academic (1 interviewee) professions. Two of the Muslim women participants were wearing the Islamic veil. Participants were between the ages of 25 and 62; half of them were married and the other half were either single or dating. Almost half of them were Muslims and the rest were Christians.

Six qualitative interviews were conducted with those who accepted invitations. The interviews made it possible to question and get detailed answers about issues that were unwritten in policy documents. The six interviewees included: (a) a policy-maker at the Higher Council for Integration (HCI), (b) a person involved in developing policies at the International Labour Organization (ILO), (c) two immigration specialists working with migrants in France, (d) one interviewee cooperating with the French government, and (e) an eminent French academic specialising in human resource management, with expert knowledge of the French institutions. The interviews lasted approximately one hour and most of the interviews were conducted in French. The interview and document data were subjected to thematic coding for the purposes of this paper. QSR NVivo software was used to code the material collected. Upon the completion of coding and analysis, selected quotes were translated from French to English. In order to attend to the problem of translation, back translation was used. In this way, collecting data in one language and presenting results in another does not influence the necessary rigour in this qualitative research.

In Germany, 30 semi-structured interviews were conducted with German equality and diversity actors coming from different subfields (for example: trade unionists, politicians, members of NGOs, academics, journalists, lawyers and diversity trainers). Fifteen of them belonged to ethnic minority groups in Germany. The other 15 were native-born Germans. Half of the participants were female and the other half were male. The study employs multiple sources of data: secondary data in the form of scholarly and practitioner literature overview, semi-structured interviews with stakeholders, and a single company case study. This field study provides an ethnic minority perspective, which certainly is not frequently considered in German equality and diversity research.

The coping strategies of migrant elites in France

Drawing on personal accounts of 43 Lebanese migrant elites, we extend Duberley et al. (2006) and Richardson's (2009) concepts of modes of engagement, and explain four dominant coping strategies that participants adopted in this study. A more detailed account of such strategies is discussed in Al Ariss (2010). These strategies are maintenance, transformation, entrepreneurship and opt-out. In order to develop their career, all participants drew on these four modes of engagement at different times. They are presented here in the mode that describes their predominant experiences.

Maintenance

Maintenance implies recognising career barriers and working within them in order to obtain a desired career outcome (Duberley et al., 2006; Richardson, 2009; Al Ariss, 2010). Overall, eight participants adopted primarily the maintenance mode. The case of Mustafa shows how he coped with discrimination at the workplace. Mustafa is an engineer in his mid-twenties. Mustafa related the story of a Moroccan Muslim woman who decided to begin wearing the Islamic veil at his workplace, knowing that no rules forbade this in the company. In fact, the company demonstrated openness and diversity in its advertising:

> Mustafa: If you go to the website of [name of the employer], you can see publicity ... as if they recruit some Mohamads, Rachidas, Stépahies ...

Yet such diversity was discouraged in practice.

> Mustafa: She began wearing a veil. People started speaking badly about her. I often heard people laughing at her and calling her – not to her face – a Ninja. I have heard much criticism, er ... really very strange! I find it really strange how people who are highly educated ... can have such negative images of people. Her supervisor didn't want her to wear the veil, so he transferred her to another department where nobody can see her. She has been working in her job, I think, for six or seven years ... and from the time she began wearing Islamic veil, we felt that people had this reaction. Therefore, they threw her aside. They didn't want to understand that there are people of other cultures or other religions who accepted her.

Mustafa's observation of this woman's experience affected his own perceptions of the implications for his own career. Instead of changing this inequality in the context of his organisation, and in an attempt to avoid discrimination, Mustafa tried to hide, in the workplace, the fact that he is Muslim. For instance, in this same organisation, he was asked about his religion but decided not to respond clearly. Instead, he attempted to explain that religion did not impact his job performance. In that way, he felt that hiding his religion allowed him to avoid being discriminated against. He reported that this allowed him to establish a good relationship with his French boss and helped him to advance his career. This reflects the way Mustafa navigated discrimination rather than changed it. The maintenance mode of engagement described here reflects the way participants in Richardson's (2009) study accepted the employment conditions in their host countries as being 'pretty much unassailable' (Richardson, 2009: 166).

Transformation

Transformation denotes identifying barriers to career advancement and trying to alter them (Duberley et al., 2006; Richardson, 2009; Al Ariss, 2010). There were 15 participants who identified various barriers to their career development and attempted to challenge them. A great many of these barriers were linked to being an ethnic minority in France, underemployment, and lacking the power (i.e. legal status) to work in France. The 15 participants perceived that challenging these barriers would give them more power to develop their careers.

Almost a quarter of the participants decided to replace their Arabic names with French ones in order to avoid discrimination. The case of François illustrates this. He first expatriated to France to escape war and to pursue graduate studies and has now been living in France for more than 20 years:

> François [talking about his initial attempts to enter the French job market]: I had to change my name so that I could access jobs easily. This means that … er … when you present your CV, I never got job offers! The fact that I had French citizenship and changed my name [to a French one], at that moment … er … what I know is that once I had French citizenship and with my new [French] name, the first CV I sent I had a job interview for. This eased my insertion into the job market.

By changing his name and acquiring a new citizenship, François felt that he succeeded in overcoming discrimination as well as legal barriers. Looking at his career trajectory, François perceives himself as a successful entrepreneur. Success for François emerges in terms of his subjective self-satisfaction in his career outcome. This success is also objective as he invests in engineering projects, owns an art gallery, teaches in universities, owns Internet cafés and rents out apartments.

Where organisations offered participants positions incommensurate with their qualifications, participants strategically resumed their studies and changed employers. This accumulation of human capital gave them a symbolic power to challenge their institutional and organisational structures and attempt to develop their careers. This was the case for Aline, a 55-year-old woman. In Lebanon, she pursued a Bachelor degree in philosophy and worked in many jobs such as journalism and teaching. In France, organisations did not fully value Aline's human capital acquired in Lebanon. Thus, she was obliged to take menial jobs:

> Aline: I studied translation at [name of the university in Paris] and got a degree. It was great to have this on my CV! Thanks to that and to relational networks, I was able to work in translation … After working in several organisations … 10 years later … I wanted to advance my career: I didn't want just to type texts as I used to do … I wanted to study law … now, I am studying law.

The experience of Aline shows how career capital gained in one country is not always valid in the international marketplace. In order to manage structural barriers to her employment and obtain valid capital (i.e. professional qualifications that are recognised) in France, she decided to pursue new studies. Along with her work, she successfully pursued several degrees. In this way, Aline felt that she succeeded in securing recognition from her several employers who promoted her.

These findings show how international careers are characterised by 'seams which must be navigated' (Richardson, 2009: 168). Accordingly, rather than accepting legal constraints as 'pretty much unassailable' (Richardson, 2009: 166), participants actively attempted to advance their careers by many ways including changing their names, changing their migrant status and acquiring valid and useful education in France.

Entrepreneurship

Compared to 'transformation', the entrepreneurship mode of engagement meant taking an additional risk in organising a new business in an attempt to avoid discrimination and legal constraints in the context of employment in France (Al Ariss, 2010). Entrepreneurship offered a possibility of career development for 13 migrants based on the structural obstacles they faced in France.

While 12 participants were entrepreneurs, one person had a career history full of entrepreneurship but was in temporary employment. Entrepreneurs used professional and personal relationships in starting their own businesses. This was useful in securing financial help and commercial cooperation as well as obtaining professional expertise.

Mahmoud, a 62-year-old man, first expatriated to France to continue his Doctoral studies. Upon receiving his Doctorate, he returned to Lebanon. He was a faculty member at the Lebanese public university. However, he decided to relocate again to France in search of better security for his family and a better economic situation. Mahmoud was allowed to study in France and later emigrate on a long-term basis. Nonetheless, the institutional and organisational contexts in public universities prevented him from working in his profession. In France, he reported that he was unable to find an academic post because of the strict legislation that regulates the employment in public universities. During his search for academic employment, he felt that professors selected their own students for jobs, even if they lacked the qualifications. By taking on the entrepreneurship mode of engagement, he succeeded in setting up his own bookshop and buying several others:

> Mahmoud: I applied for academic jobs ... but I soon realised that my attempts were blocked by selection barriers that prevented me from getting such positions! So I preferred to have my independence and decided to work in a job related to my previous profession ... So I invented and created my own employment, for myself and for my employees, and doing so, avoiding all sorts of discrimination or other barriers.

Entrepreneurship options were not always available immediately for participants arriving in France. First, they had to acquire administrative authorisations such as work permits and recognition (when possible) of their previous professional qualifications. Second, they had to accumulate education, professional experience and training in the business they chose. Third, they needed money and appropriate social contacts. With time, the 13 participants were able to accumulate these resources and fully engage in the entrepreneurship mode. For instance, entrepreneurship required that participants manage the legal barriers (e.g. acquiring work permits), accumulate career capital, and venture into new business. This three-step process made them able to deploy their career capital in managing barriers to their career development in France.

Opt-out

'Opt-out' occurs when migrants are confronted with obstacles which push them to operate outside exiting structures (Al Ariss, 2010). In comparison with the 'transformation' and 'entrepreneurship' modes, 'opt-out' results from an individual's sense of subjective and objective failure in developing a desirable outcome career. Seven participants reported that legal and discrimination barriers made them adopt an 'opt-out' mode of engagement in managing barriers to their career development. The case of Hiba illustrates this situation. Hiba is a 29-year-old woman who has been living in France for eleven years. In France, she pursued her business studies and worked for two years. After she had her second baby, she decided to suspend her career in order to take care of her family. Recently, she decided to wear the Muslim hijab.

Hiba would love to be working again; however, she feels that employers will not accept her because of her choice of dress. She decided to opt out as she felt that the French employers would not hire her:

> Hiba: I see, that even if the law protects the citizens, all these people, in the society are against us! Even, perhaps, policy-makers who make legislation! They make laws that they don't respect! [Laughing]. [When asked if she recently applied for jobs in France] ... Well, no, I didn't! I was afraid to do so!

It is important to mention that participants sometimes adopted an 'opt-out' mode of engagement prior to shifting to an entrepreneurship mode. One example was Imane who is in her mid-fifties. She is a widow and has one child. Prior to leaving for France, Imane stated that she had connections with an elitist milieu in Lebanon which was useful for her career development. For instance, she first came to France to pursue an education in engineering in a well-known university. Unlike most of the participants, the elitist reputation of her school gave her a chance, whilst temporary, to experience a brilliant career in France. When Imane was appointed as general director, she felt that being a woman made it difficult for her to convince the company's board of directors of her style of management. She therefore resigned. She decided to 'opt out' when she felt that she could no longer further her career, due to gender-based discrimination in her job. Shortly after that, she opted for entrepreneurship and created her own consulting company:

> Imane: I had the possibility of advancing in my career ... until the day I became general director of a company and then difficulties started ... In France, despite the discourse on liberty, there is a problem of discrimination ... we don't accept a woman at the presidency of a board of directors. This remains a problem in the professional sector ... This is very French, it is not linked to my origins! But it is alike for all women ... when we reach a certain level of responsibility, we have to give five times more effort ... It is a male chauvinist milieu ... statistics show it: with equivalent qualifications it is not the same ... there are cycles, so if it becomes closed, I set up my own work activities.

It is useful to see how the elitist career track of Imane played a key role in her career development. Having succeeded in an elitist French university, she had access to career opportunities more than other migrants. Nevertheless, when confronted with gender barriers, she decided to opt out. Shortly after that she decided to venture in a new business. This transition between 'opt-out' and 'entrepreneurship' shows a need to acknowledge their interconnectedness. This requires situating each of the four 'modes of engagement' in a particular historical moment of the life of an internationally mobile professional. In the next section, we discuss the findings from the study on elite ethnic minorities in Germany.

Minority ethnic elites in Germany

The aim of this section is to examine how the abilities and skills of migrant elites are undermined across various job criteria by the majority group utilised to justify their labour market exclusion. This is done using the example of alleged deficient German language proficiency on the part of migrant workers in Germany. We draw on a larger field study which set out to understand the habitus of managing ethnic diversity in Germany.

In recent years we can observe an increasing recognition of and an enormous global competition for migrant elites. However, Germany no longer receives a high number of migrants and particularly migrant elites. In the case of Germany governmental policies are in fact not setting enough incentives for highly skilled migrants to migrate to Germany. For instance, the German government introduced Green Card regulations for non-German specialists in 2000 (Bericht der unabhängigen Kommission Zuwanderung, 2001). However, the very low number of Green Card applicants and current Green Card holders indicates that Germany has a rather weak position in the global war of talent (Kolb, 2005).

Moreover, Germany misses out not only on attracting migrant elites from abroad, but also misses out in recognising home-grown ethnic minority talent, despite the fact that utilising this talent could be one means to meet future and current labour market demands. For instance, the unemployment rate among ethnic minority academics was 12.5% in 2005 compared to 4.4% among native-born academics (OECD, 2007). Discrimination, stereotypes, prejudices and negative attitudes are some of the factors that prevent members of ethnic minorities from fully participating in the labour market. The potential of ethnic minorities remains unused and the ethnic minority working population in Germany is marginalised (Ortlieb and Sieben, 2008).

Germany has received a high number of immigrants since the Second World War. Today Germany has the third largest number of international immigrants in the world (IOM, 2010). Nonetheless, neither the public and political debate, nor relevant research pays much attention to migrant elites. Research focuses on migrant elites mainly in the context of recruitment strategies (Kolb et al., 2004) or in regard of brain drain, brain gain and brain exchange (Straubhaar, 2000). Migrant elites are viewed as a homogeneous group, holding more resources, skills and capital than the average labour force, placing them in a more favourable position in the labour market than others. Paired with this notion is the assumption that migrant elites do not face problems in terms of, for instance, labour market exclusion. For example, Tanja argues:

> Tanja: The portion, which is highly or very good qualified, there I would say that the inclusion in the labour market and in the economy has been very successful. I think that these people have a very secure position in the labour market, because of their multiethnic education, whereas the others without sufficient education are the first ones to be standing on the street without a job.

All this stands in contrast to the German dominant research paradigm of integration, which is merely concerned with how to integrate lowly skilled, so-called 'problematic' migrants. This might explain why highly skilled migrants are viewed as not worthy of further investigation (Kolb, 2006).

The dominant discourse as well as the vast majority of research prefers to focus on 'problematic' ethnic minority groups or individuals, rather than on migrant elites. In this manner literature on ethnic minorities in Germany concentrates predominantly on ethnic minorities being in deficit and on how to integrate poorly educated ethnic minority individuals into German society (Esser, 1999, 2000, 2001). Thereby the focus lies for the most part on ethnic minority Turks, who are viewed as the most problematic ethnic minority group in Germany (Esser, 2006). Moreover, the dominant discourse with its focus on 'deficient' migrants influences how the dominant group perceives migrant elites.

According to interview evidence, not employing, for instance, workers of Turkish ethnicity is legitimated with internalised arguments referring to people of Turkish ethnicity being deficient across various job criteria. This deficit is particularly seen when referring to educational credentials held by migrant individuals, particularly ethnic minority Turks. This is true to some extent; educational outcomes of some ethnic minority groups, particularly ethnic minority Turks, are far below the average of native-born Germans. However, in the mainstream debate the most common argument is that migrants do lack fluency of German language, even if born in Germany in the second or third generation regardless of the educational background of the migrant individual. This is also believed to be applicable for migrant elites. This notion is reflected in all interviews held with native-born German stakeholders in Germany. For instance, Brigitte legitimates the exclusion of migrant elites in the labour market as follows:

> Brigitte: I know from my husband, who works at a University as a professor, that young persons with migration background often do not have good written German, this is one reason, and for instance diploma dissertations are often counterchecked by others, that is logical, we would surely do this too if we would be in another foreign country, but logically if you are not even capable of writing a error free email or business letter, what can I say, then it is over very fast. This is one reason. Another example is, I have a lot of schoolteachers in my circle of acquaintances, and they say that those which have a migration background, are not able to create a correct blackboard drawing in class and that I think is a barrier and I believe that if somebody with a academic background has the aspirations of taking for instance a academic job, you need to be able to speak and write the German language.

This statement reflects the strong belief that migrant elites are not capable of writing error-free German. The mainstream debate is dominated by a discourse which only views migrants as being in deficit. Certainly this dominant discourse is influencing the stereotypes and perceptions held by persons responsible for hiring workers in organisations. An additional statement from Brigitte illustrates this issue clearly:

> Brigitte: What companies are telling me is that nothing goes without German language skills. There must be a better level than only rudimentary

knowledge of the German language, an ability to read but also a certain ability to write. That does not mean that a cleaning lady should be able to write novels, but she must be at least able to read a memo for instance. Thus this attitude, which we experienced for decades, why should I learn German, I just want to work, that does not work anymore.

It appears that companies are negatively biased regarding the language skills of migrants. That is not astonishing considering the mainstream debate regarding this issue. The same was observed in the case study company, which will be discussed in more detail later. However, this statement shows that ethnic minority workers and hence also migrant elites are mainly associated with low skilled labour. For instance, Brigitte refers immediately to a cleaning lady when talking about the language skills of ethnic minority workers. Peter, who holds a similar position regarding the lack of sufficient language skills on the part of migrant elites, goes further suggesting how this assumed deficit could be dealt with:

> Peter: Though I think if we stay in the area of academics, it has become thoroughly obvious that, ehm, if the mother tongue is not German, so ehm, that even so to say in the academic area, that there are problems in putting something into writing, there are deficits. But there could be measures targeting second language learning, such as writing concepts for academics with German as second language. Such things for example. That there are particular support measures, but with the goal to create upward mobility.

The interesting point of this statement is that Peter refers to the German language as a second language for ethnic minorities. This is rather surprising considering that most of these individuals he is talking about have been born in Germany and went through the educational system in Germany and also graduated from a German university. How can one perceive the German language as a second language for ethnic minorities in this case? According to Boos-Nünning (2005) the everyday life of young ethnic minority individuals must be described predominately as bilingual. Only 11% of ethnic minority youngsters live in an environment that is solely dominated by the German language. And 17% of young ethnic minority individuals are growing up in an environment dominated by the language of the country of origin of their parents and this is particularly the case for newly arrived immigrants. Moreover, and contrary to the mainstream perception, Boos-Nünning identifies girls of Greek ethnicity as the biggest group merely exposed to the language of the country of origin and not ethnic minority Turks. Considering that the educational attainment of ethnic minority Greeks is similar to that of native-born Germans, it could be questioned whether the language argument can account for the low educational and employment outcomes of ethnic minority Turks compared to native-born Germans.

However, the language issue seems to be rather overrated in the German context. For instance, how is it possible that a significant number of foreign academics work in academic institutions all over the UK or the USA without English being their mother tongue? Thinking about attracting and accommodating migrant elites from abroad seems rather challenging in this light. Moreover, some even doubt the existence of language problems on the described level. For example Erkan argues:

> Erkan: I don't believe that they can't speak a proper German. These kids grew up in Germany. They have been socialised in Germany and they received their education here and I worked a lot with the youth. But what I believe is that there are certain stereotypes and prejudices, certain prejudices exist particularly through the media, which creates this picture steadily. The same as topics such as forced marriages, violent migrant youngsters and so on. Employers, those responsible for recruitment in a company don't employ migrants as they see them as a risk factor for their company. These are prejudices, an information deficit transported through the media.

Regarding the German language skills of migrants in Germany, a view of deficiency dominates the discourse and serves to undermine the skills and abilities of migrant elites. However, we should attempt to understand what exactly this notion is serving. A possible answer comes from interview evidence. For instance Ingeborg argues:

> Ingeborg: ... in creating pseudo criteria and in never talking about the good students for example, which do not get a job or trainee position, rather we talk always about the bad ones the ones that cannot speak German or that have other problems and we also never talk about those which cannot get a job at the university, simply because they belong to an ethnic minority, and the tricky thing is that they are not even talking about ethnicity as a criteria but instead they are saying that this and this criteria is not met. This is used as legitimation for not employing them. They would always say that migrants just do not get the jobs because they do not fulfil the requirements, because they do not speak enough German and so on.

According to Bourdieu social capital consists of two components: it is connected with group membership and social networks. 'The volume of social capital possessed by a given agent ... depends on the size of the network of connections that he can effectively mobilize' (Bourdieu, 1986: 249). It is a value produced by the sum of the relationships between actors, rather than merely a common 'quality' of the group. Thus German language proficiency as a socially constructed criterion is utilised by the dominant group to undermine the skills and qualifications of migrant elite groups. The same amount of economic and cultural capital can yield different degrees of profit, and different powers of influence to different actors (see Bourdieu, 1986; Joppke, 1987; Coleman, 1988). For Bourdieu each individual occupies a position in a multi-dimensional social space; he or she is not defined only by social class membership, but by every single kind of capital he or she can articulate through social relations. Social capital includes the value of social networks, which Bourdieu showed could be used to produce or reproduce inequality (Bourdieu, 1977). Moreover, undermining the social capital of migrant elites serves the reproduction of imbalances in relations of power and class and to secure the social reproduction of the racial and social order. Ingeborg referring to the work of Bourdieu states:

> Ingeborg: In my opinion they are clearly blocking people with migra-
> tion background, because it is about reproduction, it is always about
> reproduction. This means that these institutions are reproducing their
> young generation, and now you can relate to Bourdieu. They come up
> with indistinct criteria and alleged attributes that people should hold
> and utilise these criteria in order to exclude people with migration back-
> ground and to secure the process of reproduction.

Unfortunately this possible loss of highly skilled labour is economically detrimental, considering the recent shortages of highly skilled labour in Germany. However, this is also indicative of the racism that would rather see the minorities from undesirable ethnicities leave, when the government tries to bring in migrant elites from abroad through Green Card schemes.

Conclusions

The purpose of this chapter was to theorise the experience of minority ethnic elites in their host countries. We adopted a multi-level perspective through which we framed experiences of minority ethnic elites in pursuit of their careers. We showed how meritocracy alone, based on skills and profes-sional experiences, cannot explain the career success of ethnic minorities. By doing so, we contributed to the literature on careers, which to date fails to capture the experiences of elite minority ethnic workers.

In order to understand the experiences of migrant and ethnic minority elites, we used an interdisciplinary survey of literature in industrial soci-ology, migration and self-initiated expatriation studies, which shed light on the career experience of elites from organisational and individual level perspectives. This chapter makes two key contributions to the literature by better defining who ethnic minority elites are and how they experience their careers. First, there are particular factors which are overlooked in the current literature, including the definition of minority ethnic elites' characteristics and the professional criteria that they must satisfy in order to gain entry to positions commensurate with their skills and qualifications (Groutsis, 2003, 2006; Allsop et al., 2009). Our findings showed that the idea of an elite is created and sustained by dominant majority ethnic groups and the access to such status is ethnically marked. However, in some cases migrant and minority ethnic workers can access such positions although the route in such cases is paved with complexity and hardship.

Second, our review showed that the literature, while useful, has a tendency to focus on either micro-individual or macro-organisational levels, failing to recognise the meso level interface between them. Accordingly, we attempted to deal with this shortcoming by answering two research questions. We asked what are the coping strategies of migrant elites in their efforts to develop their careers. In addressing this question we drew on findings of a field study examining the career experience of migrant elites in France. Their experiences were hindered by discrimination and structural barriers to their career development. In response to such barriers, Lebanese elites in France used four strategies that were essential for their career development: maintenance, transformation, entrepreneurship and opt-out. In France, participants' skills, education and training alone were not sufficient to overcome the organisational and institutional barriers that restricted their full integration into the labour market. The second research question we asked was regarding how the abilities and skills of ethnic minority workers are undermined across various job criteria by the majority ethnic group. The field study from Germany explained the experiences of minority ethnic elites in the context of organisational structures. In Germany, we showed how thus far migrant elites are mostly denied access to positions representative of their skills and qualifications.

In this chapter, we were able to make distinctions between migrant and minority ethnic groups as the former surprisingly experiences less labour market discrimination than the latter in comparison. There can be multiple reasons for that. Migrant workers are less subject to racism in their lives. They often move after school or university to host countries and face minority status later in their lives. This keeps them away from structures of disadvantage which exist throughout the life span of a minority ethnic worker. The good news from France is that ethnic minority elites can challenge and break down inequalities. Further studies are needed to show how valid our findings are in different national contexts and for other minority groups. There are indications that such diversity studies are burgeoning in management and organizational research (Tatli, 2011; Tatli et al., in press).

References

Abbott, A. D. (1988) *The System of Professions* (Chicago and London: University of Chicago Press).

Aiken, L. H., Buchan, J., Sochalski, J., Nichols, B. and Powell, M. (2004) 'Trends in International Nurse Migration', *Health Affairs*, 23(3): 69–77.

Al Ariss, A. (2010) 'Modes of Engagement: Migration, Self-Initiated Expatriation, and Career Development', *Career Development International*, 15(4): 338–58.

Al Ariss, A. and Ozbilgin, M. (2010) 'Understanding Self-Initiated Expatriates: Career Experiences of Lebanese Self-Initiated Expatriates in France', *Thunderbird International Business Review*, 52(4): 275–85.

Al Ariss, A. and Syed, J. (2011) 'Capital Mobilization of Skilled Migrants: A Relational Perspective', *British Journal of Management*, 22 (2): 286–304.

Allsop, J., Bourgeault, I. L., Evetts, J., Le Bianic, T., Jones, K. and Wrede, S. (2009) 'Encountering Globalization: Professional Groups in an International Context', *Current Sociology*, 57: 487–510.

Atkinson, P. and Delamont, S. (1990) 'Professions and Powerlessness: Female Marginality in the Learned Occupations', *Sociological Review*, 38: 90–110.

Bericht der unabhängigen Kommission Zuwanderung (2001) *Zuwanderung gestalten Integration fördern* (Berlin: Bundesministerium des Innern, Öffentlichkeitsarbeit).

Berry, D. (2009), 'Expatriates, Migrants, Gender, Race, and Class', *Proceedings of the Academy of Management*, Chicago, USA, August (Ipswich: Business Source Elite), 1–6.

Boos-Nünning, U. (2005) 'Zuhause in zwei Sprachen'. In I. Gogolin et al. (eds.), *Interkulturelle Bildungsforschung: Migration und sprachliche Bildung* (Münster: Waxman), 111–28.

Bourdieu, P. (1977) *Outline of a Theory of Practice* (Cambridge: Cambridge University Press).

Bourdieu, P. (1986) 'The Forms of Capital'. In J. G. Richardson (ed.), *Handbook of Theory and Research for the Sociology of Education* (New York: Greenwood Press), 241–58.

Bourdieu, P. and Passeron, J. C. (1977) *Reproduction in Education, Society and Culture*, trans. R. Nice (London: Sage).

Bozionelos, N. (2009) 'Expatriation Outside the Boundaries of the Multinational Corporation: A Study with Expatriate Nurses in Saudi Arabia', *Human Resource Management*, 48(1): 111–34.

Brown, J. S. and Duguid, P. (2001) 'Knowledge and Organization: A Social-Practice Perspective', *Organization Science*, 12(2): 198–213.

Buchan, J. (2006) 'Migration of Health Workers in Europe: Policy Problem or Policy Solution'. In C.-A. Dubois, M. McKee and E. Nolte (eds.), *Human Resources for Health in Europe* (Buckingham: Open University Press), 41–62.

Carr, S. C., Inkson, K. and Thorn, K. (2005) 'From Global Careers to Talent Flow: Reinterpreting "Brain Drain"', *Journal of World Business*, 40(4): 386–98.

Coleman, J. S. (1988) 'Social Capital in the Creation of Human Capital', *American Journal of Sociology*, 94 (Supplement): 95–120.

Cullen, J. B. (1978) *The Structure of Professionalism: A Quantitative Examination* (New York: Petrocelli Books).

Doherty, N. and Dickmann, M. (2008) 'Self-initiated Expatriates: Corporate Asset or a Liability?' Paper presented at the 4th Workshop on Expatriation, 23–24 October, Las Palmas, Gran Canaria.

Duberley, J., Cohen, L. and Mallon, M. (2006) 'Constructing Scientific Careers: Change, Continuity and Context', *Organization Studies*, 27(8): 1131–51.

Esser, H. (1999) *Soziologie. Spezielle Grundlagen. Band 1: Situationslogik und Handeln* (Frankfurt: Campus).

Esser, H. (2000) *Soziologie. Spezielle Grundlagen. Band 5: Institutionen* (Frankfurt: Campus).

Esser, H. (2001) 'Kulturelle Pluralisierung und strukturelle Assimilation. Das Proble der ethnischen Schichtung', *Schweizerische Zeitschrift für Politikwissenschaft*, 7(2): 97–108.

Esser, H. (2006) 'Migration, Language and Integration', AKI Research Review 4 (Wissenschaftszentrum Berlin, www.wz-berlin.de).

Forcier, M. B., Simoens, S. and Giuffrida, A. (2004) 'Impact, Regulation and Health Policy Implications of Physician Migration in OECD Countries', *Human Resources for Health* 2(12). Available at www.human-resource-health.com/content/2/1/12 (accessed August 2010).

Freidson, E. (1994) *Professionalism Reborn: Theory, Prophecy and Policy* (Chicago: University of Chicago Press).

Freidson, E. (2001) *Professionalism: The Third Logic in the Practice of Knowledge* (Chicago: University of Chicago Press).

Giddens, A. (2001) *Sociology* (Cambridge: Polity Press).

Groutsis, D. (2003) 'The State, Immigration Policy and Labour Market Practices: The Case of Overseas Trained Doctors', *Journal of Industrial Relations*, 45(1): 67–86.

Groutsis, D. (2006) 'Geography and Credentialism: The Assessment and Accreditation of Overseas-Trained Doctors', *Health Sociology Review*, 15(1): 59–70.

Harvey, W. S. (2008) 'Strong or Weak Ties? British and Indian Expatriate Scientists Finding Jobs in Boston', *Global Networks*, 8(4): 453–73.

Inkson, K. and Myers, B. (2003) 'The Big OE: International Travel and Career Development', *Career Development International*, 8(4): 170–81.

International Organization for Migration (IOM) (2010) 'Regional and Country Figures' (http://www.iom.int/jahia/Jahia/about-migration/facts-and-figures/regional-and-country-figures, accessed 14 June 2010).

Iredale, R. R. (1987) *Wasted Skills: Barriers to Migrant Entry to Occupations in Australia* (Sydney: Ethnic Affairs Commission NSW, Government Printer).

Jehn, K. A. and Bezrukova, K. (2004) 'A Field Study of Group Diversity, Workgroup Context, and Performance', *Journal of Organizational Behavior*, 25(6): 703–29.

Jokinen, T., Brewster, C. and Suutari, V. (2008) 'Career Capital during International Work Experiences: Contrasting Self-Initiated Expatriate Experiences and Assigned Expatriation', *International Journal of Human Resource Management*, 19(6): 979–98.

Joppke, C. (1987) 'The Cultural Dimensions of Class Formation and Class Struggle: On the Social Theory of Pierre Bourdieu', *Berkeley Journal of Sociology*, 21: 53–78.

Kolb, H. (2005) *Die Deutsche Green Card. Kurz Dossier, Focus Migration, 3* (Hamburg: Bundeszentrale für politische Bildung and Hamburgisches Welt Wirtschafts Institut gemeinnützige GmbH (HWWI)).

Kolb, H. (2006) 'Internationale Mobilität von Hochqualifizierten – (k)ein Thema für die Migrationsforschung'. In F. Swiaczny and S. Haug (eds.), *Neue Zuwandergruppen in Deutschland* (Wiesbaden: Bundesinstitut für Bevölkerungsforschung beim Statistischen Bundesamt).

Kolb, H., Murteira, S., Peixoto, J. and Sabino, C. (2004) 'Recruitment and Migration in the ICT Sector'. In M. Bommes, K. Hoesch, U. Hunger and H. Kolb (eds.), *Organisational Recruitment and Patterns of Migration* (Osnabrück: IMIS), 147–78.

Larson, M. S. (1977) *The Rise of Professionalism* (California: University of California Press).

Larson, M. S. (1990) 'In the Matter of Experts and Professionals, or How Impossible it is to Leave Nothing Unsaid'. In R. Torstendahl and M. Burrage (eds.), *The Formation of Professions* (London: Sage), 24–50.

Lee, C. H. (2005) 'A Study of Underemployment among Self-initiated Expatriates', *Journal of World Business*, 40(2): 172–87.

Muzio, D. Ackroyd, S. and Chanlat, J.-F. (eds.) (2008) *Redirections in the Study of Expert Labour Established Professions and New Expert Occupations* (Basingstoke: Palgrave Macmillan).

Myers, B. and Pringle, J. (2005) 'Self-Initiated Foreign Experience as Accelerated Development: Influences of Gender', *Journal of World Business*, 40(4): 421–31.

Organisation for Economic Co-operation and Development (OECD) (2002) *International Mobility of the Highly Skilled* (Paris: OECD).

Organisation for Economic Co-operation and Development (OECD) (2007) *International Migration Outlook 2007*. Available at http://www.oecd.org/document/25/0,3343,en_2649_33729_38797017_1_1_1_1,00.html (accessed 10 September 2008).

Ortlieb, R. and Sieben, B. (2008) 'Diversity Strategies Focused on Employees with a Migration Background: An Empirical Investigation based on Resource Dependence Theory', *Management Revue*, 9(1–2): 70–93.

Parry, N. and Parry, J. (1976) *The Rise of the Medical Profession* (London: Croom Helm).

Richardson, J. (2009) 'Geographic Flexibility in Academia: A Cautionary Note', *British Journal of Management*, 20(S1): 160–70.

Richardson, J. and McKenna, S. (2003) 'International Experience and Academic Careers: What do Academics Have to Say?', *Personnel Review*, 32(6): 774–95.

Stilwell, B., Diallo, K., Zurn, P., Dalpoz, M. R., Adams, O. and Buchan, J. (2003) 'Developing Evidence-Based Ethical Policies on the Migration of Health Workers: Conceptual and Practical Challenges', *Human Resources for Health*, 1(8). Available at www. human-resources-health.com/content/1/1/8 (accessed August 2010).

Straubhaar, T. (2000) *International Mobility of the Highly Skilled: Brain Gain, Brain Drain or Brain Exchange*, HWWA Discussion Paper 88 (Hamburg: Hamburg Institute of International Economics).

Syed, J. (2008) 'Employment Prospects for Skilled Migrants: A Relational Perspective', *Human Resource Management Review*, 18(1): 28–45.

Tatli, A. (2011) 'A Multi-Layered Exploration of the Diversity Management Field: Diversity Discourses, Practices and Practitioners in the UK', *British Journal of Management*, 22(2): 238–53.

Tatli, A., Vassilopoulou, J., Al Ariss, A. and Özbilgin, M. (in press) 'The Role of Regulatory and Temporal Context in the Construction of Diversity Discourses: The Case of the UK, France and Germany', *European Journal of Industrial Relations*.

Tharenou, P. (2009) 'Self-initiated International Careers: Gender Differences and Career Outcomes'. In S. G. Baugh and S. E. Sullivan (eds.), *Maintaining Focus, Energy, and Options over the Career* (Charlotte, NC: Information Age Publishing), 197–226.

Vance, C. M. and Paik, Y. (2006) *Managing a Global Workforce: Challenges and Opportunities in International Human Resource Management* (New York: M. E. Sharpe).

Witz, A. (1992) *Professions and Patriarchy* (London: Routledge).

16
Urban Elites in Eighteenth-Century Northampton

Barbara Russell, Jon Stobart and Nada Kakabadse

Introduction

In recent years historians have been engaging with the concept of social capital and its uses and benefits to individuals and groups, and much of the research has concentrated upon merchant networks of the eighteenth century. Pearson and Richardson (2001: 673) and Stobart (2005: 298–307) respectively have correlated the rise of a consumer market as a positive result of the trust and reputation intrinsic within merchant networks of the eighteenth century, noting that merchants were often engaged in a civic role within a community. However, the overlapping networks of trust and reciprocity produced by the merchants or tradesmen, and the combination of their political and social networks are underdeveloped in the research of social capital relating to urban elite status. This chapter analyses the social capital of elites in Northampton during the eighteenth century, how that capital was acquired, maintained and propagated, and the political, social and business networks which were used for that purpose.

Like many towns and cities, Northampton had two worlds or layers of political elites during the eighteenth century. It is the second layer of political elites, the town's Aldermen, and not its members of Parliament, upon which this chapter concentrates. Whilst the research recognises that there were individuals with social and business status within Northampton the accumulation of political, economic and social capital networks can be seen as identifying the Aldermen with elite status within the urban community; and it is the acquisition and maintenance of their status upon which this research is focused.

Though the term 'social capital' was first introduced to the academic world in the 1920s, its contribution to academic research was largely neglected until the 1980s. Expanding upon Hanifan's (1916) research Bourdieu (1986: 241–58) concluded that social capital is the

> aggregate of actual or potential resources which are linked to the possession
> of a durable network of more or less institutionalised relationships of

mutual acquaintance and recognition – in other words to membership of a group – which provides each of its members with the backing of collectively owned capital a 'credential' which entitles them to turn to credit, in various senses of the word.

Building upon Hanifan's (1916, 1920) initial theories that social capital was the product of networking based upon goodwill, fellowship, sympathy and social intercourse, Putnam refined Hanifan's (1916: 130–8; 1920) earlier conclusions for the basis of community interaction. He suggested that social capital is primarily based in the reciprocal networks of individuals with similar conceptual understanding of norms, e.g. duty, trust, honesty, virtue (Putnam et al., 1993; Putnam, 2000). However, Putnam (2000) and Bourdieu (1984) differ in their views upon ownership of social capital. For Putnam social capital is the result of interactive networks within society and thus the property of the community. Bourdieu (1984: 157–8) contends that whilst interactive networks are the product of individual intentions the ownership of social capital stock belongs to the individual first and community second. It is towards Bourdieu's (1984) interpretation of social capital to which this chapter leans. It is important to note here that social capital is the natural resulting resource of social interaction (Putman, 2000) and is accrued throughout life, generally beginning through familial networks. Social capital, however, requires time to be expended in the attainment of new networks, the maintenance of existing ones and the severing of unproductive network ties (Bourdieu, 1984: 10). Moreover, without reciprocity between individuals social capital is lost; it must therefore be spent to be gained.

Empirical and statistical research related to social capital is generally conducted through a series of interviews and questionnaires; this study, however, is based on archival material including records relating to Northampton Borough Corporation. Data were entered into several databases before being layered into one single database for the purpose of cross-referencing and statistical analysis has been conducted. Analyses of wills, indentures and property transactions have been used in conjunction with the database in order to give a fuller picture of interpersonal relationships. Data from the records of the Northampton Infirmary and the *Northampton Mercury* have also been used as an indication of social and business network integration required in the maintenance of status. The study is set out in two sections: the first section explores the route to, and the maintenance of, elite status; whilst the second section explores the networks of two serving Aldermen of the 1770s which are typical of urban elite networks of the period in Northampton. The research maps their family, business and political connections and analyses the importance of those connections.

The route to becoming an urban elite

The urban elites in Northampton during the eighteenth century were undoubtedly the Mayors and Aldermen of the Borough Corporation who were economically and politically successful. It appears that continuity of tradition, personal economic and social status within the immediate community, and the future economic security of their respective families were the stimulus for becoming a member of the local elite. The overlapping roles of businessman and politician common to the eighteenth century (Thompson, 1991; Stone and Stone, 1995; Thompson, 2001) provided the means for the acquisition of social capital in the maintenance and propagation of elite status for the Aldermen.

Education

Bourdieu suggests that the dominant class maintain and justify their supremacy through a formal education system of school and university (Bourdieu, 1984: 177). However, for the majority of individuals living in Northampton during the eighteenth century formal education within the physical boundaries of school buildings and a nationally recognised and standardised curriculum did not exist. As Thompson has demonstrated, it was not until the nineteenth century that public schools such as Eton received, in large numbers, the sons of businessmen (Thompson, 2001: 102); the small number of public schools in the eighteenth century remained the preserve of the upper echelons of society and for those with ambition to enter the professions (Colley, 1996: 180; Thompson, 2001: 127). The town did have a grammar school; however, education for the most part remained a private affair for the majority of the local urban elite of Northampton (*Northampton Mercury*, 1762) and there is no evidence that any of the Aldermen attended grammar school prior to the nineteenth century. Home schooling and apprenticeships appear to have been the usual method of education and as such limited the opportunities for individual network expansion that was to become so commonly associated with public school and Oxbridge 'old boys' networks of the nineteenth and twentieth centuries. Why so few of Northampton's urban elite attended the grammar school is unclear, though it may simply be that the capital of a grammar school education was not seen as being a necessity for the acquisition of status in eighteenth-century Northampton.

However, all of Northampton's Aldermen of the eighteenth century served an apprenticeship. Apprenticeships provided the opportunity for instruction on town culture and tradition, and on social and business norms, values and practices. In general the apprenticeships lasted a period of seven years, and as Defoe noted, the period of apprenticeship provided for the building and extending of vital business, social and political networks (Defoe, 1726/2008: 5). It is noticeable that the majority of the serving Aldermen of the 1770s were not 'apprenticed out', though there were some exceptions, for example Alderman Edward Cole appears to have been apprenticed out to yeoman Robert Lambert in 1746 and William Gibson more than a decade later. This suggests that during the apprenticeship period the family continued to educate sons and nephews ensuring a continuity of established values and social norms, and business practices which included a degree of access to established business, social and in some cases political networks. As Defoe (1726/2008: 14) argued: 'if a young man comes from his master, and formed no acquaintance or interest among the customers whom his master dealt with, he has lost one of the principal ends and reasons for his being an apprentice'.

Politics

As in many towns in the eighteenth century, the role of the Borough Corporation as an institution was to act as a group representing the interests of the town and the townspeople (Clark, 1984: 311–38). Its purpose was to promote trade by ensuring that it was conducted according to regulations and ordinances, maintain the peace, grant all liberties and freedoms (Cox, 1898: 20), and ensure that the town received representation in Parliament. The financing of the Corporation came from charitable bequests, the rents on butchers' stalls and market tolls (Cox, 1898: 27). The Corporation met quarterly and consisted of two tiers: the first was the General Assembly where all members of the Corporation attended and the second was the Court of Mayor and Aldermen. The role of the latter was to address the administration of Corporation property and the administration of freemen and apprentices. The Court also voted pensions to its own members and exercised the patronage and administration of charities (Cox, 1898: 29). However, evidence shows that during the 1770s as with much of the eighteenth century and in contrast to similar size market towns such as Loughborough (Clark, 2005: 161, 170) the Northampton Corporation did little to enhance the town or the lives of its inhabitants.

Civic duty was a route towards elite status in the eighteenth century and it was expected that all freemen would be available to perform their duty at least once during their lifetime (Cox, 1898). The Corporation was not a united or homogeneous institution beyond that of religion (Greenall, 2000: 84). The businesses occupations of the Borough Corporation members covered a plethora of trades, from tanners and inn holders to grocers and shoemakers; no single trade group was able to dominate the proceedings either in full assembly or during the Court of Mayor and Aldermen (Cox, 1898: 554–6). However, it was the Aldermen who selected the common councillors, bailiffs, chamberlain and Mayor. The political selectiveness practised in Northampton was not dissimilar to that of Canterbury or Chester where Corporation members also originated from the business world of the town and were equally selective in their membership (Ruggiu, 2001: 157). In this respect the governance of the town of Northampton by a handful of local elites reflects a pattern and practice of eighteenth-century local governance in many towns and cities across Britain (Webb and Webb, 1963: 245). The immediate recognisable benefit was that the practice enabled the political elite to exercise exclusion, selecting those with whom they shared common bonds of trust and network reciprocity.

The first step towards recognition as a member of the political elite was to be selected by the Court of Mayor and Aldermen for service as a common councillor for the Borough (Cox, 1898: 20). However, several men who later went on to become Mayors began their civic duty outside the offices of the Corporation and in so doing were able to show their commitment, reliability and competency for office. Having served as a common councillor higher status could be conferred in being selected to serve as a bailiff of the town, whose duties were to support the Mayor, select jurors and collect debts (Cox, 1898: 51). It was generally from the ex-bailiffs or office of chamberlain that the Mayor was chosen, although there were some exceptions; for example, John Davis was in 1766 selected directly from the pool of forty-eight common councillors as Mayor for that year without having completed a period as bailiff for the town (Cox, 1898: 40). As political elite the position of Mayor was significant and announced to the wider world of the community that an individual had achieved a degree of trustworthiness and reliability recognised by his peers and to be recognised by others. However, the real power lay with the ex-Mayors, the Aldermen, whose ability as a body could dictate the political direction of the Borough Corporation and who, more importantly, had constructed political, social and business networks through which they might maintain their status within the community (see Figure 16.1).

Nevertheless it was common practice in the eighteenth century for preference to be shown to family members, sons following in their fathers' footsteps; the most noticeable is that of the Thompson family. Two of Alderman George Thompson's sons, Henry and William, had a dramatic rise through the Corporation. The average period of time between becoming a Freeman of the borough and becoming a serving Alderman of the 1770s was twenty-two years; William Thompson took ten years whilst his brother Henry completed the transition in eight. Their rapid rise into the political arena may have less to do with Pareto's (1939) definition of an elite as the 'strongest, the most able and the most active' than with their political and family network contacts. George Thompson was Lord Northampton's political agent in the town and the families were related through marriage (Hatley, 1968: 21). However, whilst family nepotism may have been common practice generally, in Northampton it appears to have been the exception in the political arena; the greater number of individuals who served in the office of Mayor between 1736 and 1780 had no direct family connections with those who gained elite status through serving as Mayor, chamberlain or bailiffs (Cox,

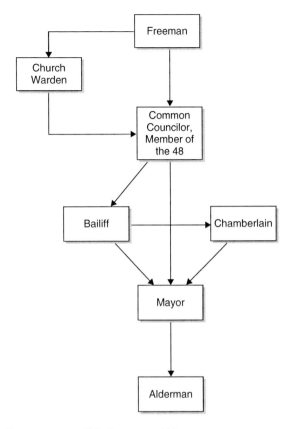

Figure 16.1 Route map to political status as Alderman
Source: Cox (1898: 554–6).

1898: 554–70). This suggests that though family networks could benefit an individual they were not essential for political office in Northampton.

Business

Northamptonshire in the eighteenth century was predominantly an agricultural county. The town of Northampton itself was small and lacked any major industry or large business. Although twentieth-century Northampton was to become synonymous with the shoe industry, the eighteenth-century town was little more than an agricultural market-town. There were numerous businessmen and various trades which were conducted on a small scale (*Universal British Directory*, 1791; Poll Books, 1768, 1774, 1796). This was, after all, 'an era of personal ownership and capitalism' (Wilson, 1995: 22), which Wilson suggests was the direct result from the introduction of the Bubble Act

1720; restrictions on the numbers of directors, non-transferable shares and the general expense of becoming an Incorporated Company severely hindered the growth of large business enterprises (Wilson, 1995: 44).

Rubinstein conducted research upon the business behaviour and practices of the nineteenth and twentieth centuries. However, his statement that 'the majority of economic activity was conducted overwhelmingly in one trade or line of business, and other interests as a side line to their main field' (Rubinstein, 1981: 58) is equally relevant to Northampton's businessmen of the eighteenth century who followed the same pattern: they acted independently within their primary business or trade and with the exception of family partnerships, only jointly or with others as a secondary economic activity. A measure of success in business was often translated into the accumulation of land and property and was a declaration of interest in elite status, and used as Thompson suggests as 'a jumping off point for power and office' (Thompson, 1991: 26).

During the 1770s, the number of serving Aldermen fluctuated between nineteen and twenty-five and their business occupations varied from merchant to tanner. Colli and Rose suggest that eighteenth-century 'family business represented a predictable response to instability, uncertainty and poor property rights and became the central pivot of a network of trust' (Colli and Rose, 2007: 197). However, only half of the Aldermen of the 1770s followed their fathers' main trade or business. This suggests that rather than the family business being pivotal to economic success and status within the community some men felt it prudent to show their independence as a badge of competency and ability and thus potential material for social recognition and power. Nevertheless William Gibson and others did receive financial assistance through inheritance of money and property from their fathers, whilst Edward Kerby and Henry Woolley received money and property upon marriage which not only gave them financial security but which raised their status and networking opportunities.

There were several routes through which a man could ultimately become successful in business. The first was simply through hard work and good business acumen, the second common practice was the use of an employer's good name and reputation upon completion of apprenticeship; for example, James Whitney utilised his connections with Alderman Edward Kerby in his advertisement of a new business on completion of his apprenticeship (*Northampton Mercury*, 1774). The third route in Northampton was to make an application to the Corporation for funds from Sir Thomas White's charity. The charity was open to all freemen between the ages of twenty-one and thirty-five and stipulated that the money could be used as part of a mortgage for a property of not more than £200, or could be used in the funding of a business venture. The sum loaned was £50, which was to be paid back over a period of nine years. Several of the serving Aldermen of the 1770s had made use of this funding opportunity, as had many of the towns' tradesmen. In 1772 serving members of the Corporation Samuel Sturgiss, William Gibson and William Davis all repaid their loans. The three routes mentioned did nevertheless require good network contacts based upon trust and trustworthiness.

The archival material examined in this research suggests that partnerships or rather alliances in business in eighteenth-century Northampton were rarely lifelong commitments outside of the family circle, and were entered into as single ventures. Family partnerships were often father and son as with the printers Birdsall or Dicey, who not only ran a printing business but produced the local newspaper, the *Northampton Mercury*. The family partnership of John Lacy and Son, Booksellers and local bank owners is an example of the integration between the business, social and political worlds of Northampton. Besides being a successful businessman John Lacy became a bailiff in 1781 (Cox, 1889: 554–6), followed by two terms as chamberlain of the Corporation. Lacy also held other positions of importance within the community; he was treasurer of the Northampton General Hospital Funds (*Northampton Mercury*, 1772, 1773, 1774), treasurer of the Joint Navigation Stock Company and trustee of All Saints Church property.

Archival records show business activity in the selling and leasing of property and land outside of the primary activity of trade by several of the Aldermen serving during the 1770s. For example, victualler William Gibson, plumber Edward Kerby, shoemaker Thomas Hall and scrivener William Gates owned and sold the Goat Inn to victualler James Miller and Stephen Gaudern and the Rev. Frost leased arable land to gardener John Gibson, victualler George Thompson and others. The sale of land and property was not limited to between residents of Northampton; in 1780 William Gibson sold land and property – business premises in Northampton – to City of London oilman William Fox for four hundred pounds, the property does not appear to have been advertised and thus suggests that Gibson had networks which extended outside of the county.

Land and property ownership whether freehold or leasehold was an important commodity during the eighteenth century. As Thompson has noted property ownership was often a prerequisite for political inclusion during the eighteenth century (Thompson, 1991: 26). It appears that short-term partnerships were not an uncommon practice and often emerged from the dense network of business, social and political connections (Wilson, 1995: 47). There are several possible reasons for this. First, there was a personal reduction in financial outlay – the more individuals involved in the scheme the less each individual stood to lose should the venture fail. Second, owning property or land, even on a short-term basis, brought economic and social recognition. Third, it was often passed on to family members, if not sold on, as a legacy. Fourth, joint ventures in property were the physical presentation of network contacts. Fifth, the property could be used against loans or mortgages. Finally, property was a display of economic success, a route into elite status in the accumulation of social capital.

A key question in all of this is the extent to which holding the office of Alderman brought tangible benefits to the individual. There were, no doubt, advantages to being part of the urban elite in terms of accumulating and articulating social capital, but there is also evidence of more direct and specific ways in which Northampton's Aldermen could profit from their position. They had inside knowledge about the expiry dates of Corporation leases including land, buildings and road tolls, and this provided the opportunity for business activity and economic gain. Once an application for a Corporation lease was expressed the body of Aldermen decided whether the application should proceed. Success was therefore a result of good network ties. For example, the Abstract of Corporation Leases shows that in 1755 Alderman John Fox leased from the Corporation grounds and stables in All Saints parish of Northampton, for the term of ninety-nine years, at a price of £2 per year. Nevertheless, new business ventures from leasing and renting corporation property was not always readily available and several of the Aldermen were required to purchase leases sometimes years in advance of their availability. In 1769 Alderman William Gibson leased all the Corporation road tolls for a period of fourteen years beginning in 1772, with the express aim of renting out each toll (Cox, 1898), whilst in the same year Henry Thompson bought the Corporation lease for a tenement in Newlands at a cost of £8 per year to begin the period of a 31-year lease in 1775. This forward planning suggests that, for recognition of elite business status to be maintained, Aldermen needed to constantly reaffirm their business ability and economic capital.

Social

Social acceptance was undoubtedly paramount in the acquisition of elite status in the eighteenth century. Being elite was not merely being acknowledged by one's social peers but also being recognised by the wider community as elite. Having the right connections and moving in the same business and social circles as established elites was also necessary for success. Marriage was one possible way in which almost immediate acceptance could be attained. Thompson points to the fact that marriages between the titled and the industrial or entrepreneurial trades was becoming more acceptable during the period (Thompson, 2001), and much the same can be said of marriages in provincial towns. George Thompson was uncle by marriage to Lady Northampton (Hatley, 1968: 21), which afforded him personal interaction with the local aristocracy and as such brought social recognition. The Rev. Woolley married the comparatively wealthy spinster Elizabeth Sewell, which brought financial stability and enabled him to enter into local politics and other social activities. However, social, business and political activities in Northampton during the 1770s were interwoven and overlapping.

Northampton, similar to other towns, held an annual horse race which many of the townspeople attended and there was regular cock-fighting in the grounds of Northampton's inns. In the summer there was cricket

(*Northampton Mercury*, 1741) and bowls, though Borsay has suggested that towards the end of the eighteenth century bowls was becoming less attractive within fashionable society (Borsay, 1989: 178). Nevertheless in 1770s Northampton it offered the opportunity for individuals to see and be seen, and provided social and business networking opportunities essential for elite status. In 1771 several Aldermen sanctioned the leasing of land in Kingsthorpe to Samuel Treslove for the specific purpose of establishing a bowling green. Membership was by subscription only (*Northampton Mercury*, 1771: 28) the effect of which was to limit membership to an exclusive group of individuals with a degree of economic freedom, and it is likely that the membership was limited to interested Aldermen and successful businessmen with established community networks and friendships.

Church attendance also offered the Aldermen and leading citizens the opportunity to display their status within society. Whilst the dissenting Baptist congregations encouraged social mingling, the Anglican churches of the Aldermen offered the opportunity to display their social status. There were areas within most Anglican churches where the local elite would sit and worship together, in clear view of but separated from the lower ranks of society, and it was not unusual for members of the elite to have purchased their pews as Edward Kirby did in 1763. All Saints Church Northampton has several plaques which name Aldermen and other leading citizens of the community. They are an outward display of the importance the church gave to those individuals but also an acknowledgement of the contribution to the wider community that those men made. Equally important, they can be seen as the physical display of family wealth and status within the wider community of Northampton.

There were other activities in Northampton where the local elite often met. For example, in Northampton there were 91 inns (*British Directory*, 1791). Though inns were open to all members of society often men met for business, social and political intercourse. Between 1771 and 1797 the Court of Mayor and Aldermen met nine times in the George Hotel and seven times at the Angel Inn (Cox, 1898: 51). In so doing they displayed not only their status as local political elites but were also able to portray a sense of Corporation solidarity and unity. Each year there were a series of Ordinaries which began during the winter months (*Northampton Mercury*, 1775). These occasions included dancing, card playing and other entertainment for many of the local elite, men and women alike, and afforded the opportunity to reaffirm established social networks. As with many of the activities of the social elite, Ordinaries or Assemblies required subscription and were limited to those of social standing as hinted at in an advertisement of 1775 (*Northampton Mercury*, 27 November 1775):

Three Assemblies for the ensuing months are proposed on the following terms at the Peacock Inn. Ladies to subscribe 10s 6d. Gentlemen 15s.

No other expense will attend to the evening. Tea, Cards, Music, Negus, Cakes etc. will be paid out of the Subscription. Subscribers will be good enough to send their servants this week to set their names down in the subscription. Non-subscribers to pay ladies 5s Gentlemen 7s 6d, and it is expected they are to be introduced by a subscriber.

Subscribing to worthy causes such as the Northampton Infirmary was a sign of economic and social status. Though the governors of the infirmary were members of the aristocracy and gentry, the subscription lists were important, the yearly publication provided written confirmation of commitment to the whole community and went towards enhancing reputation and status, it also suggested network connections with county elites which in reality may not have existed. Nevertheless subscription to worthy causes was a traditionally recognised means through which economic and social status could be exhibited and were the core of the public space (Price, 1999: 195). Surprisingly less than half of the Aldermen made donations or subscribed to Northampton's General Infirmary over the period of one decade, 1770 to 1780; this research suggests that they were excluded from the Annual General Meeting and could not therefore engage in productive networking which may have contributed to their limited involvement as a group.

Subscribing or donating to the 'deserving poor' appears to have been an annual occurrence during the 1770s. During the winter months the *Northampton Mercury* would ask that 'eminent persons' donate funds or goods such as firewood or blankets (*Northampton Mercury*, 1776: 183). Without question the local landed gentry did so and their contributions were often reported in the newspaper; the donations from other citizens was not acknowledged by the newspaper beyond that of requesting their attendance at a meeting to deliberate upon whom should receive the donations (*Northampton Mercury*, 1776: 187). In a period of history when paternalism and *noblesse oblige* were the cultural norm any established or budding elite would not only have donated but reputation would have demanded that he attend such meetings (Williams, 2000: 118) and in doing so gained capital.

Networks

Crucial to the understanding of how networks were used and maintained is the research which has been conducted by Granovetter and Burt. Granovetter (1973) considered the ways in which individual actors within networks optimised personal and group contacts to produce economic and social advantages and his research uncovered the types of network ties that existed. Granovetter concluded that networks such as family and close business associates produced 'strong ties' which bound individuals together. The members were well known to each other and often belonged to the same external networks, which produced dense overlapping connections between individuals. Granovettter's research also showed the importance of 'weak ties', those which are not familial or involving immediate work colleagues. These he suggests have the advantage of a bridging effect between individuals and groups and have the ability to maximise potential resource acquisition (Granovetter, 1973). Burt's analyses of networks identified a different form of linkage between individuals, 'structural holes' (Burt, 1992: 65–7). Used initially as brokerage mechanisms between networks they often provide an advantage against competition for the instigator of the linkage. Both Stobart and Pearson have shown in their research that businessmen not only joined existing networks but were producers of new networks. It seems likely therefore that during their normal course of business Northampton's Aldermen did instigate such ties, particularly as 'individuals do not move about in a random way' (Bourdieu, 1984: 10).

Paramount to acceptance into an established or the production of a new network was the emotion of trust, which is difficult to quantify. Researchers of social capital generally test their theories of trust using various 'game scenarios' to record participant interactional behaviour (Kanagaretnam et al., 2010). Research into eighteenth-century trust precludes the process of 'game scenarios', therefore trust is assumed following the process used by Letki who suggests a definition of 'assumed reliability, honesty, honour and truth, shared moral values and observance of social norms (Letki, 2006: 306–7). As Granovetter, Stobart, Pearson and Richardson have suggested, these become unwritten rules and practices in business, enabling greater cooperation between businessmen and social elites alike (Granovetter, 1973; Pearson and Richardson, 2001; Stobart, 2005).

'Guardianship networks'

The eighteenth century was dominated by a societal system of paternal hierarchy which valued trust, honesty and conformity to existing social norms. The period of apprenticeship proved advantageous in the production of social capital. Firstly, the apprentice was given a trade and was expected to become competent and independent Secondly, apprenticeships were a time when trust was earned, individual honesty proved and personal reputation begun and displayed to the employer, customer and the wider community. Thirdly, it was a training ground for interpersonal relationships and fledgling networks to be experimented with under the protection of the employer. Lastly and most importantly apprenticeships gave access to established networks within society, business and politics (Defoe, 1726/2008: 14). Figures 16.2 and 16.3 demonstrate the 'guardianship networks' of Aldermen William Thompson and William Gibson, respectively. Apprenticeship networks generally consisted of three main strands: familial, employer and friendship, though if apprenticed to a family member those strands were reduced to two.

Apprenticed to his father, himself an Alderman, William Thompson's 'guardianship' network clearly shows there were two main network strands.

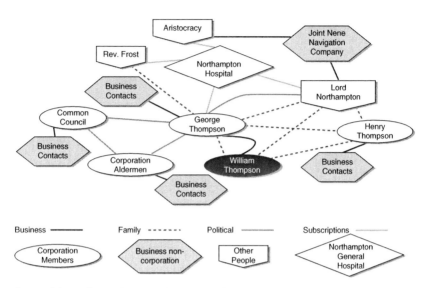

Figure 16.2   William Thompson's guardianship network
Source: Compiled from primary material.

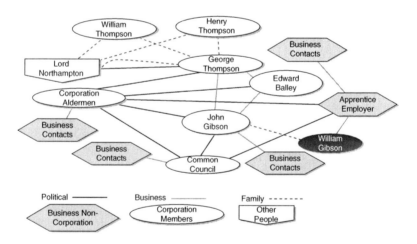

Figure 16.3   William Gibson's guardianship network
Source: Compiled from primary material.

The more influential of the two is undoubtedly family connections. It was through his father's established network that William had access to the aristocracy and landed gentry of the county, the business world and political connections. With the first of these, the network map shows that William's family connection to Lord Northampton potentially provided him with an unearned degree of social status amongst the Northampton community; an asset which could potentially be translated into usable business, social and political capital at a later period in life. As an apprentice, William was unable to conduct business in his own right and therefore relied upon indirect business links through his father's network. Whilst initially these connections were 'weak ties', over the period of his seven-year apprenticeship William had the opportunity to maximise and consolidate those connections, increasing his stock of business and social capital for future use. Similarly, William's introduction to political activity and local politicians was also experienced through the political networks established by his father (Defoe, 1726/2008: 14). It was through these connections that William had access to common councillors and the Aldermen of the town. Again, through the cultivation of his father's networks, William was able to build political alliances, thus increasing his overall stock of social capital and in particular his political capital.

Unlike Thompson, William Gibson was apprenticed out rather than to his father, so his guardianship network had three strands: family, friendship and employer (Figure 16.3). It is immediately apparent that the network distance between William Gibson and the aristocracy is greater than was the case for Thompson. Whilst the latter had an advantage of family association and thus an automatic social status, the degree of separation between Gibson and the aristocracy was such that it was unlikely to produce any tangible capital. However, he may have gained some business network advantage over Thompson's strong network ties, from the separation of family and employer. The separation had the potential to produce a more extensive network of weak ties: networking opportunities which enabled a greater accumulation of business capital. As with the guardianship network of Thompson, Gibson also had access to political networks via his father, which again offered the opportunity of building loose political and business alliances for future utilisation in the acquisition of status.

Both of these networks formed avenues for integration into existing networks and the instigation and development of new ones. They provided actual and potential social capital which was necessary for the acquisition of elite status in eighteenth-century Northampton. The structure of both networks is significant as neither presents a spider's web of connections generally associated with the research into the use and manufacture of social capital.

Established networks

There is limited archival material to show the progression of political and economic capital networks of any of the established urban elite of the period; however, data are available to suggest how elites maintained their status. Something of the social norms and values to which the Northampton civic elite adhered can be gleaned from the list of trustees for All Saints Church property. These positions were long term rather than annual appointments and the trustees were drawn entirely from members of the Corporation: five were common councillors, one was the town clerk John Jeyes, and six were Aldermen. Both William Thompson and William Gibson were trustees, suggesting that they were considered trustworthy by the larger body of the Corporation. In turn, being a trustee produced trust that could be translated into social status, and was used as a means of consolidating elite status. Further evidence of this trust and of the business ability which Gibson had accrued can be found in his involvement in a case of bankruptcy (see Figure 16.4). Along with his friend, Robert Billson, Gibson was entrusted with publicising and conducting the auction of property, goods and chattels of the innkeeper George Saunders, and the distribution of the money raised to his creditors. It is also likely that one way in which Gibson displayed his trustworthiness and business skills to his fellow politicians was the repayment of a loan from Sir Thomas White's charity, which the Aldermen administered, within the prescribed period of the loan agreement prior to becoming Mayor of the Corporation in 1771.

Economic capital was important to the maintenance of elite status in the eighteenth century. Money provided the means to interact with influential or established individuals and groups, and was a means of procuring property. Both Thompson and Gibson held property: a physical display of economic ability and security to the wider community, and a sign of status. Moreover, their political and social networks provided access to business connections through Corporation membership and interaction (see Figures 16.4 and 16.5). In 1769, whilst still a common councillor, Gibson leased all Northampton 'Road Tolls' from the Corporation for a period of 14 years at a cost of £87 half yearly. This was a large sum of money which intimates that Gibson was economically comfortable; that Gibson acquired the lease also indicates he had established strong network ties with serving Aldermen prior to gaining office as Mayor of the town.

Pearson and Richardson (2001: 673) suggest that eighteenth-century business networks were rarely centralised, appearing rhyzomic in their construct. However, the analysis presented here suggests that the networks of Northampton Aldermen had both rhyzomic and spider-web characteristics. A more nuanced and complex picture emerges when the networks of different individuals are overlain upon one another (Figure 16.6). This shows the importance of family connections in shaping the interpersonal networks between some members of the Corporation. Alderman George Thompson is the father of Aldermen William and Henry Thompson; Alderman John Gibson is the father of Alderman William Gibson, whose daughter married Councillor Samuel Treslove, and Edward Kerby's daughters married Alderman John Fox and Councillor John Sharman. Both Treslove and Sharman capitalised on their network connections to become Aldermen themselves.

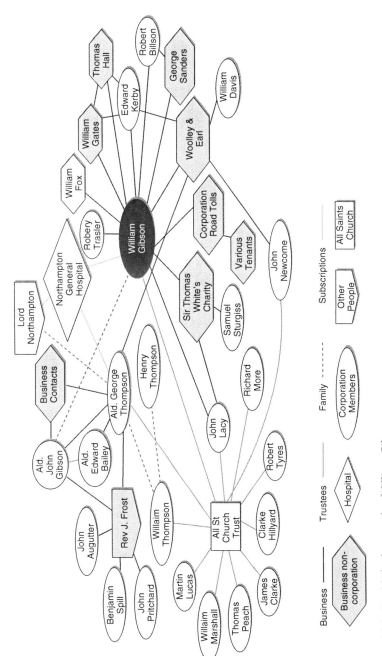

Figure 16.4 Established network – William Gibson
Source: Compiled from primary material.

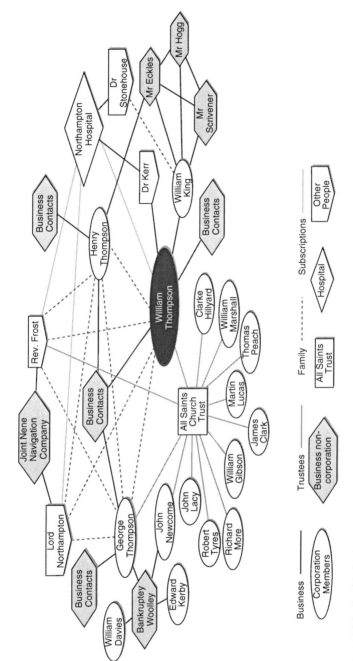

Figure 16.5 Established network – William Thompson
Source: Compiled from primary material.

279

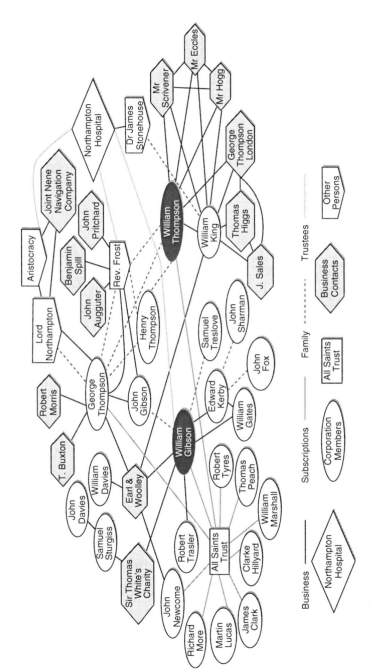

Figure 16.6 Aldermen's networks
Source: Compiled from primary material.

Historically marriage has often brought social, political and economic capital and these marriages were thus no exception.

The diagram also shows some of the business connections of the Aldermen. As discussed earlier, short-term partnerships were a common practice in the eighteenth century and often emerged from the dense network of business, social and political connections (Wilson, 1995: 47). Land and property ownership, whether freehold or leasehold, was an important commodity during the eighteenth century. It not only signalled economic capital but was also a sign of the commercial and financial ability crucial to business networking (Thompson, 1991: 26). Short-term partnerships, or rather business alliances and projects, provided not only economic benefits to those involved but increased levels of trust between them. This enhanced individual and collective reputation, making the network bond stronger; whilst successful projects could also lead to the acquisition of new networks and future business projects. At the other extreme, Figure 16.6 also shows a business networking 'structural hole' for William Thompson (Burt, 1992). Whether he acted in the capacity of facilitator between members of his established networks and the new network is unclear. However, it is important to know that the possibility existed.

Adding to the picture those Aldermen with Corporation leases suggests that several individuals, William Gibson in particular, must have established strong network ties with serving Aldermen prior to gaining office as Mayor of the town since the leases would have needed sanctioning by the Corporation. Lastly, the network map shows those who subscribed to Northampton General Hospital and those members of the Corporation who served as trustees of the property belonging to All Saints Church. There were many more interlinking and overlapping networks in operation in eighteenth-century Northampton than can be shown in the Figure 16.6. However, the visual representation does begin to give a physical dimension to the reciprocal nature of social capital.

Conclusion

This research has drawn on Bourdieu's theory of social capital and Pareto's definition of elites. The study examined the social capital of the elite of Northampton in the eighteenth century, focusing on the town's Aldermen. These men had the greatest combination of social, business and political status, and the largest stock of social capital. The evidence analysed in the study has concentrated on the means through which individuals attained and maintained elite status in eighteenth-century Northampton. It shows that, despite the presence of a grammar school and a dissenting academy in the town, apprenticeship was the main means of delivering a business education – a finding which challenges Bourdieu's theory that status is determined and justified through formal education. All of the serving

Aldermen of the 1770s underwent a period of apprenticeship, the completion of which entitled the man to register as a Freeman of the town and formally begin the path to becoming a member of the Corporation and thus part of the urban elite. Contrary to Granovettter's assertion that financial gain was the main impetus and aim of networking, the evidence for Northampton suggests that economic capital was a means rather than an end in the acquisition of elite status.

The route to becoming a member of the urban elite in eighteenth-century Northampton was, in theory at least, open to any Freeman of the town. However, they would require an accumulation of three forms of capital: social, business and political. Each required conformity to social, political and business norms, values and practices. Trust, trustworthiness and honesty were measured through the constant interaction between individuals; cultivation of and acceptance into existing networks and the establishment of new networks were essential to achieving elite status.

The most important form of capital in the acquisition of elite status was economic. Liquid assets enabled access to groups and activities where the established business, social and political elite interacted with one other; where social norms and values were exhibited and reinforced, and where network alliances were formed. Once established, these networks could yield incalculable social capital in the acquisition and recognition of elite status. Though it was common in the eighteenth century for family members to be shown preference for political office the greater number of individuals who served as Aldermen did not do so through inherited nepotistic family networks. In business too, approximately half the Aldermen followed the trades of their fathers. This implies that many individuals were required to build a greater number of new business networks to be successful and that their networks are greater in number than those with inherited networks. This offers some support to Pareto's theory that elites are those who are most active.

The evidence acknowledges that there were business partnerships in operation in Northampton; however, the Aldermen appear to have had a greater engagement with temporary business alliances than with partnerships. The available evidence indicates that several of the Aldermen formed small groups for the purpose of acquiring property. This was significant since property ownership in the eighteenth century not only constituted economic capital; it was also an important sign of social status and was essential in gaining and maintaining social capital and thus status within the wider community. The preponderance of temporary business alliances rather than formal partnerships also implies reciprocated trust between the Aldermen which resulted in a reduction of transaction cost and the building of strong bonding network ties. The evidence also shows that Aldermen engaged in economic forward planning. Membership of the Corporation opened business opportunities, and many Aldermen took advantage of 'insider' knowledge to 'pre-book' Corporation property leases, often years in advance.

Social interaction – particularly that which involved outlay of finances, engaging in subscription donations, attending 'ordinaries' and entering into sporting and other leisure activities – served to strengthen network bonds whilst at the same time defining and protecting elite status. Church attendance, meanwhile, displayed conformity to social norms and values amongst an elite drawn entirely from the Church of England.

The research highlights that networking began within 'guardianship' networks, which comprised the dense overlapping web of social, political and business connections of the father or employer. These networks confirm Defoe's suggestion that it was during the period of apprenticeship that the networks began to be more fully engaged by the apprentice. Through this engagement, the young man would also become enculturated in the unwritten rules of trust, honesty, social norms and values, and business practices discussed by Pearson and Richardson, Stobart and others. These networks comprised both 'weak' and 'strong' links between individuals. The latter primarily comprised those linking family and the Corporation, though the degree of strength between individual Aldermen and businessmen is less clear. However, it was the network links which produced the 'capital' to which Bourdieu refers: the greater the number of links, the greater the opportunity there was to produce the stock of social capital necessary for elite status.

Of course, there were far more links than can be reconstructed from the historical record or presented diagrammatically. For instance, the network maps do not reflect the actual business networks which the Aldermen would have had in operation both before and after elite status was achieved. However, they do show some temporary business alliances of the type highlighted by Wilson and Rubinstein. More importantly, they also suggest that the interlocking family, business and political networks were vital to the acquisition of a stock of social capital: business networks gave the necessary economic backing, political networks afforded access to power and status, and family networks provided support and access to status. These three came together in the bodies of the Aldermen, whose multiple and overlapping networks provided them with a reservoir of reciprocal trust which enabled them to consolidate their positions as urban elites and to gain a greater stock of social capital.

Appendix: List of Aldermen and their occupations

Information extracted from the 1774 and 1796 Poll Books and J. C. Cox, *The Records of the Borough of Northampton Vol. II*, Northampton, Northampton Corporation (1898).

1751 – Richard Moor – Business unknown
1752 – John Plackett – Tailor
1753 – George Thompson – Victualler
1754 – Henry Jeffcut – Business unknown
1755 – William Jackson – Surgeon
1756 – William Farrin – Tailor

1757 – Robert Lucas – Attorney
1758 – Lucas Ward – Butcher
1759 – John Fox – Cooper
1760 – Robert Tyres – Tinman
1761 – Robert Morris – Yeoman
1762 – William Giles – Hatter
1763 – Joseph Elston – Ironmonger
1764 – William Davis – Inn Holder
1765 – Robert Balaam – Painter
1766 – John Davies – Unknown
1767 – Thomas Breton – Apothecary
1768 – John Edwards – Gentleman
1769 – Henry Woolley – Schoolmaster
1770 – Samuel Sturgiss – Tanner
1771 – William Gibson – Maltster
1772 – William King – Grocer
1773 – Henry Thompson – Currier
1774 – Edward Kerby – Plumber and glazier
1775 – John Newcombe – Draper
1776 – William Chamberlain – Hatter
1777 – Robert Trasler – Baker
1778 – Edward Cole – Yeoman
1799 – James Clarke – Shoemaker
1780 – William Thompson – Victualler

Primary source material

Northamptonshire Record Office (NRO)

NBR indicates (Northampton Borough Records)
NBR 4/3 Book of Freemen of the Town 1730 'B'
NBR 6/2 Book of Enrolment of Apprentices Book 'B' 1721
NBR 3/5 Minutes of the Court of Mayor and Aldermen, Assembly Book 'B'
NBR 3/6 Minutes of the Court of Mayor and Aldermen, Assembly Book 'B' 1770
NBR 3/7 Assembly Book 1796–1818
NBR 8/2 Mayors Accounts 'B' 1772
NBR 9/2 Abstract of Corporation Leases 1730–1769
NGH (Northampton General Hospital) List of Subscribers
XYZ 1287a Joint Stock Nene Navigation: Western Division 1759
O3839, List of Trustees of Property belonging to All Saints Church Northampton
YZ 8014 Marriage settlement for Henry Woolley
ZA 9940 Contract of purchase of Church Pew
ZB 667/2/50 Sit Thomas White's Charity
Poll Book 1768
Poll Book 1774
Poll Book 1796

The British Directory 1791
NPL 132 Bankruptcy Paper
NPL1322B Bankruptcy Paper
ZB 142/10/1-30 George Sanders Bankruptcy Paper
NPL 511 Bankruptcy Paper
D 3698 Will of Edward Bailey
NPL 2296 Will of John Gibson
NPL 2297 Will of John Newcome
NPL 2685 Will of John Gibson
WB(N) 21 Conveyance of Property
XYZ 863 Conveyance of Property
XYZ 864 Conveyance of Property
NPL 2313/2 Conveyance of Property
YZ 3737a Conveyance of Property
YZ 3737b Conveyance of Property
YZ 3740 Conveyance of Property
ZB 542/12/7-6 Lease of Land
XYZ 2015 Lease Agreement

Northamptonshire Libraries
NM 1741 August
NM 1762
NM Vol. LIV, 1774
NM 26th September, Vol. LVI, 1775
NM 27th November, Vol. LVI, 1775
NM 29th January, Vol. LVI, 1776
NM 5th February, Vol. LVI, 1776
NM Vol. LVII, 1777
Birdsall and Son Binding Co. Northampton, Northamptonshire County Libraries ref. NPTN 686.3

References

Borsay, P. (1989) *The English Urban Renaissance: Culture and Society in the Provincial Town, 1660–1770* (Oxford: Oxford University Press).

Bourdieu, P. (1984) *Distinction: A Social Critique of the Judgement of Taste* (London: Routledge).

Bourdieu, P. (1986) 'The Forms of Capital'. In J. Richardson (ed.), *Handbook of Theory and Research for the Sociology of Education* (New York: Greenwood Press), 241–58.

Burt, R. (1992) 'The Social Structure of Competition'. In N. Nohria and R. G. Eccles (eds.), *Networks and Organisations: Structure, Form and Action* (Boston: Harvard Business School Press).

Clark, P. (1984) 'The Civic Leaders of Gloucester 1580–1800'. In P. Clark (ed.), *The Transformation of English Provincial Towns* (London: Hutchinson), 311–45.

Clark, P. (2005) 'Elite Networking and the Formation of an Industrial Town: Loughborough, 1700–1840'. In J. Stobart and N. Raven (eds.), *Towns, Regions and Industries: Urban and Industrial Change in the Midlands, c.1700–1840* (Manchester: Manchester University Press), 161–75.

Colley, L. (1996) *Britons: Forging the Nation, 1707–1838* (London: Vintage).

Colli, A. and Rose, M. (2007) 'Family Business'. In G. Jones and J. Zeitlin (eds.), *The Oxford Handbook of Business History* (Oxford: Oxford University Press), 194–218.

Cox, J. C. (1898) *The Records of the Borough of Northampton, Vol. II* (Northampton: Northampton Corporation).

Defoe. D. (1726/2008), *The Complete English Tradesman* (Milton Keynes: Tutis Digital Publishing).

Granovetter, M. (1973) 'The Strength of Weak Ties', *American Journal of Sociology*, 78(6): 1360–80.

Greenall, R. L. (2000) *A History of Northamptonshire and the Stoke of Peterborough* (Chichester: Phillimore and Co.).

Hanifan, L. J. (1916) 'The Rural School Community Center', *Annals of the American Academy of Political and Social Science*, 67(1): 130–8.

Hanifan, L. J. (1920) *The Community Center* (Boston: Silver Burdett).

Hatley, V. (1968) 'The Northampton Elections of 1774: An Eye Witness Account', Northamptonshire Historical Series, 5 (with reprint from Reports and Papers of the Northamptonshire Antiquarian Society, 1958/9).

Kanagaretnam, K., Mestelman, S., Khalid Nainar, S. M. and Shehata, M. (2010) 'Trust and Reciprocity with Transparency and Repeated Interactions', *Journal of Business Research*, 63(2): 241–7.

Letki, N. (2006) 'Investigating the Roots of Civic Morality: Trust, Social Capital and Institutional Performance', *Political Behaviour*, 28(3): 305–25.

Pareto, V. (1939) *The Mind and Society*, trans. A. Livingston (New York: McGraw-Hill).

Pearson, R. and Richardson, D. (2001) 'Business Networking in the Industrial Revolution', *Economic History Review*, 54(4): 657–79.

Price, R. (1999) *British Society: Dynamism, Containment and Change, 1680–1888* (Cambridge: Cambridge University Press).

Putnam, R. D. (2000) *Bowling Alone: The Collapse and Revival of American Community* (London: Simon & Schuster).

Putnam, R. D., Leonardi, R. and Nannetti, R. (1993) *Making Democracy Work: Civic Traditions in Modern Italy* (Princeton: Princeton University Press).

Rubinstein, W. D. (1981) *The Very Wealthy in Britain since the Industrial Revolution* (London: Croom Helm).

Ruggiu, F. J. (2001) 'The Urban Gentry in England, 1660–1780', *Historical Research*, 74(185): 249–71.

Stobart, J. (2005) 'Information, Trust and Reputation: Shaping the Merchant Elite in Eighteenth-Century England', *Scandinavian Journal of History*, 30(2): 61–82.

Stone, L. and Stone, J. (1995) *An Open Elite? England, 1540–1880*, abridged version (Oxford: Clarendon Press).

Thompson, E. P. (1991) *Customs in Common* (London: Merlin Press).

Thompson, F. M. L. (2001) *Gentrification and the Enterprise Culture: Britain 1780–1980* (Oxford: Oxford University Press).

Webb, S. and Webb, B. (1963) *Statutory Authorities for Special Purposes* (London: Frank Cass).

Williams. C. (2000) 'Expediency, Authority and Duplicity: Reforming Sheffield's Police 1832–40'. In R. J. Morris and R. H. Trainor (eds.), *Urban Governance: Britain and Beyond since 1750* (Aldershot: Ashgate), 115–27.

Wilson, J. F. (1995) *British Business History, 1720–1994* (Manchester: Manchester University Press).

17
Delicate Empiricism: An Action Learning Approach to Elite Interviewing

Nada K. Kakabadse and Eddy Louchart

Introduction

This chapter presents a practical framework useful to both young and well-seasoned researchers who are about to embark on qualitative research studies requiring interviews with the elite, 'a short-hand term for those actors who [people] perceive as more powerful or privileged than some undefined group' (Woods, 1998: 2101).

Welch et al. (2002) in their definition of elite posit that the status of individuals in organisations is a combination of several factors such as the individual's hierarchy, personal assets and degree of international exposure. Welch et al. (2002) define elite as:

> a respondent (usually male) who occupies a senior or middle management position; has functional responsibility in an area where he enjoys high status in accordance with corporate values, has considerable industry experience and frequently also long tenure with the company, possesses a broad network of relationships and has considerable international exposure.

Interviewing is one of the most powerful data collection methods for qualitative studies (Ackroyd and Hughes, 1981; McCracken, 1988; Berg, 2007). For example, McCracken (1988: 9) argues that in-depth interviews are particularly useful as they allow interviewers to enter the 'mental world of the individual, to glimpse at the categories and logic by which he or she sees the world'. Tansey (2007) suggests that elite interviewing can contribute to empirical research in political science; whereas Berry (1999) notes that scholars extensively use in-depth interviews across many social and educational research disciplines.

The authors of this chapter have over twenty years of combined experience in conducting qualitative studies and interviewing international elites (chief executive officers, board members, politicians and various categories of corporate elite) who view the elite interview process as an 'action learning' opportunity (Revans, 1982). This chapter discusses issues such as negotiation of access, interviewee/interviewer power imbalance, conversation dynamics and feedback methods.

The section below consists of a brief literature review which highlights that conducting in-depth interviews with elites is significantly different to conducting interviews with non-elites. Then we introduce the elite interviewing framework (EIF) composed of four key elements: (1) preparing for the interview, (2) conducting the interview, (3) reflecting upon the interview and (4) follow-up. For each element, we present a series of recommendations and real-life examples. The chapter concludes with a presentation of the elite interview cycles. We argue in the conclusion that elite interviewing is, in fact, a combination of internal and external processes.

Learning from the literature

Roulston (2010) argues that inquirers' approaches to interviewing depend a great deal upon the type of the study, whether phenomenological, ethnographic, feminist, oral history or dialogical. There are multiple typologies for qualitative interviews and there has been little consensus in regards to the categorisation of the interview process (Rapley, 2004). For example, Janesick (1998: 30) defines interviewing as a 'meeting of two persons to exchange information and ideas through questions and responses, resulting in communication and joint construction of meaning about a particular topic'. According to Janesick (1998), numerous factors influence the interviewing process, such as individuals' ideas and values, individuals' personalities, as well as the context in which the interview takes place.

In a special edition of *PS: Political Sciences and Politics* on elite interviewing, Aberbach and Rockman (2002), Berry (2002) and Goldstein (2002) acknowledge that there are relatively few studies which provide practical guidance on how to prepare and conduct interviews with elites. Indeed, *Qualitative Report*, an online bi-monthly journal dedicated to qualitative research since 1990, has published twenty articles on interviewing, but not a single one focused on interviewing elites.

There are significant differences between elite interviewing and non-elite interviewing. Table 17.1 summarises major characteristics of elite and non-elite interviews. Most notable is Kahl's (1957) observation that studying elites within their context has proved greatly difficult. Kahl (1957: 10) notes that 'those who sit amongst the mighty do not invite sociologists to watch them make the decisions about how to control the behaviours of others'.

Welch et al. (2002) commented that in the context of elite interviewing, professional values, seniority, gender and culture have a strong impact on the interactions between researchers and elite participants. In particular, the seniority gap between the elder elite and the researcher can result in the

Table 17.1 Non-elite and elite interview characteristics

Characteristics	Non-elite interviews	Elite interviews
Access	• Relatively easy • Negotiated through formal channels	• Difficult • Negotiated through networks
Common interview style	• Structured or standardised open-ended questions • Semi-structured or guided interview • In-depth informal conversation and/or life histories	• Open or unstructured conversation • Semi-structure or guided interview
Sampling method	• Convenience, quota, theoretical, non-probability	• Opportunistic, snowballing, non-probability
Ethical safeguards	• Explicit responsibility of inquirer	• Implicit process based on inquirer's credibility
Interview protocol	• Important – use of interviewing guides	• Less important – may or may not be used, but useful for inexperienced researchers
Interviewer's initial knowledge about interviewee	• Minimal	• Considerable, including professional and personal information
Interviewee's initial knowledge of interviewer	• Minimal	• Considerable, including professional and personal information
Expert knowledge (i.e. balance of power) with	• Interviewer	• Interviewee
Scrutiny/selection of participation rests with	• Interviewer	• Interviewee

Source: Compiled from Fitz and Halpin (1995); Knapp (1997); Goldstein, (2002); Rapley (2004).

elite behaving ambivalently. They can patronise younger inquirers and often override their comments as they try to 'enlighten' them (Welch et al., 2002). Goldstein (2002) presents a series of useful techniques that enable inquirers to gain access to elite participants with a particular focus on how to approach candidates and convince them to become involved in a research project.

Fitz and Halpin (1995) observed that the level of candour in interviews is often directly related to the interviewee's seniority, where non-elite interviewees tend to guard their responses. Elite interviewees, on the other hand, are open and transparent during the interviewing process. Knapp

(1997: 340) suggests that open-ended interviews with elite participants provides an opportunity for a 'shared agenda setting' between interviewer and interviewee; however, for this to occur, interviewers must play a variety of roles such as 'insider and outsider, subordinate and sounding board, sympathiser and critic, therapist and spy, academic and consultant' (Welch et al., 2002: 6).

Fitz and Halpin (1995: 68) note that elite interviewees are 'professional communicators' who unlike non-elite interviewees are often confronted with sensitive situations. This partially explains why inquirers involved in elite interviewing often experience a power imbalance phenomenon (Welch et al., 2002) whereby the elite interviewees dominate the interviewers.

Other contributors to the field of elite interviewing include Aberbach and Rockman (2002) whose research focused on conducting and coding elites' interviews and Berry (2002) who addressed the issue of validity and reliability in the context of elite interviewing. The researchers believe that despite their political science context, Aberbach and Rockman (2002) and Berry's (2002) contributions are highly relevant to social researchers. Indeed, political, corporate and social elite interviewees share many similarities, including a similar level of exposition to the public media. Lord (2000) notes that it is not rare for corporate elites in large organisations to pursue various extra-curricular activities which often have a political connotation (e.g. contribution to electoral campaigns, informational lobbying, advocacy advertising, constituency building).

Regarding the format of elite interviewing, as Table 17.1 illustrates, open-ended interviews are the most suitable mode of exchange and less subject to interviewers' control. However, Wong (1998: 196–7) notes that 'the ethics of ambiguity and ambivalence in research relationships will always be present and dependent on the local, strategic and tactical conditions of the field', particularly in elite interviewing. However, Powdermaker (1966) states that ambivalent and ambiguous situations can at times provide inquirers with learning and serendipitous opportunities. Whilst in non-elite interviews the inquirer needs to 'ensure the individual's mental capacity, disclose sufficient information, provide sufficient time and privacy, provide the safeguard and ensure the individual's awareness' (Antle and Regehr, 2003: 137), these issues will not surface in elite interviews. On the contrary, in elite interviews the interviewee scrutinises the inquirer's academic and social credibility before agreeing or not to an interview, whilst the interviewee's secretary usually handles the timing and all other details. By the time the interview takes place, the elite has scrutinised the inquirer who has passed his/her initial test. Hence, the interview creates an opportunity to take that relationship forward, preserve it or, if not careful, damage it. If damaged, this can also have negative consequences on the relationship with the intermediary (and possibly the whole network) who facilitated the initial introduction. This creates additional pressure on the inquirer.

The elite interviewing framework (EIF)

Our experience suggests that there are four critical stages to conducting elite interviews (Figure 17.1). We argue that the preparation, reflection and follow-up phases are equally as important as conducting the interview itself. This is a dynamic, iterative and cyclical process (the arrows in Figure 17.1 represent the dynamics between each stage) which follows, in many ways, the collaborative inquiry cycle as described in Kakabadse et al. (2007), and reinforces action learning (Lewin, 1942; Revans, 1982; Kolb, 1984). According to the collaborative inquiry cycle, knowledge is created through a cycle of concrete experiences, personal reflection on given experiences, application of knowledge and establishment of ways of modifying the next occurrence of a given experience (Lewin, 1942; Kolb, 1984).

The preparation stage establishes a strategy to gain access to elite participants and objectively assesses the strength of one's professional network in respect to accessing elite participants. The preparation stage for elite interviews is crucial and inquirers need to focus on setting the scene, reinforcing their credibility and awareness of conversation dynamics (Stage 1). Conducting interviews with elites can involve power imbalance between inquirer and participants (Stage 2). Elite interviewing is first and foremost a tremendous learning opportunity; hence, inquirers need to spend time after each interview conducting a thorough and objective analysis of their own behaviour and the participants' behaviour during the interviewing (Stage 3). This reflection process then enables inquirers to build on their experience and develop their interviewing skills. Finally, following up on elite interviews and providing feedback enables inquirers and participants to expand their professional networks (Stage 4).

Stage 1: Elite interviewing preparation

Securing an interview with an elite participant is a subtle mix of luck, audacity and ability to network. For example, Goldstein (2002: 669) suggests that

Figure 17.1   The elite interviewing framework (EIF)
Source: Compiled by the authors.

gaining valuable data from elite interviews requires inquirers to 'be well prepared, construct sound questions, establish a rapport with respondents, and know how to write up their notes and code responses accurately and consistently'. Inquirers preparing for elite interviewing soon find that the preparation phase is a tricky and time-consuming exercise.

Negotiation of access

Before deciding to conduct a study requiring elite participation, one needs to objectively gauge accessibility to elite participants. Does the inquirer have direct access to potential participants, and realistically, will they participate willingly? This requires a thorough scrutiny of the inquirer's personal and professional networks. Our experience shows that this assessment phase may require talking with various members of one's network and asking for support. Granovetter (1992) suggests that trust is a major feature of social capital and enables actors to pursue their goals within a network. The 'mode of entry' into the elite network has a direct impact on the level of openness during conversations. Personal trust is very important in elite interviewing. Equally, the extent of one's network is of great importance. As Bourdieu (1986) notes, networking is paramount for both the acquisition and the use of social capital whether these are cognitive, relational or structural.

If upon the initial assessment the accessibility to elites via personal and professional networks is not guaranteed, one must revisit and revamp the research project. We have seen many frustrated inquirers and studies fail because the lack of elite participants resulted in wasted time, resources and efforts. If upon analysis the inquirer is confident that accessing elites will not pose a major obstacle, we recommend that the inquirer starts preparations to initiate the research study.

Once the inquirer has established access to elites, he/she must convene with the elite participants. Gaining access to elites is not purely a matter of luck, personality, class, gender or nationality, but very much depends on the level of interaction that inquirers and participants have had over a period of time (Ward and Jones, 1999). One must bear in mind that politically sensitive research studies may render participation even more problematic (Goggin et al., 1990), thus requiring the inquirer to take extra caution when approaching potential participants.

At this stage inquirers must write a short and concise summary of their research study. Goldstein (2002) suggests that the letter should clearly state the basic outline of the study and how much time participants must spend with the inquirer. Our experience shows that the introductory one-page letter (or email) should address the following six key points:

- Aim of research study
- Reason for asking for participation
- Interview format

- Length of interview
- Assurance of confidentiality and anonymity
- Benefits to participants

Most importantly, when making contact with potential participants for the first time, the introduction letter/e-mail should focus on what the elite respondents will gain by participating.

Many scholars realise that executives are incredibly busy individuals. Schoenberger (1991: 183) notes that a 'busy manager is prone to interruption and preoccupation with the exigencies of his or her job'. Hunter (1993: 167) argues that elites are 'relatively unstudied, not because they do not have or are not part of existing social problems, but precisely because they are powerful and can more readily resist the intrusive inquisition of social research'. Hunter adds (1993: 167) that 'researchers rarely study those more powerful than themselves, preferring instead to engage with the relatively powerless'.

Aristotle (1908) noted that all men, by nature, desire to know and individuals are, by nature, curious. We also found that often elites like to know what other individuals in the same position think about certain issues. In our recent study of C-level executives, we used the flowing technique to entice elite participation and to increase the participation rate. We offered to share preliminary findings of the study even before dissemination through academic journals. By emphasising privileged access to newly created knowledge, we were able to secure twenty-five in-depth interviews within a matter of weeks.

Inquirers widely recognise that it is easier to secure a conversation with elite participants when one can justify a certain number of years working for prestigious organisations or conducting research in conjunction with a well-respected university (Aberbach and Rockman, 2002). Welch et al. (2002) suggest that in order to increase the study participation rate, inquirers should package and present the study to the interview subjects so that it appears relevant, and more importantly, non-threatening. The second section of this chapter addresses this critical point.

Assuming that one has gained access to elites through recommendation or personal contact, it is incredibly important that inquirers take the time to introduce themselves and their research study to the individuals surrounding potential participants. Inquirers should give a courtesy call and briefly introduce themselves to personal assistants, who play a gatekeeping role and often control the elites' diaries. Aberbach and Rockman (2002) support this observation and recommend that the inquirer prepare a short introduction for the attention of the personal assistant or appointment secretary. Morill et al. (1999) add that securing gatekeeper cooperation also enables the inquirer to understand the vocabulary and terminology within a given organisation, which ultimately could increase the inquirer's level of personal credibility.

We recall a situation where the personal assistant advised us to request a face-to-face meeting instead of a telephone interview with a particular executive, since the individual's preferred method of interaction was face-to-face meetings. This anecdote presents a perfect example of a vital piece of information that we would never have been able to gain without the trust of the personal assistant. Similarly, we know of many good interview opportunities that inquirers have lost because they paid very little attention to gatekeepers. Despite this, Lee (1995: 16) observes that 'the access to a research setting is never a given. What is open at one juncture can close at another time or in different circumstances.'

Background information collection

One positive aspect of interviewing elites (apart from the stimulating conversation) is the relative ease of gathering personal and professional data prior to the interview. Some would argue that this is particularly relevant in political science, but we argue that this is also relevant when conducting interviews with executives. It is important to collect information related to the elite's career history. Inquirers may find, for instance, that they have things in common with interviewees. Perhaps both inquirers and interviewees studied at the same university, attended a similar seminar or have acquaintances in common. Davies (2001: 76) stresses that it is crucial for inquirers to gain professional information prior to the interview. 'When going in to talk to someone about his/her career, it is crucial to know what that career was and, if possible, its most important features relevant to the interview.' Several professional networking websites enable inquirers to gain valuable information about the participants in a non-intrusive manner.

However, inquirers should not be surprised if interviewees have done their research too and read the interviewers' latest book or published article before relinquishing some of their precious time. Inquirers must prepare themselves to answer questions such as 'What is your interest in this subject?' or 'What are you going to do with the results?' Inquirers ought to bear in mind that they are under scrutiny. If inquirers do not pass the scrutiny test, it is very likely that the interview will be short. If they are successful, inquirers should expect an intellectually stimulating dialogue.

Using the pilot study as a training platform

Conducting in-depth interviews with elites can be an overwhelming experience for inexperienced inquirers. We suggest that inexperienced inquirers use the pilot study as a training ground for the more complex and intense interviews. We recommend that they conduct interviews for the pilot study (three to four interviews) face-to-face and with participants with whom the inquirers have had previous contact to build up self-confidence.

The use of a research protocol

Three types of interview techniques are available to qualitative inquirers: (1) structured, (2) semi-structured and (3) open interviews (Ackroyd and Hughes, 1981; McQueen and Knussen, 2002; Bryman, 2008). From our experience, we recommend only semi-structured and open interviews with elite interviewees. Open interviews are very powerful, but require inquirers to have a strong understanding of their research topic and be comfortable having this kind of interaction. Open interview or 'guided conversation' is a very fruitful data gathering method; however, only experienced inquirers are able to guide conversations with elite participants within their area of interest. The open interview has a non-standardised flexible format, and is likely to produce a qualitatively rich array of personal insights. Guided conversations rely less on specific questions, but more on a series of topics to cover during the interview. If inquirers are not experienced in guided conversations, the elite can quickly turn these into 'unguided reminiscence'. Inquirers should focus on asking questions that are directly relevant to the research study. Notwithstanding, even experienced inquirers may encounter some challenges. We recall an interview with an ex-defence minister and chairman of a number of enterprises who spent the first four hours over lunch telling us about his political influence before we could ask him to talk about the leadership challenges he experiences in his boardroom. One needs patience, tactfulness and focus in order to gain the information that one seeks.

Inquirers often consider a questionnaire as a discretionary matter in qualitative research; however, McCracken (1988) argues that in the context of in-depth interview, the use of interview protocol is indispensable. Our experience in elite interviewing suggests that the time one spends designing a well-constructed protocol is a non-negligible investment.

Similarly, McQueen and Knussen (2002: 204) note:

> the process of formulation can highlight problems: some questions may not in fact be 'researchable' and although it is not always possible to spot this at an early stage, the more thought and deliberation that goes into planning, the less likely it is that the study will fail.

Elites evolve within micro-communities where each and every single individual is connected to each other. The last thing that inquirers would want is to finish an interview and leave the interviewee with the feeling that the inquirer was unprepared and that the interview was not a good use of his/her time.

Our experience proves that guided conversations and semi-structured interviews allow for higher, better and more meaningful interaction with participants, which is particularly relevant since individuals vary in their ability to articulate their thoughts and ideas (Berry, 1999). Ackroyd and Hughes (1981) assert that semi-structured interviews allow for more flexibility and enable interviewers to probe beyond specific questions. Rodham (2000) notes that semi-structured interviews allow for a certain level of structure and still permit sufficiently flexible spontaneous contributions. The level of structure varies from one inquirer to another and depends greatly on personal preferences. From our experience, we recommend designing semi-structured interviews in a flexible way that allows inquirers to alter the questions while conducting the interview.

Political scientists recommend that, when conducting elite interviews, inquirers should opt for semi-structured interviews with open-ended questions. Aberbach and Rockman (2002: 674) point out that interviewees should have the latitude to fully articulate their responses. By doing so, inquirers ultimately increase the validity of the collected data. 'Elites especially, but other highly educated people, do not like being put in the straightjacket of close-ended questions. They prefer to articulate their views, explaining why they think what they think' (Berg, 2007). McQueen and Knussen (2002) note that despite following a structured set of questions, participants in semi-structured interviews have the freedom to digress and use real-life examples as illustrations.

Stage 2: Interviewing elites

Factors such as the intensity of the interaction, the expectations that respondents hold of the interviewer, as well as the conversation dynamics make elite interviewing a challenging exercise. The literature on elite interviewing reveals a power imbalance between interviewees and interviewers. Welch et al. (2002) note that this phenomenon begins from the moment academic inquirers seek access to elites. Welch et al. (2002) argue that elites' perception of academia's relevance in the development of industry practice plays a key role in securing an interview with elite subjects.

In elite interviewing, power and control phenomena are very dynamic. We found that Schoenberger's (1991) term 'locus of control' denotes the control of research agendas between inquirer and study participant are static. In our experience, we found that agenda control, tone, lengths and other dimensions of the interview are dynamic. This dynamic process can be challenging for novice inquirers who can be overwhelmed and in awe of the experience, power and trappings surrounding participants. For instance, interviewing a chief executive on a private jet on a flight from Milan to Larnaca required a certain level of concentration to focus on the conversation without being distracted by the scenery or succumbing to the power of French 'bubbly'. We also recall drinking the customary rice wine with ministers in the Chinese province of Hunan, which required a strong stomach and a great deal of recovery the day after. Although these instances are exceptional rather than a rule, they can easily overwhelm inexperienced inquirers. In elite interviewing, interviewees can often dominate conversations.

Fitz and Halpin (1995) judiciously point out that elite interviewees are professional communicators involved on a daily basis in situations which require them to develop powerful and elaborate arguments. Yeung (1995: 322) notes that in the context of elite interviews, 'there is always a tendency for the interviewee to impose his/her meta-communicative norms on the interviewer'.

We have experienced these phenomena and the section below presents a series of recommendations and techniques that inquirers can use to limit this power imbalance phenomenon. We suggest that quickly establishing one's credibility is the key to a successful interview with elite respondents. Welch et al. (2002: 6) corroborate this by suggesting:

> The challenge for researchers in elite settings is somewhat different. There, the issue is rather a matter of proving one's professional credentials and standing. Researchers must demonstrate they are worthy of the time and support of busy and often powerful individuals.

The literature on elite interviewing suggests that the first step into redressing the power imbalance is to demonstrate professionalism and a strong understanding of the discussion topics (Peabody et al., 1990; Richards, 1996).

Setting the scene for the interview

Our experience with elite interviews suggests that before starting the interview, it is beneficial if inquirers introduce themselves (see Box 17.1 below). By means of an introduction, we suggest a short description of past and present academic/professional experience and current research area.

Inquirers should spend some time to reintroduce the research study (including research aims, research questions and key research assumptions), but most

Box 17.1: An example of interview introduction

Good afternoon / morning / evening, Mr. X. First of all, I would like to thank you for your time today. I understand how busy you are at the moment, so I really appreciate that you took some time to meet with me today. Make reference to an earlier encounter (e.g. We, in fact, had the chance to meet about three years ago at the ...) or a mutual friend who had brokered the meeting (e.g. John sends his regards...).

As you already may know, I am currently a researcher at the University of [name of your university]. Prior to joining the University of [name of your university], I spent x years working at [name of your previous organisation]. During this time, I have had the chance to work closely with about ... (e.g. 60 Chief Executive Officers).

importantly inquirers ought to remind interviewees of some of the key aspects of interview protocols (i.e. informed consent). Welch et al. (2002) point out that it is not rare for elites to answer questions in a guarded manner through fear that the interviewer may use some of their comments out of context and against them. Inquirers have a duty to inform interviewees whether they will keep the conversation confidential, and what steps they will take to ensure participant anonymity. McQueen and Knussen (2002: 208) state:

> The researcher should discuss or consider beforehand the issue of disclosing personal information within the interviewing setting. Self-disclosure can help establish a comfortable and open relationship between the researcher and the interviewee and it can facilitate certain topics.

The interviewee–interviewer relationship

A day in the life of a company executive or politician involves back-to-back meetings, important conversations with key stakeholders and important decisions that have broad-spectrum impact. Mindful of the allocated time, inquirers (especially inexperienced ones) can easily dive straight into interviewing mode. We suggest that inquirers spare a few minutes for idle chatter with interviewees. McCracken (1988) suggests that idle chatter plays a critical role in establishing a sound relationship between the interviewer and the interviewee. McCracken (1988: 38) notes that:

> whatever is being said in the opening few minutes of the interview, it must be demonstrated that the interviewer is a benign, accepting, curious (but not inquisitive) individual who is prepared and eager to listen to virtually any testimony with interest.

Inquirers use idle chatter extensively both as a way to relax the atmosphere and to sense the responsiveness, assertiveness and current stress level of the respondents.

Idle chatter is usually more effective in face-to-face interviews when the interviewees invite inquirers to share their private space. When proceeding into the elite's agreed interview place, often (but not necessarily) his/her offices, we recommend that inquirers look for clues that would enable the start of an informal chat. We remember a particular meeting with a C-level executive, where after a few minutes of informal chatter, the executive was comfortable enough to share with us information related to his family. One ought to be cautious and not generalise, as not every single elite interviewee would be comfortable with this kind of informality. Our experience, however, shows that in situations where we informally chatted for a few minutes, the tone and the dynamics of the conversation and ultimately, the overall relationship between the inquirer and the interviewee change. McCracken (1988) argues that starting the conversation with simple opening questions (e.g. biographical) is an excellent way to build a rapport between inquirers and elites. Asking people to talk about themselves is a very flattering experience.

We posit that the way an inquirer presents a project influences the dynamics of the interview process. As a matter of principle, we make a point when talking with elites of not using the word 'interview', as this word could subconsciously create or reinforce the power imbalance. We always refer to interviews as *conversations*, which appears to have a more colloquial connotation. Welch et al. (2002: 11) suggest that inquirers should position interviews as an intellectual discussion and reflection and note that 'the challenge in an interview situation is to create a space for intellectual discussion and reflection which is clearly separate from the manager's day-to-day routine of meetings, deadlines and administration'.

Conversation dynamics

From our experience, we suggest that in-depth interviews with elites are amazingly rewarding both in terms of the collected data and stimulating conversations. The reason for this is simple: the dynamics of the conversation are somehow different. Berg (2007) notes that participants agree to participate for various reasons including curiosity, potential therapeutic benefits or a desire to share experiences that they have not felt comfortable sharing with anyone else before. Ackroyd and Hughes (1981: 80) also acknowledge the therapeutic aspect of some research studies, suggesting that:

> the interviewer is giving the respondent a chance to talk anonymously without fear of contradiction, signs of boredom, disagreement, or disapproval, often about deeply personal matters. [This is] a temptation that few of us would not be able to resist.

Trying to understand why elites consent to participate in a research study can help inquirers prepare for the interview. Our experience shows that it is not rare for elites to seize the opportunity to update themselves on current thinking in a particular field or benchmark themselves against other participants. Welch et al. (2002: 12) also noted this and state:

> Elites like to use the interviewer, who is up-to-date in the academic literature which they themselves often have little time to read, as a facilitator of their own thinking and a sounding board for ideas.

In recent discussions with C-level executives, we often found ourselves sharing insights into theories of leadership. This did not have a negative effect on the interview process, but served as an opportunity for inquirers to increase their personal credibility and reinforce their status as theorists. In order not to be caught off balance, it is important for inquirers to recognise beforehand that this exchange of ideas and opinions constitutes a key aspect of elite interviewing.

Often research method manuals recommend that inquirers, in order to enhance the level of consistency in the answers (standardising stimuli effect) (Ackroyd and Hughes, 1981), conduct each interview in the same way and ask each question in the same order. Our experience shows that inquirers should not attempt to standardise interviews with elites, as it is very unlikely that every single interview will take place in the same conditions and atmosphere, or even under similar circumstances. Aberbach and Rockman (2002: 674) support this view and note that interviewers 'may not have necessarily asked questions in the same order', but in our own experiences, we found that the advantages of conversational flow and depth of response outweigh the disadvantages of inconsistent ordering. Berry's (2002: 681) observations corroborate this statement. He notes, 'your time with a subject is a scarce resource. Try to determine early on in an interview what part of the protocol is likely to yield the best answers.'

We suggest that inquirers during elite interviews should make an effort so that conversations do not happen in a linear way. Aberbach and Rockman (2002: 674) noted that 'elites do not like to be put in the straitjacket of close-ended questions'. Our experience shows that one way to make the exchange of ideas more interesting and challenging is for inquirers, when appropriate, to use unscheduled probes. Berg (2007) asserts that probing questions are particularly useful to inquirers to draw out complete stories. Berry (2002: 681) confirms the importance of probing in interviewing elites and argues that probing can also be non-verbal:

> Skilled interviewers know how to probe nonverbally as well. When a subject gives an answer that does not appear to contain all the information needed, the immediate response on the part of the interviewer should be to say nothing and stare expectantly at the subject.

Time management

Finally, one of the most crucial aspects of the elite interview is time management. As the literature suggests on countless occasions, inquirers are constantly seeking to meet elites who are working in busy and fast-changing environments. We recommend that inquirers respect their allocated time when interviewing. Herz and Imber (1995: 3) note that gaining the trust of individuals in interviewing settings requires 'a sympathetic understanding', thus understanding and appreciating their time constraints is critical.

Time management is also important in situations where interviewees digress or are quite talkative. Monitoring elapsed time allows inquirers to react instantaneously and change the focus of the conversation back to the research interest area. Berry (2002) recommends that inquirers use a series of bridges to re-channel the discussion to the subject area. Our experience demonstrates that writing down interviewees' keywords helps inquirers pull the conversation back on track. By doing so, inquirers also demonstrate that they have paid attention during the conversation and allow them to improvise a short summary to conclude the interview. However, if a participant is willing to give extra time, inquirers should be prepared to reciprocate and gracefully accept this opportunity. Inquirers can learn a great deal from prolonged interviews providing they keep the focus of the conversation.

Stage 3: Personal reflection: making sense of interview experience

As Carlson and McCaslin (2003) observe, all too often inquirers forget to reflect upon the initial interview protocol. Yet, it is our belief that this process is mandatory since qualitative inquirers, in order to gain contextual sensitivity, must explore, discover and connect the empirical material to the environment. Carlson and McCaslin (2003: 551) argue that reflexivity moves the inquirer into an 'inductive mode that involves reflection on the homogeneous informants' data grounded in the ecology'. Elite interviewing is a learning opportunity and a personal development experience. Elite interviews often reveal insightful and potentially sensitive information. Making sense of an elite interview experience requires both in vivo and post hoc reflexivity from the inquirer. This process is necessary for the inquirer's understanding of theoretical key practice, the identification of standpoints and to build a relationship and trust with interviewees. Inquirers need to move from an epistemic or 'scientific' (Aristotle's *episteme*) interview with a focus on knowledge, belief, acceptance, verification, justification and perspective during interviews to a 'phronetic' (Aristotle's *phronesis* or practical wisdom) interview with a focus on deliberation and values that the elite interviewee considers good or bad. Theoretical reflexivity is a key concept and practice in the identification of inquirers' standpoints. In vivo reflexivity allows the inquirer to reflect on his/her situation and gain an understanding of it. Self-reflexivity is also important during interviewing, 'even though little has been written about this unspoken, inner or self-dialogue' (Arendell, 1997: 342). The inquirers need to remain cognizant of and cope with several activities simultaneously: the conversation with the interviewee; responses and changes in the line and direction of discussion; the anticipation of transitions to new topics; and the reflection upon strategies to return to discussion topics for additional information (Arendell, 1997). This 'in vivo' self-reflexivity is much more emotionally demanding than the post hoc reflexivity, so much so that at times after prolonged interviewing the inquirer may feel exhausted. For the novice interviewer the whole experience may feel overwhelming. Moreover, in an open-ended dialogue the inquirer first needs to understand, then to be understood. This calls for empathy in the dialogue. Empathy in the dialogue requires that the listener enter another person's frame of reference, understand his/her philosophy and understand how he/she feels. It requires listening for feeling, meaning and behaviour using abilities of sensory intuitiveness and feeling (Covey, 1992). Empathy allows for personal connections with others (the art of relationship is to enter into an encounter or to recognise and respond fittingly to people's feelings and concerns) and ability for social analysis (the ability to detect and have insights about people's feelings, motives and concerns). It also requires demonstration of emotional intelligence (EQ) when conducting interviews with elites. Mayer and Salovey (1997: 10) define emotional intelligence as:

> the ability to perceive accurately, appraise, and express emotion; the ability to access and/or generate feelings when they facilitate thought; the ability to understand emotion and emotional knowledge; and the ability to regulate emotions to promote emotional and intellectual growth.

Even the most famous public figures respond positively to empathy, as they too desire that their interlocutor understand them. As utterances create opportunities for shared understanding of the world, showing a cognitive understanding of feelings expressed by these utterances confers dignity to sentiments such as compassion and respect. One can thus conceptualise elite interviews in Goethe's (1781/2003) terminology as delicate *empiricism* (*zarte Empirie*) where the inquirer is required to exert much effort in understanding and co-creating meaning with the co-locator through prolonged empathetic examination. In Goethe's scientific work, to understand phenomena by perceiving directly 'as such' rather than through hypotheses inferred from actual phenomena, 'there is the germ of a systematic investigation of phenomena by way of participation' (Barfield, 1988: 137).

Undoubtedly, in-depth interviewing is a draining process, both physically and mentally (McCracken, 1988), but at the same time also very rewarding as it acts as a developmental process for interviewees. In our experience, we have found that successful interviews with elites are intellectually challenging, and often result in a feeling of exhilaration. However, interviewing elites can also be a tremendous source of frustration. We remember a specific example of an interview with a sought-after executive. It took months of endless phone calls and meeting scheduling, only to result in a disappointingly mediocre conversation. It was apparent that the interviewee was preoccupied with other matters on that particular day. Inquirers interviewing elites must prepare themselves for potentially draining and disheartening experiences. Emotional awareness allows inquirers to objectively reflect upon their own performance and behaviours as well as the interviewees'. Hence, we recommend that inquirers take a moment after each interview to reflect post hoc on the experience by asking themselves the following questions:

- Was the conversation fruitful?
- Are the data gathered useful?

- What would I do differently during the next interview?
- What will I do the same during the next interview?
- What have I learned from this interaction from a personal development standpoint?
- Are they any additional questions that I ought to raise during the next interview? Are there issues that I need to address?

Stage 4: Elites interview follow-up

In the previous section we examined why individuals accept to participate in research studies. We concluded that these are varied. Our experience reveals that often elites, when accepting participation into a research study, aim at developing their own network.

Professional network expansion

In addition to traditional clubs and associations, professional networking websites provide new tools for interviewees and interviewers to keep in touch (this is particularly relevant with the younger, techno-savvy executives). As a way to conclude the discussion, we always take some time to explain the course of action, and when interviewees should expect to hear from us again. This is also the opportunity to thank the participants for their time and answer any questions they may have.

One can gather an amazing amount of information after the interview. The last few minutes of the interview are also the appropriate time for inquirers to ask elites whether they would be willing to introduce the inquirer to some of their peers. This method, known as the *snowball effect*, is well known in qualitative research manuals, and very much applicable to elite interviewing. Welch et al. (2002) concluded that snowballing proved an efficient way of identifying potential participants. Although inquirers widely use the snowball sampling method in qualitative research today, Tansey (2007) argues that inquirers should exercise caution with this method as respondents may suggest interviewing individuals who share similar opinions.

Providing feedback

We recommend that inquirers follow up and send a courtesy letter or an email to participants with the results of preliminary findings of the research study. Inquirers also need to ask whether participants would like to have the interview transcript and whether they would like to review/comment or edit it. From our experience, a majority of interviewees choose not to; however, some participants rigorously review their interview transcript to make amendments and suggestions. Welch et al. (2002: 13) argue that:

> Perhaps the least reliable feedback process was that of returning interview transcripts to interviewees for factual verification. The majority of

transcripts were not returned, which presented the interviewer with the dilemma of whether to interpret silence as consent.

Our experience suggests that it is important to offer a full interview transcript and a short executive summary. There are no right or wrong formats; however, Hirsch (1995) suggests that inquirers present the feedback and findings to elites in a different format than that required in the academic world. Given the informal character of the feedback, inquirers can afford to be creative and use presentations, podcasts or screen casts as a way to present preliminary findings.

Conclusion

Goldstein (2002) judiciously notes that when it comes to elite interviewing, there are no silver bullet solutions, and from our experience it is nearly impossible to anticipate and be fully prepared for elite interviews. This view accords with Berry (2002: 682) who notes that 'even the most experienced research can't anticipate all the twists and turns that interviews take'. Indeed, as this chapter highlights, inquirers often face a multitude of situations and must be able to adapt their behaviour accordingly. Our experience shows that often participants are engaged and genuinely interested in the research study. However, sometimes senior executive participants have mixed feelings about spending any time with academic inquirers, especially when the request comes directly from the CEO or chairman. This requires considerable skills and preparation to build relationships and gain the trust of the interviewee. On other occasions, unforeseen events take place which interrupt, postpone or cancel interviews. This requires flexibility, patience and understanding on the part of the inquirer.

Inquirers also must be aware of a misconception that gathered data in elite interviews are systematically of superior quality because of their source; however, Ackroyd and Hughes (1981) suggested that individuals can occasionally say things to maximise their self-esteem. Berry (2002: 680) supports this view and argues that:

> Interviewers must always keep in mind that it is not the obligation of a subject to be objective and to tell the truth. We have a purpose in requesting an interview, but ignore the reality that subjects have a purpose in the interview too: they have something they want to say.

Kakabadse and Kakabadse (2009) note that elite interviewing is a cyclical process and depending on the stage of the interview, inquirers alternate between an internal or external focus (Figure 17.2).

The elite interview cycles framework demonstrates that there is a strong element of personal development involved and suggests that inquirers

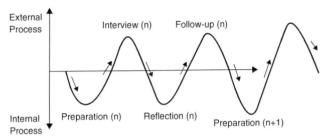

Figure 17.2 Elite interview cycles
Source: Kakabadse and Kakabadse (2009).

Box 17.2: Ten practical recommendations for elite interviewing

1 – To improve the participation rate, offer to share preliminary findings with elite interviewees.
2 – Secure the cooperation of gatekeepers by introducing yourself and your research study.
3 – Do your homework and gather relevant information about study participants before the interview.
4 – Opt for guided conversation and/or semi-structured interviews, which allow for more meaningful and fruitful interactions with elites.
5 – Several minutes of idle chatter between the inquirer and the interviewee allows inquirers to get a sense of the responsiveness of elite participants.
6 – Position the interview as a guided conversation as opposed to a formal interview.
7 – Conversation dynamics vary drastically with elites interviewing; however, inquirers should prepare themselves for elites to ask them for personal opinions and help in articulating their thoughts.
8 – Make the most out of interviewing techniques such as probing, which make for more stimulating and challenging discussions.
9 – Writing down a series of keywords will help inquirers re-channel the discussion and/or probe the interviewee to discuss a specific issue further.
10 – Use the last minutes of their conversation to (1) explain to participants the course of action, (2) check whether interviewees have any questions and (3) ask participants whether they would be willing to open their network to the inquirer.

Source: Compiled by the authors.

should capitalise on their experience. With each cycle of elite interviewing, inquirers increase their spiral of understanding. This spiral of understanding is only limited by the inquirer's willingness to learn. Elite interviewing provides more opportunities for learning and re-learning to occur as it allows for insights from more than one angle.

Finally, Box 17.2 presents ten practical recommendations drawn from our experience in interviewing elites. We believe that these recommendations can help young inquirers address some of the issues this chapter raises.

No matter the challenges an inquirer encounters in order to secure an elite interview, one should remember that no other data collection method makes one privy to experience the kind of information, emotions and intimacy of meaning making with a recognised expert. Even this brief encounter can ultimately lead to one's learning.

References

Aberbach, J. D. and Rockman, B. A. (2002) 'Conducting and Coding Elites Interviews', *Political Sciences and Politics*, 35(4): 673–6.

Ackroyd, S. and Hughes, J. A. (1981) *Data Collection in Context* (London: Longman).

Antle, B. J. and Regehr, C. (2003) 'Beyond Individual Rights and Freedoms: Metaethics in Social Work Research', *Social Work*, 48(1): 135–44.

Arendell, T. (1997) 'Reflections on the Researcher–Researched Relationship: A Woman Interviewing Men', *Qualitative Sociology*, 20(3): 341–68.

Aristotle (1908) *The Works of Aristotle*, ed. D. Ross, 12 vols. (Oxford: Clarendon Press).

Barfield, O. (1988) *Saving Appearances: A Study of Idolatry* (2nd edn.) (Middletown, CT: Wesleyan University Press).

Berg, B. L. (2007) *Qualitative Research Methods for the Social Sciences* (6th edn.) (London: Pearson International Edition).

Berry, J. M. (2002) 'Validity and Reliability Issues in Elite Interviewing', *Political Sciences and Politics*, 35(4): 679–82.

Berry, R. S. Y. (1999) 'Collecting Data by In-depth Interviewing'. Paper presented at the British Educational Research Association Annual Conference, University of Sussex at Brighton, 2–5 September.

Bourdieu, P. (1986) 'The Forms of Capital'. In J. Richardson (ed.), *Handbook of Theory and Research for the Sociology of Education* (New York: Greenwood Press), 241–58.

Bryman, A. (2008) *Social Research Methods* (3rd edn.) (Oxford: Oxford University Press).

Carlson, N. and McCaslin, M. (2003) 'Meta-Inquiry: An Approach to Interview Success', *The Qualitative Report*, 8(4): 549–69.

Covey, S. R. (1992) *The Seven Habits of Highly Effective People: Restoring the Character Ethic* (New York: Simon & Schuster).

Davies, P. H. J. (2001) 'Spies as Informants: Triangulation and the Interpretation of Elite Interview Data in the Study of the Intelligence and Security Services', *Politics*, 21(1): 73–80.

Fitz, J. and Halpin, D. (1995) '"Brief Encounter": Researching Education Policy-Making in Elite Settings'. In J. Salisbury and S. Delamont (eds.), *Qualitative Studies in Education* (Aldershot: Avebury), 65–86.

Goethe, J. W. von (1781/2003) *Wie herrlich leuchtet die Natur: Gedichte und Bilder* (Berlin: Insel Verlag).

Goggin, M. L., Bowman, A. O., Lester, J. P. and O'Toole, J. L. (1990) *Implementation Theory and Practice: Toward a Third Generation* (London: Scott, Foresman).

Goldstein, K. (2002) 'Getting in the Door: Sampling and Completing Elite Interviews', *Political Sciences and Politics*, 35(4): 669–72.

Granovetter, M. (1992) 'Problems of Explanation in Economic Sociology'. In N. Nohria and R. G. Eccles (eds.), *Networks and Organisations: Structure, Form and Action* (Boston: Harvard Business School Press).

Hertz, R. and Imber, J. B. (eds.) (1995) *Studying Elites Using Qualitative Methods* (London: Sage).

Hirsch, P. M. (1995) 'Tales from the Field: Learning from Researchers' Accounts'. In R. Hertz and J. B. Imber (eds.), *Studying Elites Using Qualitative Methods* (London: Sage), 40–64.

Hunter, A. (1993) 'Local Knowledge and Local Power: Notes on the Ethnography of Local Community Elites', *Journal of Contemporary Ethnography*, 22(1): 36–58.

Janesick, V. (1998) *Stretching: Exercises for Qualitative Researchers* (Thousand Oaks: Sage).

Kahl, J. (1957) *The American Class Structure* (New York: Rinehart).

Kakabadse, N. and Kakabadse, A. (2009) 'Thinking about Research', Research Seminar, Copenhagen Business School (CBS), 19 March.

Kakabadse, N., Kakabadse, A. and Kalu, K. (2007) 'Communicative Action through Collaborative Inquiry: Journey of a Facilitating Co-Inquirer', *Systemic Practice and Action Research*, 20(3): 245–72.

Knapp, N. (1997) 'Interviewing Joshua: On the Importance of Leaving Room for Serendipity', *Qualitative Inquiry*, 3(3): 326–42.

Kolb, D. A. (1984) *Experiential Learning: Experience as the Source of Learning and Development* (New Jersey: Prentice-Hall).

Lee, R. (1995) *Dangerous Fieldwork*. Qualitative Research Methods Series, vol. 34 (London: Sage).

Lewin, K. (1942) 'Field Theory and Learning'. In K. Lewin, *Field Theory in Social Science: Selected Theoretical Papers*, ed. D. Cartwight (Chicago: University of Chicago Press), 238–303.

Lord, M. (2000) 'Corporate Political Strategy and Legislative Decision Making', *Business and Society*, 39(1): 76–93.

Mayer, J. D. and Salovey, P. (1997) 'What is Emotional Intelligence?' In P. Salovey and D. J. Slayter (eds.), *Emotional Development and Emotional Intelligence: Educational Implications* (New York: Basic Books), 3–31.

McCracken, G. (1988) *The Long Interview* (Newbury Park, CA and London: Sage).

McQueen. R. and Knussen, C. (2002) *Research Methods for Social Science: An Introduction* (New Jersey: Prentice-Hall).

Morrill, C., Buller, D. B., Buller, M. K. and Larkey, L. L. (1999) 'Toward an Organisational Perspective on Identifying and Managing Formal Gatekeepers', *Qualitative Sociology*, 22(1): 51–72.

Peabody, R. L. et al. (1990) 'Interviewing Political Elites', *Political Science and Politics*, 23(3): 451–5.

Powdermaker, H. (1966) *Stranger and Friend: The Way of an Anthropologist* (New York: W. W. Norton).

Rapley, T. (2004) 'Interviews'. In C. Seale, G. Gobo, J. F. Gubrium and D. Silverman (eds.), *Qualitative Research Practice* (London: Sage), 15–33.

Revans, R. W. (1982) *The Origin and Growth of Action Learning* (Malabar, FL: Krieger Publishing Co.).

Richards, D. (1996) 'Elite Interviewing: Approaches and Pitfalls', *Politics*, 16(3): 199–204.

Rodham, K. (2000) 'Role Theory and the Analysis of Managerial Work: The Case of Occupational Health Professionals', *Journal of Applied Management Studies*, 9(1): 71–81.

Roulston, K. (2010) *Reflective Interviewing: A Guide to Theory and Practice* (London: Sage).

Schoenberger, E. (1991) 'The Corporate Interview as an Evidentiary Strategy in Human Geography', *The Professional Geographer*, 43: 180–9.

Tansey, O. (2007) 'Process Tracing and Elite Interviewing: A Case for Non-probability Sampling', *Political Science & Politics*, 40(4): 765–72.

Ward, K. G. and Jones, M. (1999) 'Researching Local Elites: Reflexivity, "Situatedness" and Political-Temporal Contingency', *Geoforum*, 30(4): 301–12.

Welch, C., Marschan-Piekkari, R., Penttinen, H., and Tahvanainen, M. (2002) 'Interviewing Elites in International Organisations: A Balancing Act for the Researcher', Paper presented at the 25th Annual Conference of EIBA, Manchester School of Management, 12–14 December.

Wong, L. M. (1998) 'The Ethics of Rapport: Institutional Safeguards, Resistance and Betrayal', *Qualitative Inquiry*, 4(2): 178–99.

Woods, M. (1998) 'Rethinking Elites: Networks, Space, and Local Politics', *Environment and Planning*, 30: 2101–19.

Yeung, H. W. (1995) 'Qualitative Personal Interviews in International Business Research: Some Lessons from a Study of Hong Kong Transnational Corporations', *International Business Review*, 4(3): 313–39.

18
Leadership Hubris: Achilles' Heel of Success

A. G. Sheard, Nada K. Kakabadse and Andrew P. Kakabadse

Introduction

Rooted in mythology, ancient Greek society considered hubris as man's capital sin (Wiener, 1973). Hubris (or hybris) is the pretension to be godlike, and thereby fail to observe the divine equilibrium among god, man and nature. The essential element of hubris is extreme confidence that can lead to arrogance and other dark side leadership attributes. In ancient Greek mythology, the gods relentlessly struck down those who were excessively confident, presumptuous, blindly ambitious or otherwise lacking humility (Grimal, 1986). Scholars have defined hubris as:

- A state of mind in which man thinks more than human thoughts and later translates them into act. It is an offence against the order of the world (Grene, 1961: 487).
- The arrogant violation of limits set by the gods or by human society (North, 1966: 6).
- Having energy or power and misusing it self-indulgently (MacDowell, 1976: 21).
- Behaviour that is intended gratuitously to inflict dishonour and shame upon others or to the values that hold a society together (Fisher, 1979: 32, 45).

In other words, hubris is the capital sin of pride, and thus the antithesis of two ethics that the Greeks valued most highly: aidos (humble reverence for law) and sophrosyne (self-restraint, a sense of proper limits). Descriptions of leaders with hubris include: overwhelming pride, self-glorification, arrogance, insolence, over-confidence in one's ability and right to do whatever one wants to the point of disdaining the cardinal virtues of life, ignoring other people's feelings, overstepping boundaries and impiously defying all who stand in the way.

In Greek literature, hubris often afflicted rulers and conquerors who, though endowed with great leadership abilities, abused their power and authority and challenged the divine balance of nature to gratify their own vanity and ambition. Thus, hubris was no common evil. It led people to presume that they were above ordinary laws, if not laws unto themselves, and to presume they deserved to exceed the fate and fortune ordained by the gods.

In ancient Greek mythology, acts of hubris aroused envy among the gods on Mount Olympus and angered them to restore justice and equilibrium. Nemesis, the goddess of divine vengeance and retribution, might then descend to destroy the vainglorious pretender, to cut man down to size and restore equilibrium. Today we say that a leader 'has met his Nemesis' when his/her own actions result in his/her eventual downfall.

Leaders with hubris meet their Nemesis precisely because they believe themselves to be and present themselves as virtual messiahs or saviours who are on a crusade and have a fate, destiny or mission that is historic, both timeless and time-changing in its implications (Ronfeldt, 1994). They politicise everything in the name of the mission and the high principles it engages.

Combining constructive with destructive tendencies, a leader with hubris proposes to accomplish monumental projects that will confirm his/her individual or organisation's greatness. Such projects, if achieved, may bring material progress, but their purpose extends beyond. They symbolise the leader's desire to direct vast energies at constructing something awesome that commands widespread respect and honour and enhances people's feelings of pride and dignity, thereby validating the leader's leadership and conception of his/her individual or organisation's abilities. Meanwhile, the leader seeks to blame and attack the chosen enemy and its imperious ways for his/her individual or organisation's weaknesses and failures to live up to hopes and capabilities.

How easy it is for leaders' self-knowledge and confidence to spiral beyond their control? This article presents four case examples that illustrate different aspects of leadership hubris. We illuminate how corporate activities have discretionary motives and how they impact those occupying leadership roles. First, we present an overview of critical literature, followed by a description of the methodology adopted during the study. Next, we present four mini exemplary cases to illustrate four forms of leadership hubris. A discussion of results presents the overarching dimensions of hubris that emerged from the analysis and the forms of hubris we consequently identified. The chapter then discusses how to cope with each form of hubris, making strategic suggestions leaders can adopt to mitigate the worst effects of hubris in both self and others. The discussion concludes with a summary of the main findings of the study.

Relevant literature

Analysis of corporate scandals in the USA and elsewhere suggests that corporate practices have suffered from CEO dominance with incommensurate controls (Felton, 2004; Keasey et al., 2005; Keay, 2006). Some scholars (Walsh and Seward, 1990; Berkovitch and Narayanan, 1993) have posited that there are three main motives for takeovers, namely, (1) poor target company management, (2) synergy and (3) leadership hubris. Whilst scholars have paid substantial attention to the first two motives, underscoring the importance of individual and social factors in takeover pricing, they have neglected the investigation of the third motive, hubris.

Roll (1986) has argued that in many merger and acquisition events, the acquiring managers overestimate their ability to extract value from the acquisition because of their hubris. Roll (1986) advanced a hubris hypothesis, stating that takeovers occur because bidding leaders imbued in hubris overestimate their ability to manage the target firm and hence overpay for it. Prior research (Firth, 1980; Berkovitch and Narayanan, 1993) assumed that a negative market reaction indicates hubris and thus used aggregate stockholder returns on the acquisition announcement as a surrogate for hubris. As such, the hubris hypothesis assists in overcoming the limitations of other perspectives. The hubris hypothesis explicitly considers transactions from the perspective of the decision-maker, namely, the leader, and is consistent with market evidence that premiums are excessive.

When considering the hubris hypothesis a leadership paradox becomes apparent. In order to perform certain actions, such as mergers and acquisitions, leaders must have self-knowledge and confidence that goes beyond Aristotelian moderation. However, the personality traits that enable a leader to go beyond this easily result in extreme confidence that, in turn, results in the individual highly overestimating his/her ability. When a leader overestimates his/her ability to extract value from a merger or acquisition, the resulting tendency is to pay a large premium and become infected by hubris or the dark side of leadership.

Leaders' individual success, or as a consequence of organisational success attributed to them, often results in hubris (Kelley, 1971; Meindl et al., 1985). Research suggests that there is a strong propensity to credit leaders with organisational success even when we can attribute such success more objectively to other factors (Meindl et al., 1985). The greater the recent success of an individual leader or the organisation they lead, the more likely they will suffer from hubris. The leader whose company has been recently successful is likely to receive favourable attributions which build their confidence and as such, the development of even greater expectations about his/her own ability (Jacobs et al., 1971; Brockner, 1988).

Whilst a leader may start his/her career with healthy levels of self-esteem, favourable events and organisational success may become material sources of self-esteem and prestige, feeding ever more assurance to the leader's attributed success and stature (Brockner, 1988; D'Aveni, 1990). Also, we often attribute equally poor organisational performance to the leader, resulting in a decrease in their power, stigma and demise of his/her authority and confidence (Sutton and Callahan, 1987; Eisenhardt and Bourgeois, 1988).

Chen and Meindl (1991) suggest that successful leaders often place undue emphasis on the efficacy of their leadership ability and in turn, their infallibility. The more successful the organisation, the more likely it is to develop patterns of beliefs or 'givens' and justification of its leader (Festinger, 1954; March and Simon, 1958; Staw, 1976). In turn, leadership attributions tend to be self-serving rather than self-critical, and their ability beyond the perspectives, attitudes and styles associated with their success (Starbuck and Milliken, 1988; Schweiger, et al, 1986; Clapham and Schwenk, 1991). A self-serving culture can, in turn, lead to the leader taking unnecessarily risky decisions in order to perpetuate success, unethical decisions as well as abuse of power, arrogance, self-exaggerated abilities and narcissistic behaviour (Kets de Vries and Miller, 1985).

The study

Throughout the inquiry we use a narrative approach for the study of leadership hubris as human action. Narrative is an interpretive approach in the social sciences. It involves a storytelling methodology where the story becomes an object of study. The story focuses on how individuals and/or groups make sense of events and actions in their lives, whilst inquirers capture the informant's story through ethnographic techniques such as observation and interviews. This methodology is well suited to study subjectivity such as individual and cultural influences on identity and the human condition (Polkinghorne, 1988).

Since the narrative movement began during the late twentieth century, scholars have progressively viewed language as deeply constitutive of reality, rather than merely a device for establishing meaning. Stories do not reflect the world 'out there' but are constructed, rhetorical and interpretive (Riessman, 1993). Stories give attention to experience which is a part of the reawakening interest in narrative. This has occurred since cognitive psychology recognised narrative as reflecting a cognitive structure (Polkinghorne, 1988).

In a similar manner to therapists in psychoanalysis who listen to individual clients' narrations of their lives and transform these narrations into alternative narratives that are more adaptive, coherent and functional (Polkinghorne, 1988), we also listen to our study participants' stories, recasting their narratives in a more coherent framework. We also utilise narrative therapy with our study participants in order to shift the dynamics of their narrative to achieve more socially functional behaviour.

We can use narrative to gain insight into individual, organisational and cultural change (Boje, 1998; Faber, 1998; Beech, 2000) and provide insight into decision-making (O'Connor, 1997). Whilst storytelling can help in transferring complex tacit knowledge and also serve as a source of implicit communication (Ambrosini and Bowman, 2001; Linde, 2001), at the same time storytelling aids an individual's development (Abma, 2000; Cox, 2001) and sense making (Gabriel, 1998) and in so doing, comprises a source of understanding (Cortazzi, 2001).

Six CEOs, each leading organisations that operate globally in a single sector of the manufacturing industry, agreed to participate in this study. Each recounted his/her experiences of working with leaders who exhibited the extreme confidence and arrogance which we classically associate with hubris. The narrative approach illustrated the subjects' particular decisions and dilemmas. This highlighted many forms and facets of hubris and the influence of emotions and environment in the arising conflicts.

We recorded and then later transcribed and read our interviews which yielded rich qualitative data. We analysed them using a system of open coding. From this, themes emerged. We adopted an interpretive, inductive approach to the analysis to respect the 'wholeness' and 'meaningfulness' of the data (Dey, 1993; Bryman and Burgess, 1994). This approach allows clusters to emerge from the data without pre-specifying the categories (Miles and Huberman, 1984; Lincoln and Guba, 1985; McCracken, 1988). Rather, we defined and clarified emerging concepts afterwards by referring to relevant concepts in the literature, in particular, Jungian concepts. This process aligns with qualitative content analysis methods of reduction and interpretation (Rubin and Rubin, 2005).

We base the findings in this chapter on narratives with the six CEOs participating in the study. We interviewed them on three separate occasions with each interview focusing on a different experience. Consequently, we base our findings on eighteen CEO narratives. Following the interviews, we talked with the individuals the study participants described in their narratives. Accessing these individuals presented us with a challenge. First, only half the people described by study participants could be both tracked down and allowed us to interview them. Second, we reasoned that questioning the individuals about their excessive self confidence and arrogance was unlikely to elicit either a positive or helpful response. Although difficult to direct these interviews, by focusing questions around a specific time in their life, we were able to elicit some form of explanation regarding events that study participants described.

After conducting the interviews, analysing the data and identifying emergent themes, we combined study participant narratives into four case study segments. Each segment comprises a story about a single leader who exhibits one form of hubris from the perspective of a composite character, Harry, a self-starter with a great capability. Energetic and youthful, this 42-year-old director has a reputation for relentless effort. The case study segments reflect a cognitive structure within which Harry both represents the combined experiences of study participants and also a voice of sanity within each organisation.

Discussion of results

Two overarching and independent dimensions to hubris emerged from the data analysis: (1) reinforcement and (2) success. We used these to identify four forms of hubris (see Figure 18.1). Study participants identified reinforcement as an event, a circumstance or a condition that increases the likelihood that a given response will recur in a situation like that in which the reinforcing condition originally occurred. Reinforcement theory is an established behavioural theory of learning and motivation focused on the effect that the consequences of past behaviour have on future behaviour (Skinner, 1953; Tucker et al., 1998).

The source of reinforcement could originate either externally from the organisation or internally within the organisation. Hence, consistent with an entity perspective, this model describes processes that are located in the perceptions and cognition of the individuals involved in the relationship.

The four forms of leadership hubris are:

1. Self-greatness: internal reinforcement and individual success.
2. Sovereign greatness: external reinforcement and individual success.
3. Presidential greatness: external reinforcement and organisational success.
4. Assumed greatness: internal reinforcement and organisational success.

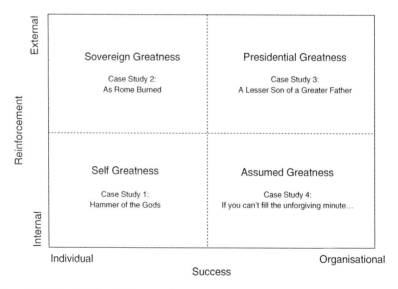

Figure 18.1 Leadership hubris model conceptualising the forms leadership hubris takes depending on the leader's need for reinforcement and success

The self-greatness form of hubris is a blatant attempt of a leader to present him or herself as more than he/she is in an arena where he/she is not easily challenged. We argue that the sovereign form of hubris is better grounded in reality than the self-greatness form, as it is dependent on reinforcement by those outside the organisation over whom the leader does not have direct authority. The presidential form of hubris is perhaps the most subtle form, with study participants associating it with leaders who had become preoccupied with their legacy. The assumed greatness form of hubris marks a return to an internal arena where individuals do not easily challenge the leader who takes credit for organisational success that could be attributed more reasonably to the work of others at lower levels of the organisational hierarchy or favourable market conditions.

This hubris model applied to the experiences of the study's participants but did not constitute a hierarchy of endeavour. Leaders exhibiting one of the four forms of hubris did not generally change over time, apparently preferring either internal or external reinforcement, individual or organisational success and consequently, one of the four forms of hubris.

Leadership hubris: self-greatness

Self-greatness manifests itself in a leader who has too much interest in and admiration for his/her abilities. We classically associate this personality trait with narcissism. Such a leader seeks constant attention, hates to be upstaged or ignored and if he/she is ignored, may brood on how to regain attention. He/she is intolerant of rivals as he/she perceives him or herself to have a God-given right to do whatever he/she wants.

If rivals prove persistent, he/she is sidelined though a process that regards the truth as highly flexible and something to manipulate as the ends always justify the means. Whether the self-great leader deals with allies or enemies, he/she refuses to be humbled. Like any successful leader, he/she is capable of pragmatic behaviour, yet he/she never relents in his/her ambition for power.

Two years after the events we asked Bud to reflect on his experiences organising the factory move. Because Bud had moved on before the full consequences of his decisions became apparent, combined with the passage of time, he was able to present an idealised version of the past that put him in an unfailingly good light.

> 'It was a great experience for me to work in England. It's so important to have real international experience on your CV these days if you are to get to the very top. I spent a little over one year straightening out a factory move, you know, getting the plans sorted out, deciding how the factory should be laid out. It was great to be able to do that and I am really proud of the result. I mean, how many new factories are being built in England these days? Most are being shut and moved to the Far East.' (Bud)

Case study part one: Hammer of the gods

Harry gazed out of his office window, wondering why he was so upset that he would no longer be the youngest board member. Perhaps it was because the new manufacturing director was younger by a full ten years. There was more to it than just age, Harry thought to himself. William (or 'Bud' as he preferred to be called) had irritatingly good looks and looked down upon Harry. You could not blame Bud for looking down on Harry. He looked down on almost everyone given his height of six foot seven inches.

Others did not seem bothered 'being looked down upon', particularly the ladies. For example, Harry's secretary was spellbound by Bud, and would do anything to accommodate him. The finance director was little better, extolling the virtues of their young warrior and how he could turn around any failing team. Harry objected to colleagues suggesting that he was part of a 'failing team', but had enough sense to keep his mouth shut.

How on earth did a former Olympiad end up on the same board as he? Rowing for the USA in an 'eight' one learns a thing or too about team work. Bud told Harry that the first time they met, with a handshake that could crush rocks and a look in his eye that told Harry he wanted to. However, the group chairman liked him. He had hired Bud nine months ago, sent him roaming around the group as his 'Mr Fix It' and now he was here to 'fix' the forthcoming factory move.

If he were honest, Harry knew he was not actually angry with Bud, but with the group chairman. Why had he not consulted Harry about the change in manufacturing director? Granted, the old manufacturing director had never managed a factory move and over the last year it became progressively more obvious that he did not have the necessary capabilities to do so. However, that the manufacturing director was not up to his job did not mean the rest of the board was not capable.

Harry had spent the last three years preparing for this factory move. He had converted over one million drawings and reports into electronic format which were stored in a web-based application. He had implemented new systems to create a genuinely paperless office, motivated by a desire to ease the move to the new factory. 'Well,' Harry thought to himself, 'It is what it is. Better make the best of it.'

As the date for the new factory move approached, it became increasingly difficult to 'make the best of it'. Management had approved the factory planning application over two years ago, but now it seemed that they were building a different building. Harry only discovered this when his staff complained that they had to fit into 30% less space than they had been promised. Also, now the laboratory location would be along the back of the building, not at the far end as originally agreed. The laboratory needed to be away from heavy manufacturing equipment in order for the anechoic chamber used to measure product noise to work. There was no point in having a new factory with the new laboratory location. It would be impossible to demonstrate that anything manufactured in it complied with applicable legislation; therefore, any shipments from the new factory would be illegal.

Harry decided it was time to take the new plans he had acquired from his staff and visit Bud in his office. As Harry entered, he noticed on the wall behind Bud's desk awards and plaques – not for his rowing, but for the various leadership qualifications and awards he had amassed. They assaulted the senses as you walked in. 'What do you see when you walk into my office?' Harry thought. He had one framed certificate presented to him for outstanding service to an engineering institute to which he had dedicated himself for over twenty years. That the two of them valued such different things was not a good omen.

'Let me tell you something, Harry ...' As Bud continued to recount tales of past glory, Harry could feel himself losing the will to live. It was like trying to find a way into a sphere. Every attempt to speak about specifics or get into detail was swiftly and expertly deflected. Finally, Harry forced the issue. 'Just for once, shut up and listen. The lab can't go where you have decided to put it. It will not work.' Harry expected some reaction, but not the one he got. 'I would love to help you Harry, but the group chairman insists we have a straight-through flow of work. Modern manufacturing processes, Harry. My hands are tied.'

Back in his office, Harry reached for the phone to call the group chairman, then thought, 'What's the point?' A call would do nothing more than show that he was not competent to manage his own working relationships. The group chairman had put his favourite hero in charge of the move without consulting Harry. What was there to talk about? He might as well look at more effective ways to acoustically isolate the lab. He would find a way to make it work. He always did.

Six months later, the factory move was a total disaster. The concrete floor was not strong enough to hold the heavy machinery and it promptly started to sink. That was before they added the weight of acoustic enclosures, none of which Bud had thought worth ordering. As a direct consequence, the council health and safety inspector shut down the factory as the noise was damaging workers' hearing. It did not really matter. The anechoic chamber in the new lab was vibrating so badly that the technicians could not test anything anyway.

On time delivery during the first month after the move was zero per cent. On time delivery was still zero at the end of the second month. As the beleaguered staff struggled towards the end of the third month, Bud stuck his smiling face round Harry's door. With his trademark bone-crushing handshake and that glint in his eye, he told Harry he was leaving. 'A big promotion back in the USA. My work here is done.' As Harry watched his retreating form, he heaved a huge sigh of relief.

Eighteen months later on time delivery was finally back to where it should be. That news resulted in the first board meeting Harry could remember that had not been a 'blood letting' session. After lunch over coffee, Harry found himself standing next to the group chairman. Spontaneously, he blurted out, 'Why did you insist on moving the laboratory?' 'Laboratory?' replied the group chairman. 'We have a laboratory on this site? I'd like to see what you do in it.' Without thinking Harry spoke again. 'Well, we do much less as a consequence of you insisting it was put in the wrong place.' The group chairman looked genuinely bemused. 'I never commented on any aspect of the layout. That was all left to Bud.'

With a long pause, Harry glared at the group chairman who shuffled his feet and tried to look anywhere but at Harry. Finally, after inspecting all eight corners of the room, the silence was too much for him. 'I know, I know. I sent a boy to do a man's job.'

The case study illustrates what the capital sin of pride means in practice. The self-glorification and overconfidence in his own abilities marked Bud as a leader with hubris. In this example, the hubris manifested itself in a charming individual and an apparently good team player. That exterior covered a ruthless focus on personal success with absolutely no remorse for the organisational consequences of his actions. The concerns for how good the factory move looked on his CV illustrate that internal reinforcement mattered to him; the opinions of others were simply irrelevant.

Leadership hubris: sovereign greatness

Sovereign greatness manifests itself in a leader who insists on virtually absolute power and loyalty in ways that resemble military discipline. Such a leader hates to be upstaged and does not tolerate abandonment by subordinates. He/she is intolerant of rivals who are crushed, especially if they challenge his/her power or vision, imperiously defying all who stand in his/her way. He/she is disdainful of the rules and regulations by which lesser persons must live. He/she is a law until him or herself, utterly selfish in his/her behaviour; nothing is too good for him/her. We can sum up his/her preoccupation with presenting the world with a vision of success with the mantra 'there is only one thing worse than being broke and that is looking broke'. This type of leader is the ultimate consumer.

Case study part two: As Rome burned

Harry stood contemplating the view. 'They all look the same to me,' he thought to himself. His new Audi was parked on the end of a line of new Audis, all exactly the same model and colour, with the exception of the car closest to the main door. That was a Porsche, and not just any Porsche, but a lightweight and very limited edition racing car. It was the first time Harry had seen this particular model, or at least he thought it was. It was difficult to be absolutely sure as Jack (the CEO) had five different Porsche 911s, none of which you would find in a dealer showroom.

The row of cars was symbolic of Jack's attitude generally. During his interview three months previously, Jack explained to Harry the logic behind the factory floor plan. It was not configured for efficient work flow, but to maximise the visual impact for visitors. Shortly after starting with the company, Harry met the local mayor and the bank manager. Both were key stakeholders in the organisation and needed to know how Harry's new operation would build both regional employment and organisational profitability. As Harry watched their corporate video for a third time, Jack leaned over to him and confidentially whispered that he used the same production company as Roll-Royce – all part of a measured package to impress the right people.

As Harry walked along the row of cars parked prominently by the main entrance, he wondered why he was there. Every Monday was the same. The week started with a board meeting during which the members would listen in respectful silence as Jack spoke at length about whatever he wanted. However, these strange sessions could, and often did, turn nasty. Last week he attacked the manufacturing director. A couple of weeks before that he launched into the project director. Harry couldn't understand why Jack would transform from Jekyll into Hyde over the most trivial points and spend two hours relentlessly mentally abusing people. As Harry climbed the steps to the first floor board room, he could not help but think that today was not going to go well.

As he entered the board room, Jack was already in full flow. Harry checked his watch – he was five minutes early, but apparently the meeting had already started. The ranting that followed was directed at all of them. Jack had fired the project director for an act of unspeakable treachery. Harry poured himself some coffee and tried to remain focused on the meeting and not mentally leave for the beach. After the meeting adjourned, Harry dropped by the finance director's office to find out what had really happened. The project director had resigned that morning. The CEO had torn up his letter of resignation and then had him thrown off site. He was not even allowed to collect the CDs he had unwisely left in his company Audi. As Harry drove back to his own office, he was sorry that the project director had gone. The two of them had got on well together.

Harry was the general manager of a satellite office that specialised in instrumentation. Jack had hired him as he wanted to expand the organisation from manufactured components to complete test rigs. Those test rigs needed to be instrumented and then fitted with a control system. That was where Harry's operation came in; his team did the 'clever bits' that turned the components manufactured in the main factory into a complete test rig.

Occasionally, Jack would arrive at Harry's office unannounced. After about three months a pattern started to emerge. First, Jack would arrive in apparently good spirits. Second, he would spot some minor error and make something of it. Third, he would pick up on a poorly worded response from an unsuspecting member of staff and then proceed to rip him/her to shreds and publicly humiliate him/her for about an hour.

Despite the risk of Jack dropping in, other members of the board progressively found increasingly flimsy excuses to visit Harry. It did not take a rocket scientist to work out that they chose to do this when Jack was in a particularly dysfunctional mood. Jack liked sacking people when he was in these moods, so Harry could not blame his colleagues for wanting to present the enemy with a moving target.

The following Monday Harry arrived as usual at the main factory and noticed the absence of the Porsche. 'I wonder if Jack is ill,' Harry thought to himself. 'Nothing trivial, I hope.' As Harry walked in an accountant from a firm of administrators accosted him. The company was bankrupt. What did Harry know about the state of the company finances? Realising that Harry ran a satellite office and was not involved in any aspect of the company's finances, the administrators quickly lost interest in him. Harry wandered into the board room on auto-pilot where another accountant promptly terminated his employment contract.

As Harry waited for a bus to take him home, he looked at the CDs he had emptied from his car into an old supermarket carrier bag. 'Well,' he thought to himself, 'looks like I did better than my friend. At least I got my CDs back.'

No one particularly likes discussing the times when he/she has presided over a very public organisational failure. As such, getting more than vague generalisations from Jack about the events that resulted in the organisation he was entrusted to lead going into administration was never going to be easy.

> 'You need a special kind of person to build a business. It's what I do. Racing cars and running an engineering company are two sides of the same coin for me. I need an engineering company to rebuild my cars between races and of course, clients just loved going to track days. It's the only time they get close to a real car. I never let them drive mine, but there are always cars you could rent by the lap. A few laps and a few drinks and the rest takes care of itself.' (Jack)

The case study illustrates the results of overconfidence in one's ability. Believing that he had a fundamental right to do whatever he wanted marked Jack as a leader with hubris. In this example, the hubris manifested itself in a bully who was, nevertheless, astute enough to ensure that he would present external stakeholders with a polished and positive professional image on the rare occasions when they actually met. However, the polished performance served as a cover for an utterly selfish individual focused only on his own gratification. Whatever Jack might have said about the reasons for his business failing, the primary cause of businesses failing is management incompetence.

Leadership hubris: presidential greatness

Presidential greatness manifests itself in a leader who may look outwardly confident, but in reality, is deeply insecure. He/she purports to have a humble reverence of the law and a sense of restraint and proper limit, but in actuality, is vain and puritanical in his/her attitude towards others. As a consequence of his/her vanity he/she seeks constant attention – the bigger the audience and the larger the stage, the better. He/she never relents in his/her ambition for power, spending hours brooding over the composition of his/her 'court' and the decisions as to who is 'safe' enough to hold a position of real power. All who work with him/her must be deeply respectful in public and in private and ensure that they discuss and approve all important matters before presenting them publicly. The net result is that public meetings, such as board meetings, do nothing more than rubber stamp previously made decisions.

It was not easy encouraging Harold to speak about the events described in the case study. The events had occurred five years prior to his interview and the passage of time has enabled him to either forget or simply gloss over the reality of what had occurred. Implementation of a web-based conference

Case study part three: A lesser son of a greater father

'Sometimes,' Harry thought, 'a sense of humour can be a liability.' The chairman of the board, Harold, certainly thought so as he explained to Harry, as if he were a small and rather stupid child, that their great and venerable organisation depended on the good will and support of its volunteers. Harry must thank them for their effort. Under no circumstances was he to fire any of them and he absolutely would not suggest that volunteers who did not do what they had committed to do were 'persistent offenders' or that they should be 'nailed up'.

Harry had recently been appointed technical program chairman of the biggest conference in the industrial sector within which his business operated. It was a great honour and he regarded this as a stepping stone on to the board where he would get to know the movers and shakers in his industry on first-name terms. However, following his first board meeting, the prospect of further advancement seemed remote.

Despite the negative board meeting, Harry remained resolutely optimistic about the future. He got on exceptionally well with the organisation's staff who would actually orchestrate the conference he was to chair. Whatever the board members might like to think, the staff actually did the work and made all the key operational decisions. Sitting in a bar that evening with the staff, they started laughing about the day's events. One of the longest serving staff members observed that Harold hates any comment or suggestion that the conference volunteers are anything other than perfect. Keep in mind, most of the volunteers work for one or another board member. To criticise volunteers is to criticise the board. The success of the organisation is in a very real sense linked to the support it receives from its board.

Incensed, Harry thought to himself that it was not just Harold who was obsessed with the external perception of the organisation's success. Harry had known three of the current board members for years, each of whom had approached him after the board meeting with essentially the same message: perception is reality. They were a professional society. Their organisational success was dependent of the external world's perception of the organisation.

Despite a poor start, Harry found organising the following year's conference a surprisingly enjoyable experience. The staff were keen to move to a web-based conference management tool, something the board had not exactly blocked, but had endlessly debated for over five years without providing any direction or guidance to the staff. Harry did not care about the lack of board direction or guidance. He got stuck into the detail of developing a new web tool. Not as easy as it first appeared, the staff ended up doing much more work behind the scenes than Harry anticipated. Despite its imperfections, the web tool came with an unexpected benefit. It could generate data that enabled Harry to track operations in a level of detail that was previously impossible.

For the first time ever, Harry as technical program chairman could see if volunteers were doing what they should, when they should. When they did not, Harry sent them polite emails asking why they were not doing their job. Out of many thousands of emails Harry generated via the web tool, he received only one reasonable excuse for lack of previously promised action. The individual concerned had suffered a heart attack and unfortunately died. The rest were just not performing, a point that Harry felt compelled to mention.

News of Harry's enthusiasm for contacting volunteers about their lack of action, rather regrettably, reached Harold's ears. The big boss bluntly told Harry that if he did not stop 'harassing' volunteers, he would be sacked as conference technical program chairman. Harry listened without retaliating. He sent out his last batch of 'get-your-act-together' emails that morning. Harry had no intention of 'insulting our most loyal friends' further. There was little point putting up a fight.

The staff, however, took a very different view. Finally someone said what they all knew – if you volunteer to do a job then you should do it and not make excuses. As the date for the conference drew near, Harry forgot about the organisational aggravation. There would be the usual 'large group' meeting the day before the conference where Harold would present preliminary plans for the following year to the volunteer organisers and in turn, those same volunteers would comment on their experiences over the previous year. It would be Harry's first chance to obtain real feedback on his organisation of the conference.

To his complete surprise, the large group meeting was a huge success. With the involvement of over 2,700 volunteers, it was difficult for anyone to really judge the collective consensus between conferences. Nevertheless, it was astonishing that everyone did not just like, but loved the new web tool, particularly the 'helpful' reminders that 'it' generated. With a sense of mounting irritation and indignation, Harry sat and listened as Harold took credit for the outstanding success of what was now apparently a board initiative to further develop the web tool. The following week Harry was not surprised to learn that he had not been elected to the board.

tool was something that he had fought against until it was overwhelmingly obvious that it was a success with the key organisational stakeholders.

> 'The organisation was, and still is today, about service to our community. I don't believe that service should be recognised, as to recognise individual service is to risk motivating people for the wrong reasons. I have always taken my pride in the success of the organisations I have run, the legacy I have left of an organisation in better shape when I completed my term of office than it was when I joined.' (Harold)

The case study illustrates the arrogance we associate with self-glorification. In this example, we see self-glorification epitomised by a negative attitude towards change, followed by taking credit for that change once others embraced and endorsed it. Claiming the work of others as part of one's own legacy oversteps a boundary that any leader with a shred of humility or self-restraint would never contemplate doing.

The hubris in this example is manifested in a deeply conservative individual with an apparent respect for authority and the establishment in general, but who in reality is deeply insecure. The presidentially great leader is constantly looking for ways to manipulate reality to ensure that people see them in the best possible light. The neurosis such a leader feels feeds a desperate desire for power, but the power he/she has is like a drug that quickly wears off. There is a proverb that says 'happiness is not getting what you want, but wanting what you have got'. This is particularly applicable to a leader with this form of hubris. He/she is never happy with what they have.

Leadership hubris: assumed greatness

Assumed greatness manifests itself in a leader who has absolute confidence in his/her world view. It is not so much that he/she is contemptuous of the opinions of others, more that it simply does not occur to him/her that there might be another perspective or point of view. All leaders with hubris ignore other people's feelings; however, it is a particularly prominent personality trait in a leader with assumed greatness. His/her behaviour is callous and uncaring, which partly explains his/her success as leader. Business requires tough decisions and they can be even tougher to implement.

Speaking about three months after the events described in the case study, Derek showed no sign of recognition regarding any linkage that might exist between his own behaviour and the employees' poor reaction to his magnanimous Christmas bonus. Neither did he recognise that the increasing staff turnover might be a consequence of his management style.

Case study part four: If you can't fill the unforgiving minute ...

The global recession had affected everyone, but those companies quick enough to respond could still make money. Harry listened to Derek, the company's CEO, as he lectured the board on best practice in cost management. Derek did not discuss or debate, he made speeches, ignoring other people's feeling with the attitude that he had an absolute right to do whatever he liked. 'When it came to other people,' Harry thought, 'Derek does not just overstep boundaries – he does not even recognize that they exist.'

Other board members shared Harry's negative view of the boss, but they were unwilling to vocalise. These were recessionary times and the company needed to manage costs. The sales director was closest to Harry in his concern for business practices. Clients were tiring of increasingly poor customer service, but the sales director irrationally justified the 15% decrease in sales saying that at least, we have business; competitors are going out of business completely. Compared to those failing businesses, Jack's organisational performance was nothing short of miraculous.

Harry tried to remain mentally engaged, knowing that eventually, there would be a point to the rhetoric. After an extended power point presentation covering every aspect of the company's excellent financial position, Derek finally moved to the main agenda item. A child's toy? Not just any toy, Derek quickly pointed out, a tower of wooden blocks. The tower represented the company (it was a very tall tower) and the wooden blocks represented the people in it. Look how many wooden blocks you can take out without the tower falling down! The board members sitting around Harry nodded their heads in agreement. You could take out far more wooden blocks than you would have thought at first sight. Brilliant! How many more people could they remove from the organisation to better manage cost in these troubled times?

As Harry left the board room he was deeply uneasy. It was madness. They could not cope with the current work load, but there had been no interest in the warning signal. Board members felt the illusion of invulnerability and excessive optimism that they could slash another 20% from the overall head count and still survive.

Over the next week Harry approached each board member, expressing his alarm regarding the increased number of people signed off with stress-related illness. When Harry finally spoke directly to Derek about this, his concern was simply swept aside. 'These are challenging times, Harry. We must think about the ongoing viability of the organisation, not one or two weak individuals.' It came as no surprise when the redundancy list included everyone who had a medical excuse for not working.

Within a week of the redundancies the strain started to show. No one else had signed off sick yet, but the number of people coming to see Harry for confidential discussions about their current difficulties keeping up with their own jobs started making it impossible for him to do his job. Harry approached the finance director with his concerns. This resulted in another lecture about the difficult market conditions and the need for board members to stop complaining and get on with implementing change. 'That,' he informed Harry, 'is what leadership is all about – change. Management is about running the business and that is what the managers are paid to do. Leadership is about changing the business, and that is what board members are paid to do.'

Each week's board meeting presented an illusion of unanimity. Members assumed that the majority view and judgements were unanimous. Harry knew that he and the sales director had deep reservations about staff morale, but it was not possible to express doubts or concerns. They both felt pressure not to express any argument about the board's position.

As the year end approached, staff members started signing off sick with stress-related illness at an increasingly rapid rate, putting those who remained under even more pressure. However, the year end results showed no sign of stress. Profit was actually 40% above budget. As a consequence, Derek decided to make a magnanimous gesture. He granted members of staff an additional £100 in their December pay packet in recognition of their contribution to the organisation's outstanding success. He conveyed the good news to the workforce at a mass meeting in the factory, but was greeted with sullen silence. One more week to go before the Christmas factory shut-down and the workforce was clearly hanging on to the promise of time away from this dreadful place with grim determination.

The following Monday Harry took two phone calls from his two best project managers who had received doctor's notes indicating stress. They were ordered six weeks' rest. As Harry contemplated how to manage this turn of events, his Chief Engineer walked in and handed Harry his letter of resignation. He had landed a job that paid less, but in an organisation 'that actually welcomes human beings'. 'It looks like we took too many wooden bricks out of the tower,' Harry thought to himself, as he opened a Christmas card that promptly started to play 'God Rest Ye Merry Gentlemen'.

'Leadership is about taking action. You have to take action, there has to be a plan and the plan has to be implemented. Four times out of five it is better to have a plan implemented quickly then the best plan implemented late. That is why my organisation is successful; I take action and I get the job done. I have no time for the bleeding hearts and their pathetic quest for work/life balance. If you want a "work/life balance" get a job with a charity.' (Derek)

The case study illustrates that ignoring others' feelings and impiously defying all who stand in the way ultimately leads to broken morale and, consequently, unproductivity. Derek's supreme arrogance marked him as a leader with hubris. In this example the hubris manifested itself in an apparently hard-headed business man. That exterior covered a cold, thoughtless and inconsiderate man who cared nothing for anyone except himself. By creating group pressures that resulted in the deterioration of reality testing and moral judgements, Derek dehumanised other groups within the organisation he headed. Deterioration of reality testing and casting moral judgements are two symptoms of groupthink (Janis, 1972) and comprise a way in which a leader with hubris can extend his/her control beyond healthy limits.

Coping with leadership hubris

The four parts of the case study illustrate how two overarching dimensions, reinforcement and success, combine into four distinctly different forms of hubris. Part one profiles a 'self-great' leader who used charm and charisma to get his way and when that failed, he simply ignored his critics. Part two profiles a 'sovereign great' leader who epitomised the corporate bully, using the threat of imminent dismissal to ensure compliance. Part three profiles a 'presidential great' leader with severe sensitivities about pride, dignity and honour, respect plus an insatiable lust for power. Part four profiles an 'assumed great' leader who created a board affected by groupthink to enable him to impose his will.

In addition to illustrating the four forms hubris can take in leaders, the case study demonstrates that leaders with hubris have a spectrum of personality types. The case studies cannot be used to infer that we can associate one form of hubris with a particular personality type. However, there is one aspect of personality that runs through all four parts of the case study that marks out a leader as being prone to hubris: narcissism.

The psychoanalytic concept of narcissism extends from the myth or Narcissus. This youth had an inflated love of his beauty. He was filled with a pride so fierce that, in a form of hubris, he disdained the advances of admirers, notably the nymph Echo. At the prompting of spurned nymphs, Nemesis descended and made Narcissus fixate on his reflection in a pool, which led him to wither and die.

Narcissism runs though the four parts of the case study. Each features an individual with grandiose ideas who longs for adulation. There are three points relevant to the rationality and reasoning of narcissistic individuals that are indicative of a leader with hubris (Ronfeldt, 1994: 21). First, it is hard to identify a narcissistic personality with any consistent beliefs, because his/her beliefs shift. The only central and stable field of the narcissistic leader is the centrality of self. Second, a narcissistic leader is not 'crazy'; he/she is functional, with a sharpened sense of rationality enhancing his/her ability to attack an enemy. Third, narcissistic grandiosity in a leader results in his/her inclination to treat crises as opportunities and to take risks that ordinary, pragmatic leaders would avoid (Post, 1993: 112).

When we reflect on the rationality and reasoning of leaders, authority, power and superior–subordinate relationships comprise recurring themes. These are the political issues involving the activities of rulers and rules (Morgan, 1997: 154). We can consider organisational politics a shadow side of leadership that we can conceptualise in terms of emotionality (Sheard et al., 2009). Parts one and two of the case study profile leaders who quickly moved on at the point where doing so served their best interest. Their success was not emotionally linked to the organisations they headed. In contrast, parts three and four profiled leaders who regarded the organisation they headed as their own private property. They did not move on as circumstances changed, demonstrating a deep level of emotional engagement.

The success dimension of the leadership hubris model in this chapter characterises success in terms of individual and organisational success. The world-view of a leader with hubris focused on individual success is emotionally disengaged from the organisation he/she heads. The organisation is merely a vehicle to progress self-interest. In contrast, the world-view of a leader with hubris focused on organisational success is emotionally engaged with the organisation he/she heads. The organisation is an extension of the leader. When we reflect on what success means to a leader with hubris, it is apparent that in combination with a narcissistic personality, an assumed great or presidential great leader fixates on organisational success, behaving as if he/she owns the organisation. When fixated on individual success, the self-great or sovereign great leader behaves as if he/she does not care who owns the organisation.

The reinforcement dimension of the leadership hubris model characterises reinforcement in terms of reinforcement internal to, or external from, the organisation a leader heads. The world-view of a self-great or assumed great leader focused on internal reinforcement characterises the trappings of success as of paramount importance. In contrast, the world-view of a sovereign great or presidential great leader focused on external reinforcement characterises the support and cooperation of key external stakeholders as critical.

Kakabadse et al. (2007) observe that throughout history, scholars have characterised individuals attracted to and successful in leadership roles as displaying a strong desire to pursue personal interests in addition to that of the cause or organisation they head. Hedonism, power and posterity are overarching categories of temptation. We define hedonism as the pursuit of personal pleasure through the accumulation of material goods, consumerism or sensual pleasure. Power refers to control over environment. Posterity is a drive to establish a legacy sustainable beyond an individual's term in post.

All four parts of the case study profile leaders who exerted an excessive control over their environment; however, parts one and four profile leaders who were also hedonistic. Both were 'party animals' who took full advantage of the opportunities their leadership roles facilitated. In contrast, parts two and three profile leaders with no apparently hedonistic tendencies, but a brooding obsession with the world and its perception of them and the legacy they would leave. A focus on a leader's tendency towards hedonism in the present or what he/she will leave for posterity can assist in differentiating between the self- and assumed great leaders and the sovereign and presidential leaders.

A consideration of the success and reinforcement dimensions of the leadership hubris model helps in the identification of a leader as a self-great, sovereign great, presidential great or assumed great leader. Although helpful in identifying the form of hubris a leader exhibits, this knowledge does not provide a road map for managing, working with or for a leader with any of the four forms of hubris. It would be naïve to suggest that there can be hard and fast rules when contemplating the self-, sovereign, presidential or assumed great leader. However, Post's (1993) observations are instructive. The behaviour of a leader with hubris depends on whether advisers are sycophants or independent thinkers accurately informing a leader about political reality. Independent thinkers who focus on reality assist a leader in evaluating the completeness of a plan and in making mid-course corrections. In so doing, we can, at least, moderate the worst excesses of a leader with hubris.

Concluding remarks

Hubris is one of the less attractive sides of leadership, but nevertheless, it is a real issue. It is naïve to pretend that there is a cure for hubris. However, insight into the forms of hubris can assist a leader in his/her efforts to mitigate the worst effects of hubris of others and by recognising his/her own hubris provides the insight he/she needs to mitigate the worst effects of hubris in him/herself.

The leadership hubris model affords insight into the nature of hubris. We identified four forms of hubris that result in what we have named the self-great, sovereign great, presidential great and assumed great leader. Knowing the forms hubris can take in others and self provides some protection. By observing a leader, we can identify his/her preference for individual or organisational success and internal or external reinforcement. Once we have established preferences, then the model enables us to identify the form of hubris to which a leader is prone. Additionally, self-examination can provide the same insight for self.

To assert that specific responses to a leader with hubris are appropriate in every situation is unrealistic. Despite the caveat that action is inevitably situation-dependent, we can generally observe that behaviour of a leader with hubris depends on whether advisers are sycophants or independent thinkers accurately informing a leader about political reality (Post, 1993). By remaining grounded and resilient, always focusing on reality and ignoring the worst excesses of others' behaviour, an individual can, at least, mitigate the worst effect of hubris in a leader.

Rules and other organisational mechanisms may lean towards constraining a leader's action such that he/she has more difficulty responding in ways that escalate hubris. Bearing in mind the introduction of governance safeguards against personal excess and desire, still some of the control must come from within the leaders themselves (Kakabadse et al., 2007). Learning how to question oneself and analyse actions is the start to reviewing self-motivation and the impact that has on followers. Leaders need understand their own will and how they perceive the outside world as according to Socrates (Plato, 1981) – an unexamined life is not worth living.

A more effective response for effective governance than rules and regulations is Kakabadse and Kakabadse's (2005) 'shared leadership' model. This provides a sound infrastructure where power is not invested in one individual. It will not eliminate the hubris of others, but should mediate against any abuse of leadership position.

References

Abma, T. A. (2000) 'Fostering Learning-in-Organizing through Narration: Questioning Myths and Stimulating Multiplicity in Two Performing Arts Schools', *European Journal of Work and Organizational Psychology*, 9(2): 211–31.

Ambrosini, V. and Bowman, C. (2001) 'Tacit Knowledge: Some Suggestions for Operationalization', *Journal of Management Studies*, 38(6): 811–29.

Beech, N. (2000) 'Narrative Styles of Managers and Workers: A Tale of Star-Crossed Lovers', *Journal of Applied Behavioral Science*, 36(2): 210–28.

Berkovitch, E. and Narayanan, M. P. (1993) 'Motives for Takeovers: An Empirical Investigation', *Journal of Financial and Quantitative Analysis*, 28: 347–62.

Boje, D. M. (1998) 'The Postmodern Turn from Stories-as-Objects to Stories-in-Context Methods', *Research Methods Forum*, 3. Available at http://www.aom.pace.edu/rmd/1998_forum_postmodern_stories.html (accessed 23 May 2002).

Brockner, J. (1988) *Self-esteem at Work: Research, Theory and Practice* (Lexington, MA: Lexington Books).

Bryman, A. and Burgess, R. G. (eds.) (1994) *Analyzing Qualitative Data* (London: Routledge).

Chen, C. C. and Meindl, J. R. (1991) 'The Construction of Leadership Images in the Popular Press: The Case of Donald Burr and *People's Express*', *Administrative Science Quarterly*, 36: 521–55.

Clapham, S. E. and Schwenk, C. R. (1991) 'Self-serving Attributions, Managerial Cognition and Company Performance', *Strategic Management Journal*, 12: 219–320.

Cortazzi, M. (2001) 'Narrative Analysis in Ethnography'. In P. Atkinson (ed.), *Handbook of Ethnography* (London: Sage), 384–94.

Cox, K. (2001) 'Stories as Case Knowledge: Case Knowledge as Stories', *Medical Education*, 35(9): 862–6.

D'Aveni, Richard A. (1990) 'Top Managerial Prestige and Organizational Bankruptcy', *Organization Science*, 1: 123–42.

Dey, I. (1993) *Qualitative Data Analysis: A User-Friendly Guide for Social Scientists* (London: Routledge).

Eisenhardt, K. M. and Bourgeois, L. J. (1988) 'Politics of Strategic Decision Making in High Velocity Environments: Toward a Midrange Theory', *Academy of Management Journal*, 31: 737–70.

Faber, B. (1998) 'Toward a Rhetoric of Change', *Journal of Business and Technical Communication*, 12(2): 217–43.

Felton, R. F. (2004) 'What Directors and Investors Want from Governance Reform: A Survey of Directors and Institutional Investors Shows that Board Governance Has a Long Way to Go', *McKinsey Quarterly*, May.

Festinger, L. (1954) 'A Theory of Social Comparison Processes', *Human Relations*, 7: 117–40.

Firth, M. (1980) 'Takeovers, Shareholder Returns and the Theory of the Firm', *Quarterly Journal of Economics*, 94: 235–60.

Fisher, N. R. E. (1979) 'Hybris and Dishonour: II', *Greece and Rome*, 26(1): 32–47.

Gabriel, Y. (1998) 'Same Old Story or Changing Stories? Folkloric, Modern and Postmodern Mutations'. In D. Grant, T. Keenoy and C. Oswick (eds.), *Discourse and Organisation* (London: Sage), 84–103.

Grene, D. (1961) 'Herodotus: The Historian as Dramatist', *Journal of Philosophy*, 58(18): 477–87.

Grimal, P. (1986) *The Dictionary of Classical Mythology* (New York: Blackwell).

Jacobs, L., Berscheid, E. and Walster, E. (1971) 'Self-esteem and attraction', *Journal of Personality and Social Psychology*, 17: 84–91.

Janis, I. L. (1972) *Victims of Groupthink* (New York: Houghton Mifflin).

Kakabadse, N. K. and Kakabadse, A. P. (2005) 'Discretionary Leadership: From Control/Coordination to Value Co-Creation'. In C. L. Cooper (ed.), *Leadership and Management in the 21st Century* (Oxford: Oxford University Press), 57–106.

Kakabadse, A. P., Kakabadse, N. K. and Lee-Davies, L. (2007) 'Three Temptations of Leaders', *Leadership & Organization Development Journal*, 28(3): 196–208.

Keasey, K., Short, H. and Wright, M. (eds.) (2005) *Corporate Governance: Accountability, Enterprise and International Comparisons* (Chichester: John Wiley).

Keay, A. R. (2006) 'Enlightened Shareholder Value, the Reform of the Duties of Company Directors and the Corporate Objective', *Lloyd's Maritime and Commercial Law Quarterly*, 3: 335–61.

Kelley, H. H. (1971) *Attribution in Social Interaction* (New York: General Learning Press).

Kets de Vries, M. F. R. and Miller, D. (1985) 'Narcissism and Leadership: An Object Relations Perspective', *Human Relations*, 38(6): 583–601.

Lincoln, Y. S. and Guba, E. (1985) *Naturalistic Inquiry* (Beverly Hills, CA: Sage).

Linde, C. (2001) 'Narrative and Social Tacit Knowledge', *Journal of Knowledge Management*, 5(2): 160–70.

MacDowell, D. M. (1976) 'Hybris in Athens', *Greece and Rome*, 23(1): 14–31.

March, J. and Simon, H. A. (1958) *Organizations* (New York: Wiley).

McCracken, G. (1988) *The Long Interview* (Beverly Hills, CA: Sage).

Meindl, J. R., Ehrlich, S. R. and Dukerich, J. M. (1985) 'The Romance of Leadership', *Administrative Science Quarterly*, 30: 78–102.

Miles, M. B. and Huberman, A. M. (1984) *Qualitative Data Analysis: A New Sourcebook of Methods* (Beverly Hills, CA: Sage).

Morgan, G. (1997) *Images of Organisation* (London: Sage).

North, H. (1966) *Sophrosyne: Self-Knowledge and Self-Restraint in Greek Literature* (Ithaca, NY: Cornell University Press).

O'Connor, P. A. (1997) 'Decisions Made in the Absence of Formal Delegation of Power', *Local Government Law Journal*, 2, LBC Information Services, Sydney, NSW: 225–34.

Plato (1981) *Apology*, ed. J. J. Helm (New York: Bolchazy-Carducci Publishers).

Polkinghorne, D. E. (1988) *Narrative Knowing and the Human Sciences* (New York: State of New York University Press).

Post, J. (1993) 'Current Concepts in the Narcissistic Personality: Implications for Political Psychology', *Political Psychology*, 14(1): 99–121.

Riessman, C. K. (1993) *Narrative Analysis* (Newbury Park, CA: Sage Publications).

Roll, R. (1986) 'The Hubris Hypothesis of Corporate Takeovers', *Journal of Business*, 59: 197–216.

Ronfeldt, D. (1994) *Beware the Hubris–Nemesis Complex: A Concept for Leadership Analysis* (Santa Monica: Rand).

Rubin, H. J. and Rubin, I. S. (2005) *Qualitative Interviewing: The Art of Hearing Data* (2nd edn.) (Thousand Oaks, CA: Sage).

Schweiger, D. M., Sandberg, W. R. and Ragan, J. W. (1986) 'Group Approaches for Improving Strategic Decision Making: A Comparative Analysis of Dialectical Inquiry, Devil's Advocacy and Consensus', *Academy of Management Journal*, 29: 51–71.

Sheard, A. G., Kakabadse, A. P. and Kakabadse, N. K. (2009) 'Organisational Politics: The Shadow Side of Leadership', *Proceedings of the 5th European Conference on Management, Leadership and Governance*, Hellenic American University, Athens, Greece, 5–6 November, 232–41.

Skinner, B. F. (1953) *Science and Human Behavior* (New York: Macmillan).

Starbuck, W. H. and Milliken, F. J. (1988) 'Executives' Perceptual Filters: What They Notice and How They Make Sense'. In D. C. Hambrick (ed.), *The Executive Effect: Concepts and Methods for Studying Top Managers* (Greenwich, CT: JAI Press), 35–66.

Staw, B. M. (1976) 'Knee-deep in the Big Muddy: A Study of Escalating Commitment to a Failing Course of Action', *Organizational Behavior and Human Performance*, 16: 27–44.

Sutton, R. I. and Callahan, A. (1987) 'The Stigma of Bankruptcy: Spoiled Organizational Image and its Management', *Academy of Management Journal*, 30: 405–36.

Tucker, M., Sigafoos, J. and Bushell, H. (1998) 'Use of Noncontingent Reinforcement in the Treatment of Challenging Behavior', *Behavior Modification*, 22: 529–47.

Walsh, J. P. and Seward, J. K. (1990) 'On the Efficiency of Internal and External Corporate Control Mechanisms', *Academy of Management Review*, 15: 421–58.

Wiener, P. P. (1973) *Dictionary of the History of Ideas* (New York: Scribner).

Index

Note: entries in **bold** refer to figures, tables and boxes.

Bowman, J. 84
Box, R. 106
Bozionelos, N. 244
Brady, M. H. 220
Brannen, M. Y. 162
Braybrooke, D. 91
Brenner, R. 90
Bretton Woods 57–8
Brewer, G. D. 88
Brint, S. 94
British–American Project 2
Brockner, J. 310
Brovkin, V. N. 12
Brown, J. S. 242
Brownlee, J. xiv
Bryman, A. 294, 312
Buchan, J. 242
Buchstein, H. 27
Bugra, A. 150
bureaucracy 4, 39, 40, 49, 63, 94, 209, 217
Burgess, R. G. 312
Burnham, J. **6**, 19
Burt, R. S. 139, **147**, **149**, **152**, 272–3, 280

Calhoun, C. 98
Callahan, A. 311
Calvinism 130
Campbell, J. L. 89
Cannadine, D. 4
Cao, C. 179, 183, 185
capital
cultural 23, 140, 141, 143–4, 145, **147**, 148–53, 155, 257
economic 138, 139, 140, 142–3, 145, 146, **147**, **149**, 150, 151, **152**, 153–5, 270, 275, 276, 280, 281
social xviii, 4, 5, **17**, 22–5, 47, 139–41, 143, 146–54, 242, **243**, 256–7, 262–4, 269, 270, 273, 275, 280, 281, 282, 291
capitalism
delocalisation 62
global 55–9, 61–4, 65, 66, 70, 71
nation state 57–9
theory of 54–72
transnational 54, 55–6, 58, 63, 64, 65, 71
see also global accumulation; global production

capitalist 12, 29n12, 45, 55, 90, 141, 174
alliances 140
class 9, 56, 63
enterprise 41, 129
revolutions **18**
Carlson, N. 300
Carr, E. H. 13
Carr, S. C. 245
Carroll, W. K. 141
Carver, J. 158
Castells, M. 60, 143
Cerny, P. G. 90
Chandler, A. D. 38
Chen, C. C. 311
Chen, J. 183
Child, J. 158
Chinese Academy of Engineering (CAE) 178
Chinese Academy of Science (CAS) 178
Chinese People's Political Consultative Conference (CPPCC) 185
Chisholm, H. 11
Chomsky, N. 94, 110
church(es)
All Saints Church, Northampton 121, 269, 271, 276, **277–8**, 280, 283
Anglican **15**, 271
Church of England **15**, 282
Protestant 40
Roman Catholic 11, **16**, 105, 107
Clapham, S. E. 311
Clark, P. 265
class
capitalist 9, 54, 56, 63, 71
compromise 57, 58
convergent 1–32
dominant **6**, 116, 264
economic 10
educated 119
global 9, 62
inequalities **17**, 67, 117, 128–9, 257
interests 63, 66, 72, 133
leisure 77–8, 107
lower/working/popular **17**, 25, 56, 57, 58, 61, 62, 70, 71, 203
middle 10, 12, **16**, 55, 62, 68, 70, 71, 77, 83, 84, 203
mobility 54, 83, 138
moneyed 2, 8